HELLGATE MEMORII
WORLD WAR II

GREEN HELL

The Battle for Guadalcanal

William J. Owens

We few, we happy few, we band of brothers;
For he today that sheds his blood with me
Shall be my brother. Be he ne'er so vile,
This day shall gentle his condition;
And gentlemen in England now abed
Shall think themselves accursed they were not here.

— Shakespeare, Henry V, Act IV, Scene 3

Hellgate Press
Central Point, Oregon

GREEN HELL: THE BATTLE FOR GUADALCANAL

Published by Hellgate Press, Memories Series

HELLGATE PRESS
a division of PSI Research
P.O. Box 3727
Central Point, Oregon 97502-0032
(541) 479-9464
(541) 476-1479 fax
info@psi-research.com e-mail

Editing and typography: Editype, Jackson, MI
Cover design: Steven Burns

Library of Congress Cataloging-in-Publication Data
Owens, William J., 1932–
Green hell : the battle for guadalcanal / William J. Owens. – – 1st ed.
p. cm.
Includes bibliographical references and index.
ISBN: 1-55571-498-6 (pbk.)
1. Guadalcanal (Solomon Islands), Battle of, 1942-1943.
I. Title.
D767.98.084 1999
940.54'26 – – dc21 98-54597
CIP

Printed and bound in the United States of America
First Edition 10 9 8 7 6 5 4 3 2 1
Printed on recycled paper when available.

For my son John
grandson Justin, and
my daughter Adrian—
who persevered, and wondered if
this book would ever be written.

FOREWORD

The Battle for Guadalcanal was a microcosm of the United States' participation in World War II, which took place in two distinctly different theaters of war—in the Pacific Ocean against Japan, and in Europe against Germany and the Axis powers. In both areas war resulted from the inability of modern governments to achieve political solutions to their pressing problems. While it is doubtful that a political settlement acceptable to Nazi Germany was ever possible, the situation between America and Japan might have been resolved short of outright hostilities.

The American landings on Guadalcanal—Operation Watchtower—took place on a remote island, one of a chain of similar islands in the South Pacific that very few people in the entire world even knew existed. This first American offensive, in response to an immediate Japanese threat, began despite the Allied political agreement that the United States would first help Great Britain, the USSR, and the Free French win the war in Europe before turning to defeat the Japanese.

Further, the various branches of the armed forces within each nation were politically motivated to secure their own supremacy. The American Joint Chiefs of Staff (JCS), who seemed to accept the principle of "Europe first," were engaged in bitter infighting as to which commander in which service would command which area. The Army didn't want to have a Navy admiral in command of its forces, the Navy abhorred the thought of working under an Army general, and the Army Air Force wanted to operate independently without having to answer to the Army or the Navy. The Marines (considered part of the Navy) would have preferred to be led by Marine generals, but favored Navy to Army leadership.

The situation existing in Japan was even more disruptive. The Army and Navy rarely saw eye to eye, and each had its own air arms. The Imperial Army did not even know their Navy was building a forward air base on Guadalcanal. That was the Navy's problem, not theirs. A large, experienced, and well-trained Army was held back in Manchuria—far from the Pacific battles—until long after they might have contributed to a Japanese victory. While the Imperial Army and Navy had very little to do with each other, their common disdain for the civilian government was monumental. Emperor Hirohito, in whose name the war was being fought, never had the power to reconcile fully the differences between the branches of his armed forces.

In both Japan and the United States the political basis and the perceived need to go to war were far ahead of the ability to provide the actual means with which to fight a war. The American Congress had effectively stripped the military of the funds necessary to build a modern fighting force until war was almost upon the nation. There was a strong feeling that once a war was over, there was no need to maintain an adequate military—a verdict pronounced after World War I and again after World War II. That situation manifested itself again in the Korean conflict. The crippled armed forces had to start over from scratch in both cases.

War Crimes

The term "humane war" is an oxymoron, an absurd attempt to reconcile two totally contradictory ideas. War is essentially inhumane. When any nation agrees to the rules of war, it does so under the assumption that it will be victorious. No nation, no army or navy, or group of fighting men, will willingly give up the "right" to do whatever it takes to achieve victory.

No one goes to war with the intention of losing, nor with the intention of engaging in prolonged hostilities. The enemy is always so weak, unprepared, cowardly, and incapable of resisting the overwhelming spirit, superiority, and power of "our magnificent Army" that the fighting will be over in six weeks.

One of mankind's most powerful instincts is that of survival, which appears to be imbedded in the cerebral cortex. It has nothing to do with morals—the rules devised by social groups to facilitate living together. There is no ideal way of dying. A man or woman who dies to preserve a group's survival is dead, and no longer capable of defending the group. The desirable objective, then, is *survival*—to remain among the living.

This ideal can be altered to some degree by the society in which one lives. The Japanese *Way of the Warrior* imposed on its fighting men a code of conduct in war contrary to that imposed by the Western world. To the Japanese their way was both civilized and chivalrous, the highest ideal that a man could attain. Consequently, they could not understand nor accept a foreign ideal that clashed with their accepted way of conduct.

After the Japanese conquered a new territory, they sought to impose their concept of honor and civilization upon their new subjects, which meant bowing to the new and different authority of their masters. Of course, this was not an attribute unique to the Japanese. Nazi Germany expected to make loyal subjects of those swept up in their conquests. Indeed, Britain did precisely the same thing in creating its empire, as did the Spanish, Russians, French, and Dutch. Throughout history subjugated peoples either accepted whatever subservient role they were assigned by the new authority, or they died.

The Europeans who settled North America subjugated the native population and nearly eliminated them from the face of the earth. Africans were brought to the Americas, much against their will, to serve as slaves. Whatever brutality and cruelty a master thought necessary to force them to do what he wanted them to do was acceptable. In the truest sense of the word, the spoils of war belonged to the victors.

Revenge

At the end of World War II, when the Allies had totally defeated and all but destroyed their enemies—a vengeance in itself—there seemed to be a psychological need for further vengeance. That is, there was a need to "rub the noses of the vanquished in the mess they had made." In legal terms this is the equivalent of committing a crime in cold blood.

The punishment of war crimes can be conducted only by the victors. The losers have no similar recourse. The leaders of the losing nations accused of crimes against humanity were brought before legal tribunals, and were often convicted and killed. The same acts defined as crimes against humanity were frequently committed by leaders and fighting men of the victorious nations, but the war crimes trials were not concerned with how the winners had achieved victory.

Many of the more thoughtful citizens in the victorious nations thought these public trials were little more than extraneous exhibitions of power. The wars had ended on terms set by the victors. To these observers, a terrible precedent was being set that would impact on future military confrontations. The imposition of "impartial" legal judgments on the conduct of the war made no sense unless the victors were judged by the same criteria. The implication is absolutely clear: a nation can get away with anything it wants or needs to do so long as it wins the war.

When North Korea and China in the early 1950s, and later the North Vietnamese around 1970, set up and conducted war crimes trials, the Western nations were incensed that these smaller countries would attempt to claim a legal basis for such uncivilized behavior. The fact that the Allies had done exactly the same thing at the end of World War II has been conveniently forgotten.

During World War II the determined quest for victory led to a deliberate act that had never before been acceptable: the waging of total war encompassing the civilian populations. The morally and ethically objectionable concept of unconditional surrender as the only basis for ending the war led directly to the idea of destroying the enemy's capability to wage war. The practice of unrestricted bombing of enemy cities, including defenseless civilians, was a repugnant result of that decision. The "crime" of Germany's policy of unrestricted submarine warfare for the destruction of enemy shipping necessary for the Allied continuation of the war pales almost to insignificance when compared to the Allied bombing of German and Japanese cities.

These inhumane acts were decreed by the leaders of the warring nations, not the men who did the actual fighting. Yet pleas by many military and civilian personnel that they were following orders were summarily rejected. This implies that individuals had the option of refusing to obey an order they thought objectionable without any threat of punishment.

Such a possibility never existed for Americans, British, Russian, or other Allied troops, for in these "humane" nations an individual who refused to serve in the armed forces was held to be beneath contempt and subject to whatever punishment a government decided to impose. Refusal to obey the orders of superiors in the armed forces could not be and was not tolerated. Elaborate and brutal rules and regulations were devised to deal with such individuals, with the infliction of punishment up to and including death. The fact that all nations forced men into their armies and navies under the threat of dire punishment, to fight against enemies that did the same thing, must be recognized in assessing guilt.

The essential truth is that any nation struggling for survival will, and should, do anything necessary for survival. When an enemy escalates warfare with the development of better weapons, with more destructive killing power, the nation at peril must respond or face certain defeat. The antiquated concept of chivalry involving individual honor and responsibility remained an ideal far beyond its origins. Improvements in the implements of mass destruction—rifles, machine guns, artillery and aerial bombs—removed from individuals any onus of destroying an enemy in combat. Not that killing an enemy ever really was considered deplorable. Men, and now women, go to war to win, not to display gallantry toward a foe. This was as true when ancient tribes fought each other as it is now.

War, the ultimate partisan function invoked to achieve a nation's purposes, is not usually an uncomplicated end in itself. Warfare is not and can never be free of political considerations. It is a governmental action. The armies and navies do not possess a higher moral stance or place of honor than the citizens of the nation they represent. If a government accepts the necessity of waging war, that government must accept whatever actions are necessary to win that war. Total war means that civilians must accept the same dangers as the uniformed men and women compelled to fight that war. The ultimate front line is the chair in which the foremost leader sits.

Many leaders, thoroughly isolated from the field of battle, may proclaim that their fighting men will not resort to the types of behavior exhibited by the enemy, evoking a higher sense of morality of purpose. This is an obscene falsehood, a lie that soldiers engaged with a determined enemy will reject out of hand. The military arm of any government has one purpose, and that is to defeat the enemy using any possible means.

Wars are fought for reasons of power and economics. The men in the trenches, on the ships, and flying the airplanes fight to survive. They know that if they are to live, they must kill the enemy. The ordinary privates, seamen, and airmen do not vote on whether or not to go to war. Usually they have no voice in the matter. These men and women are compelled to fight on behalf of their nation regardless of whether they want to be in uniform or not. Compulsion is another facet of power.

The truth is that there is no real problem in jumping on the back of a tiger for a wild ride. The crisis begins when we want to jump off. Beginning a war isn't difficult, but ending one before we are destroyed physically or economically is nearly impossible. Anyone going to war must be prepared to kill, maim, and destroy the enemy.

If morality were the issue, there would be no wars.

Acknowledgments and Many Thanks

Much has been written over the years about the Battle for Guadalcanal. Richard B. Frank's *Guadalcanal: The Definitive Account*, must be considered the most reliable source. Robert Leckie's *Challenge for the Pacific*, and his personal story, *Helmet for My Pillow*, are must reads for the human side of the battle. Perhaps the best written account is *The Battle for Guadalcanal* by Samuel B. Griffith, II, who was there with the 1st Raider Battalion. *The Guadalcanal Diary* by Richard Tregaskis and *Into the Valley* by John Hersey are remarkable books covering a small portion of the campaign. Eric Hammel's *Starvation Island* and his later account of Navy actions are quite useful.

My first serious thought of doing a history of this prolonged campaign came in 1969. It was not until 1997—at age sixty-four—that I finally decided it was time to sit down and start writing. After a few months of floundering, the way of presenting my material to make it different from previous books fell into place. This meant new research and a revamping of what I had already written.

Contrary to the main thrust of several of the more popular and widespread accounts, the Battle for Guadalcanal did not end with the relief of the 1st Marine Division. Two more bloody months remained before the Japanese were driven off the island. If only the land battle were considered, the U.S. Army was there early with fighter planes, and with troops from mid-October until the finish. The U.S. Navy was deeply involved at all times. This battle, above all, was truly a combined effort of all the armed forces.

With a solid plan to work with, I found that there are many willing hands who shared my vision. The simple fact that many of the veterans of Guadalcanal and other WWII battles will not be with us much longer, that they deserve to be remembered as once ago we promised, was probably the single greatest motivation for their help.

The coming of age of the Internet and the World Wide Web made it is easier to make individual contacts than in the past. Fred Swain, born after WWII but with an avid interest in the Coast Guard and the Pacific Battles, found me by e-mail, and still contacts me several times a week with new information and suggestions. This singular connection led to a close working relationship that resulted in my trekking out to the Swansboro, North Carolina area near Camp LeJeune. He put me in contact with that dynamo retired chief warrant officer, Gunner Jack Parks, who persuaded three other veterans of the campaign nearby to share their memories with me. Nearing eighty years old and still an active eagle-eyed marksman, Jack can leave younger men in his dust.

Dave Roper, who loaned me his priceless copy of *Fighting on Guadalcanal*, was discovered by Swain. An amateur historian and an expert on Japanese weapons, Roper joined the effort to produce this book, as did several veterans and relatives who shared some personal remembrances and photographs.

My dearest friend Liz Aley devoted hours of her time to reading and editing the various drafts of the manuscript. Her pointed questions regarding fact and meaning helped immensely, preventing me from appearing to be ignorant about things that really mattered.

For any errors, mistakes, misinterpretations, or distortions of events that remain, the blame must fall solely upon myself. All those mentioned above, as well as those who helped anonymously, tried their best to keep me on track.

TABLE OF CONTENTS

CHAPTER 1

The Prelude to World War II

A military man can scarcely pride himself on having "smitten a sleeping enemy"; it is more a matter of shame, simply, for the one smitten.

—Admiral Isoroku Yamamoto,
Commander-in-Chief, Combined Fleet,
after the stunning Japanese raid on Pearl Harbor

One Japanese woman, after the end of World War II in the Pacific, simply could not understand why the United States had been so determined to destroy the Japanese Empire. Her heartfelt belief was that the supremely enlightened Japanese had generously offered to extend the beneficial and divine rule of the Emperor to non-Japanese peoples. This is much like the Spanish claim of bringing the beautiful joy of Christianity to the New World to justify their acts of exploitation and extinction.

This bountiful overture began in earnest at a few minutes before eight o'clock on Sunday morning, December 7, 1941. On what President Franklin Delano Roosevelt called "a date which will live in infamy," 360 dive bombers, torpedo planes, fighters and high-level bombers from the six-aircraft-carrier Striking Force of the Japanese Imperial Navy, under Vice Admiral Nagumo, plunged down from the peaceful skies in a tragic and devastating surprise attack on the American Pacific Fleet moored at Pearl Harbor and the Army forces on Oahu, in the then Territory of Hawaii. Catching the sleepy peacetime American Army and Navy personnel at their bases and on their ships in the middle of a weekend, Japanese bombs, torpedoes, and machine guns killed 2,335 servicemen and 68 civilians, and wounded 1,178 individuals. On the battleship USS *Arizona* alone 1,104 men were killed after a 1,760-pound bomb penetrated the forward magazine, causing catastrophic explosions that sent the vessel to its now enshrined eternal resting place. One hundred and eighty-eight American naval and army aircraft were destroyed.

The citizens of the United States were enraged by the sneak attack on Pearl Harbor, but according to newspaper polls, only about 10% of the populace even knew where Pearl Harbor was. In late 1941 Hawaii was an exotic and foreign South Seas paradise to the inhabitants of the continental 48 states. Even fewer people in the world had ever heard of the now legendary island of Guadalcanal.

The American Navy's formidable battleships, long thought of as the backbone of the fleet, were destroyed or badly damaged. They turned out to be easy stationary targets moored in neat rows for this long-planned and well practiced sneak attack by Japanese aircraft launched from a battle force that had crossed the northern Pacific undetected. This attack has been thoroughly documented in a number of authoritative books that are well worth the reading, but their subject is beyond the scope of this book.

The "divine rule" of Imperial Japan in Asia did not in any way imply equality. Even within Japan equality did not exist, and the unyielding caste differences, from the divine royal family to the lowest untouchable, were wide and deep. Japan, at the time, had raised the feudal system to a lofty level, with the majority of common citizens classified as workers, serfs, or outcasts.

An attack such as that carried out at Pearl Harbor does not occur on the spur of the moment or by whim. It was a deliberate confrontation on the part of the Imperial Japanese government, which was completely dominated by the Army and the Navy, to force the United States to accept Japanese aggressions in the western Pacific—incursions and attacks on Manchuria and China begun in the early 1930s that resulted in the occupation of large portions of those nations. Korea had been a Japanese colony since 1910. Later, in a belated attempt to justify its Asian aggressions, Japan proclaimed the creation of the Greater Asian Co-Prosperity Sphere—essentially, Asia for Asians.

When apologists bewail the American dropping of atomic bombs on Hiroshima and other Japanese cities during August 1945, they often assert that these terrible attacks were acts of racial aggression. They attempt to cultivate the impression that World War II in the Pacific was only a few months or a year or two old. The all-out Pacific War had been raging since that reprehensible moment when Japanese attack planes flew over Hawaii. That is, the United States–Japanese conflict had existed from December 7, 1941 until the surrender documents were signed on September 2, 1945, encompassing forty-four months—or more than three and a half years—of some of the bloodiest and most brutal combat of WWII.

In retrospect, "the bomb" would just as surely have been used against the Germans to end the fighting in Europe—had the weapon been ready. It simply wasn't available at that time. The European Axis powers were subjected to the same concept of unconditional surrender, with the same brutal devastation as that visited on the Japanese nation. The deliberate and horrible fire-bombings of several German cities were essentially inhumane actions taken to destroy the Nazi will to fight. Americans, before the war, thought the idea of massive offensive bombing of civilian production and government centers despicable. There is nothing noble or chivalrous about modern war.

It is important to understand that the Japanese Imperial Army and Navy hadn't waited until the Pearl Harbor assault to begin their history of militaristic conquest and all but inexplicable atrocities against other nations and people—Asian, European, and American. The undeniably brave but often insensate soldiers of Nippon had been attacking, occupying, and destroying cities and civilian populations about eight years before they instigated hostilities with America.

In August 1945 America may have known the Japanese were beaten, and the Japanese may have known they were beaten, but the Japanese military showed few signs of capitulating. How much longer the war would have gone on is a matter of conjecture, simply because we did use the bomb and that usage did bring the war to an end. A realistic estimate established that the American invasion of Japan would have cost 500,000 American and Japanese casualties, in addition to inflicting even greater destruction and ruin upon that already ravaged nation.

"When word got around that the bombs had forced the Japanese to surrender, we knelt in the sand and cried," admitted one veteran of the vicious Pacific fighting. "For all our manhood, we cried. We were going to live. We were going to grow up to adulthood after all." This marine had been scheduled to land on the southern island of Kyushu in one of the opening assaults on the home islands. He could have been speaking for all the Allied soldiers, sailors, and marines headed for the big fight—and their families back in the States—and the Japanese populace as well.

Had Japan lost the will to fight despite the enormous loss of men and materiel, despite the savage bombings of its mainland? No, the Japanese military forces were committed to fight for the glory of the Emperor and Japan every bit as much as the woefully desperate Americans, who had sworn vengeance for Pearl Harbor. At the beginning of the war, once isolationist America lost the bulk of its Pacific Fleet, its large contingent of troops in the Philippines and elsewhere had been defeated, and it possessed inadequate military resources with which to continue the war against the Japanese.

Prior to the outbreak of hostilities, there was a strong presence of Western powers in Southeast Asia, with Great Britain, France, and the Netherlands "possessing"—that is, exploiting—colonies rich in natural resources. America had a strong interest in the Philippines, but claimed no colonial rights—it had already been mandated before the war that full independence would take place in 1946. Germany's colonies in the southwest Pacific had been stripped away as a result of the First World War. The United States was particularly disturbed when the formerly German-held island chains of the Carolines (Truk and the Palaus with Peleliu) and the Marshalls (Kwajalein and Eniwetok) were claimed by Japan. These islands were then turned into heavily fortified military bases, a direct threat to the Americans' Hawaii–Philippines supply and communication line. Japan's only true goal in Asia was to replace the European dominance with their own. Japan was striving to take their self-proclaimed rightful position as ruler of Asia and the western Pacific.

"Even more frightening than the collapse of the Allied defense," said leading WWII historian Walter Lord in his powerful book *The Lonely Vigil*, "was the collapse of a great many preconceptions that had stood inviolate for a century: the invincibility of the Royal Navy; American technological supremacy; the limitations of a purely imitative Japan; the innate superiority of the Western fighting man; a conviction that the oil, tin, rubber, and other resources of Asia somehow belonged by inheritance—if not by divine right—to a few European powers; and an abiding faith that the Far East would always accept this state of affairs."

Japan particularly disliked the fact that the area was referred to as Southeast Asia, or the Far East, which suggested that England and Europe were the center of the universe. The area in question was really the Southwest Pacific, seen from the United States. If you look at any map of Asia, the nations of a large portion of China, Burma, Indonesia, Vietnam, Malaysia, the Philippines, Borneo, and New Guinea do make up southeastern Asia. The Japanese Empire simply wished to replace the influence of the Western powers and claim the natural resources of the Asian colonies for their own use.

Japan's claim for expansionism was based on their conviction that the racial Japanese were superior to any other people on the face of this earth and in heaven. They possessed a self-proclaimed spiritual and holy mandate to rule the world—the part not ruled by Hitler's Nazi Aryan supermen, whom they also distrusted. "Liberation" of the masses of Asians then under Western dominance meant only that Japan would become the absolute master, with the rest to serve as slaves to the needs and desires of the Empire of Japan.

The only Western nation left with the strength and resources to oppose Japanese expansionism in the Pacific was the United States. Japan's traditional nemesis, Russia, was fully occupied fighting the Nazis. Japanese military planning had anticipated an armed confrontation with America or Russia for several decades. Likewise, America knew the only nation with whom war in Asia was really possible was Japan, and had created a number of plans for a possible military collision. The American plans were rehashes of obsolete previous plans, all of which failed when war began.

In the two decades following WWI, the United States' national policy was based on isolationism, with minimal concern for political or military participation in affairs beyond American borders. The thinking was that if we maintained an aloof neutrality, nothing that happened in Asia, Africa, or Europe could affect our well-being. The concept of widespread and influential isolation promoted by the America First advocates—and grasped by a large number of Americans—lasted until the very moment the first bomb fell at Pearl Harbor.

Conversely, by the early 1930s the heady wine of militarism was intoxicating the Germans and Italians in Europe, as well as the Japanese in Asia. A strong militaristic stance was restoring a sense of pride to nations humiliated or bankrupted by the First World War. Almost any keen and intelligent observer of the time recognized that a large-scale war was all but inevitable. The malignant rise of aggressive militarism throughout the world during the 1920s and 1930s has no counterpart today.

During this period the American Army and Navy armed services were run more on a corporate structure—complete with internal power struggles—than as fighting forces. Only in early 1940 did our government recognize that involvement in the European and Asian wars was a real possibility. Congress then authorized increases and funding for additional manpower and materiels of war. Only time revealed that the military higher commands possessed many high-ranking officers who had succeeded in running the gauntlet of peacetime promotion practices, but who were totally incapable of wartime leadership.

The Japanese had a better grasp of the emerging doctrine of air warfare at a time when most American military planners still considered aircraft carriers as an adjunct to the battleship fleet, not as a primary front line combat weapon. This the Japanese proved in their enormously successful raid on Pearl Harbor, which was actually a declaration of war.

Despite this stunning initial success, the Japanese bombers failed to achieve the most important objective—the destruction of the American carriers. While the American battleships were trapped in a confined harbor, the fleet aircraft carriers were at sea and were totally untouched in the initial onslaught. The realization that the true combat striking power of the U.S. Navy in the Pacific had not been destroyed was not long in coming.

Yet, even with this prophetic demonstration of naval airpower, many of Japan's high-ranking naval officers were as obsessed with the idea of the classic confrontation of a battleship-led surface battle as the American leadership was. Japanese air arms constituted an elite corps that stressed supreme quality of flyers over quantity. The nature of future battles—the actual war of attrition that was in the offing—was ignored. Imperial strategic plans were based on the assumption that the United States would want to arrange a peaceful settlement after the initial devastating and humiliating setbacks. Most members of the Japanese high command couldn't conceive of a prolonged war with the United States. They should have been concerned after their experience with the ill-prepared, scantily equipped, and often poorly led Chinese armies, which did not quit fighting despite frightful losses.

The very success of the surprise attack may well have caused the Japanese to lose the war. To Japanese military thinking the utter technical success of the surprise air raid should have been so complete that a panicked American public would demand that its government make a peaceful settlement rather than fight. Instead, those bombs dropped in the first minutes of the war ignited a firestorm of moral fury and hatred that turned on Japan and eventually consumed it.

The Foundations of Worldwide War

Seeds for the conflicts that would escalate into the Second World War had been sown with the defeat of Germany and the imposition of the vengeful peace that ended the First World War—"the war to make the world safe for democracy." Not only was Germany devastated by the war, they were humiliated and ravaged by the peace, resulting in an infection that festered and grew into a fierce desire for revenge.

Japan, an ally of the Western powers in the First World War, was primarily concerned with the threat from Russian armies to their west. Russia had withdrawn from the big war with Germany in 1917 when the Communist party overthrew the government of the Czar and began the internal war to consolidate Russia and the nascent Soviet Union. Japan perceived Russia as an enemy, partially because Japan had repulsed the Imperial Russian 1905 attempt at expansion into Manchuria. Whether Russia was ruled by a Communist or Imperial government, that huge land was Japan's most threatening antagonist.

The powerful Western nations of the United States and Great Britain, in an effort to ensure and preserve world peace in the 1930s, imposed arms limitations on the other nations of the world. Naval armament—the number of warships—received great attention. In the first decades of this century there seemed to be a contest for the glory of building the world's largest seagoing battleship. The possession of a battleship became the symbol of a nation's power and prestige and wealth for even the smallest of nations. Britain, the United States, Japan, France, and Italy signed this naval disarmament treaty.

In these arms reduction and limitation treaties, ratios based on the size of forces fielded by England and America were established, and the size of the ground forces and the numbers and types of aircraft were prescribed. If America had ten of something, Japan could only have six. Though the numbers of soldiers in traditional armies were considered important, concern about the types and numbers of aircraft was almost totally disregarded. Airplanes were considered by the land and sea branches of the military to be little more than a sideshow in war. This remained true even after some of America's air-minded officers—"renegades" to the traditional military establishment—demonstrated how easily even a battleship could be sunk by aerial bombs.

The Road to War

By the 1930s, the emerging militaristic states of an ambitious Japan and a struggling Germany—former enemies, technically—considered the arms limitation treaties an insult to their national prestige and power. Great Britain asserted it needed its larger fleets and armies to maintain its widespread empire, including the possessions in Southeast Asia. America, on the other hand, was increasingly isolationist, drawing away from international involvement and obligations. The isolationists, speaking for many Americans of the time, sensed that more international conflict was on the rise, and believed we could and should avoid its entangling complications.

By 1930 the government of Imperial Japan was totally dominated by its Army and Navy, and civilian control of the armed forces was nonexistent. Further, the Army and Navy worked independently of each other, following their own agendas. In September 1931 the Japanese Kwantung Army manufactured the Mukden Incident as a justification for overrunning Manchuria. A year later, in September 1932, a puppet government had been set up, answerable only to the Kwantung Army. The Japanese Imperial government accepted a meaningless apology from the army, but the army did not give up nor leave Manchuria. From these aggressions, several direct armed conflicts with the Soviet Union were generated that could have turned into an all-out war. It was evident to international observers and critics that Japan's civilian government was a weak third party of the government. Japan withdrew from the League of Nations in 1932—a move dictated by the dominating influence of its aggressive military leaders.

The Rise of Fascism

Fascism—total dictatorship, or the total control of a nation by a strong central government elite—was on the rise. Adolph Hitler was creating a powerful fascist dictatorship under the Nazi party. Benito Mussolini was doing the same thing in Italy. Both these movements resulted in the overthrow and ousting from power of the remnants of royal and imperial families. In Japan Emperor Hirohito probably identified himself with the militaristic goals of the military, but nonetheless was compelled to support their aims to maintain the sanctity of his throne.

The worldwide depression that mushroomed in 1932 was a major contributor to unrest. Economies collapsed and money lost its value. Russia was enduring famine and mass starvation. Nations such as Germany, Italy, and Japan became convinced that the only way to solve their problems was by expanding, which simply meant the conquest of weaker nearby lands. The fundamental attitudes of these dictatorships were based on the belief that these nations were superior races who had been denied their true place in the world by the machinations of lesser beings. Japan believed that by divine right only their small island empire was qualified to rule over all other Asians. Nazi Germany believed to the core of their souls that their Aryan nation of supermen were destined to rule the world. The so-called wars for liberation of suppressed races were, in reality, a move to forever control those races.

One prominent statesman of the time observed that Germany was an army looking for a nation. Early in 1933 Hitler was appointed German Chancellor, and within the year was granted total dictatorial powers. Jews were boycotted and their activities proscribed, while labor unions and all political parties other than the Nazi party were suppressed. The first concentration camps were constructed. Hitler's efforts were validated when 92 percent of the German electorate voted for him. In Italy Mussolini was succeeding in his efforts to solidify his own dictatorship.

In an effort to tighten his total grip on the government, Hitler authorized the massive bloodbath and assassination of thousands of faithful followers who had helped him in his rise to power—those he determined unworthy of the honor of belonging to his Third Reich. Not long after, a German plebiscite voted Hitler as Führer. Japan renounced the Washington treaties of 1922 and 1930. In 1935 the Saarland, bordering France, was incorporated into the German state.

Hitler's Germany repudiated the Versailles Treaty, which had ended WWI. He reintroduced compulsory military training and service, and created the Luftwaffe, Germany's powerful modern air force. Mussolini, dreaming of the power and glory that once was Rome, ordered the invasion of the African state of Abyssinia (Ethiopia), despite protests, condemnation, and sanctions by the League of Nations.

The Rhineland, bordering France, was occupied in 1936 when German troops simply marched in and took over. New German elections consequently gave Hitler 99 percent of the popular vote. For Italy the Abyssinian war ended with the annexation of the country as a colony. Germany and Italy then proclaimed the Rome-Berlin Axis and agreed to the Anti-Comintern pact, expressing solidarity in the fight against international communism. Widespread Comintern—the Communist International movement—inspired challenges to royal monarchies, such as the overthrow of the Spanish monarchy in 1931. This precipitated the Spanish Civil War, in which the leftist revolutionaries were opposed in 1936 by Francisco Franco on behalf of the Spanish throne. Franco who was then elected Chief of State—placing another dictator on the European scene. Germany and Italy actively supported the rightist Spanish Royalists by furnishing weapons, modern fighter and bomber aircraft, and pilots to fly the planes against the leftists. It was an unparalleled testing site for their new weaponry.

In reaction to the Japanese incursions and incidents in China in 1937, the most powerful of the warlords, Chiang Kai-shek, declared war on Japan from his headquarters in Canton. This declaration was like whistling in the wind, for soon the Japanese armies seized and occupied Peking, Tientsin, Shanghai, Nanking, and Hangchow on the Chinese mainland. The brutality of Japanese troops against the civilian populations, in the absence of Chinese military resistance, shocked the world. It also forced an uneasy Chinese alliance between Chiang Kai-shek and Chou En-lai, the communist leader. A truly united Chinese resistance against the Japanese never existed, however, as these factions were too busy maneuvering for internal power and influence.

The American gunboat USS *Panay*, conspicuously flying the Stars and Stripes while patrolling the Yangtze River, was deliberately sunk on December 12, 1937 by a Japanese air attack from the aircraft carrier *Kaga*. A week earlier the British gunboat *Ladybird* was fired on by artillery of Colonel Kingoro Hashimoto and then seized. The Imperial Navy, not wishing to bring the U.S. Navy into the Chinese situation, relieved the commander of *Kaga*, who was responsible for the ruthless and apparently pointless bombing of *Panay*. On the other hand, Hashimoto was not even reprimanded for his attack on *Ladybird*, and entered the fallen city of Nanking with his regiment.

A few days later the Japanese occupied Nanking after all resistance had ceased. The Japanese commanding General Iwane Matsui, physically ailing and soon to be retired, had announced while still in Japan that he was "going to the front not to fight an enemy, but in the state of mind of one who sets out to pacify his brother." He ordered his troops to demonstrate the wonderful glory and honor of Japan to gain the trust of the Chinese.

This demonstration of brotherhood consisted of looting and burning the city, and raping and murdering helpless citizens. Noncombatant men and women and children were hunted down and butchered with no military justification. On hearing reports of gross breeches of discipline and morality on the part of his troops, Hashimoto reiterated, perhaps facetiously, that with the Japanese flag flying over Nanking, "the Imperial Way is shining forth in the area south of the Yangtze. The dawn of a renaissance is about to take place."

When the barbaric atrocities abated more than a month later, in January, about a third of the city had been burned; tens of thousands of women and young girls had been raped, murdered, and mutilated; and more than 20,000 young men had been taken out of the city for sacrifice in bayonet and machine gun practice. Later, personal Japanese descriptions and photographs of babies being bayoneted and tossed around were produced as evidence at the war crimes trials, which took place from May 3, 1946 to June 1948. Estimates of as many as 300,000 civilians being slaughtered by the marauding Japanese Army—enlisted men and officers—belied the dawn of a magnificent renaissance for Asians. Even the Germans—who were sympathetic to Japan—condemned the Japanese Army performance in an official report as bestial.

Before the Japanese military minds turned to other matters, the vastness of China had become a quagmire, swallowing up men and resources at an unimaginable rate. One reason given for the Rape of Nanking is that the Japanese troops were distressed at having lost so many of their comrades to unexpectedly heavy resistance. All in all, the Japanese suffered about 600,000 casualties in China *before* turning to take on the European and Western powers.

USSR Premier Josef Stalin signed a nonaggression pact with Hitler on August 23, 1939—a pact to divide Poland between them. Stalin firmly believed the agreement would deter German eastern expansion into the Soviet Union, and in a secret protocol promised to supply Germany with raw materials and to help suppress Polish "agitation" once that nation had been occupied.

World War II Begins

Eight days later, on Friday, September 1st, World War II officially began when German troops invaded Poland. On the 3rd, to Hitler's great surprise, Great Britain, France, Canada, Australia, and New Zealand declared war on Germany. When Russian forces invaded Poland, completing the division of Poland, Warsaw quickly surrendered unconditionally to Germany and Russia.

In response to indiscriminate and unrestricted sinking of neutral cargo ships by German U-boats, President Roosevelt ordered the Navy's Atlantic Neutrality Patrol to track any belligerent air, surface, or underwater naval forces approaching the Atlantic coast within 300 miles of the United States or the West Indies. Merchant shipping of all nations was being attacked and torpedoed within sight of the American coast. An additional "limited national emergency" was proclaimed and the number of naval enlisted men was increased from 110,813 to 145,000; Marine Corps enlisted strength was increased from 18,325 to 25,000 men authorized. Retired naval and marine officers, men, and nurses of corps were recalled to active duty despite the protests of America First leaders.

When the United States–Japanese Trade Treaty of 1911 expired in January 1940, the Pacific Fleet was ordered to remain in Hawaiian waters indefinitely because of the increasing unrest in the Pacific. On May 16th the president asked for $1,182,000,000 in national defense funds, stating that the Army and Navy should be given 50,000 new aircraft a year, and announced plans for recommissioning thirty-five more old destroyers.

Germany invaded Denmark and Norway in April, followed soon after by the Netherlands, Belgium, and Luxembourg. The main objective was France; the German armored blitzkrieg soon turned south, broke through French lines, and raced toward the English Channel.

The Nazi forces reached the English Channel at Abbeville, France on May 21st, pinning the Allied armies on the beaches. Belgium surrendered to Germany. Evacuation of British, French, and Belgian troops from Dunkirk, France began in early June, and the Allies also evacuated Norway. Italy declared war on France and Great Britain, then joined in the invasion of France.

Hitler had avenged Germany's humiliating 1918 loss, as France capitulated and German troops occupied Paris. On Saturday June 22nd the French–German armistice was signed at Compiègne, at the very spot where Germany had surrendered in 1918. The new Vichy puppet French government opened northern Indochina to a Japanese military mission and its supporting troops. On June 12th the Japan–Thailand Non-Aggression Pact was announced and Prince Konoye formed a new cabinet with General Hideki Tojo as Minister of War.

The Export Control Act, passed on July 2nd, allowed President Roosevelt, whenever he deemed it "necessary in the interest of national defense," to prohibit or curtail the exportation of military equipment, munitions, tools, materials, and other strategic supplies. He invoked that act against Japan by prohibiting the exportation, without license, of strategic minerals and chemicals, aircraft engines, parts, and equipment. Aviation gasoline and certain classes of iron and steel scrap were added to the list a few days later, effectively halting the flow of these critical exports to Japan. The U.S. advised all civilians to leave the Far East.

The Vichy government of occupied France consented to a full Japanese military occupation of ports, airfields, and railroads in northern Indochina, and ceded its airfields. It agreed to the admission of Japanese troops into northern Indochina. Germany,

Italy, and Japan signed the Tripartite Pact at Berlin, and were soon joined by Romania and Hungary.

Early in 1941 Germany announced that ships of any nationality bringing aid to Great Britain would be torpedoed and sunk without warning. Roosevelt declared a state of unlimited national emergency in the Atlantic, announced that the Atlantic Neutrality Patrol had been extended, and transferred units of the Pacific Fleet to the Atlantic Ocean.

Submarines had been relegated—along with aircraft carriers—by all the major powers to a minor support role between the wars. With a few stunning U-boat feats early in the war—after the German surface fleet proved totally inadequate to counter Britain—Hitler became enthusiastic about this important weapon as a tool for economic warfare. In World War I the U-boat had nearly brought Britain to its knees. At one point in the spring of 1917, England possessed only three weeks of food supplies—German U-boats had destroyed nearly 900,000 tons of shipping in the month of April alone. Suddenly, the nearly forgotten ugly weapon of WWI became Germany's only serious naval threat.

Japan "mediated" the undeclared war between France and Indochina. France ceded territory to Thailand and gave Japan a monopoly on the Indochinese rice crop and the right to use the airport at Saigon. On April 13th the Russo-Japanese Non-Aggression Pact was signed, which eliminated the threat of an immediate war with the USSR and freed Japan to confront the U.S. In May Ambassador Nomura presented the Secretary of State with the Japanese proposal for establishment of a "just peace in the Pacific."

Germany Invades the Soviet Union

On Sunday June 22, 1941, German tanks spearheaded the massive and totally unexpected invasion of Russia along a front extending from the Arctic to the Black Sea. Stalin was stunned by this sudden betrayal by his "friend" Hitler. Italy, Romania, Finland, and Hungary also declared war against the USSR and participated in the colossal invasion.

Japan recalled her merchant ships from the Atlantic Ocean, and began mobilizing more than one million army conscripts. The U.S. Army Forces, Far East (USAFFE) were organized under the command of General Douglas MacArthur, and the Philippine military forces were called up to serve in the United States Army. British and Russian forces, now allies, invaded oil-rich Iran from the south and north, respectively.

September 17th General Hideki Tojo became the Japanese Premier as the Konoye government resigned. Japanese troop transports, en route to invade Thailand and Malaysia, were sighted off Formosa. Admiral H.R. Stark, Chief of Naval Operations, sent a "war warning" message to the commanders of the Pacific and Asiatic Fleets. Japan assured the United States that her increased troop movements in French Indochina were only a precautionary measure. Japanese forces decided to remain in China to protect their flanks against Western aggression.

World War II Comes to the Pacific Ocean

The December 7th sneak attack on the American fleet at Pearl Harbor was the opening gambit in the Pacific. The next day the Congress of the United States declared war on

Japan. Japanese aircraft in other widely scattered operations bombed Guam, Wake, Hong Kong, Singapore, and the Philippine Islands. Japanese forces invaded Thailand and occupied Bangkok, and conducted amphibious landings on Tarawa and Makin, in the Gilbert Islands. China declared war on Japan, Germany, and Italy. Germany and Italy, on December 12th, declared war on the United States, and in return the United States declared war on Germany and Italy.

In the vast Pacific Ocean area during 1942, the seemingly invincible Imperial Japanese Navy and Army achieved great victories in their drive to conquer and annex the American possessions and European colonies in Asia bordering the Pacific. The vital American outpost in the Philippines held out for five months before surrendering, and what was left of the embattled and battered U.S. Asiatic Fleet headquartered there finally straggled back to Australia and to India. British and Dutch outposts fell before the Japanese tidal wave. With those early successes, there seemed to be no way to prevent the western Pacific Ocean from becoming a large, private lake ruled over by Japan.

To solidify their gains and protect their eastern flanks, the Japanese began moving across the Pacific. The plan was to occupy and secure all of the islands on which the Allies might establish bases from which to launch offensive operations against Japan. The elimination of the extended and vulnerable communications and supply lines from America to Australia became an urgent priority. There was even a hope in the Japanese high command that Hawaii could be occupied and the U.S. military presence forced back to the American continent.

A now barely adequate American fleet managed to win a marginal victory in the Battle of the Coral Sea in May, in the waters east of New Guinea and slightly southeast of the Solomon Islands—so marginal, in fact, that Japan also claimed it as a victory. The American fleet did succeed in turning back the first Japanese move to sever the Australia–U.S. lifeline—a temporary postponement so far as the Japanese were concerned. The most significant consequence of this virtual stalemate is that one Japanese light carrier was sunk, and a first line fleet carrier was so badly damaged it was forced to return to Japan for repairs, along with another unharmed third fleet carrier that had lost too many flight crews to return immediately to combat operations. All three had been designated to take part in the Midway invasion.

The original force designated for the Combined Fleet's attack on Midway would have consisted of more than 200 ships, including eight carriers with about 700 planes, eleven battleships, 22 cruisers, 65 destroyers, and 21 submarines. "These ships participating," wrote Mitsuo Fuchida with Masatake Okumiya after the war, "were to consume more fuel and cover a greater distance in this one operation than the peacetime Japanese had ever done in an entire year." Looking back, the loss of the carriers and flight crews as a result of the Coral Sea melee quite possibly crippled the attack planned by Admiral Isoruku Yamamoto. Still, the Combined Fleet possessed a substantial supremacy in combat strength that should have completely overwhelmed the makeshift American fleet.

While the American force had only three carriers—one hastily repaired in only three days after suffering serious damage at the Battle of the Coral Sea—and precious few surface ships capable of standing up to the Japanese force, they had one critical edge. They knew the Japanese were coming and when they would arrive—an intelligence coup of gigantic proportions. They set a trap to lure the Japanese carriers into a position where they could be destroyed. In the fierce air battle, marked by mistakes on the Japanese side and uncanny luck for the Americans, four Imperial Navy Fleet carriers were destroyed at a cost of only one U.S. carrier. Many of their most experienced and nearly irreplaceable air crews, attempting to defend the carrier force, were rescued and lived to carry on the fight elsewhere, but most of the aircraft employed were lost in the battle.

This astounding and decisive defeat—on June 4–5 of the powerful Japanese fleet—bringing a landing force to occupy Midway Island—put an end to any serious thought about taking the Hawaiian Islands and forcing a negotiated peace. Many feel this battle was possibly the turning point in the Pacific war. Despite the remarkable prior success record compiled when relying on carrier aircraft, the basic Japanese plan at Midway was to draw the American fleet out and destroy it in a great surface battle. Big ships and big guns head-to-head.

At the end of July 1942 the Allied armies of the United States, the British Empire, and Russia were engaged in desperate combat around the world with the Axis armies of Germany, Italy, and Japan. In Russia millions of men were engaged in fierce fighting with the Nazis in individual pocket battles, created by German pincer movements designed to envelop and destroy the then-isolated Soviet armies. Great Britain was besieged by Germany in its home islands, as well as in the Atlantic Ocean and the Mediterranean Sea. It was also under attack in Libya and Egypt by the rampaging German armored forces. Its Asian possessions, including an increasingly rebellious India, were under assault by the Japanese.

U.S. Commands in the Pacific

It can be confusing to readers when the Pacific operational area involving the Philippines, New Guinea, the Solomon Islands, Indonesia, and what was once Indochina is called the Southwest Pacific when discussing this area in—WWII under the military command of General MacArthur. The same area is now often called Southeast Asia. From London or western Asia looking toward that part of the world it does lie to the southeast. However, from San Francisco, the same area lies to the southwest. Adding to the confusion of naming the location is the fact that all military forces in the Pacific operational area, including the Central Pacific Area—headquartered in Hawaii—were under the overall command of Admiral Chester W. Nimitz. Only the forces in the Southwest Pacific Area, headquartered in Australia, were under Army command. A totally unified command under one leader was considered impossible considering the personalities of Nimitz and MacArthur in the Pacific, and Admiral Ernest Joseph King, Chief of Naval Operations, and General George C. Marshall, Chairman of the Joint Chiefs of Staff, in Washington.

This artificial command boundary structure made for confusion and conflicts that—in the early part of the war at least—confounded the successful prosecution of the war, usually to the detriment of the soldiers, sailors, and airmen caught up in this inter-service high command rivalry. Later on, when availability of personnel and the production of ships, planes, and armaments began to fill the pipeline and provide sufficient materials of war for extended and widespread operations, the situation improved, despite the command problems.

Admiral King, who was often said to be so tough he shaved with a blow torch and who thoroughly distrusted the Army, understood better than most military leaders that lack of action in the Pacific was an anathema to the public. His heart was in the Pacific because this was the Navy's war. Japan had started the war and was loathed by most Americans. When the Japanese occupied Tulagi and Guadalcanal in the lower Solomon Islands and began the construction of a major airfield that posed a dire strategic threat to continued American presence along the long and vulnerable U.S.-to-Australia supply line, the stubborn King grabbed the opportunity to take the offensive. He convinced the Joint Chiefs of Staff that further expansion of the Japanese Empire should not be tolerated.

The 1st Marine Division was ordered to assault and capture the remote and unknown island of Guadalcanal. In the early stages of the Guadalcanal campaign—indeed for nearly six months—this jealous rivalry and often deliberate lack of communication and cooperation very nearly doomed the first American offensive in the Pacific. Only the even more serious and continuing jealous territorial rivalry existing within the Japanese high command made it possible for the Americans—initially isolated on Guadalcanal—to hang on long enough to achieve a victory.

The awesome potential of the American and Allied Combined Operations concept was finally achieved despite the continuing pressures of personal jealousies. The consolidation of air, land, and sea elements necessary for the assault of Japanese-held island outposts was the ultimate beneficial result of the Guadalcanal campaign.

Indeed, the Army and Marines needed the Navy's ships to transport the men and materiel over immense ocean distances to make the many island assaults, which in turn allowed the construction of air bases to permit relatively safe operation of the fleets. Air supremacy was essential to continued advancement along the perilous road to Tokyo, but it required ground troops to seize and protect strategic bases. As in no other WWII theater of operations, meaningful interservice cooperation in the unique Pacific battles was mandatory. No one branch of the armed forces alone could have achieved this remarkable victory.

Chapter 2

The South Pacific

The words "South Pacific" conjure up magical romantic images of enchanting palm tree–studded South Sea islands, peaceful waters, and congenial natives. For most of the locations occupied during the war, this was far from true. This area consisted of foul-smelling jungle islands frequently swept by torrential rains, and hotbeds of a multitude of devastating and debilitating diseases. The Pacific area of operations consisted of great distances between uncounted small islands that precluded the kind of massive land battles that occurred in Europe and Africa.

The northern tip of the Solomon Islands is only 5 degrees south of the equator and the approximately 675-mile-long chain is one of the wettest areas of the world. Near the southern tip of the chain, and below the equator, lie the islands of Tulagi and Guadalcanal.

The first Westerners to sail into these remote seas were led by Álvaro de Mendaño de Neyra, a Spanish explorer. He gave the string of islands, an archipelago, the name Islas de Salomón, reflecting the hopeful dream that their riches would surpass those of the fabled King Solomon's mines. After his birthplace in the province of Andalucia, Spain, he bestowed the name of Guadalcanal on one large island. The ancient city of Guadalcanal is situated in a valley irrigated by the River Sotillo. Because of its strategic location it was heavily fortified; the remains of its castle and medieval walls still stand.

No Westerner knew of the island before de Mendaño de Neyra visited in 1597, and very few others afterwards. Not until the arrival of the Japanese Navy in 1942 and the later arrival of the 1st Marine Division on its shores did it become known worldwide. While there never was a canal on the island, Marines soon were calling it "The Canal."

The Pacific Ocean Areas, consisting of the North, Central, and South Pacific, were commanded by Admiral Nimitz. The South Pacific Area, under the command of the Navy's Rear Admiral Robert L. Ghormley, was that area east of a north–south line that barely encompassed Guadalcanal, and an east–west line that jogged north once again at the far western tip of New Guinea, and back west again to the very southern tip of China. U.S. Army Forces in the South Pacific Area were commanded by Major General Millard F. Harmon. It was strictly an artificial border that separated New Guinea—and especially the Philippines—and areas further west and south into the Southwest Pacific Area, under the command of General MacArthur. The North Pacific Area was a separate operating area that included the Aleutian Islands and Alaska.

When it was discovered that the Japanese were building an airstrip on the virtually unknown island of Guadalcanal, the Supreme American Commanders felt compelled to take action to stop that Japanese advance. Neither the Navy nor the Marines were in any way prepared to confront the rampaging Japanese forces, but there was literally no alternative other than the isolation of Australia by the Empire of the Rising Sun. The Americans and Australians felt it necessary to initiate some kind of military reaction that would take some of the heat off the bitter and heavy Australian–Japanese fighting taking place on New Guinea and at least slow down the enemy advances.

When the Japanese Navy was engaged by the U.S. Navy in the Battle of the Coral Sea, they were on their way to occupy Port Moresby in southern New Guinea, which would have effectively removed Australia as an allied staging, training, and operations area. The outcome of this first naval aircraft carrier battle—a virtual draw in terms of losses—was critically important, as it caused the Japanese fleet to withdraw and postpone the occupation of New Guinea—temporarily, so the Japanese thought.

Admiral King learned soon after the Battle of the Coral Sea that the Japanese were building a new airfield at the lower and eastern end of the Solomon Islands. Moreover, the Japanese Army was on the move overland, across the mountain spine of Papua, New Guinea, and was determined to capture Port Moresby from the Australians. King fully realized that immediate and drastic action was needed in the South Pacific.

The large (at the time) Allied invasion fleet—which included a few Australian ships—was hurriedly thrown together to meet the threat, but lacked the critical military intelligence to formulate a solid operational plan. There was no discernible continuity of purpose, and no understanding of the tactics of the Japanese fleet, which would have greatly minimized the grievous losses of ships and manpower in the six months ahead.

U.S. naval strategy and tactics had been based on the battleship column, right up to the morning of December 7, 1941. A few hours later the focus had shifted to naval airpower and the few aircraft carriers. Old salts—longtime battleship sailors—had difficulty accepting the airplane as the prime offensive naval weapon. But now the once dominant battleship fleet lay on the bottom at Pearl Harbor in mute testimony to the reality of airpower. This change in naval warfare was irretrievably driven home by the Battle of the Coral Sea in May 1942, and the stunning American victory at Midway a month later in June. These were battles in which the enemy ships never sighted each other.

Guadalcanal

Sharing the first impression of many first-time visitors, Martin Clemens, a Royal Australian Navy Coastwatcher who had spent many years on Guadalcanal, admitted that the island was beautiful on the outside.

"On the inside she was a poisonous morass," he later wrote. "Crocodiles hid in her creeks or patrolled her turgid backwaters. Her jungles were alive with slithering, crawling, scuttling things; with giant lizards that barked like dogs, with huge red furry spiders, with centipedes and leeches and scorpions, with rats and bats and fiddler crabs and one big species of landcrab which moved through the bush with all the stealth of a steamroller."

The desperate and brave men of all Allied services and nationalities who fought and died for the quagmire called Guadalcanal bought the time necessary for American industry to gear up and begin producing the materiel of war. The final victory over the Japanese Empire was as much as anything else a victory of logistics and supply.

Guadalcanal, lying 6,000 miles southwest of San Francisco, at 9 degrees 30 seconds below the equator and 160 degrees east longitude, was an enigma. From the sea it looked inviting, and seemed to fulfill all the delightfully enchanting images of a South Sea island.

According to military historian Dan van der Vat, in his *The Pacific Campaign*, "Even before one drop of blood had been spilled on its fecund soil or a single corpse buried in it, Guadalcanal stank...a queasy quagmire of superabundant vegetation, swift to rot, on a bed of primeval slime humming with malarial mosquitoes and nameless bacteria. Rich in mud and coconuts, the Solomons were wet from May to October, wetter from November to April and diabolically humid all the time." It was the home of a few hardy Melanesian natives, a handful of Western settlers who had provided the government or operated coconut groves, and the natural habitat of huge fierce rats, deadly snakes, and a large, very repulsive breed of frogs. Insects, including centipedes that left a painful trail when they crawled across human flesh, plagued the troops. Worse were the pervasive mosquitoes that spread devastating tropical fevers and debilitating illnesses such as malaria and dengue fever, bedeviling the Americans and Japanese alike.

Tulagi was the capital, in 1941, of the British Solomon Islands Protectorate, under supervision of the Australian government. The resident commissioner was William S. Marchant, who supervised the activities of roughly 500 Europeans, 200 Chinese, some Japanese, and a native population of nearly 100,000 Melanesians. These ferocious-looking black, woolly-haired inhabitants—frequently with bones stuck through their noses—had a long history of cannibalism.

Not far from the few open areas lay the pestilential rain forest, with hardwood trees that reached 150 feet high with spreads of limbs and leaves that blocked out the sun. Even without the sun burning down onto the jungle floor, the heat and humidity were stultifying and enervating. Around the massive trees, frequently 40 feet across at their base, their huge snaky roots grew in an assortment of vines, creepers, and other exotic plants and brambles that slowed any human progress through the jungle. One writer mentioned at least eleven different kinds of thorn bushes that existed alongside the bushes and ferns growing in a profusion that defied marines trying to hack their way through with their machetes. At least one vine had large razor-sharp thorns like hooks that ripped through uniforms and human flesh.

Frequent and heavy rains drenched this wretched area of the Pacific. According to British records the annual rainfall on Tulagi was about 165 inches per year. Sudden storms could produce what the Americans would call "gully washers"—an awful lot of rain in a short period of time. Because the ground rarely had time to dry out, fresh rains could not be absorbed by the already saturated muddy sod. The excess accumulated even on flat land, like a shallow pond, until it ran off into any of the innumerable creeks, rivers, and other waterways that drained the islands.

Geographically, Guadalcanal has little to recommend it to Westerners except the coconut groves planted for the production of copra prior to WWII along a small section of the northern coastal plain near the Lunga River. Constant and never-ending erosion from thousands of years of heavy rainfalls had created a sandy plain on the northern side of the island, between Aola Bay and the Matanikau (pronounced Mah-*tan*-ee-cow) River. This Lunga plain was where the Japanese began building a vital airstrip and where the

Marines landed to drive away the Japanese. Twice the size of New York's Long Island, the island is about 92 miles (148 km) in length and 33 miles (53 km) across at its widest part—2,180 square miles (5,648 sq km) of mostly pestilence and rot. It had no good harbors as did Tulagi, and only a few small ones that could be used at all. The island was not a hospitable place to fight a prolonged military action for either side.

"Each of the major topological features of the area created extraordinary challenges..." observed Eric Bergerud in *Touched With Fire*, his remarkable study of the land battles in the South Pacific. "...[ ]it is enough to note that both New Guinea and the Solomons are home to some of the most rugged mountain ranges and ridgelines on the globe. Precipitous ridges fan out, dissecting the landscape further. Near the coast are densely forested swamps and acres of tall, razor-sharp kunai grass."

Mount Austen, mistakenly thought to be a grassy knoll a short distance inland, and one of the first day's objectives, was 1,541 feet high and more than six miles away from the Lunga Plain. The spiny Kavo Mountain Range crossed the length of Guadalcanal, with the highest peak, Popomanasiu, towering 7,648 feet over the sea. On the south side the island is marked by plunging cliffs protected by reefs difficult to navigate.

The proximity of Guadalcanal and Tulagi—the last worthwhile military locations at the southeast end of the Solomon island chain—to the eastern tip of New Guinea and the approaches to Australian-held Port Moresby gave the location a limited military value. When the Japanese Navy landed on Guadalcanal to build an airfield to support further expansion in the area—after establishing a fleet anchorage at Tulagi about twenty miles across Sealark Channel—Guadalcanal suddenly gained substantial importance. The Japanese were suddenly in an excellent position to cut the main supply route from the United States to Australia, then foster Japan's ambition to isolate or conquer the Australian continent. Considering all the conquests of economically invaluable lands and resources in Southeastern Asia, Japan would have had a virtually unbreakable stranglehold on the area Japan called the Greater Asian Co-Prosperity Sphere.

In many respects, Tulagi was more important than Guadalcanal. The waters around Tulagi could provide a deep-water anchorage for handling the largest ships of any fleet. The combined bases on Tulagi and the Lunga Plain were extremely convenient, as the harbor at Tulagi Island—enclosed by Tulagi, Gavutu, and Tanambogo—is deep and spacious. Since the Imperial Navy had spearheaded Japan's aggressive expansion throughout the Pacific, the airfield being built on Guadalcanal would be able to support fleet operations by providing fighters and bombers as air cover. Surprisingly, the independent-minded Japanese Army and Navy leaders weren't coordinating their efforts to produce a cohesive long-range plan.

What is enlightening to the reader, looking back, is that the Imperial Army did not even know the Imperial Navy was building the airstrip to support the New Guinea operations and a second attempt to occupy Port Moresby. Even after the Americans captured Tulagi and established a beachhead on Guadalcanal, the previously immensely successful but divided Japanese high command continued to squabble about the disposition of their separate forces in response to the totally unexpected invasion, which would disrupt their plans of conquest. It seems the high command was certain the Americans and their Allies would need at least six more months of preparation to mount any kind of counteroffensive.

By that time, according to precise timetables carefully worked out in high-level planning sessions, Japan would have seized New Guinea—with the important site of Port Moresby—and several key island bases from the Allies. Then, for all practical purposes, the war in the Pacific would be over. Even after it became obvious that the Americans intended to hold Guadalcanal, the Japanese Imperial Army refused to believe the invasion was a serious threat to their expansion plans.

CHAPTER 3

THE PARTICIPANTS: AUSTRALIA/NEW ZEALAND, JAPAN, AND THE UNITED STATES

What the United States—with a population of about 132,000,000—did have was a historically and geographically unique national presence. Ranging 3,000 miles from the Atlantic to the Pacific—great natural defensive barriers—and bordered on the north by its great ally Canada, and on the south by an effectively neutral Republic of Mexico, its sheer immensity defied invasion and capture. Within the borders of its forty-eight states, and its valuable territories of Hawaii and Alaska, the United States had the greatest treasure of bountiful natural resources and manufacturing facilities in the entire world.

In contrast, Japan was a small island empire with a population of about 36,000,000 citizens, with no significant basic natural resources. Admiral Yamamoto, even as he planned the attack on Pearl Harbor, knew full well that in any prolonged war of attrition Japan was doomed. At the time of the Guadalcanal landing the American industrial and military might that would eventually prevail in the Pacific had not yet begun to fill the military supply pipelines.

Australia and New Zealand's military, popularly known as the ANZAC forces, taken from a population of about 7 million citizens, were already in the war, having declared war on Germany when Great Britain became involved in 1939. The ANZAC participation was more out of their respect for the British Commonwealth than for any pressing regional military necessity. Before Japanese hostilities began in late 1941 against the West, their nations were not in peril.

ANZAC sent three highly regarded army divisions to aid Great Britain, and were fighting alongside British troops in the Mideast theater, North Africa, and Greece. When the Japanese did declare war in the Pacific, Australia was in serious trouble, having only a small regular force and a well organized militia left to defend their homes. When Japan drove southward in force, Australia was compelled to recall their divisions from Africa and Europe.

One division remained in North Africa fighting in the climactic desert campaign, in exchange for three American divisions being sent to Australia. The other two came home in 1942 and within months were engaged in fighting Japanese advances over the Owen Stanley Mountain Range of Papua toward Port Moresby. This terrible campaign—which began in July 1942 and was fought across the Kokoda Trail—has never been appreciated nor fully understood. It is rarely acknowledged by military historians to this day, though it had a momentous impact on the American defeat of the Japanese at Guadalcanal. Port Moresby on the other side of the island from Papua, was the main objective of the Japanese army, who regarded Guadalcanal as a minor sideshow. In retrospect, these parallel Allied fights were the first major steps in the ultimate defeat of the Japanese Empire.

The United States—Marine Corps

On December 8, 1941 the enlistment offices of all the armed services had long lines of young men waiting when they opened for business. In quiet Santa Barbara, California, the lines were a block and a half long. In Philadelphia, New York, and Chicago the lines wound around the block.

A furious surge of patriotism inspired the American populace. From the mountains of North Carolina, 15-year-old Jim McCarson fudged on his age and joined up. Robert Leckie and Al Schmid were among the first to volunteer in Philadelphia. Despite cherished regional differences, men rallied to the flag from North and South, East and West. Even after being accepted, volunteers often had to go home and wait for weeks until facilities could be found to train them.

Old men, boys, able-bodied men and sickly ones lined up ready to go. Some hoped to be given a rifle on the spot and be sent somewhere, anywhere, to fight the sneaky Jap cowards. Instead, they were sent to training camps—Marine enlistees found themselves at New River, South Carolina, or at Camp Pendleton, California. Training was brief, chaotic, and disorganized, as well as demanding, tough, and brutal. The Army and the Navy were no better prepared for what was to be a massive influx of manpower.

"I'm pretty sure my boot camp was ten weeks," said McCarson. "It used to be sixteen weeks, with a whole month on the rifle range alone. We spent three weeks on the rifle, pistol, machine gun, BAR, and hand grenade—all of them.

"We fired rifles for qualification at 500 yards. It still hurts me to think about it. When I kept getting Maggie's Drawers [a flag indicating a miss] my instructor kicked me between my legs, in the back, and it like to have killed me. Now, I grew up in the mountains and my daddy and my uncle they all hunted...God knows I was shooting a shotgun and rifle when I was hardly big enough to hold one. I started raising the sights, shooting at the top of the target and still didn't hit it. The next day I slipped off and went to the captain's office without talking to the drill instructor. The captain asked what was wrong with my rifle and I told him I couldn't hit anything with it. He said it wasn't usually done but he would have another rifle issued to me before we went back to the rifle range.

"God knows that when my platoon sergeant heard about that he never let up on me the rest of the time. He kept asking me if I was old enough to be in the Marines, and when I answered that I was, he told me I was nothing but a damned liar.

"I qualified as sharpshooter with my new rifle. The old one must have been worn out or something. I knew doggoned well I could shoot better than I had, and never got another Maggie's Drawers. Shooting was the only part of boot camp that I enjoyed. It was always the .30 caliber I worked with. The only time I ever fired a .50 caliber machine gun was in boot camp. "

Some recently formed reserve units, which had gone through basic and advanced training, were called up. One such was a 37-mm antitank gun unit from Michigan that included George Herbert, who had joined the reserve in 1939. Their ranks were swelled by enlistees after a hurried and harried six weeks of boot training.

A widely believed concept in the Japanese Imperial military high command was that the Americans were effete, more interested in their comfort than in fighting, and terribly afraid to fight at night. With those basic characteristics, the American troops would panic and run at the mere sight of a Japanese warrior. Consequently, fighting U.S. troops would hardly be a challenge for the competent Japanese soldier or sailor.

The average age of the invading marines was nineteen, and the force was as green and untested as that figure suggests. Few of the career marines in the 1st Marine Division had ever been in combat. The rigorous training of the Marine Corps is well known, but it was still hard-pressed to condition the hastily assembled force for the battle of attrition they would endure in the months ahead. The division was poorly prepared, poorly equipped, and Major General Alexander Archer Vandegrift had been assured by the Joint Chiefs of Staff that he would have about six more months for the training needed to make the Division fully combat ready.

The less than 10,000 career and reserve marines making up the hard core cadre of the Corps when the war began were tough men, many of whom would have likely been in jail if they had not been in the USMC. Many were alcoholics and what today are called "hard cases"—ideally suited to be marines when WWII broke out. Education was not high on the pre-war list of priorities for enlisted personnel. Regardless, the major problem was that there were not enough of them. Handfuls of career men were assigned to form the cadres of new units being trained. Their strength was diluted in the hope of forging a new and larger fighting force down the line. Career privates were promoted and in some cases kept their stripes until they had done their job. But this program was woefully incomplete when the presence of the 1st Marine Division was suddenly required at Guadalcanal.

The famed Marine boot camp was of dire necessity not really long enough to forge their basic individual skills and certainly inadequate for essential unit (company and battalion level) training. Physical and mental conditioning—along with a close familiarity with the rifle and the bayonet—were about all that could be touched on during this brief training period. The senior officers were desperately seeking qualified junior officers and noncommissioned officers (NCOs), but often their selections didn't work out in combat. The transition from a peacetime organization to one capable of fighting a war was an enormously difficult process.

Compounding the state of readiness necessary for combat was a lack of materiel. The individual weapons issued to the incoming marines were bolt-action 1918 vintage Springfield rifles, few of which were in good condition. This rifle required that after each shot a fresh cartridge be fed into the breach manually from a five-round clip. The Garand M-1 semi-automatic rifle with eight-round clip—the standard firearm for the Army and available since 1936—was supplied to the Army. The basic sidearm issued to officers was the 1917 model .45-caliber Colt automatic pistol. The helmets to be worn in combat were the new steel pots that had replaced the flat WWI bowls worn on December 7th. The availability and quality of combat equipment such as machine guns and mortars left much to be desired. Even the ammunition and hand grenades were suspect—duds and misfires were all too frequent. A marine fighter in combat hoped when he pulled the trigger at one end of the rifle that a bullet would come out the other end.

Individual combat training procedures were hurried and not always effective. No officer or noncommissioned officer had firsthand experience fighting the Japanese. The critical survival lore gained only from actual combat against the enemy was abysmally lacking. The great majority of the officers and men in the American armed forces had no idea of the capabilities of the enemy they would be fighting, except that the Japanese were all but invincible. That perception of the enemy was not a very good morale builder.

Senior officers, despite their career longevity, were inexperienced in the ways of war. Yet a significant handful had seen action in WWI and in the various Caribbean and Central American uprisings between the world wars. On Guadalcanal many staff marine officers on the field of combat, from major through colonel, were relieved because of incompetence and sometimes cowardice. Unfortunately for the troops who served under them, the only way to tell if an officer was capable of leading in combat was to put him into combat. Consequently, Major General Vandegrift never hesitated to remove hesitant or unfit officers from combat commands.

In the Spotlight

Major General Alexander Archer Vandegrift, USMC

Alexander A. Vandegrift, commanding general of the Marine forces at Guadalcanal, would be known as "Vandegrift of Guadalcanal," proclaimed one distinguished military analyst, if America bestowed titles of nobility as they do in England. Such a formality would not have been accepted by this soft-spoken, modest, and most uncommon man.

He was a sturdy, handsome man, with a dimple accentuating his firm, hard jaw. He had a soft voice, but he was aggressive, a keen judge of men, and a gentleman long before an act of Congress made him one. The historian Dan van der Vat observed that Vandegrift "seems to have inherited a full measure of stubbornness from his Dutch forebears—a modest model of a fighting general who was also no slouch at staff work." His steady, optimistic attitude even when on the brink of disaster made him the ideal leader for the critical Battle of Guadalcanal. Vandegrift's headquarters were as exposed to the same enemy attacks, bombings, and shellings as his men. On the second day of the bloody fight for Edson's Ridge several Japanese soldiers flashing their bayonets charged to within a few feet of him before being killed by nearby marines.

That marine morale remained uncommonly high despite the constantly threatening disaster of crippling sickness, malnutrition, and death can be attributed to his remarkable reassuring presence. Even the saltiest "Old Breed" noncoms and enlisted men knew instinctively they were in the presence of an uncommon man possessing an enormous inner strength. They had not been any place or done anything he hadn't.

Later, when he was commandant, General Vandegrift, comparing the marines with the Japanese fighting man, noted that the Japanese soldier "was trained to go to a place, stay there, fight, and die. We train our men to go to a place, fight to win, and to live. I can assure you, it is a better theory."

For his aggressive leadership while commanding the 1st Marine Division, Reinforced, on Guadalcanal from August 7 to December 9, 1942, Major General Vandegrift, fifty-five years old at the time of the landing, was awarded the Navy Cross and the highest award possible for any fighting man, the Medal of Honor.

One important reason Vandegrift chose to accept a commission in the Marine Corps as a second lieutenant on January 22, 1909 was the sharp blue uniform. Born March 13, 1887 in Charlottesville, Virginia, where he also attended the University of Virginia, many of the men in his family had served in the Confederacy. He was certain that if his late father could have known he had put on a blue uniform he would have rolled over in his grave. Yet his southern ancestors would certainly have approved of his selection of the military as a career.

Like so many marines of the time, he had seen action in the Caribbean and Central America. From August 1916 to December 1918 he served in the Haitian Constabulary at Port-au-Prince, which prevented him from service in WWI France. Six months later he returned to Haiti and served as an Inspector of Constabulary until April 1923.

During the late 1920s he was stationed in China until 1937, except for a couple of short stateside assignments. He was promoted to colonel in 1936.

Upon his return to Washington, DC in June 1937 he became Military Secretary to Major General Commandant, USMC. In March 1940 he became assistant to the commandant, and was appointed to the rank of brigadier general a month later.

In 1941 Vandegrift was assigned to the 1st Marine Division, before being promoted to major general in March 1942 and named commanding general of the division just before it sailed for the South Pacific in May. Assured that the division would not be committed to action before early 1943, he was incredulous when he was suddenly ordered to lead the landing on Guadalcanal. He lived in close proximity to his marines during the heaviest and worst fighting on the island, and endured much the same privations as his men.

Later, on November 1, 1943, commanding the First Marine Amphibious Corps, he led the landing to establish a beachhead at Empress Augusta Bay, at Bougainville in the Northern Solomons. Once this goal had been achieved, he was ordered to Washington as marine commandant-designate.

On January 1, 1944, now a lieutenant general, he was sworn in as the eighteenth Commandant of the Marine Corps. Vandegrift became the first four-star general ever to serve in the Marine Corps on April 4, 1945, the promotion retroactive to March 21, 1945. He retired from the Marines in April 1949.

During his forty-year career, Vandegrift won the Medal of Honor, Navy Cross, and Distinguished Service Medal, to wear along with three Presidential Unit Citations and a host of American service and campaign ribbons. In addition, his foreign awards include being named Honorary Knight Commander, Military Division of the Most Excellent Order of the British Empire, and a member of the Legion of Honor (Grand Officer) from France.

After his retirement Vandegrift and his wife Mildred lived most of their final years in Delray, Florida. He died on May 8, 1973.

The United States—Navy

The Navy, the best prepared of the armed forces, wasn't in much better shape than the other branches. Because of the scarcity of ships the old line cadres were not as scattered among a multitude of units and had time to train new crews who knew the front of a ship from the back. Also, service in the fleet attracted a better-educated manpower pool. Because of the peacetime draft, many young men enlisted in the Navy rather than take the chance of being assigned to the Army or the Marines.

Still, the enlisted career personnel of the peacetime Navy was not all that different from the Army or the Marines. Only the iron discipline of the services had kept many of these men in line. The officer corps of the Army and Navy suffered the same malady as the Marines—the few that had seen any combat were carryovers from the First World War. Too often the main thrust of career officers had been to keep their noses clean and not do anything that would interfere with their promotions.

Military doctrine in all the services was still more or less predicated on WWI principles. The Navy had planned for the big, decisive confrontation of battleships in clear daylight. Despite rumbles from some of the more aggressive officers, little serious thought was given to the tactical use of aircraft and their carriers as a primary battle weapon. The submarine was not considered a serious offensive weapon by the dominant battleship sailors, nor by the Japanese. Consequently, no realistic doctrine concerning antisubmarine warfare existed—a lack which nearly cost the Allies the war.

As "America's first line of defense," the Navy did not do too well in the opening months of the war. The Japanese drove back any American fleet that turned to face them. Along the Atlantic coast German submarines—once Hitler recognized their cost-effective value—were waging highly successful, unrestricted economic warfare against Allied shipping, the critical lifeline of Britain's island home. Identifying competent combat officers for the few ships possessed by the Navy was a sobering experience. Finding the right mix of men, ships, and aircraft to fight the war almost took too long.

Naval Construction Battalions

Because of their mission as an amphibious assault force, the Marines did not have combat engineering units comparable to those of the Army. When the war began, the

Navy created the Naval Construction Battalions—the fighting Seabees as they came to be known—to clear ground and build airfields, docks, and the housing, warehouses, roads, and sanitation facilities necessary to maintain the ground units. Journeyman construction workers and engineers quickly volunteered to do the work they were already trained for.

"The difficult we do immediately; the impossible takes a little longer," was the often demonstrated motto of these tough men long inured to hard work. While the Seabee mission was to build, they proved time and time again that they could fight if the need arose. There are instances where bulldozer operators attacked and destroyed Japanese machine gun positions, using the big blade to deflect bullets fired at them. Even when under fire, the Seabees continued to work on their assigned projects. Later in the war the Seabees provided stevedore battalions to handle the huge quantities of supplies moving up to the forward positions.

The Seabees

Commander Joseph P. Blundon, a wiry 45-year-old engineer from Keyser, West Virginia, in charge of the 6th NCB (Naval Construction Battalion), landed in a PBY off Lunga Point the same day the combat aircraft arrived. After conferring with Vandegrift he requested that two companies of Seabees, along with specialists in water purification and machinery repair and maintenance, be moved immediately from Espiritu Santo to Guadalcanal.

"I guess I was the first Seabee to go under fire," he recalled. "The marines had been on Guadalcanal thirteen days, and they had a tiny beachhead around Henderson Field. While I was reporting to General Vandegrift, the Jap bombers came over and I hit my first foxhole. I just lay there and trembled with patriotism while the bombs fell around us.

"We realized at the outset that the battle was going to turn on how fast we filled up the holes and how fast we could develop that field. When the Jap bombers approached, our fighters took off; the bombers blasted the airstrips; and then if we couldn't fill up those holes before our planes ran out of fuel, the planes would have to attempt to land anyway, and they would crash. I saw seven of our fighters crack up in one bitter afternoon. From our point of view the battle of Guadalcanal was a race between the Jap artillery and air force and the Sixth Seabee Battalion."

When the older men making up the Seabees came ashore a few days later, the age difference was noted by the much younger marines. "What the hell, Pop! Are we running out of men at home already?"

"So, this is the Seabees! The Confused Bastards! What the hell are you doing here?" chided another. American construction workers have never been exactly thin-skinned, so they joined in the banter.

"What are we doing here? Why, goddammit, we were sent in here to *protect* you goddam marines!"

Soon the marines were getting a laugh from another comment they liked to make: "Never hit a Seabee, because he might be your father!" The mutual disparagement gave way to respect after the Seabees saw how the marines wiped out a Japanese machine gun nest and the marines witnessed the new sailors working under falling bombs and shell fire on Henderson Field.

The "tankers" were immediately grateful when a Seabee machinist spotted the open sprocket over which the tread revolved. The Japanese had learned they could jam a crowbar through the spokes of the sprocket and stop the tank dead. The machinist simply cut the top out of a fuel drum and welded it to cover the sprocket—cheap protection for a valuable vehicle.

The United States Air Arms—Navy, Marine, and Army

The groups most ready to fight the war were the army pilots and the navy and marine aviators. They were young, aggressive, and well trained...far better than the equipment they had available for use. The American Navy and Marine Wildcat fighter planes were inferior to the fast, maneuverable Japanese Zero fighter plane, or "Zeke" as it came to be called. The Army P-39 and P-40 fighter planes were no better than those of the Navy. Dive bombers and torpedo planes were decent, but the torpedoes were all but useless. Newer aircraft were in production but hadn't reached the squadrons. One fact is remarkable—not one American aircraft used in WWII was designed *during* the war. All were either in production (limited) or already on the design board designated for production. The B-17 Flying Fortress was originally designed for long-range reconnaissance or as an adjunct for coastal artillery. Hence its name, as in a defensive flying fortress. As highly effective and invaluable as the later modified versions came to be in Europe for high-level bombing of fixed targets, it proved of little value against moving targets such as ships. In the battle for Guadalcanal, the B-17 Flying Forts did a great job bombing the fixed facilities at Rabaul to take some of the heat off the marines fighting on the ground. This remarkably rugged aircraft had the ability to defend itself even while conducting long-range patrol and photo reconnaissance missions.

The United States—Army

Although the Army had more than four and a half million men on its rolls when the war began—rapidly expanded from a peacetime low of about 130,000 men—there was a startling disparity in the quality from top to bottom. Even the regulars, along with the National Guard units and Reserves that had been called up, did not possess nearly enough weapons, equipment, and materiel needed to fight a modern war.

Moreover, the training effectiveness ranged from excellent in the regular forces—such as the 25th Division in Hawaii—to pitifully poor in some of the Reserve and Guard units. The career officers and enlisted men were professionals who had been provided with a well-thought-out training and operational doctrine despite a lack of equipment. As in the other armed services, there were many who were adequate in peacetime but unsuited to command in war. Still, there was a small hard core who had seen action in WWI and survived the vicissitudes of peacetime service.

The Reserves and National Guard units, with some members who had served in WWI, were often far less militarily than politically minded. Many of the senior officers obtained their rank through personal family, political, and economic connections instead of their ability to lead troops. The structure within these units accurately reflected the local and regional social structures, in that the so-called higher class and better educated citizens became officers and the lower class and working citizens filled the enlisted ranks.

The peacetime draft had suddenly swelled the Army's ranks with several million men who had to be forged into soldiers. The expanded college Reserve Officer Training Corps (ROTC) and service Officer Candidate School (OCS) programs were hard pressed to provide sufficient numbers of junior officers, much less lieutenants with proven leadership qualities. Often, when Reserve or National Guard units were called up, their junior officers—lieutenants and captains—marginally trained as they were, were transferred to newly formed units consisting mostly of recent conscripts.

The conversion of this uneven mishmash of men into companies, battalions, regiments, divisions, and corps making up a good, solid Army—a force of nearly 6 million strong with a core of less than 200,000—has to rank among the military miracles of all time. Much of this can be attributed to the attitude of the young men of the time—the United States was just emerging from a devastating economic depression.

The men and women in all the services were accustomed by the rigors of the depression years to hard work. They had no fantasy that the world owed them a living, but embraced the idea that everyone had to take care of himself. For most, service in the armed forces was a necessary step in fulfilling their patriotic obligations to their country. Not all liked the idea of becoming soldiers as the peaceful world they'd known fell apart, but they stepped forward and did it anyway.

The Japanese sneak attack on Pearl Harbor focused their minds and gave them an almost holy crusade to pursue. Today it is all but impossible to believe that such a transformation from peace to total war could ever occur again. The Army was not a volunteer force in the same sense as the Navy and Marines, but performed their duties very well. The initial differences, primarily of mission, were soon reconciled to produce an effective fighting machine of varying capabilities. This transformation of millions of Americans indicates that the young men and women of America were basically more alike than they were different.

The Australians and New Zealanders—The ANZACs

A few Australian warships participated in the Guadalcanal action, and the nation's vulnerability to Japanese invasion prevented their army from furnishing a large number of troops. Still, some who had been fighting with other British Commonwealth armies in Egypt and the Middle East were called home. The hardy and feisty Australian Army troops quickly became involved in brutal jungle fighting in New Guinea, repelling the Japanese onslaught toward Port Moresby across the incredibly rugged Owen Stanley Mountain Range.

As few as they were, the Australians—the acclaimed "Diggers"—were justifiably noted as among the best soldiers in the world, despite MacArthur's disparaging contempt. Physical hardiness and athletic pursuits had produced independent-minded, physically active, and rugged men who thrived in the martial arts. The seasoned divisions returning to defend their homeland had been battling in the North African desert. Like the other Western armies, they were well prepared to fight a European type war, but unprepared for debilitating jungle fighting. Regardless, they learned fast and quickly became the nemesis of the highly touted Japanese South Seas Detachment.

The arrogant Japanese had divided their forces, and their consequent inability to fully focus on either the New Guinea or the Guadalcanal campaign was the major factor in their final defeat. Without the Australian army forces fighting in this little known but critical battle, the outcome on Guadalcanal would likely have been a terrible defeat for the Americans.

At this point in time, Australia and New Zealand, with their critically needed bases and staging areas, were all but isolated in a wretched battle to prevent a full-scale Japanese invasion and occupation. Even with the hurried appearance of three under-equipped and inexperienced U.S. Infantry Divisions, and limited aircraft and ships to bolster their defenses, there was little hope these stars of the British Empire could repel a determined Japanese invasion alone.

Considering the vulnerability of these British Commonwealth countries, it was a jolting surprise to the Americans when the civilian dockworkers in Wellington, New Zealand went on strike and refused to reload the cargo and equipment of the 1st Marine Division headed for combat. Perhaps they would have reconsidered their position had they known the division was headed for an invasion. Because of security reasons, they couldn't be told.

Not only did the dockworkers insist on their regular tea breaks, but they absolutely refused to work during the three weeks of rain that fell during the unloading, resorting, and reloading of the cargo on ships headed for Guadalcanal. Marines destined for combat—many suffering from a flu epidemic—were forced to work eight-hour shifts during even the most torrential rains to reload the materiel necessary for the landing so that the most urgently needed combat equipment and supplies could be unloaded first.

The ANZAC Coastwatchers

One of the most significant contributions made by the ANZACs in the battle for Guadalcanal was the handful of naval reservists and selected white and native civilians living in the Solomons who made up the Coastwatchers. Under the auspices of the Royal Australian Navy (RAN), these brave, resourceful, and rugged individuals created a mystique of courage and hardiness that still intrigues people today. Their ranks were filled with intrepid mavericks who had often spent most of their adult lives living and working in the jungle. They knew they were being asked to risk their lives doing a dirty, difficult, and dangerous job that needed to be done.

Their observation positions formed a 3,500-mile arc around Australia for the express purpose of reporting Japanese air and naval movements toward Australia back to their headquarters. Many were assigned to islands already occupied by victorious Japanese troops, who hunted them down and killed them—when they could find them. The bravery of these men was a significant contrast to the large numbers of white government and commercial residents who panicked and ran in the face of the advancing Japanese military.

Keep in mind that the natives of the region didn't really differentiate between the British "old" whites and the Japanese "new" whites—both were foreign intruders. Whoever they were, they weren't the native black Melanesians. Because of the rapid expansion of the Japanese Empire, when the Coastwatchers found large numbers of the native population who could be trusted to help them they deemed themselves lucky. Many of the population adapted to the change of "whites" for reasons of simple survival. A handful—who thought the coming of the Japanese meant they could finally rule their own destiny—were elated and willing to help expedite the departure of the British and Australian administrators.

One Western feature the British had brought to these remote islands—which helped prevent an all-out conversion to the Japanese cause—was religion. The Christian missionaries, remarkably, had proven not only tolerant of native ways, but helpful. The "white man's medicine," such as inoculations against the disease yaws, was especially useful. There were, of course, prejudiced and intolerant missionaries who alienated the natives, but they didn't last long. The deadly jungles of the Solomon Islands were no place for religious tyrants. A remarkable interdependency developed among the unique blend of unlike peoples. In the 60,000 square miles of the Solomons when WWII came there were approximately 650 whites—mostly missionaries and planters—living among more than 100,000 natives. Among the whites were a handful of wastrels, beachcombers, and drifters who could not tolerate the civilization from which they had escaped.

The durable and bulky teleradios furnished by the RAN had a range of 450 miles for voice transmission and about 600 miles when using Morse code. Each unit weighed close to 800 pounds, and even when broken down into smaller components required at least eight and often a dozen men to carry them back into the bush. The speaker, receiver, and transmitter wouldn't work without heavy batteries and recharger engines that ran on benzene. Without the invaluable assistance of a small handful of the native population, the Coastwatchers would have been out of business. Had the Japanese been more tolerant and respectful of the rights and welfare of the Melanesians, this exceptional operation would have failed.

The network of Coastwatchers was established by Australia after the First World War because of the thousands of miles of its unguarded coast. This was a haphazard organization until 1939 brought war to Europe. Lieutenant Commander Eric Feldt, RAN, was selected by the RAN's first full-time Director of Naval Intelligence, Commander R.B.M. Long. Feldt was an acclimated islander, having lived long in the wilds of New Guinea, and by 1941 he had established more than 100 Coastwatching stations in a crescent-shaped "fence," all ultimately reporting to his headquarters at Townsend, Australia.

Ferdinand was the name given to this operation, after the popular peaceful "Ferdinand the Bull" who didn't like to fight. The mission of the Coastwatchers was to observe and report, not to fight. Their primary means of communication were the teleradios, specially designed and built to survive the sweltering and rugged jungles in which they were to operate. What arms they did carry were for personal defense.

On Guadalcanal the primary Coastwatcher was Martin Clemens, a young government official who chose to stay behind at Aola, the government seat, when the Japanese displaced the British on the island. RAN Pay Lieutenant Don Macfarlan moved his teleradio to the northern coast with the assistance of Kenneth Dalrymple Hay, who had managed the Berande coconut plantation. F. Ashton "Snowy" Rhoades, another old-timer on the island, concentrated his efforts on the western end of Guadalcanal. On May 1st, with the Japanese heading for Tulagi, the three teams headed into the bush.

Two Coastwatchers were placed on Bougainville, and one in the mid-Solomons. At Malabita Hill above Buin, on the southern end of Bougainville, was Paul Mason, who had been in the Solomons since 1915. It was Mason's terse reports, such as "forty bombers heading yours"—in reference to Guadalcanal—that most characterize the legendary Coastwatchers. Jack Read, who had served on New Guinea for twelve years, was on the northern end of Bougainville at Aravia, across from Buka, where the Japanese eventually built a vital airstrip.

Donald Kennedy located his station at Segi on New Georgia. Then Henry Josselyn, formerly assistant district officer on Guadalcanal, volunteered to go to Vella Lavella. These were the leaders of the stations and they were assisted by many trustworthy and loyal native-born Solomon Islanders. In the early days of the fight for Guadalcanal, these rugged individualists were worth several regiments of soldiers. Years later, when asked why he or any other sane man would volunteer to work on an island full of Japanese troops, Snowy Rhoades said he had asked himself the same question a thousand times and still didn't know the answer.

"The intelligence signaled from Bougainville by Read and Mason saved Guadalcanal, and Guadalcanal saved the South Pacific," Admiral William F. Halsey later wrote.

The Japanese

During the interval between World War I and World War II, ardent Japanese militarists gained ascendancy, and then came to control the entire political structure—all in the name of the Divine Emperor. In 1931 Japan began its overt military adventurism by invading and conquering Korea and Manchuria. The early successes on the Asian mainland simply fueled the dream for further expansion of the empire.

Imperial Japan struck the first blow against the United States at Pearl Harbor the morning of December 7, 1941, and a few hours later in the Philippines. From then on—for more than six months—the awesome Japanese Army and Navy attacked and conquered at will. Their rapid territorial acquisitions elated the Japanese population. They fully believed they would soon achieve *Hakkichiu*, their catchphrase for bringing the eight corners of the world together under one roof. The war effort was pursued with a religious zeal.

The Japanese differed from the Europeans not only in stature, but in their distinctive culture and psychology as well. Their fighting spirit and physical strength allowed them to endure where others might falter. The Asian xenophobia—the hatred of outsiders—applied not only to the white Westerner, but to anyone not of their family, clan, or nation. In many respects the whites were able to get along with portions of the Japanese, Chinese, Filipinos, and Malays better than they were able to get along with each other. The ancient racial hatreds of the Chinese for the Japanese and the Japanese for the Koreans, for example, remain to a surprising extent even today.

The Imperial Navy and Army men who fought in the terrible battles of Guadalcanal were experienced, seasoned troops. Most of the units had fought and won in China and the other early battles of WWII, and a substantial number had participated in the Manchurian campaign. These prior successes gave the military a careless confidence that bordered on arrogance. Many of the leaders were absolutely certain that the indomitable Japanese spirit, combined with advanced armaments, would prevail over any opposition. There can be no doubt that this same almost mystical spirit allowed the Japanese fighting man to endure terrible hardships in the name of the Emperor.

During the 1920s and 1930s, the resurgent samurai spirit of militarism—the way of the warrior—began calling for a return to ancient values that guided fighting men. The animosity of the Japanese ruling classes—military and civilian—toward the Western nations ran deep. War had always been the accepted way of settling matters. Cooler heads with an appreciation of the world understood that such egocentric pugnacity by a small island nation lacking most of the basic natural resources for conducting a large-scale war against larger and richer nations was doomed to failure. Those realists who persisted in such "defeatist" thinking were apt to be assassinated or totally disgraced unless they learned to keep their mouths shut.

Historically, Japanese society derived from a feudal structure, more or less held together by the samurai—warrior caste. Attempts had been made by the central government to suppress the influence of the samurai by legislative fiat, but without lasting success. The ideal of the warrior was all but etched into the national character. Bushido, "the way of the warrior," was an ancient code of conduct prescribing that the most honorable and desirable death was to die for the clan lord, and by extension, for the Emperor. Death was the ultimate challenge of the samurai. The Japanese family (nation) had been specially created by the sun god, and the Emperor was the worldly father.

Among the values required of the warrior—steeped in the Japanese culture for hundreds of years—were loyalty, self-sacrifice, martial spirit, honor, and justice. Failure to live up to these rigid expectations would evoke an enormous shame that could be expiated only by the prescribed suicide ritual. When it came to personal honor, this code—shaped by an old Confucian principle—dictated, for example, that a son could not live under the same heaven with the murderer of his father. Vengeance for such an act, as well as for insults and slights, required the death of the offender. In modern times, as in old, the warrior was expected to endure, to prevail over personal pain and discomfort.

Training for the Japanese enlisted men and junior officers was rigorous and often brutal. Noncommissioned officers were empowered and encouraged to use corporal punishment, including beatings with bats, to humiliate and discipline their underlings. The unquestioning obedience of the troops was, at the same time, their greatest strength and their fatal weakness. The existence of the typical soldier and sailor was reduced to the level of single-minded and instant obedience to orders from superiors.

Major General Kiyotake Kawaguchi, on the ocean trip to Guadalcanal for an all-out assault on Henderson Field, saw a young lieutenant standing out on deck smoking a cigarette when he should have been in a meeting with his peers getting pumped up to fight the Americans. Deciding the young officer did not have the right attitude, the general pushed him overboard in the middle of nowhere. It may be assumed that the wayward lieutenant drowned.

Yet, the determined, obedient, and capable Japanese soldier was not perceived as such by Western eyes. "Many of them wear sneakers and swarm up the boles of the coconut trees to the feathery fronds at the top and act as snipers." *The New York Times* ran this comment at the time of the fall of Malaysia in early 1942. "They swing from the jungle lianas like monkeys. They wade through the swamps and become part of them. They infiltrate the British strong points dressed in native clothes or in few clothes at all." These were the troops, who adapted to the necessities of jungle fighting, that defeated and humiliated the supposedly superior British Commonwealth Army.

The European perception of the Japanese imperial troops as "sneaky" and "deceitful," as one English newsman wrote, and having a monkey-like affinity for the jungle, may have helped salve the sting of being humiliated and thoroughly beaten by the physically smaller Japanese warriors. In the American press, the Japanese were stereotyped as bandy-legged men moving with the agility of monkeys, grinning with heavy protruding buckteeth while peering at you through thick glasses that would hardly transmit light. Characterizations such as these may have helped the morale at home, but the American men fighting these highly motivated and well trained troops found out they were quite untrue.

What the Japanese did in Malaysia, of course, was to defeat the British by choosing not to assault head-on the heavily fortified positions, which were usually on or very near paved roads. Who were the Japanese "imitating" when they fought in an unorthodox manner? Why attack impregnable positions when it's so much easier just to bypass and get behind them? They took to the jungle to bypass the conventional fortress defenses. Where does it say in the manuals of warfare that you have to play by the other side's rules? This kind of innovation did not carry over into later battles, when the more conservative Japanese commanders chose to fight in a more traditional manner.

Though the Japanese seemed to favor night attacks, this may have been true because their enemies preferred to fight in the daylight hours. Imperial troops learned to move through the unmarked jungle on foot because their foe preferred to be near the tracks and roads that would support motorized vehicles. The Japanese were especially skillful in the use of infiltration tactics, slipping in among the enemy at night to harass and kill, even when they knew the infiltrators might die in the effort.

The concept of surrender was totally extraneous and unacceptable to the Japanese soldier and sailor. When you went into a battle, you either won or you died. This idea was ruthlessly imposed from the top down and had existed for so long that there was no question of it being right or wrong. As a consequence, the Japanese couldn't understand that their enemies might be hard-pressed enough to give up a fight. They considered surrender cowardly and beyond consideration by the true warrior. This same duty to die was not always demanded of civilians and conscripted workers, but these were not really warriors at all. A civilian leader or military commander who failed to complete an important task was sometimes expected to commit suicide as an act of atonement to the Emperor.

The Emperor was the ultimate father figure—not merely a god living on earth—in a land where the family was dominant. Every Japanese life, regardless of personal feelings, was bound to the divine being of the Emperor. Duty to the Emperor and Japan was "lighter than a feather and heavier than a mountain." To embarrass or fail in one's duty to the family was the extreme disgrace, which only death could expiate. Moreover, it was an accepted belief that the Japanese peoples ranked highest of all human beings on the face of the earth, in all endeavors. A well entrenched nobility and aristocracy ruled absolutely over the masses of the people. Only in death was there equality.

Individual Japanese were frequently a mass of contradictions fused into a whole. A samurai could shed tears while executing a brave enemy, yet felt deep contempt for a warrior who consented to surrender. A simple, straightforward, and predictable man was considered dull and worthless. An enlightened Japanese could contemplate the beauty in a sunrise one moment and have no qualms about beheading a helpless enemy the next.

When the Emperor permitted the militarists to conduct a war for the establishment of a widespread empire, the nation implacably went to war. Not everyone in the empire considered going to war—especially against the United States and the Western powers—a realistic or sensible idea. But when ordinary citizens were ordered to fight, they obeyed. When in 1945 the Emperor ordered his people to lay down their arms—to end the war—the war ended. Not all high-ranking commanders liked that decision to quit fighting—they wanted to fight on despite the certainty of total destruction—but in the end they obeyed the Emperor's edict.

The Imperial Navy's pilots were probably the best in the world at that time. Along with Army pilots, they were about 2500 strong. Rigorous training and extensive combat experience placed them far in front of their enemies. But, as few members of the Imperial high command envisioned fighting an extended war, Japan failed to produce sufficient numbers of pilots and crews. In one naval aviation class, only twenty-five of seventy meticulously screened candidates gained their wings. When pilots and crews were lost in battle, there were precious few replacements, no matter how brave or motivated by the Japanese spirit. The severe attrition of effective pilots and crews was a far more serious proposition than the loss of aircraft.

The Imperial Navy was led by many of the best qualified admirals in any fleet. The men were highly trained and usually belonged to their ship until retired or killed. Moreover, between the world wars Japanese naval doctrine was thoroughly modified to incorporate the airplane. More significantly, the fleet was trained in highly realistic maneuvers, especially in night fighting techniques. They learned to use their great Long Lance torpedoes by actually using them. Often sailors were lost or killed in these realistic training operations, but the ultimate effectiveness was unquestioned.

Most Japanese boys were so poor they could not get higher education except by qualifying for one of the military academies. In January, 1928, Zenji Orita and more than 4,000 other boys took the week-long written exams to qualify by merit only for one of the 130 appointments open for Etajima, Japan's Annapolis. No one who wore glasses, or who was missing more than a couple of teeth, would even be considered.

Before graduation each midshipman had to complete a 10,000 yard swim (about five and two-thirds miles). Most who failed to finish flunked physically, not from poor academics. "A Japanese officer was socially acceptable anywhere, a most unusual thing in class-stratified Japan," said Orita. The family background of each young man had been thoroughly checked by the police before being allowed to even take the competitive examinations.

WWII SNAPSHOT—AUGUST 1942

Egypt—British Prime Minister Winston Churchill selects General Bernard L. Montgomery to command the British 8th Army defending Cairo and the rest of Egypt. The famed German Afrika Corps, under General Erwin Rommel, is closing in on Egypt, eyeing the rich prize of a takeover of the Suez Canal. If the Suez falls into German hands, the shortest communications and supply line between Great Britain and Australia will be cut, forcing long trips down and around the tip of South Africa.

Germany—The Nazi effort to eradicate the Jewish population of Europe is moving forward. On August 9, Catholic nun Sister Bendicta, a converted Dutch Jew formerly named Edith Stein, dies in an Auschwitz gas chamber. On the 11th Germany begins the deportation of Frenchmen they have drafted as forced laborers to eastern Europe.

Southern Russia—The German Southern Army Group is attacked south and west in a massive effort to capture the great oil fields of the Caucasus region. The Nazi summer offensive is running in high gear despite a year of wear and tear on men and machines, and the Soviets appear to be incapable of stopping them.

The North Atlantic—Off Newfoundland, Nazi U-boat "Wolfpacks" send five merchant ships to the bottom in three minutes. The one offensive naval weapon that appears to be successful for the Germans is the submarine fleet. American and British navies work overtime to stop the U-boat attacks, but with little success. It is conceded that if German submarine warfare succeeds in stopping the flow of men and supplies by ship from America to Great Britain (and it is coming perilously close to doing so) they can defeat the British.

The Japanese submarine *I-8* arrives in Lorient, France, from Sasebo, Japan for a visit. The Germans are interested in obtaining more information and details about the Japanese Long Lance torpedo, the best in the world. This is part of a proposed Axis exchange of raw materials and expertise, which has limited success.

The South Pacific—On Papua, New Guinea, an attack by the three relief companies of the Australian Imperial Force (AIF) of the 39th Battalion reaches Kokoda but, unable to hold that position, the battalion is again forced to fall back to Deniki. For the equipment-laden men to climb even a few hundred yards over the steep gradients of the primitive rudimentary track that winds across the mountains through dense rain forest and narrow passages of ravines with walls overgrown with thick bush is physically excruciating and heartbreaking.

The equally struggling and under-supplied South Seas Detachment of the Japanese 17th Army valiantly presses the AIF, and although their attacks on August 9th and 10th are beaten off, the Australian position has become isolated, with food and ammunition running low. Because of an inadequate supply line along the Kokoda Trail, the entire AIF operation in the Owen Stanley Mountains is in danger of collapse.

In the nearby Solomon Islands, a mostly American force, aided by what few ships and men the desperate ANZACs can supply, is closing in on Tulagi and Guadalcanal for the first Allied amphibious assault landing of the war. As this makeshift force approaches their target, Vice Admiral Richmond Kelly Turner, commander of the landing force, reflects on the words of the noted British military theoretician Liddell Hart.

> "A landing on a foreign shore in the face of hostile troops has always been one of the most difficult operations of war. It has now become almost impossible."

The hard-driving, opinionated, and often ferocious Turner, who rarely accepts the opinions and expertise of others, has reason to be worried—the small invasion force he commands expects fierce and determined resistance from the Japanese Imperial troops defending the islands. American casualties are expected to be high.

Vandegrift, also aboard the flagship *McCawley*, has planned for this battle as well as he possibly could, and feels satisfied that whatever the day brings it is too late to worry about the prospects. He writes to his wife:

> "Tomorrow morning we land in the first major offensive of this war.... Whatever happens you'll know that I did my best. Let us hope that best will be enough."

Expectations for the very worst outcome—the destruction of the Guadalcanal invasion—are prudent and realistic. The American commitment to the Allied invasion of North Africa in late 1942 has priority for men and materiel over the Pacific arena. The Japanese are convinced that an American offensive can not possibly be mounted for at least another six months, an estimate consistent with the American high command's own appraisal. As haphazard, hastily planned, and poorly equipped as Operation Watchtower—the first Allied offensive of the war—turns out to be, it is hoped this desperate operation will at least succeed in bloodying the Imperial Navy's nose.

CHAPTER 4

FRIDAY, AUGUST 7, 1942 THE LANDINGS

Large force of ships, unknown number or types, entering the sound. What can they be?

On the morning of August 7, 1942, there were nearly 2,600 Japanese working on Guadalcanal to complete an airstrip by the end of the month, when the 26th Air Flotilla would begin flight operations. About 400 riflemen were there to protect the laborers from raiding forces. This soon-to-be-hotly-disputed airstrip was designed to handle 60 aircraft, including bombers.

Rabaul (pronounced "rah-'bow-el"), on New Britain, at the northern end of the Solomons chain of islands, was home to several of Japan's first-line army and naval forces. Among these units were the 25th Air Flotilla of the 11th Air Fleet (land-based fighters, bombers, and patrol planes), the 8th Fleet, and a formation of submarines, as well as the 17th Army. Their primary objective was the total subjugation of New Guinea—until the irritant of American forces on Guadalcanal divided their efforts. They had occupied the northern New Guinea coastal area, only about 440 miles south of Rabaul. The Japanese were determined to capture Port Moresby on the southern coast to deprive the Allies of an air base—from which B-17 Flying Fortresses could easily reach Rabaul—and then use that base to mount air attacks against Australia.

In the Solomon Islands only two airfields were considered capable of handling bombers as well as fighters. One was at Rabaul; the other was Guadalcanal. On May 3rd the Yokohama Air Group (seaplanes) occupied Tulagi. By May 18th the local commander, Captain Miyazaki Shigetoshi, reported that the Lunga Plain on Guadalcanal was a good location for an advance airbase. The first troops of the permanent party arrived on June 8th to set up tents and construct a wharf—all under the interested eyes of Martin Clemens, an Australian Coastwatcher, and his crew.

A twelve-ship convoy arrived on July 6th to unload men and heavy construction equipment. The 1,350 men of the Imperial Japanese Navy's Kanae 13th Construction Unit under Captain Tei Monzen, and the 1,221 men of Commander Okuma Tokunaga's 11th Construction Unit were to build a new airfield. This news was already known to U.S. Admirals King in Washington and Nimitz in Hawaii. Plans for a retaliatory strike to end the Japanese incursion on Guadalcanal were hastily drafted. A startled radio report from the garrison on Tulagi to the Japanese headquarters in Rabaul was the first indication an American fleet was anywhere near the area. In a fortuitous instance of good luck, the Marine landing force had achieved what any military commander hopes for—total tactical surprise.

By the time the radio station was destroyed in the overwhelming naval bombardment, the few messages reporting the surprise invasion force had aroused considerable anger and confusion among the command staff of the Imperial Naval Forces at Rabaul. Since Japanese intelligence backed the conviction that the Americans and their Allies were presently incapable of a full-scale invasion, the area commanders concluded that this was just another exasperating raid. The American forces would spend a few days destroying supplies and equipment, and reducing the defensive force—then they would withdraw.

Totally unaware that a contingent of the Imperial Japanese Navy (IJN) had begun construction of an airfield on Guadalcanal and fleet facilities at Tulagi, several high-ranking officers of the Imperial Japanese Army (IJA) openly wondered what the Americans could possibly want with such an insignificant island in the South Seas inhabited only by natives. Similarly, many of the Americans headed for the island were equally mystified, and wondered simply, "Just where in hell is this Guadalcanal?"

The American invasion fleet, consisting of more than 80 ships, had slipped into the Guadalcanal area from the south and west, splitting into two wings as it passed Savo Island. The north wing of ships sailed toward Blue Beach on Tulagi, while the south wing—the main force—moved south of Savo toward the main landing area at Red Beach, near Lunga Point, on Guadalcanal. They spotted the large looming silhouette of the island just before the tropical dawn erupted into full daylight.

Plans for the invasion had been made with a minimum of reliable intelligence. Three weeks earlier, when no up-to-date maps could be found to work with, Lieutenant Colonel Frank Goettge, the division's intelligence officer, accompanied a B-17 reconnaissance mission over the island and had a large, detailed photocomposite made of the invasion area. The package containing the only accurate map of Guadalcanal and Tulagi was lost in the Auckland post office. Thus the assault forces went in with an abysmal lack of useful information.

Dawn at Sea

On board the USS *Enterprise*, cruising about 100 miles to the south, reveille was sounded an hour and a half before sunrise to make sure the crew had time for a fairly relaxed and hot breakfast before they went to general quarters. The day promised to be hectic—with the ship's crew buttoned up in their battle stations—just as it would be for every other ship in the invasion formation. The air crews would be flying missions almost continuously in support of the marine landings. Combat Air Patrols (CAPs) would stay over and around the ships to protect the fleet from Japanese retaliation. The aircraft carrier task force was commanded by Vice Admiral Frank J. Fletcher.

"Be absolutely ruthless, show the enemy no quarter. You know that they'll give you the same treatment. The Jap pilots will kill you without blinking an eye," one air officer briefed his combat crews. "We've been hanging on, but now we are ready to strike back. Go get 'em!"

Pilots and crews were in their planes by 5:15 A.M. when the order came to start engines. As the coughing engines caught and began turning over, blue smoke erupted from the exhaust pipes. When the exhaust combined with the heavy moisture being thrust backward by the fast-turning propellers, each plane was enveloped in what some described as a blue cocoon. There was concern that the Japanese would be able to spot the blue rings. This phenomenon also greatly reduced pilot visibility and presented a uniquely dangerous launch situation in the early dark.

At 6:14 the naval shelling planned to destroy fortifications and soften up the resistance of the defenders began, with the yellow flashes of the big guns and red rockets shattering the darkness. The thudding reverberations and the rumble of explosions rolled back out to sea from the impacted target areas. As overpowering and destructive as the naval bombardment seemed to the eyes and ears of the attacking force, it proved to be ineffective against the experienced Japanese combat troops occupying well prepared and adequately fortified defensive positions.

Twenty-year-old Corporal James R. "Rube" Garrett, from Edinburg, Texas, ammo chief for I Battery, 3rd Battalion, 11th Regiment, was on deck with the thousands of marines of the landing force when the ships' guns roared with the first major offensive shots fired by our side in World War II. The men of the 1st Marine Division would never forget that they were there.

Colonel Pedro del Valle commanded the 11th Marines, the 1st Division's artillery regiment. This scion of an aristocratic Puerto Rican family was possibly the first from his island to graduate from the Naval Academy. Fiery and outspoken in his ultraconservative views and criticism of Roosevelt and the New Deal, he was very nearly removed from his post. Whatever his political views, he was an outstanding marine officer in combat.

Navy fighters and dive bombers from the supporting fleet aircraft carriers *Enterprise*, *Saratoga*, and *Wasp* swarmed down from the skies, attacking any Japanese shipping they could find, as well as preselected ground targets. A grim mood of apprehension was widespread among those waiting to hit the beach, and most hadn't felt much like eating breakfast. Still, many of those still aboard ship watching and listening to the spectacular show were thinking: "Payback time at last!"

The grimness of combat operations was sometimes softened, such as when a fighter pilot from *Saratoga* admitted he had strafed and killed about ten cows. His first perception was that he had attacked a column of Japanese infantry on the move to their fighting positions, until he went back to examine his work and realized his error.

Operation Watchtower—soon to be called Operation Shoestring—was launched, and America's first WWII offensive fight was under way. The frantic preparations of the last few weeks to get troops ashore in the lower Solomon Islands had proceeded much better than expected. Memories of the recent bungled practice landing on Koro Island in the Fiji Islands couldn't have soothed anyone's mind. Less than a third of the marines actually set foot on the beach in this badly needed "dress rehearsal." Reefs had blocked the approach of the landing boats and the engines of many broke down or failed to start.

The X-ray transports reached the unloading area off Lunga's Red Beach at 6:54. The order to "Land the landing force," was passed along by bullhorns, and the anxious pack-laden marines clambered down the sides of the transports to load up for the rough tossing and turning 9,000-yard (more than five miles) trip to the beach. The men had finished what breakfast their stomachs would handle.

Private Jim McCarson, the underage North Carolina mountain boy, who was now an ambulance driver, went in on an early wave. Navy Lieutenant (Junior Grade) Kenneth Morgan, a dental officer who had graduated from Ohio State University, wondered why they needed a dentist in the opening assault.

Sergeant George Herbert, a reservist from Michigan, went in with his 37-mm antitank gun crew, and was among the most experienced marines to land that day. Coming ashore in the 1st Marine Battalion was Al Schmid, a young machine gunner from Philadelphia, Pennsylvania. Private Robert Leckie from Rutherford, New Jersey, who later wrote *A Helmet for my Pillow* about his adventures with the 1st Marines on the Canal, was a wild kid who wanted to fight. Pharmacist's Mate 3rd Class William H. Laing from Shreveport, Louisiana, and fellow corpsmen attached to the 1st Battalion, 5th Marines, shouldered their first-aid bags and medical gear, and waded through the warm, blue-green water onto the beach. Traditionally, Navy pharmacist's mates served as medical corpsmen to marine combat units, and were frequently shifted from one unit to another according to the demands imposed in battle.

Just after sunrise fifteen Wildcat fighters from *Wasp*'s Fighting Squadron 72 and fifteen dive bombers had attacked and destroyed the seven Kawanishi "Mavis" flying boats and nine Zero "Rufe" float planes still sitting on the water at Tulagi Harbor. Attack aircraft from *Enterprise* flew in direct support of the Guadalcanal Red Beach assault. Planes from *Saratoga*, flagship of the Expeditionary Force, flew protective cover over the entire fleet. The existing doctrine was to keep the ships of the landing force far enough away to keep them from being destroyed by shore-based gunfire and airborne attacks.

Steaming close in to shore, destroyer *Monssen* opened up with five-inch naval gunfire at 7:27 on a promontory of Florida Island, west of Tulagi, expending sixty rounds on the target in five minutes. *Buchanan* and *San Juan*, the latter an antiaircraft cruiser, fired 100 rounds each into nearby targets. *Buchanan* concentrated its shells at a position east of Haleta, on Florida Island, while *San Juan* blasted a small island to the south of that position. In a later evaluation of the results, experts concluded that substantially more intensive naval gun bombardment over a longer duration would have been required to have had a significant destructive effect on entrenched enemy positions.

"Japanese aerial reconnaissance had bungled incredibly," wrote James and William Belote in their *Titans of the Seas*, "in allowing an invasion force of more than 80 ships, plus three carrier task groups, to slip up to Guadalcanal undetected literally until the moment that the pre-invasion gunfire and bombing began."

Blue Beach—Tulagi—Gavutu—Tanambogo

Though the main landing force, on Guadalcanal proper, met only very light resistance from the 2,571 Japanese and Korean conscripts making up the airfield construction units, the approximately 3,000 marines landing on Tulagi were the first Americans to confront the bitter, fight-to-the-death resistance that typified Japanese Imperial troops on the defensive throughout the remainder of the war.

Some 880 of the Yokohama Air Group and the 3rd Kure Special Naval Landing Force defending Tulagi and the nearby islets died in this fierce early fighting lasting about thirty-one hours. Reportedly, only three of the twenty-three Japanese taken captive surrendered voluntarily. Most were captured only after they had been badly wounded or knocked unconscious by explosions.

The meager gunfire laid down by the ships had little effect. The Japanese were concealed in dugouts and caves that could be eliminated only with a direct hit. There hadn't been any direct hits. The enemy, holed up in the hilly southeastern terrain, had to be killed with grenades and explosives placed by hand. At best this was slow and highly dangerous work. By early afternoon it was obvious that Tulagi was not going to be secured by dark.

Company B, 2nd Marines, reinforced by 4th Platoon, Company D, and twenty-one men from headquarters company, led by Captain Edward Crane, at 7:40 A.M. were the first Marines to set foot on land in the new offensive. The 252 queasy men, in eight landing boats, clambered over the sides and sloshed ashore unopposed at Haleta on Florida Island, twenty minutes before H-hour in a screening maneuver to cover the left flank of the forces hitting Blue Beach on Tulagi. Unopposed, this force secured its objective in forty minutes.

While this covering force raced inland to secure its objective, the remainder of the 1st Battalion, 2nd Marines under Lieutenant Colonel Robert E. Hill conducted a similar protective screening landing at Florida's Halavo Peninsula near Gavutu and Tanambogo. The landing party drew some fire from Gavutu without suffering any casualties. They returned to their ships without encountering any enemy forces.

The landing force that went ashore on Tulagi's Blue Beach at 8:00 A.M. consisted of the 1st Raider Battalion, commanded by Lieutenant Colonel Merrit A. "Red Mike" Edson, followed by the 2nd Battalion of the 5th Marines, commanded by Lieutenant Colonel Harold E. Rosecrans.

Edson was a tough, slender man, with a jaw like cast iron, and cold pale eyes that pierced deeply into a man's soul. His voice was soft, but possessed a compelling authority. He was just the man to lead the Raiders, an organization many marines disliked and didn't see the need for. The idea of an elite force within an already elite force didn't sit well with other officers and men.

Still aboard the Yoke transport group was the Marine Parachute Battalion, scheduled to seize the islets of Gavutu and Tanambogo later that day. There simply were not enough of the clumsy landing boats available to get all the troops ashore simultaneously in the designated landing areas. All Blue Beach land operations were under the command of Brigadier General William B. Rupertus, Vandegrift's assistant commander.

The LCPs (Landing Craft, Personnel), manned with Navy crews, were 36 feet long, with a beam of 10 feet 8 inches and a draft of 2 feet 6 inches. Troops had to unload over the sides, as very few of the boats with front drop-ramps had reached the Pacific. Each boat was powered by one 225-horsepower diesel or gasoline engine. The top speed of 13 knots was not enough to get them out of serious trouble, even with two machine guns aboard installed in ring mounts. The crews and passengers were extremely vulnerable to any kind of concentrated enemy fire.

The Raiders of Companies B and D of the main force landing in the first wave had to wade in to the beach from 30 to 100 yards away through water as much as armpit deep. By the time the men touched dry land their uniforms and equipment were waterlogged. Some men suffered cuts from the coral, which ripped their hands, knees, and fatigues. All the landing boats got hung up on or were stymied by coral reefs and formations. These invaders, stunned by the searing heat and humidity, had no idea what kind of resistance to expect from the Japanese. Fortunately, the landing was unopposed.

The enemy forces, concentrated in the southeastern third of the island—by now fully aware that an assault was under way—still didn't know if it was just a hit-and-run raid or an invasion in force. At 8:00 Japanese messages said shells were falling near the radio installation. Ten minutes later, the final message went out: "Enemy troop strength is overwhelming. We will defend to the last man."

As Companies B and D reached the beach and began moving inland, the landing craft carrying Companies A and C encountered the same problems on the coral reefs. The Weapons Company, landing later, assumed responsibility for beachhead security.

The first companies ashore, now sopping wet and gasping for air, with cramping muscles aching, and sweating profusely in the oppressive heat, climbed up a steep, heavily wooded coral slope, the southwestern portion of the 350-foot ridge that forms an almost unbroken backbone along the island. The green marines were in only fair physical condition, weakened after weeks at sea. Company B pushed across to the far coast of the island and, opposed by only the verdant jungle itself, overran the native village of Asapi. Here they swung right, linking up with Company D and Companies A and C, who had come ashore and moved up alongside. Forming a line across the island, they began hacking their way through the thick underbrush toward the harbor area in the southeast. Dripping sweat in the sweltering heat, they advanced steadily, warily, and without opposition until Company B reached Carpenter's Wharf at 11:20, halfway down the east shore of the island. At this point shots were exchanged with a series of enemy outposts and the company commander, Major Justice Chambers, was wounded by mortar fire and relinquished his command to Captain William E. Sperling.

Second Battalion Fifth Marines, bringing the number of infantrymen ashore up to 1085, were landed and ready to go by 9:16. Their job was to clear the north and west and protect the main advance to the east. Tulagi was about 4,000 yards (2¼ miles) in length by 1,000 yards (a little more than ½ mile) at its widest point. The heaviest fighting was expected to take place on the southeastern third of Tulagi around the areas cleared of jungle growth—Government Wharf and the former government residency grounds. Early estimates of Japanese strength on Tulagi-Gavutu-Tanambogo were put at 7,125 to 8,400 men. Actually, only a small detachment of about 350 members of the 3rd Kure Special Naval Landing Force, commanded by Commander Masaaki Suzuki, was on Tulagi.

Many Japanese military units bore the name of the province or area from which most of their members were recruited. Hence, of the defending force, those wearing the anchor and chrysanthemum emblem of the Imperial Navy on their helmets had come from in or around Kure, near Hiroshima. Despite their designation as Special Naval Landing Force they were not the equivalent of the American marines. These units served in defensive positions around naval facilities, such as the seaplane base at Tulagi. They were there to protect the seaplane base, and in typical defensive fashion had expanded into tunnels and caves arranged in a staggered alignment. These positions were impervious to almost any blow other than a direct hit, and had hardly been touched by American naval gunfire and dive bombing conducted by carrier-based aircraft.

Traveling light because of their special assault mission, the marines carried little gear other than ammunition. "Don't worry about the food," Edson had told them. "There's plenty there. Japs eat, too. All you have to do is get it." The Raiders found out just after noon how difficult it would be to seize that food when they moved up to the resistance line about a mile from the southeastern tip. Company A advanced down the hill toward the old cricket grounds.

Japanese snipers and machine gun emplacements, concealed in camouflaged tunnels and caves, frequently let the point men pass by and then opened up on the main force following, delaying the advance. "If they had been good shots few of us would have survived," said one marine. Slowly, one by one, those nests were destroyed and the defenders killed.

By dusk, despite persistent sniper fire that seemed to come from every tree and building, the marines owned all but one corner of the island, where the protectorate government center was located. They moved into a three-sided shovel-shaped ravine where the Japanese, burrowed in countless caves, delivered a continuous cross fire over the flat space the British had once used as a cricket field. After the Raiders dug in for the night the Japanese counterattacked with the first *banzai* charge of the war on Americans. Filled with liberal amounts of sake and whiskey, shouting obscenities in Japanese, or in what little English they knew, they charged through the darkness against the American lines.

"Banzai!" and "Hurrah!" they screamed from the inky tropical night, their banshee-like yelling designed to stab terror into cowardly American hearts.

"Japanese boy drink American boy's blood!"

The marines roared back obscenities, accompanied by the hammering punctuation of heavy U.S. machine gun and Springfield rifle fire that ripped enemy flesh apart. Some marines were so gifted with the salty vocabulary that they were reputed to be able to cuss nonstop for an hour without ever once repeating themselves. Grenades exploded and tore bodies apart, killing and maiming, and lit up the pitch-blackness with red and yellow flashes. Screams of the wounded and dying assaulted the ears. Five times the howling Japanese charged, and five times they were stopped. When dawn came on the 8th, Private 1st Class John Ahrens, one of Company A's Browning Automatic Rifle (BAR) men, was found bloody and dying from two shots in his chest and three bayonet wounds. The dead bodies of a Japanese officer and a sergeant had fallen on him, and thirteen other dead Japanese riflemen lay in front of him. Captain Lew Walt, the company commander, holding the youth in his arms, heard his final words.

"Captain, they tried to come over me last night, but I don't think they made it."

"They didn't, Johnny. They didn't," replied Walt in a soft voice.

Fighting continued during the day, and while corpsman William Buchman and surgeon Lieutenant (Junior Grade) Samuel Miles were working on three seriously wounded Raiders, they were killed by the blast and shrapnel from a mortar shell, which also critically wounded a company commander. On that second day Laing and three other corpsmen were rushed to Tulagi across Sealark Channel to set up a crude battle aid station and assist the corpsmen already there with the Raiders of Company B. A day later they began evacuating the seriously wounded to the beach for transfer to the designated hospital ships.

The fewer than 350 Japanese had to be blasted out of their caves and defensive positions with grenades and dynamite charges. Individual marines crawled forward under covering rifle fire, climbed the hills, and swung improvised satchels of explosives down into the caves.

On Hill 208 Major Kenneth D. Bailey, Danville, Illinois, commanding Company C, was wounded in the leg after he scurried to the top of a cave, from which a Japanese machine gun nest was raking the area, to kick away its cover so it could be destroyed with rifle fire and hand grenades.

Gunnery Sergeant Angus Gauss quickly understood that the best way to neutralize the bitterly defended caves was to blow them up. He loved to blow up things, and an explosion was music to his ears. Assembling a small crew, they improvised pole charges—no Bangalore torpedoes, flamethrowers, or tanks were available. Two men would slide forward under cover of machine gun, smoke grenade, and rifle fire, shove the dynamite charge into the cave and set it off.

Edson reported that, "We pulled out thirty-five dead Japs from one dugout. In another we took out thirty. Some of those people had been dead for three days, but others were still in there shooting.... In none of these places was there any food or water."

Company A counted twenty-six dead Japanese within 20 yards of the defensive line. By afternoon the only living Japanese on Tulagi were a half-dozen badly wounded enemy soldiers. They had fulfilled their vow to fight to the last man.

In the brisk fighting on Tulagi, thirty-six Raiders were killed and fifty-four wounded—a light casualty list compared to Japanese losses. About forty defenders swam to nearby Florida Island, where they were later hunted down. Among the supplies and materiel captured were trucks, ammunition, gasoline, radios, a couple of antiaircraft guns, and ten machine guns.

Big Show for the Coastwatchers

Across the channel, on Guadalcanal, Martin Clemens was disgusted and depressed with the lack of any reaction to the airport rising on the plain far below his lofty mountain observation point. "Is nothing going to happen after all?" he wrote in his diary on August 6th. In the meantime, the Japanese were increasing their patrol activity to locate and destroy these vital observers.

Startled awake the next morning by his exuberant comrades and the sound of naval gunfire and bombs blasting the Japanese positions, Clemens saw that the channel between Tulagi and the Lunga Plain was swarming with ships and attacking Allied airplanes. His deliverance from the Japanese was at hand, as was that of his fellow Coastwatchers Don Macfarlan and Snowy Rhoades and the other civilians who had remained behind. Their terrible wait was over.

"Calloo, calley, oh, what a day!!!" This joyful expression of glee was his diary entry at noon. He and the others listened in rapture over the combat network to the chattering between ships and airplanes, the endless short bursts of American slang. Now the work of Clemens and his mates stationed along the Solomon Islands was just beginning.

Already the Japanese were readying warships and airplanes at Rabaul to strike back hard at the intruders on Guadalcanal. The direct flight route was over these islands, where the Coastwatchers had established their observations posts. These men were also in an excellent position to view ship movements through the "Slot" between the islands. Within the next few months the Coastwatchers would write, all alone, a new chapter in the book of heroic legends.

Red Beach—Guadalcanal

At 9:10 A.M. the first of the 10,000 men of 1st Marine Division, commanded by Major General Vandegrift, vaulted and crawled over the sides of the landing craft to splash ashore onto the beaches of Guadalcanal, exactly as scheduled. Full of foreboding about what the day would bring, their sweat dripping in the oppressive heat, the invaders hadn't been able to eat the storied breakfast of steak and eggs served aboard ship. Some marines reported they were served up only a sandwich and coffee as their departing breakfast.

Private 1st Class Robert Stiles, from the Bronx, enlisted the day after Pearl Harbor at age 29, weighing only 140 pounds. Assigned to Company L, 3rd Battalion, 1st Marines, he was given only a steak sandwich before going down the cargo net to board a Higgins Boat. The small boats began circling the mother ship in the choppy sea, and soon many of the passengers started throwing up. The others tried to "keep the pukers on one side of the boat, but it really didn't help. It was just a mess."

"Thank God there weren't any Japs firing at us. I understand the water was even rougher over at Gavutu," Stiles recalls, "and when some of those paramarines went in, they didn't even care if the Japs hit them or not."

Captain William Hawkins, a graduate of Tufts University from Bridgeport, Connecticut, was in the first wave of the 1st Battalion, 5th Marines. He was likely the first American to set foot ashore on Guadalcanal. The landing force moved off the beach slowly, partly from apprehension of the coming fighting, partly because they were hot and sweaty and worn out from the exhausting sea voyage. Vandegrift and the senior commanders were incensed at the lack of progress toward the first day's objectives.

Red Beach, several miles to the east of Lunga Point, was to be used only for the actual landing. Once ashore, in a hopefully less defended zone, the marines would then move westward to capture the airfield and "Grassy Knoll." Mount Austen, the Grassy Knoll, was much too far away from the field and quickly dropped from the target list, as it could not have been defended by the men available within the Lunga Perimeter.

On Guadalcanal proper there were about 2,300 Japanese troops—mostly Korean conscript laborers just rising for the day's work—when the naval bombardment began. They scurried into the questionable shelter of the adjoining jungle. Without weapons and food, they posed virtually no threat to the Marine landing force. Small numbers of the laborers surrendered rather than endure almost certain starvation in the dense, dank jungle. Months later American and Japanese patrols continued to come across small groups of wretchedly ill and malnourished workers, their clothing rotted away, wandering lost in the endless jungle.

The failure of the inadequate naval bombardment to level Japanese defensive positions and supply dumps—which would prove deadly in later island landings—actually worked in favor of the Marine landing force here. The barely damaged and still intact food, supplies, and equipment left behind and captured by the invaders would prove to be a godsend.

"The Canal"—as it came to be called by the men who fought there—was about 20 miles from Tulagi across what would later be called Iron Bottom Sound. This was the broad opening for three smaller sea channels, the larger Sealark, Nggela, and Lengo, situated east of Savo Island between Guadalcanal and the southeastern edge of Florida Island. Any reference to the Sealark Channel separating Tulagi and Guadalcanal generally includes the other two channels.

The primary objective on Guadalcanal—the unfinished landing strip being built by the Japanese—was quickly overrun and captured early on the second day with scarcely any exchange of gunfire. Three weeks of heavy work remained to be done before the first American planes would be able to land and begin air operations. Capture of the airfield was a direct response to the crisis created when the Japanese selected Guadalcanal as the site for a major new air base. The base was needed to support their projected envelopment of New Guinea, as a stepping stone toward the invasion of a highly vulnerable Australia, as well as the American-controlled islands further to the east.

The airfield was the key to continued American Navy operations in the area, and, as it turned out, it was absolutely essential in holding the island against frequent and increasingly larger-scale counterattacks. Without the air support to fight off air and ship forays down the Slot, and to cover ship movements attempting to reinforce the fighting foot soldiers barely clinging onto what little bit of the island they occupied, the island would surely have fallen once again to the Japanese.

The most pressing problem on Guadalcanal was that supplies and equipment began piling up on the beach. The unloading party was far too small to handle the incoming cargo. Considerable hostility was aroused when combat commanders refused to allow their apparently idle troops to turn to and help out.

At this point no one knew when and if there would be a Japanese counterattack, and it would have been disastrous to have to fend it off with riflemen exhausted from helping in the unloading. Yet, looking back, this reluctance to help move the cargo inland left those same combat marines with precious little food and ammunition for the weeks ahead. The transports were compelled to leave Sealark Channel after unloading about half the cargo they had brought to Guadalcanal. The unmoved piles and stacks of boxes and gear on the beach prevented the incoming boats from getting close enough to unload. The major snag was not getting the cargo off the ships, but rather clearing the unloading area.

Tanambogo and Gavutu

The 1st Parachute Battalion, which attempted its assigned landing on much smaller Gavutu islet at noon of the 8th, had completely lost the element of surprise. There the

Japanese—about 400 members of the elite naval troops—were waiting to resist the assault. The reason given for attacking Gavutu before Tanambogo was that Gavutu's hill was 148 feet high, against Tanambogo's hill at 121 feet. It was thought it would be better to take the high ground, which would allow the marines to fire down on the resisting troops. The same idea had occurred to the defenders.

Gavutu had to be assaulted from the northeast because of reefs. Again *San Juan* bombarded the landing area for four minutes, a 14-gun salvo every twelve seconds, for a total of 280 shells. Twelve SBD dive bombers from *Wasp* made a ten-minute attack on the defenses. Once again, the destructive effect was negligible.

Company A in the first wave, and Company B in the second, landed without any sign of trouble. Apparently the Japanese let them land without much opposition, knowing that with marines on the beach, American air and naval support would be suppressed. Father James J. Fitzgerald, a Chicago priest, came ashore on Gavutu. The man just ahead of him was killed. He moved about on the beach administering last rites to twenty-seven dead, and encouraging the forty-seven wounded. He figured he led a charmed life that day, because none of the snipers firing at the beach hit him.

When Company C and a few miscellaneous detachments came in, they landed under heavy fire from the enemy dug in on the face of Hill 148, and from Hill 121 on Tanambogo. Major Robert Williams, commander of the 1st Parachute Battalion, was shot through his lungs and two of his staff officers died at his side. The gunfire and fighting in the resistance were fierce, but by 2:30 P.M. most of the island had been taken. It was quickly evident that before Hill 148 could be secured, Hill 121 on Tanambogo must be taken to eliminate the accurate and aggressive fire support. The two islets were connected by a 300-yard causeway.

At 6:00 Captain Crane's Company B, who had landed earlier on Haleta, was ordered to move in as night fell and seize Tanambogo, believed to be held by only a handful of snipers. This small landing force was supported by an airstrike from *Wasp* and gunfire from destroyers *Buchanan* and *Monssen*. One landing boat got hung up on the coral in the approach while the other four moved toward a small pier on the northeast side. The first platoon managed to land without drawing any fire, but then a shell from the bombarding ships exploded and set fire to a fuel dump, which highlighted the landing boats moving in.

The invaders were raked by heavy rifle and machine gun fire, which inflicted serious casualties among the marines and the navy boat crews. Crane managed to make some order out of the fiasco and get most of his men, including the wounded, back aboard the damaged boats. The assault company was then forced to withdraw under heavy fire and limp back five long, exhausting hours later to the Marine lines on Gavutu. Twelve marines, including Captain Crane, were forced to cross the exposed causeway to reach the safety of Gavutu. Two other marines boarded a rowboat and made their way to safety.

At the request of Rupertus, the 3rd Battalion, 2nd Marines was ordered to Gavutu on the 8th to reinforce the men already there. The relief battalion, supported by naval gunfire from a destroyer stationed about 500 yards offshore, came ashore on Gavutu at 10 A.M. against some of the original opposition, supplanted by survivors from Tulagi and Florida Island.

Captain Harold L. Torgerson, Valley Stream, Long Island, New York, was credited with blasting more than fifty caves with bombs made from thirty sticks of dynamite tied together. The fuses were lit after he had rushed the cave and placed the bomb in the mouth of the cave. War correspondent Richard Tregaskis, in his book *Guadalcanal Diary*, reported that, "In his day's work Captain Torgerson had used twenty cases of dynamite and all the available matches. His wrist watch strap had been broken by a bullet which creased his wrist." Once he attached a five-gallon can of gas to one of the bombs, which exploded with such force that his trousers were blown off his huge frame. His comment on the blast: "Boy, that was a pisser, wasn't it!"

The American eastern group drew fire from a few enemy riflemen and machine gunners on Gaomi, a tiny islet a few hundred yards east of Tanambogo, but that was quickly silenced at 5:00 P.M. by *Gridley*. One American tank, rushing ahead of its infantry, was disabled by a desperate but clever defender who jammed an iron bar into the track mechanism, and then set the vehicle afire using oily rags. Later forty-two dead Japanese were found piled up around the tank.

The tank assigned to cover the other side of the hill was successful in its mission, but tank commander Lieutenant E. J. Sweeney was killed in the heated action. Even with armored support the progress was slow. Rooting out the holed up Japanese troops required the rest of the day.

Corporal Ralph W. Fordyce, Conneaut Lake, Pennsylvania, cleaned out six gun emplacements, each with at least six Japanese defenders. From one dugout, which he entered blasting away with his submachine gun, he dragged out eight dead. Corporal Johnnie Blackman accounted for five dugouts blown apart with TNT charges. Sharp-eyed Sergeant Harry M. Tully, Hastings, Nebraska, fired his rifle at great range to pick off the three enemy soldiers manning a machine gun nest.

A very weary Captain George R. Stallings, Augusta, Georgia, spoke softly to Tregaskis, almost as if he did not want to reveal his position, about the fighting on Gavutu. He told about Corporal George F. Grady, New York City, who alone had charged a group of eight Japanese, killing two with submachine gun fire. With the gun jammed, he clubbed another defender to death. He dropped the useless gun, drew his sheath knife, and stabbed two more before he was killed by one of the survivors.

At 4:20 P.M. Company I landed and formed two attack groups. One worked up the southern slope of the Tanambogo hill while the other, moving to the right and then inland, attacked up the eastern slope. Japanese fought fiercely from caves and dugouts, and the eastern group drew fire from a few enemy riflemen and machine gunners on Gaomi. Naval gunfire from USS *Gridley* was directed on Gaomi at 5:00 and positions on the small island were silenced. At this time the 1st Platoon of Company K attacked across the causeway from Gavutu, secured the Tanambogo end of the causeway, and took up positions for the night with the southeastern two-thirds of the island secured. At 11:00 P.M. a light machine gun platoon from Company M reported to Company I to serve as support against enemy counterattacks.

Occasional but vicious close-in fighting took place during the night with Japanese who infiltrated Marine lines. The Japanese defenders gained nothing more than an honorable death, and by late the next day continued fighting and mopping up operations secured the island. Nearly 400 Imperial troops had perished in the intense action, and only twenty were taken prisoner. The marines lost 108 killed, and 140 wounded.

The Gavutu–Tanambogo landing was, as a matter of fact, the first *opposed* landing by American amphibious troops in WWII. In his excellent book, *Storm Landings*, Joseph H. Alexander perceived, "...the Gavutu-Tanambogo landing represented a microcosm of the opposed landings to come in the Central Pacific. All the promise and frustration peculiar to forcible seaborne assaults appeared to some degree in this crude little preview—including the excruciatingly difficult task of conducting a ship-to-shore assault against a determined foe."

A large number of Japanese troops died in *banzai* charges—essentially suicidal frontal attacks—a unique tactic frequently employed until the last days of the war. The heavier firepower of the Americans invariably massacred these wildly screaming groups—the only alternative to being themselves overrun and slaughtered by these fanatically brave but sadly misused Japanese soldiers. There were no survivors to report back to Japanese headquarters that a *banzai* attack was a hopelessly inadequate and wasteful tactic when exercised against disciplined and heavily armed opponents.

Still, the U.S. troops did take serious casualties. During the fighting to secure the islets, 144 Marines were listed as killed or missing in action, and nearly 200 more were wounded. The inexperienced American fighting man had much to learn about combat from his combat-hardened Japanese counterpart.

Tulagi and the surrounding area was now organized into a defensive posture to guard against a counterlanding. Except for an occasional shelling from passing Japanese warships, however, Tulagi was effectively isolated from the war zone. Several times American ships as large as cruisers that had been badly damaged in the nearby sea battle sought refuge there until they could be patched up sufficiently for the slow return to a major repair base.

Japanese Strike from the Air

The first retaliatory response of the Japanese took the form of an air attack on the invasion fleet. Fighters and bombers made the 560-mile (one way) trip from Rabaul to Guadalcanal, at almost their maximum operational range. There would be time to make only one run over the assembled American fleet before the planes had to turn back. As it was, many Japanese pilots ran out of fuel on the return leg and were forced to crash land their planes far short of Rabaul.

The air strike that left Rabaul at about 8:30 A.M. consisted of twenty-seven medium Betty bombers, eighteen Zero escorts, and nine Val Aichi D3A1 dive bombers, all from the 25th Air Flotilla of the 11th Air Fleet, commanded by Rear Admiral Sadayoshi Yamada. The Vals were on a one-way suicide trip, as they did not have enough fuel to return to base. Yamada warned his fighter pilots that the approximately 1,100-mile round trip would be the longest fighter operation in history. The range of the Zero—called the Zeke by the American identification system—when equipped with a supplemental belly fuel tank, was three times that of the American Wildcat fighter.

Sakai Saburo, a senior flying noncommissioned officer and Japan's leading ace—with 3,000 hours in fighters and fifty-seven planes shot down in combat, including combat in

China and against the Americans in the Philippines—was in the crack Tainan Air Group, led by Lieutenant Commander Tadashi Nakajima. Also in the group was humorless, cold-eyed killer Hiroyoshi Nishizawa, Japan's second ranking ace. These first-string Imperial Japanese Navy air units—previously assigned to air operations over New Guinea in support of the South Seas Detachment capture of Buna and the advance over the Kokoda Trail to Port Moresby—were immediately sent to destroy the Guadalcanal landing force.

An air raid by Japanese Betty bombers flying in a beautiful "vee" formation attacked at about 1:30 P.M. Pilot Joseph Daly of *Saratoga*'s Fighting Five was surprised to see the Zekes, not truly believing that any fighter could make the round trip to and from Rabaul. This counterattack was driven off by Wildcats and other aircraft from Fletcher's three carriers, operating to the southwest of Guadalcanal. Of the nine Val dive bombers, six were shot down during the attack. Three splashed into the sea on the return flight before they could reach an emergency landing field at Buka, on New Britain. Five Betty bombers were sent down in flames. One American destroyer, *Mugford*, was hit on an aft mount.

Lieutenant Vincent DePoix, from *Enterprise*'s Fighting Six (VF-6) was first to spot the vee formation of thirty twin-engine bombers coming in at 180 knots over Florida Island. The famed Zekes flew escort. Four Wildcats moved in to attack the force. DePoix got within range of a bomber, fired off a burst, and knocked down a Betty. Lieutenant (Junior Grade) T.S. Gay's attack brought smoke from another. On the return, about 35 miles north of Savo Island, six Wildcats from *Enterprise*, including that of Lieutenant Raleigh E. Rhodes—who shot down a Zeke—attacked from either side of the formation. Three of his attacking group failed to return from the fight.

Eight Wildcats and an SBD were shot down. Daly had shot down two Betties when his Wildcat took a 20-mm shell hit from a Zeke that set fire to his cockpit. He managed to bail out, and several hours later he was plucked, badly burned, from the sea. Five planes from *Saratoga*'s Fighting Five were downed by Nishizawa alone. "I don't know how many Wildcats there were, but they seemed to come out of the sun in an endless stream," he related. Regarding later missions, Nishizawa said: "We never had a chance.... Every time we went out we lost more and more planes. Guadalcanal was completely under the enemy's control.... Of all the men who returned with me, only Captain Aito, [Lieutenant Commander Tadashi] Nakajima and less than six of the other pilots who were in our original group of 80 men survived."

Sakai was one of nine fighters in the other section of Zekes that escorted the Betties attacking the fleet. Sakai was drawn into a dogfight, and managed to shoot down a Wildcat, flown by Lieutenant James J. Southerland from *Saratoga*'s Fighting Five, in what he called the hardest dogfight he had ever experienced. A few minutes later Sakai made a mistake. He and his wingman went after eight planes he thought were Wildcats, but actually it was a flight of Dauntless dive bombers from *Enterprise*'s Bombing Six led by Lieutenant Carl Horenburger.

The rear gunners on the Dauntlesses laid in a devastating concentration of .30-caliber bullets that smashed Sakai's windscreen, wounding him in the face, scalp, and eyes. When his Zero plunged toward the sea, the American gunners thought he was done for, but he was able finally to pull his plane out of its nearly vertical dive. Badly wounded, continually blacking out from loss of blood from his wounds, he made it back to Rabaul and managed to land his plane. In this heroic effort—one of the most determined and dramatic by any airman in the entire war—Sakai lost an eye and Japan lost its leading pilot. He was returned to Japan, where much later he would be promoted to Lieutenant Junior Grade but not permitted to fly again until the last desperate days of the war.

Within a few days the three lost pilots of Rhodes's group were accounted for. Lieutenant Gordon Firebaugh was safe on Santa Isabel Island. He was credited with three Zeroes before he found himself in the water, spending hours swimming to the little island. He had been found by a Coastwatcher. Machinist's Mate Warden had been found by another Coastwatcher at Guadalcanal's Biarro Bay, and Machinist's Mate Achten was picked up by *San Juan* after ditching off Tulagi. (Warden and Achten were enlisted aviators assigned to combat units.)

Digging In

While Vandegrift and his staff were appalled at the seemingly languid advance of their troops, much blame can be attributed to the brutal 100-degree-plus heat and dripping humidity. The men had been aboard ship experiencing forced inactivity too long to make the needed instant transition to fast-moving aggressive infantry. The availability of drinking water quickly became a problem as the thirsty men emptied their single canteens.

"I have been in the Marines 16 years, and I have been in three expeditions to China and five engagements since I have been in the Solomons," complained Gunnery Sergeant H.L. Beardsley, Company G, 5th Marines. "I will say that this 1942 model recruit we are getting can drink more water than six old timers. We have to stress water discipline all the time. They don't seem to realize what water discipline is."

Recognizing that the availability of water would continue to be a problem, 2nd Lieutenant Andrew Chisick of the 5th Marines said, "I think that in the regimental supply there should be extra canteens so when an outfit gets in a place like the 'table plateau' where there is no water, an extra canteen of water can be issued."

That first torrid night the dirty and rain-drenched marines dug into the slimy mud and prepared to meet their most deadly enemy—the island itself. New and strange sounds assaulted their ears—the screeching of a macaw or a monkey would evoke a fusillade of rifle fire from the jittery troops. Huge land crabs crawled around and burrowed under the sand, and the men became targets of a vast array of spiders and a multitude of creepy-crawly insects. The persistent and ever present flies made eating even the most meager of rations difficult. Even the torrential rains didn't suppress the hordes of pestilential insects. Squadrons of large malaria-bearing mosquitoes became an almost unbearable scourge. Later an airman asserted that he had poured 50 gallons of aviation gas into one such mosquito before he discovered it wasn't an airplane.

"I could hear the darkness gathering against me and the silences that lay between the moving things. I could hear the enemy everywhere about me," related Private Robert Leckie, recalling the terror of that first night, "whispering to each other and calling my name. I lay open-mouthed and half mad beneath that giant tree. I had not looked into its foliage before darkness and now I fancied it infested with Japanese...."

Sergeant Windish, an artilleryman, was accidentally killed by his instrument section commander. He had left the bunker for a moment and when he returned he spooked the officer, who shot him twice with a .45-caliber pistol. Some marines who wandered only a few yards away from their buddies simply disappeared into the jungle, forever lost in the nearly impenetrable thickets of rotting underbrush, entangling vines, and root systems of the rain forest. Once isolated in that quagmire, men lost their sense of direction. They yielded to the sheer terror, which drove them into frantic, hopeless attempts to escape that green hell. This was the everlasting day and night threat the men endured for more than four seemingly endless months once they were away from the narrow strips of relatively open spaces near the beach and plain around the airfield.

"I hate to admit it, but its the truth," Master Gunner E.S. Rust reported later. "When we got here, a lot of our young men were confused at night. They were not used to jungle at night. They could not use their compasses at night, and we did not have enough compasses." Another marine asserted that every man should have been issued a compass and taught how to use it.

August 8–The Second Day of Guadalcanal

Moving through the stands of coconut trees, encountering a few brief skirmishes, the marines captured the airfield, their primary reason for landing at Lunga Point. The 2,600-foot landing strip was nearly finished. Aircraft revetments, bunkers, and repair shops were in place, along with quantities of fuel and supplies. The new invaders feasted on canned meat and fish and tons of rice left behind by the routed construction troops.

Lieutenant Colonel Samuel B. Griffith (later Brigadier General) later related: "Daily the engineers extended the runway. With Japanese dynamite they cleared obstructing trees from the north end, and with three earth tampers operated by Japanese air compressors laboriously packed new fill excavated by Marine-powered Japanese picks and shovels, and brought to the site in Japanese trucks fueled with Japanese gasoline.... Marines queued up to use latrines built of Japanese lumber and protected from flies by Japanese screens. When Japanese sirens announced the approach of Japanese planes, Marines dove into holes dug and roofed by the Japanese."

In contrast to the ease with which the airfield had been captured, hanging on to that valuable piece of real estate would prove infinitely more difficult. Still, it was American aircraft that first touched wheels down on the landing strip.

Yamada's remaining nine Val torpedo bombers roared into the transport area the next afternoon, along with twenty-three Betties and a veteran escort of Zeroes. Flying in low from the north, the attack group evaded radar detection until they were almost upon Savo Island. Six patrolling Wildcats attacked, shooting down four Betties and a Zero in the first confrontation. A burning Betty crashed into *George F. Elliott*, inflicting enough damage to the transport that it had to be abandoned and sunk. Eighteen Betties were destroyed, and two Zeroes.

Japanese Navy Reacts

From the Japanese fortress of Rabaul, on the Gazelle Peninsula of New Britain, the new Japanese 8th Fleet under Vice Admiral Gunichi Mikawa sortied to inflict havoc on the meager Allied naval invasion fleet, and shell the land forces on the beaches. The most direct route was down the Slot, a sea passage between Santa Isabel and New Georgia in the Solomon Islands and ending at Savo Island. Mikawa was one of the very few to surmise that this was a major landing attempt. The Japanese 17th Army commanded by Lieutenant General Harukichi Hyakutake was inclined to dismiss the initial reports as frantic overreaction by the naval personnel in the Tulagi area. The conquest of New Guinea and capture of Port Moresby were his overriding concern. The disturbances at Tulagi–Guadalcanal were the problem of the Imperial Navy, as the Army had played no part in occupying those islands in the first place.

Jack Coggins, author of the illuminating book *The Campaign for Guadalcanal*, summed up the Japanese reaction. "...Seventeenth Army was not particularly interested. Both they and the Navy consistently underestimated the strength and fighting ability of the American invasion forces. Mikawa's dispatch of the ill-fated handful embarked on *Meiyo Maru* was only the beginning of a haphazard method of reinforcing the islands by dribs and drabs, putting ashore units never strong enough or well enough supplied to do the job assigned. This had been put down by a Japanese naval writer to 'victory disease'—a combination (born of a series of almost uninterrupted victories) of blind arrogance, supreme confidence, and utter contempt for the enemy. This may be a splendid thing in the individual fighting man but at the tactical and strategic level it can prove a serious handicap. In Japan's case it was fatal."

Mikawa's first move was to send the transport *Meiyo Maru*, with light escort, loaded with about 410 sailors armed with rifles and a few machine guns to help out at Guadalcanal. Just before midnight she was spotted and sunk about 14 miles off Cape St. George by torpedoes from the American submarine *S-38*, commanded by Lieutenant Commander Henry G. Munson. About 350 of the would-be fighters were lost.

Mikawa submitted a hastily devised emergency plan to launch a nighttime surface attack to Admiral Osami Nagano, who thought the action rash, but passed the request along to Admiral Yamamoto, commanding the Combined Fleet, who approved the plan. He didn't consider Mikawa a reckless commander at all, and immediately sent off the signal: WISH YOUR FLEET SUCCESS. Aboard his flagship, the heavy cruiser *Chokai*, Mikawa headed south to destroy the American transports.

His intelligence reports from his search aircraft were timely and accurate. He knew that his eight ships were going up against twenty-six Allied warships, split into two groups, but was convinced he could inflict the greater damage on one group. Making up his attack column were heavy cruisers *Aoba*, *Kako*, *Kinugasa* and *Furutaka*, light cruisers *Tenryu* and *Yubari*, and the single destroyer *Yunagi*. They assembled in St. George Channel at about 7:00 P.M. after deceptive maneuvering to confuse enemy observation.

The Japanese column had been spotted at about 10:30 that same morning by an Australian pilot, who failed to break radio silence and report his observation. Instead, the pilot finished his patrol, returned to base and had tea before relating his find. The American submarine that had put a torpedo into the relief transport had almost been run down off the mouth of St. George Channel by the eight-ship column steaming south, and found itself too close to fire her torpedoes. It was approximately 7 P.M.—more than eight hours later—before Turner was informed of the sightings. His steel gray eyes blazed in furious anger under his bushy black eyebrows. He detested incompetence.

Vice Admiral Fletcher had abruptly decided to remove the carriers and their essential air cover from Guadalcanal, without consulting Turner or Vandegrift—an action which placed the entire Operation Watchtower in dire peril. The amphibious force had not been able to unload even half the needed basic supplies and materiel, which had been brought to the island at great risk.

Turner recognized that the sea on either side of Savo was the shortest and most natural entry to the invasion fleet area. A marauding fleet from the northwest could steam in through the entry to Sealark Channel, swing around Savo Island and then head back up the Slot. Any sailor with a map could have figured that out. Prudently, Turner had ordered that a PBY Catalina flying boat make an aerial reconnaissance of the area in which Mikawa had assembled his fleet. What no one bothered to tell Turner was that the PBY never left the water for the patrol mission.

The Australian commander of the screening force, Rear Admiral Victor Crutchley, Royal Australian Navy, was on his flagship, *Australia.* His operational plan was for the northern force to cruise independently but to conform to the movement of the southern force. Crutchley, head of the southern contingent as well as the entire patrol force, signaled Captain Howard D. Bode on *Chicago* to assume temporary command of the southern group when he withdrew his flagship *Australia* to attend an urgent meeting with Admiral Turner. Bode did not bother to signal Captain Frederick L. Riefkohl on *Vincennes* in the northern force, now the senior officer with Crutchley's departure, to take overall command. Nor did Bode move *Chicago* ahead of the *Canberra* to lead the southern column as he should have done.

In preparing their ships to fight, Mikawa's forces had thrown overboard those items that would be useless in battle, but a prime source of fire, debris, and shrapnel if hit in combat. The cruisers had a weapon the Allies had not reckoned with: intensively trained night observation teams of keen-eyed spotters equipped with highly efficient low-light-gathering 20-power pedestal-mounted binoculars. Another advanced weapon the Japanese possessed, which had proven itself as early as Pearl Harbor, was the Long Lance torpedo, which could cruise 11 miles at 49 knots per hour. Powered by oxygen instead of air, it did not leave the familiar air bubble trail of standard torpedoes. All Japanese cruisers as well as destroyers were equipped to fire and reload and fire again. These deadly and accurate underwater missiles contained 1,090 pounds of TNT. No American heavy cruisers and only a few light cruisers were equipped with torpedo launchers, although destroyers were so equipped. The most significant difference was that American torpedoes at that time rarely worked properly. Not until 1943 did the U.S. begin producing a torpedo comparable to the effectiveness of the Long Lance.

American naval doctrine had been based on the Big Battle between ships of the line in bright clear daylight. Night operations training was all but totally neglected. When there was any semblance of night training, the results were rigged to make it appear the forces actually had performed well and knew what they were doing. Early in the war Americans did not want to fight at night, and could not fight effectively in night combat. The U.S. Pacific Fleet learned to fight at night by necessity from the Japanese, who not only trained seriously in night surface operations, but planned to use them whenever possible. Lookouts on Japanese warships received rigorous training with highly efficient German Zeiss optics. At the time of the encounter at Savo these human lookouts were considerably more effective than American radar.

American ships had recently been equipped with the new technology of radar, which would detect intruders far enough away for the fleet to prepare for battle. In addition, when the Allied ships did go into action, they would have the benefit of new rapid-firing guns and the recent TBS radio development—Talk Between Ships—that all but precluded enemy eavesdropping. On the simple nontechnological side, the Allied ships had failed to eliminate flammable materials such as wooden lifeboats and decks, their exposed seaplanes—of absolutely no use at night—and fuel caches. Prewar amenities, such as linoleum, interior paint—and even pianos, in the captains' staterooms—also contributed to the spread of fire after enemy shell or torpedo hits.

Twenty miles away at Lunga Roads, Crutchley, who had taken *Australia* out of the screen and away from the patrol area, was attending an urgent meeting aboard *McCawley* with Turner and Vandegrift. They were aghast with disbelief, and needed to discuss the enormous problems created by the planned abrupt departure of Fletcher and his carriers. When told it would take five days to land the marines and supplies, Fletcher, commander of the expeditionary force, proclaimed that the carriers would leave after only two days "because of the danger of air attacks and because of the fuel situation...if the troops can't be landed in two days, then they should not be landed."

"There were those in the Marine Corps who thought that Fletcher wanted to add a fourth color to the American flag," historian William Manchester observed later. In effect, the Navy did desert the seriously pressed Marines at a crucial junction.

Fletcher and Ghormley were not the only high-ranking American officers who thought the first offensive would fail. MacArthur thought the plan to take Guadalcanal "was open to the gravest doubts." Major General Millard F. Harmon, chief of the Army Air staff and serving under Ghormley, shared their misgivings. General Henry H. "Hap" Arnold, chief of the Air Force, refused to send the new high-altitude fighters to Guadalcanal, on the ground that they would be needlessly sacrificed. On the other hand, the Imperial Japanese Navy was extremely confident it could easily smash this brash incursion.

It is little wonder that the minds of the shocked leaders actually involved with the landing were diverted from possible local threats to the beachhead. As the earlier sighting reports were discounted or ignored, these commanders were also completely unaware of the Japanese force sweeping down the Slot between the northern and southern rows of the Solomon Islands and headed directly for the Allied fleet.

What Mikawa did not know and could not have guessed was that Fletcher had removed the *Enterprise*, *Saratoga*, and *Wasp* from the area. This precipitous and unexpected move left the still partially loaded transports standing off Guadalcanal with hardly any protection against an enemy attack. Fletcher was concerned about air attacks on his carriers, and did not appear to appreciate that any Japanese air retaliation in force could not have been launched from Rabaul before dawn and would not have reached the Allied ships until about noon the next day. Even then they would have been at maximum range and would most likely have missed the carriers entirely if they had waited until dawn to depart.

What is a virtual certainty is that if Mikawa had known the carriers were gone, the intrepid Japanese fleet could have easily destroyed the remaining transports standing off Guadalcanal and Tulagi and swiftly terminated the invasion then and there. The Japanese commander feared the presumed presence of the carriers, not of the surface fleet.

CHAPTER 5

AUGUST 9
THE NAVAL BATTLE OF SAVO

Around Savo Island the early morning blackness was oppressive and stifling hot as rain squalls swept the area. The air of enervated complacency that infused the U.S. and Australian ships of the screening force, its commanders, and crews resulted from near exhaustion resulting from nearly two days at action stations. The supercharged energy brought on by the actual landing had worn off. Worse, it appeared no one afloat that night seriously thought the Japanese would attack, although there was no realistic reason why they shouldn't—the Allies were definitely in enemy waters. When the attack did come, the weary captains of the heavy ships had gone to bed.

Lieutenant Commander Edmund Billings on board *Quincy* was awakened by Quartermaster 2nd Class Thomas Morris to take the watch. With no activity reported, Billings got dressed and prepared his pipe. Thoughts of a quiet night off Guadalcanal were pervasive, for if there was trouble, someone would sound the alarm—but by the time the alarm was sounded it was too late. When the screening force patrolling the waters north and south of Savo Island did wake up they were already victims of a ferocious all-out attack from Japanese torpedoes and accurate gunfire that struck at about 1:30 A.M. and virtually blew the big Allied warships out of the water.

A third group of two light cruisers and two destroyers under Rear Admiral Norman Scott were on station between Tulagi and Guadalcanal guarding the transports, and never got into the fight. All the men in the Allied naval defense force this night were as totally overwhelmed as the late Japanese contingent on Tulagi had been the morning of the American invasion.

Three Japanese seaplanes were launched from Mikawa's cruisers at 11:10 to scout the Allied screening force. At 11:45 P.M. the destroyer USS *Ralph Talbot* heard and reported the three unidentified planes, which droned over the sleepy Allied vessels for an hour and a half providing position reports, ready to drop brilliant flares to aid Japanese gunners in selecting targets. The report never reached Turner, and moreover, the American commanders on patrol assumed the planes were from the American aircraft carriers, *which had already departed the scene.* Turner would have known instantly that the planes were Japanese, because no American aircraft remained to fly over any fleet.

On the leading HMAS *Canberra*, Sublieutenant Mackenzie Gregory had taken the conn in anticipation of the watch change, while below decks Stoker 2nd Class George Faulkner was about to be relieved in the engine room. In the Y-turret handling compartment, Able Seaman Stephen St. George removed his antiflash gear before sitting down to play cards with his mates. Surgeon Lieutenant Kenneth Morris was trying to take a nap on one of the mess tables.

Mikawa's battle force had slipped by the unsuspecting American radar-equipped picket destroyer *Blue*. At 1:33 A.M. Mikawa's battle force, taking advantage of passing rain squalls, used the ship's blinkers to send the message: ALL SHIPS ATTACK. When *Chokai* lookouts spotted the two cruisers *Canberra* and USS *Chicago*, accompanied by the American destroyers *Bagley* and *Patterson*, to their starboard at 1:36, Mikawa issued the order to commence firing. A couple of minutes later four Japanese Long Lance torpedoes with half a ton of TNT in the warheads splashed into the water headed for *Canberra*. The attackers themselves weren't spotted until they opened fire with their 8-inch guns. Until that instant the Allied ships didn't suspect the presence of the hard-charging Japanese ships. When *Chokai*'s guns opened fire on the patrol column at 1:43, Commander Frank Walker on *Patterson* finally sighted the intruders and sent the signal: WARNING, WARNING, STRANGE SHIPS ENTERING HARBOR!

The enemy float planes dropped brilliant flares—much better flares than any the Americans had—as the Japanese big guns opened fire on the hapless patrol vessels. The Allied ships stood out in stark contrast to the sultry sea. With the Japanese ready at their guns, there could not have been easier targets.

"Stupid bloody Yanks. What the hell are they up to? Why are they dropping flares?" muttered Able Seaman Henry Hall on *Canberra*, talking on the phone before his headset disintegrated and the man next to him was killed in the first salvo.

Two of the torpedoes launched earlier ripped gaping holes in *Canberra*, and twenty-four shells fired from less than a mile away tore the ship apart. Steel splinters and shrapnel tore through sailors, killing or maiming in an instant. Captain Frank Getting joined his crew in rushing to battle stations. Getting, who had been selected for the rank of Admiral, arrived on the bridge as shells tore into the boiler room, knocked out the ship's power, and brought the ship to a halt.

Another shell smashed into the pilot room, mortally wounding Getting and killing his navigator and gunnery officer. While the ship's surgeon tended the fallen captain, command was passed to his executive officer, Commander James Walsh, who was told, "Fight her till she goes down, Jim!" But *Canberra* was in ruins; her boiler rooms were destroyed and she was unable to fight, and with the radios wrecked the devastated ship was unable to broadcast a warning.

Below decks were in shambles and the situation was desperate. Seaman Albert Warne climbed into his antiflash gear and struggled through the deadly oven-hot heat and dense smoke and licking flames up three decks to safety. There a rain shower cooled him, easing the assault on his throat and lungs. Sublieutenant Gregory ordered his men to jettison ammunition into the bloody sea before the consuming flames fired it off. The big guns were out of action. Walsh ordered all hands on deck to flood the magazines, dump the torpedoes over the side, and empty all fuel tanks.

Surgeon Morris was tending the wounded with a flashlight strapped to his head. Stoker George Yates tried to get to his feet, saw a severed limb lying on deck and shouted, "Look! Someone's arm has been shot off!" Ship's Butcher John Quigley, coming to the stoker's assistance, shouted to him, "Lie down and be quiet! It's yours!"

The American cruiser *Chicago* was similarly surprised, and turned hard to starboard when lookouts spotted the torpedoes fired from *Kako*. Two hit the bow of *Chicago;* one failed to explode and the other sent a column of water high above the deck and damaged the main battery director. Wounded Lieutenant Commander Cecil C. Adell crawled aft, where dentist Lieutenant Commander Benjamin Ostering sewed up a slice in Adell's neck, without the benefit of anesthesia.

Captain Bode, temporary commander of the southern force, apparently dazed and not knowing what to do—including sending the emergency warning signal to all ships—literally took *Chicago* out of the battle when he turned and chased after *Yunagi*, Mikawa's only destroyer. Several months later the disgraced Bode, when an inquiry indicated that he had not done anything right in the fight, committed suicide. He was not the only incompetent Allied commanding officer on a bridge that night.

Seaman George John Sallet, aboard the destroyer *Bagley*, in the southern column, recalled the battle with horror. After *Canberra* took two torpedo hits amidships followed by a barrage of 8-inch shells, absolute confusion reigned. "On our bridge our ever so nervous captain turns us away from the battle to head for the retirement position. The executive officer relieves him of his command and turns *Bagley* back into the fight, firing four torpedoes at the enemy." *Patterson*, after sounding the alarm, got in a shoot-out with the enemy light cruisers and had her aft 5-inch guns blasted away. Once the destroyers were shoved aside, Mikawa's route to the second Allied echelon was unimpeded. Had Bode gotten off word that the southern column was under attack, the ships in the northern column might have made a better showing.

After putting *Canberra* out of action and driving off *Chicago* and the destroyers, Mikawa's force then inadvertently split to create a pincer movement against the northern column. American cruisers were blocked from the action of the southern group by a rain squall and did not know what to make of the underwater explosions heard at 1:44 from the south. At 1:48 *Chokai* launched a spread of torpedoes at *Astoria*, the first ship they spotted as they swung north from 12,000 yards. They were well within range but the torpedoes missed. Gunnery officer Lieutenant Commander William H. Truesdell saw *Vincennes* and *Quincy* come under fire, and he trained his guns toward the enemy. Lieutenant Commander James R. Topper, supervisor of the watch, hesitated before giving the order to "Stand by to sound general quarters." Quartermaster 3rd Class R.A. Radke went ahead and sounded general quarters without permission, and Truesdell opened fire. Then Captain William Greenman appeared on the bridge and demanded to know who gave the order to fire. Ordering cease fire, Greenman and Topper thought they were firing on their own ships until they saw geysers caused by shells bracketing the ships ahead in line.

"Whether our ships or not," Greenman said belatedly, "we would have to stop them. Commence firing." Four long minutes had gone by, giving the Japanese gunners time to adjust their range. The next salvos were on target and began tearing apart the American ships. Shell hits set fire to the hangar and boat deck, cut power to Turret Number 3, and smashed into the bridge, as Greenman steered a hard left to avoid a collision with *Quincy*. Shrapnel and steel splinters from the exploding superstructure cut down men struggling to fight back. Greenman himself received eleven pieces of shrapnel during the carnage.

Astoria was fighting back despite the horrific damage and mauling of men. One of her shells destroyed *Chokai*'s main gun battery, killing 15 gunners. Still, the fight was decidedly one-sided, with the losers getting in a lucky blow or two but not inflicting comparable heavy damage. With *Astoria* in dreadful trouble and taking water from the sea, Greenman collected 400 sailors on the bow and formed them into a bucket brigade. Unknown to the captain because of the fires raging amidships, another 150 survivors on the stern were also trying to keep their ship afloat. They all felt the ship could be saved, despite the fact that the powder magazines had not been flooded and the fires were headed that way.

Quincy, astern of *Vincennes*, came under fire and took the worst beating of all, but in the opinion of the Japanese it put up the best fight. Captain Samuel N. Moore reached the bridge just as the ship went to general quarters. He ordered "fire at the ships with the searchlights on," but Quincy's guns were not ready. "Fire the main battery!" he shouted, just as Japanese shells hit the fantail and set off the ammunition for a 5-inch gun, killing all hands on the left side of the gun. A minute later a Japanese shell shattered a float plane in the well deck, and burning gasoline quickly ignited the other four planes. Caught in *Chokai*'s searchlights, and with her guns unlimbered, she did manage to bring her batteries into play and fire off two 9-gun salvos. Two shells that hit *Chokai* narrowly missed Admiral Mikawa but destroyed the staff chartroom.

Swerving to avoid a collision with *Vincennes*, her fantail ablaze from her own destroyed seaplane, *Quincy* came under fire from the two Japanese columns. Her own Number 1 and Number 2 Gun Turrets fired salvos before Number 2 Turret was blown away from a direct hit. Heavy and accurate gunfire from port and starboard slammed into the ship to wreck the steering and nearly wipe out everyone on the bridge. The executive officer, navigator, damage control officer, and numerous enlisted men were killed. Lieutenant Commander Billings staggered from the bridge, his face half shot away, trying to encourage the men before he crumpled to the bloody deck.

"We're going down between them—give 'em hell!" gasped the dying Moore, whose last order was to attempt to beach his shattered ship on Savo Island. Before that could happen Lieutenant Commander Harry Heneberger, the surviving senior officer—seventh in the chain of command—was forced to give the order to abandon ship.

Quartermaster 2nd Class Morris regained consciousness at his station, his left hip broken by an exploding shell. Crawling over dead bodies to reach and pull himself up and over a gun shield, he grabbed a rope and was told to drop down onto Turret 3. There Chief Boatswain's Mate George Strobel patched up Morris's wounds as best he could and helped him safely off the ship and into the water. At 2:35 A.M. *Quincy* rolled over and sank.

The leading ship in the northern column, *Vincennes*, was the last to be taken under fire by the Japanese. When searchlights highlighted the three cruisers at 1:50, Captain Riefkohl, now on the bridge, still wondered about *Patterson*'s warning and what all the flares and gunfire meant. Thinking the searchlights were beamed from *Chicago*, he signaled for the lights to be shut off, as "there might be enemy vessels around." The sudden salvos of 8-inch shells and deadly torpedoes that ripped into his ship and caused the steel plates and beams to reverberate in a deafening crescendo let Riefkohl know that there *were* enemy ships in the area. He had just ordered a starboard turn when a torpedo hit destroyed the Number 4 Fireroom, knocking out the engines. *Chokai*'s guns poured salvos of 8-inch shells into the American cruiser, which went dead in the water and became a flaming hulk.

Vincennes's guns got off an 8-inch shell that damaged the steering gear of *Kinugasa*, which began to straggle behind. Lieutenant Commander R.L. Adams, the gunnery officer, continued to issue firing directions even with an unexploded Japanese shell at his feet. Signalman George Moore, seeing the flag shot away, hoisted up a new Stars and Stripes over the luckless ship, which staggered under 85 direct hits from close range on both sides. Realizing his ship was doomed, Riefkohl gave the order to abandon ship. *Vincennes* swayed over on her port side, her silent deck guns awash from the merciless sea. With 342 sailors still trapped below decks, she joined *Quincy* beneath the waves of Iron Bottom Sound.

Bagley chased the action northward at top speed, where flashing lights on the water revealed a group of sailors on an upturned seaplane that had been blown off *Quincy*. As Sallet recalls, "They say that they are OK and tell us to help the burning cruiser just ahead. As we close on the cruiser, not knowing if it is an enemy, we see a man waving to us from the water. *Bagley* stops dead as he swims towards us and in the glare we can see sharks around him. We open fire on the fins with rifles and he panics and swims away with only one arm. Our loudspeaker convinces him that we are friendly and he swims back as two men jump into the water to put a rope around him to haul him inboard. He was a fire-control man from the cruiser *Vincennes*, blown from his position when concentrated fire sank his ship in seconds. He still had his battle telephone on under his helmet and his left arm was shattered."

The cruiser listing to her port side with fires raging amidships was *Astoria*, and at 4:30 *Bagley* moved alongside to help remove the wounded. Her antiaircraft batteries, now an inferno, cooked off 5-inch and 20-mm shells, exploding them like a long string of big firecrackers, throwing hot shells, debris, and shrapnel in all directions. After looking down and seeing the sea swarming with sharks, says Sallet, "our executive officer takes us alongside, our starboard bow to her port bow. Gun Number 1 and the handling room crews of Gun Number 2 are secured to assist. I go into the handling room and bring out a heaving line; others are bringing up a hawser and getting the capstan working. I stood in the bull nose and tossed the line out as I had never done before. It sailed out to the bitter end—*too short.* I rewound and another line was added; this time, with my adrenaline running high, I tossed it completely over their Number 1 Gun Turret." Just then Sallet was "whomped in the back by a flying piece of metal that ripped open my life vest before sailing over the side. The heavy kapok packing saved me from a nasty wound. I felt for blood but could only find sweat under the vest."

Wounded sailors were passed over from *Astoria*. Captain Greenman was standing at the rail directing and shouting orders, even while a corpsman was trying to patch the shrapnel wounds on his bleeding left side. Flames were snapping out from Number 1 Turret. Sallet began assisting the wounded, and the first he helped was in shock, his midsection torn open about the waist. The sailor held a large compress against his stomach to hold his internal organs in place. They struggled down a passageway slippery with blood to the ward room, now the operating theater.

"My next casualty came wrapped in a blanket," Sallet continued. "A shipmate took hold under his armpits and as I put my arms under his legs I found a protruding bone—his left leg had been blown off at the knee and a tourniquet was tied around the upper thigh. As we carried him round Number 1 Gun one of his officers told us to put him comfortably behind the turret with two others. As I put a life jacket under his head I saw this milky white face trying to talk to me with a sort of smile that I can remember to this day. He was saying 'Thank you.'"

Sallet assisted another sailor with part of one arm shattered to the passageway, stained red on both bulkheads. Surgeons were forced to use a sterilized electrician's hacksaw to amputate limbs, as nothing else was available. "A sick feeling came over me as I saw two trash cans with legs and arms outside the wardroom door. I can still see them today. [Back on deck] I hear terrible screaming as the sailor at the hole [on the side] has his head out and flames are blowing out around it."

Nearing the end of this terrible ordeal, said Sallet, "Someone above shouted for all able-bodied men to abandon ship and they jumped over to *Bagley*'s decks in waves of ten to fifteen at a time, slipping and sliding on the wet decks. Midship repair crews arrived with fire hoses and started flushing down the decks. I looked at the marine behind the gun turret, resting peacefully with two others in their final sleep. I asked one of the hose men to flush me off. The salt water loosened the material from my skin until I could part my fingers. I went below aft and found sailors in every bunk and crevice. Some were sobbing, others were comforting their shipmates. One sailor was in dungarees that were all burned off his body. Dabs of salve covered his burn spots. I gave him my third set of dungarees."

Sailors were laying wherever there was an open space. With 400 extra bodies on board, *Bagley* was riding only three feet out of the water. After the furor of the night, the sea was as calm as a lake. Circling around to the fiery cruiser's stern, forty more survivors were taken off.

At 5:45 A.M. Greenman, the engineering officer, and the chief petty officers wished to return to *Astoria* to try to save her—325 men made up the repair party. Not even this heroic effort could save the cruiser. The attempt to get up steam, put out the fires, and correct the list came to nothing when the forward 5-inch magazine blew up. Another destroyer came up at 12:05 P.M. to take off the work party just before she rolled over and went down by the stern with 274 dead. The 400 able-bodied survivors and the wounded were transferred to the AP-37 *President Jackson*.

"As we move out into the bay I see ten bodies laid out on deck in front of Number 1 Gun. They are being sewn up in canvas with a 5-inch shell between their legs. Their open wounds, naked in the blistering sun, stay with me to the present day. At 17:15 hours all hands come to attention as taps are sounded and ten *Astoria* shipmates are committed to the deep in Iron Bottom Sound off Guadalcanal. With my shipmates I fell into a deep sleep around the gunmount until wakened at midnight to man the gun."

Meanwhile, with Captain Getting dying, *Canberra* was still afloat but listing heavily and unable to get the raging fires under control. *Patterson*, which came alongside to assist, passed over water hoses and a hand pump to help the bucket brigade fight the fires. A rain squall helped quench part of the fires, but it was not enough.

Seaman Hall carried wounded down the slippery ladders from the bridge to the forecastle. Surgeon Morris still worked with the flashlight strapped to his head to help find the wounded. The ship's chaplain and some of the crew passed out cigarettes and beer to the wounded, while the able-bodied jettisoned the remaining ammunition over the rails.

Crutchley was ordered to scuttle *Canberra* if the ship could not join the retreat by 6:30 A.M. It became increasingly obvious that the ship was not going anywhere but down. At 5:15 Walsh gave the order to abandon ship, which—because of the super hot fires blocking the escape route—was a death warrant for those sailors still trapped in the engineering compartments. The able-bodied men on deck refused to leave until the wounded were transferred to safety.

USS *Selfridge* was assigned the onerous task of sinking *Canberra*. Of the four torpedoes fired, only one hit the wasted ship. Then as *Selfridge* fired 263 rounds with her 5-inch guns, another destroyer, *Ellet*, turned her guns on *Selfridge*, thinking it was the enemy blasting away at *Canberra*. After the exchange of a few unpleasantries, *Ellet* fired the torpedo that finally sent the flagship of the Australian Navy and eighty-four dead to the bottom.

Sent to the bottom in the brief battle were the American cruisers *Astoria*, *Quincy*, and *Vincennes*, as well as the Australian heavy cruiser *Canberra*. This bitter and costly loss was a product of the Japanese superiority in night fighting and an endless sequence of stupid mistakes by the Allied ship commanders. The Japanese depended on the keen night eyesight, superior night telescope, and binocular optics used by the trained spotters, who were isolated in total darkness before being put on station.

At 2:15 A.M., after taking only thirty-two minutes to eliminate the Allied screening force, the Japanese fleet was in position for an unopposed attack against the now unprotected transports.

But by the time Mikawa could reassemble his force, get to Tulagi, and attack the transports in Sealark Channel, it would be dawn. Since that meant he would be vulnerable to air attack by planes from the American carriers, he prudently decided to turn back for Rabaul. Fortunately, the Japanese were still unaware the American carriers had abruptly hightailed it out of the area, else they could have destroyed the landing force and inflicted a terrible defeat on the first American invasion of Japanese-held territory.

Because of one mistake after another, and the absence of a sensible operating plan, 1077 Allied naval officers and men—mostly American—were killed in the action and more than 700 were wounded. In a tragedy of errors, the American ships were totally unprepared to engage the enemy fleet. The Allied cruisers made up a screening force whose single purpose was to intercept and repulse Japanese warships, which were fully expected to attack the vulnerable landing beaches.

This particular site, at the northwestern end of Guadalcanal across from Savo Island, quickly became known as Iron Bottom Sound because of the many Allied and Japanese ships that were sunk there during the campaign. Bleeding and wounded men floating in these waters faced another, more personally intense peril: any swimmer or helpless survivor in the warm tropical waters was likely to be attacked and killed by sharks, among the most vicious of nature's predators.

Battles at sea are particularly harrowing once shells and bombs start tearing ships apart. There are no foxholes, bunkers, or trenches—no place to hide, no place to run from the killing and maiming explosions or the screeching clangor of steel being torn apart like sheets of paper. The number of higher-ranking officers killed or badly wounded in sea battles may seem disproportionately high when compared to land units, but in any emergency the captain of a ship and his officers are expected to be on the exposed bridge directing the action. The ship's skipper is totally responsible for everything that takes place, and his entire career is judged by decisions made and actions taken in only a few minutes of mortal combat.

In the first light of morning approximately 1,000 survivors were in the water, clutching life rafts, wooden crates—any drifting debris that would keep them afloat. Doctors and corpsmen swam around trying to render aid to the seriously wounded, tying off bleeding wounds. Human blood in the water attracted schools of sharks, and many men screamed as they were attacked and then suddenly disappeared under the oil-coated waters. More than 700 survivors were picked up and rescued by circling ships or taken to the beach. The burn cases were particularly gruesome, and at least seventy-six were given 4,000 cc's of plasma, and 2,000 cc's of saline and glucose solution within the first seventy-two hours. None of these died. The corpsmen had some unappreciative words for the ships that had taken off with desperately needed medical supplies.

"I saw the Battle for Iron Bottom Bay when we lost five cruisers," Rube Garret wrote later in his memoirs of the campaign. "I nearly had a beach side view.... It was raining like the dickens and I got under a truck. When you watch a naval gun battle eight miles away, you see tremendous flashes in the gloom. When you see continuous flashes like lightning, what that is is 16-inch guns. We didn't realise it at the time but that was our ships getting blown to hell. But we thought we were winning the battle, and every time a ship would go down we'd start cheering 'Rah, Rah, that's the good guys'...and they were kicking our butts every time."

The Supply Unloading Problem

The 1st Pioneer Battalion, about 490 men strong on Guadalcanal, had been assigned the task of unloading supplies on Red Beach on the 7th. This was exhausting work in the extreme heat and caused nausea and severe headaches, because all supplies had to be manhandled over the sides of the Higgins Landing Boats. Because the landing force lacked the trucks necessary to move the quickly piled-up supplies off the beach as fast as the boats brought them in, a massive logjam soon occurred. Japanese air attacks compounded the problem. When night fell there were a hundred boats on the beach waiting to be unloaded and another fifty standing offshore. Finally the unloading from the transports had to be curtailed until 10:00 the next morning.

The destruction of the screening force and the precipitous departure of the carriers created new problems. The transports were now vulnerable to Japanese air attacks because there were no American planes to engage the enemy planes and drive them off. The ten transports, one cruiser, and four destroyers had to depart at 3:00 the afternoon of the 8th for the return to Nouméa.

Almost 17,000 men of the landing force of more than 19,000 were ashore, but 1,390 men of the 2nd Marines, Reinforced, and companies of the 2nd Amphibian Tractor and 2nd Service Battalions, and the 10th Marines with their 75-mm pack howitzers were taken to Espiritu Santo. More important to the forces ashore on Tulagi and Guadalcanal were the unloaded supplies and equipment.

In the effort to expedite the landing, only sixty days of supplies and ten units of fire had been loaded in New Zealand. Only four units of fire had been off-loaded on the two islands, including 6 million rounds of .30-caliber ammunition and 800 90-mm shells. Only eighteen spools of barbed wire were on hand. When food supplies were inventoried on the 15th, only enough for thirty days was available—a seventeen-day supply of B rations, three days of C rations, and captured Japanese rations for ten days. This imposed a two-meals-a-day regimen for the troops—far less than needed.

Heavy construction equipment such as power shovels, bulldozers, and dump trucks had not been landed, nor the 2½-ton trucks needed to move artillery and supplies. There were no aircraft of any kind—not even seaplanes from the cruisers—for aerial reconnaissance. Small wonder that many marines began to feel they would never get off the island alive. They had been deserted by the Navy.

Despite the frequent bombing raids, the underfed and inadequately equipped 1st Engineer Battalion began work on the airfield, adding 1,178 feet to the 2,660 feet already constructed by the Japanese, for a total of 3,778 feet by the 18th. This involved movement of 100,000 cubic feet of dirt to fill in a 196-foot gap in the middle of the runway—using hand shovels, trucks, and captured dump cars. The airfield was absolutely essential if the Marines intended to stay on Guadalcanal. Running east and west, the 150-foot-wide field lay about a mile from Alligator Creek on the east and the Lunga River on the west. While the dispersal and servicing areas had been improved, the airfield lacked taxiways and revetments needed to make it fully operational.

The Ill-Fated Goettge Patrol

In response to the discovery of some "termites," surviving and now leaderless Korean laborers, Vandegrift ordered more aggressive and probing patrols along the Matanikau River to locate the original Japanese garrison. A handful of these dispossessed and relatively harmless wanderers eventually chose to surrender instead of starving to death in the unforgiving jungle. On August 9th and 10th the 5th Marines encountered a determined resistance that suggested the presence of regular Japanese combat troops.

First Sergeant Steven Custer, senior NCO (noncommissioned officer) in the division intelligence section, became determined to lead a combat patrol through the Japanese lines to get a better idea of what the troops on the river were facing. Custer had joined the Marines in 1918 at the age of fifteen, and had since served in China, the Caribbean, and aboard the USS *Arizona* prior to Pearl Harbor. He'd taught marksmanship to FBI agents when they received their first firearms. The fact that he had been a Marine recruiter on "The Grand Ole Opry" radio program beamed to the Deep South from Nashville is a good indication of what kind of marine he was. Nearing forty years of age with twenty-five years in the Corps, and recalled from retirement, he was without doubt well schooled in intelligence and sabotage techniques.

At the same time the more determined Japanese fighters were discovered, a surly captured Japanese sailor, a warrant officer, when primed with a few drinks, told his interrogators that others in his group that had been left behind would probably surrender.

Considering the fact that Japanese troops who gave themselves up had never been told not to reveal military intelligence, the information was probably true. Further, some Marine and Navy personnel reported that they thought they had seen a white flag displayed in one area. In truth it was probably a Japanese battle flag that had wrapped itself partly around a pole, and not a ruse to lure marines into an ambush.

Lieutenant Colonel Goettge, division intelligence officer, thought this would be a chance to gather some good intelligence and a few prisoners as well. He expanded Custer's probe into a group of twenty-five, including Lieutenant Commander Malcolm Pratt, a surgeon, to treat the Koreans needing medical care. Lieutenant Ralph Corry, who had lived in Japan and was a proficient Japanese translator, was also taken along. Vandegrift wasn't happy about the project, but he did let them make the dangerous trip along the hostile coast. He had been in the Marines long enough to know that if something could go wrong it probably would go wrong.

In the early evening of August 12th, at about 6 P.M., the patrol set out from Kukum in a Tank Lighter craft with the warning from Colonel William J. Whaling not to land between the Matanikau River and Point Cruz. In some kind of mix-up, the boat was recalled and then departed again at 9:00. At about 10 P.M. Goettge ordered the boat ashore short of its destination, and far too close to the Matanikau River. Two-hundred yards inland is an approximately 200-foot-high coral ridge, Vayaya. Japanese sentries detected the landing craft, and soon armed soldiers took position near the base of the ridge and were ready for a fight when Goettge went over the side with the prisoner, Captain Wilfred Ringer, and Custer. Japanese gunfire from the brush at the edge of the beach killed Goettge and critically wounded Custer, who Ringer helped back to the defensive perimeter. Heavy fire from the hidden positions pinned down and began decimating the hapless patrol, now under Ringer's command. Sergeant Frank L. Few recommended they send Sergeant Charles C. "Monk" Arndt for help. Spry and agile, Monk received his nickname at Calebra, Puerto Rico in 1939 after he shinnied a coconut tree to reap some of the ripe nuts.

"If anyone can get through, it'll be Arndt," Few said.

The small wiry sergeant from Okalona, Mississippi slipped into the water around 10:30 P.M. and headed for Lunga Point, five miles away. At the besieged position, the wounded Dr. Pratt, tending Custer's grievous wound, was hit again, in the lower back, and killed. The Japanese, possibly led by a platoon commander named Sakurai, were increasing their pressure at the extremity of their flanks.

In the deep dark Sakurai sent up flares so his men could get a clearer view of the marine position, allowing heavier Japanese machine gun fire against the small marine perimeter huddled behind the beach abutment at the high tide mark. The Americans sought concealment behind the mangrove tree roots and coconut palms with broad protrusions—good protection from the nearby frontal firing.

"They must have had muzzle flash suppressors on their machine guns," Frank Few recalled later." We could almost feel the muzzle blast of their weapons, but could not locate their fire."

Corporal Joseph Spaulding checked the positions and reported to Ringer. The captain told him he was afraid that the marine he'd sent for help hadn't made it, and asked

Spaulding if he thought he could get through if they pinned the enemy down here on the beach with concentrated firing. Spaulding thought he could, but took a moment to say "so long" to his close buddies on the left flank, then took off along the hard sand at the water's edge as the thin line laid down a heavy cover fire.

The first man had gotten through, but too late to bring help. Exhausted and badly cut up by the coral formations, Arndt staggered ashore to the safety of the marine lines at dawn to report the massacre. He swam the entire distance wearing his heavy ankle-high work boots (his boondockers) because he had double-knotted the laces and couldn't kick them off and didn't dare take the time to cut them free. Once he started on his mission he continued with a single-minded resolve.

Spaulding had shed his dungarees and boondockers when he began his swim east. Once when he came ashore for a brief rest, he saw a bonfire in a bivouac area. Assuming he had reached the marine perimeter, he almost stumbled onto a group of Japanese soldiers sitting around talking. Luck was with him, and he slipped unseen into the water again. He came ashore again at 7:30 A.M., when he arrived exhausted at Kukum, inside the perimeter, where he was almost shot by a marine guard. These messengers arrived far too late to help the patrol.

As dawn came up on what was left of the embattled patrol, only four men able to fight were left. Sergeant Few—a twenty-two-year-old half-Indian from Buckeye, Arizona—and Sergeant Caltrider, along with Captain Ringer and a corporal, knew they were trapped on the beach and tried to move inland to effect an escape. The corporal quickly was cut down by enemy fire. As the remaining three dashed for the protection of the coconut trees Ringer and Caltrider were killed.

Sergeant Few, with fierce dark eyes gleaming and now the sole survivor, glanced back and saw a Japanese soldier firing his rifle into the fallen marines. He rose, steadied himself, and squeezed off a round from his forty-five, dropping the soldier in his tracks. He killed two others of the enemy that night. Possibly the first soldier was the commander, Sakurai, reportedly killed near the end of this skirmish. Few escaped into the sea despite rifle and machine gun fire, and eventually managed to make it back to the safety of the Lunga perimeter.

Still horrified, angered, and nearly exhausted from their ordeal, the survivors related an eyewitness account of the wounded marines on the beach being hacked to death with swords and bayonets. Official reports indicate that none of the victims were ever found—dead or alive—and only a few helmets and the doctor's medical bag indicated they had ever been there.

To the contrary, Private 1st Class Donald R. Langer, I Company, 3rd Battallion, 5th Marines, stated, "I was a lead scout sent to find Colonel Goettge's patrol. We were a rifle platoon. Went up the Matanikau River, water up to our chests. We found the patrol—bodies all cut up." Another patrol later on discovered a mass grave with marine boondockers sticking out, which could have been the final resting place of the patrol, but the patrol was driven off before they had a chance to examine the bodies.

Langer went on to fight in several other campaigns between hospitalizations for malaria, a common ailment of the marines in jungle warfare. When he was discharged from the Marines in 1944, he had suffered twenty-two episodes of malaria.

Walla Walla?

The marine rumor mill—the ubiquitous "scuttlebutt"—was buzzing that a Japanese counterinvasion force was on its way. This was the greatest fear for the men on Guadalcanal. There were not enough men available to stop a determined beach landing. This situation was called "Condition Black." Additional foxholes were dug around the division command post, and more troops were moved to the airfield to take up defensive positions.

Warned that the Japanese were experts in nighttime infiltration, special passwords had been devised. Words with combinations of the letter "L" were preferred, such as lollipop, Lilliputian and Walla Walla, which the enemy had difficulty pronouncing. One incident involved a jeep approaching from the beach with its lights off that didn't answer the challenge to halt and give the password. The alert sentry fired at the strange sound, apparently hitting the vehicle. At this time the driver did respond, yelling out in a southern drawl, "Hallelujah, brother, Hallelujah!" He was allowed to proceed.

That same night the command post of the 1st Marines was overrun by the completely unexpected stampede of nearly 300 head of terrified cattle that had been frightened by a Japanese bomb. In their flight, the bovine detachment managed to inflict some destruction on the position. There were no official reports of casualties on either side. The walking food supply was on the loose because the marines had removed the wire from their enclosures. Everything said and done, "Hallelujah Night" would long be remembered.

Not all fared as well. Marines were killed during the night by friendly fire. Men leaving their foxholes to relieve their natural functions were gunned down by over-nervous sentries in that night of panic. In several instances, best friends killed best friends. To move around at all, for any reason, was to invite sudden and certain death. It is difficult to imagine the mental stress faced by scared, weary, and heat-exhausted men during that first, never-ending night. Nothing they had done before could have prepared them for the unique and harrowing reality of a jungle war.

Not only had the Japanese learned well the lessons of jungle fighting—for which neither they nor the Allies were prepared until the demands of war made it necessary— they had also trained in night operations. Every soldier in every army hated moving around or fighting at night. It was dangerous and difficult work—but it had to be done.

Considering their weaponry, for the highly disciplined Japanese light infantry it was a necessary tactic. They didn't like the idea of night movement and fighting in the jungle any better than their adversaries, but they quickly became masters of the art. Small units—such as platoons and squads—used the protective darkness of night to their advantage, at least to the extent of harassing their opponents and keeping them in a continual state of alert.

The Japanese desire, however, to make terrifying large-scale night assaults against the entrenched enemy proved to be a grand concept that failed in actual practice. Moving large numbers of troops in the dark was infinitely more difficult than maneuvering those same troops in daylight—especially in the unforgiving jungle. Close coordination and basic communications were all but impossible to achieve. Adequate maps detailing fundamental features of the often trackless and thick jungle did not exist for either side.

The American air supremacy, with its endless fighter patrols during the daylight hours, buttressed the need for night movement of large numbers of troops. Difficult as these movements would have been over open terrain, advancing at night through the dense rain forest and over steep, ragged, and muddy ridges while keeping units together and in correct alignment was impossible. In almost every instance the Japanese failed to move sufficient artillery, ammunition, and food to support large assaults.

A simple solution would have been to move the units into position at the point of attack, and then regroup to ensure they were where they were needed and that the necessary supplies and equipment were on hand. Then they could launch the attack in daylight, when the troops could see where they were and where they were going, with a greater possibility of success. Many Japanese field commanders recognized the adversities inherent in making a night attack, but they had no choice but to do so once orders had been issued by the high command far from the scene.

These same field commanders were loathe to request, much less order, delays that might have given them victory. "Loss of face"—the embarrassment of failing to make a scheduled attack—was much more repugnant to field commanders than the possibility of failure. The abysmal lack of communications and coordination virtually guaranteed a fragmented night attack. Some units would attack too early or too late, or not at all. The nocturnal movements that worked so well for squads and platoons proved impossible on a larger scale.

The Japanese Army simply lacked the heavy weapons possessed by the Allies. The basic infantry weapon, the Arisaka Model 38 .256-caliber rifle, was not a match for the larger-caliber Allied rifles. It was roughly finished, with poor sights, a pound heavier, and possessed a barrel 6 inches longer than the Springfield. With the bayonet attached, it was taller than most of the troops carrying it. The only redeeming feature was that the rifle and ammunition were cheap to produce—a critical consideration.

Further, the inferior, heavy, and often unwieldy Model 11 Nambu light machine gun fired an even less powerful version of the standard .256-caliber bullet because the Japanese Army could not afford the expense of replacing it. Because of the design compromises required to produce cheap personal weapons, the bullet of both weapons exited the barrel with a slight wobble that produced messy, tearing wounds at close range, compensating for its lack of weight.

With all their faults, both the Arisaka rifle and the Nambu light machine gun proved ideally suited to close-in jungle fighting. Then there was the propellant powder, which, when combined with the longer barrel, gave off hardly any flash or smoke when fired. In the darkness this was a vital advantage. Allied rifles, on the other hand, emitted both smoke and a distinct flash that an enemy could target in on, with the result that many Allied casualties suffered head wounds. Steel helmets did not offer great protection against direct rifle fire.

Considering the equipment furnished to Japanese light infantry—never an even match against Western forces—special tactics had to be devised. Night movement demanded discipline, individual bravery, and patience, which characterized the Japanese soldier. One deadly result of this tactic was to magnify the readiness of nervous Allied troops to fire at any perceived movement or noise in the dark. This skittishness often resulted in the killing or wounding of friendly forces. Even those suffering from severe dysentery learned they could not leave their foxholes to relieve themselves without great risk to their lives. Sleeping with one eye open while having to exist in cramped, exposed, muddy, and filthy positions grinds men down to a barely functional level.

The undermanned marines defending the Lunga perimeter were spread over large areas in small pockets, which left considerable open space between them—an invitation for the infiltration of Japanese patrols and probes. So it was only natural that the weary defenders had itchy fingers. In time the hardened survivors learned to use grenades instead of rifle or machine gun fire to discourage intruders.

In retrospect it appears the Japanese used night infiltration tactics to deprive the defenders of badly needed sleep as much as to secure information and intelligence about enemy positions. In the long run, however, large-scale night attacks on land cost them dearly in human lives and squandered opportunities.

On August 13 the Imperial High Command in Tokyo ordered the 17th Army under Lieutenant General Harukichi Hyakutake to take over ground operations on Guadalcanal from the Navy. This was to be called Operation Ka, taken from the first syllable in the Japanese word for Guadalcanal. The Combined Fleet was directed to support the army to oust the marines clinging to the island. Hyakutake designated an elite combat team from the 28th Infantry, along with artillery and engineers, to land and drive off the presumptuous invaders.

Fast American destroyer transports (APDs) sailed into Sealark Channel on August 15th to deliver the advance element of the Navy's CUB-1, the code name for an advanced fuel and supply base. The element consisted of five officers and 118 enlisted personnel—navy petty officers wearing aviation support ratings—and equipment to support operations at Henderson Field. Ensign George B. Polk commanded this first group of Seabees (from the Navy's *C*onstruction *B*attalions—CBs). They brought with them and unloaded without enemy opposition 400 drums of aviation gasoline, 32 drums of lubricant, 282 assorted bombs from 100-pounders to 500-pounders, ammunition, and tools and spare parts for the planes. These were the first supplies to arrive since the departure of the invasion fleet on the 9th.

The Seabees not only went to work on the airfield, but began constructing other needed facilities, such as roads, storage areas, and fortifications. Another significant but not officially sanctioned contribution to the marines' welfare was the unique beverage distillation units they fabricated. These construction men generally were older by as much as a decade, but many had come from the mountains of Appalachia, where the distillation of moonshine was an honorable, albeit illegal, profession. A handful of the Old Breed marines had known how it was done, and produced an awful-tasting brew that was very much in demand.

The same techniques used to distill clean water applied to making alcoholic beverages. Soon after their landing, a few of the more entrepreneurial Seabees had their equipment up and running. Their product was usually better than that previously available, and could be produced in larger quantities to satisfy the huge demand. The price of as much as $50 a quart was no obstacle to men who had no place else to spend their pay. Best of all, the suppliers were local and could be counted on. The stills, vulnerable to air raids and the nightly ship bombardments, were as securely protected as fuel supplies, howitzers, or any other necessary equipment. After all, the unappròved distillation apparatus had to be concealed from accidental discovery by the prying eyes of officers, who might have shut them down.

The ingenious construction workers soon found that the disabled amphtraks (amphibious tractors—landing vessels) had ample quantities of copper tubing, and that the gas tanks were made of copper. By cutting the top off the tank, rigging the tubing as a condenser, and cooking the chopped cane sugar, a product very much like rum can be produced. They had also learned a native trick: drill a hole in a fresh coconut, fill it with raisins, close the hole and bury it in the ground for five days. When served to thirsty troops, it was a remarkable cure for many ailments, the worst of which was homesickness.

Incoming pilots brought in bottles of whiskey, which most often wound up in the hands of the officers. There was a flourishing trade between the thirsty men on the rotten island and the souvenir-seeking crews of ships bringing in supplies. A favorable but liquid rate of exchange for converting Japanese rifles, helmets and, above all, battle flags was quickly established.

On that same day Coastwatcher Captain Martin Clemens, dressed in ragged clothing but with his shoes brightly shined, led two files of Guadalcanal natives past astonished marine sentries into the marine perimeter. His offer to provide reconnaissance scouts to gather intelligence and serve as guides was readily accepted by Vandegrift. The services of these Melanesians, thoroughly acclimated to the mysteries of the jungle, were worth a regiment of marines. The Japanese couldn't make a move without the information being passed on to the Americans.

While the situation on the Canal was still vulnerable, it was not yet precarious. The men knew what to do and were doing it even if they had to improvise. A jeep was used to tow a 75-mm howitzer and carry a gun crew. To move a gun across a stream, it was broken down and carried over piece by piece. Three or four men were needed to carry the barrel and the main block alone.

Supplies continued to trickle in, but not in sufficient quantities to relieve the pressure. The lack of an adequate diet for the force was beginning to show. Night blindness, caused by the lack of vitamin A, was affecting performance of duties. In effect, the few supply ships—bringing in mostly ammunition, but little in the way of food—were running a Japanese naval blockade.

News from the home front was not encouraging. The U.S. State Department issued a statement, for international consumption, that the government was spending more money on housing and feeding uprooted Italian-American civilians than on fighting the Japanese. A particular issue of *The New York Times* that managed to reach the Canal reported that the marines were TIGHTENING THEIR GRIP...AS NAVY KEEPS SUPPLIES FLOWING.

Considerable attention has been given to the Japanese "propaganda machine," which continued to proclaim great victories over the hapless Allies. Grossly inflated reports of sensational victories, with spectacular lists enumerating the ships sunk, planes shot down, and men killed (often more men, ships, and aircraft than possessed by the Allies in an area at the time) by the unbeatable warriors of Nippon continued throughout the war. At home in Tokyo it didn't take a rocket scientist to figure out that if the reports were true, the Imperial Japanese Empire should long ago have won the war.

Yet, William Manchester found a story on page 25 of the August 24th issue of *Time* magazine reporting on the Battle of Savo, which said that: "Japanese cruisers and destroyers tried to smash the invasion fleet. Then came what the U.S. Tars had long waited for: the first real gun-to-gun test of the U.S. and Japanese surface sea power. Result: a licking for the Japs." It was several months before the powers that be in the government and military considered the public capable of handling the dismal news of that naval disaster.

Rear Admiral Raiso Tanaka, newly appointed commander of the Guadalcanal Reinforcement Force, sortied from Rabaul August 16th with a destroyer transport group carrying a detachment of elite infantrymen to reinforce Guadalcanal. This small contingent of about 900 soldiers was to reconnoiter the area—and wait for the second part to arrive before attacking Marine positions.

The next day, August 17th, Henderson Field was ready to begin air operations. The Pagoda, a tall building left behind by the Japanese, was set up to provide air direction and control. A captured siren was mounted on the Pagoda to sound the alert. The American war planes so desperately needed were already at sea and nearing the besieged island.

There were few buildings that could be used as housing. The basic protection from the elements was the two-man pup tent. It could be rigged to provide a cover over open holes. Some created more elaborate bunkers by digging into the mud and using logs for the floor and sides. Considerable Japanese lumber was appropriated for the same purpose. Sandbags, when they could be had, added some protection from naval shells and aerial bombs, but narrow slit trenches dug in the ground were much safer when bullets and shrapnel were flying. The high-explosive shells from Japanese ships gouged out many holes, which were simply converted into slit trenches.

Tanaka's six destroyers landed 900 men of the first-class, battle-hardened Ichiki Force at Taivu Point, 20 miles to the east of the marine perimeter, during the night of August 17. This was the vanguard of the famed 28th Infantry Regiment led by Colonel Kiyono Ichiki. In 1937, as an impetuous company commander in China, his actions helped provoke the sensational Marco Polo Bridge Incident, which many historians consider the beginning of WWII. After conducting successful combat operations in China and in the jungles of Borneo, this proven amphibious assault unit had been designated to land on Midway in early June had not the Imperial Navy been repulsed in a decisive and devastating defeat by a hastily assembled and daring American fleet.

Colonel Ichiki was devoutly dedicated to the idea that Japanese Spiritual Power could and would overcome any resistance. Other Nipponese commanders referred to it as "the school of bamboo spear tactics." All his men had to do was beat their spears against their shields, scream defiantly, and show their savage teeth to frighten away the cowardly Americans.

Marine sentries along the coast, judging from the heavier lapping of water on the beach, which suggested ships passing close in, suspected a landing. This was confirmed the next day when a marine patrol led by Captain Charles Brush ambushed a Japanese work party laying telephone wire. Thirty-three Japanese, led by Captain Shibuya, died at the cost of three marines. The dead officers were carrying accurate maps that pinpointed Marine positions, which did not extend very far inland. Moreover, they wore the Star of the Imperial Army on their helmets, rather than the anchor and Chrysanthemum of the Navy landing forces.

Because of the discovery of his landing force, or more probably because of his supreme self-confidence, Ichiki decided to disregard the recommendation to wait for the remainder of his regiment. Not noted for his restraint, he decided to begin his attack immediately, as he was certain the Japanese would easily drive the marines off the island. After all, he knew that the Americans were soft, that Americans would not fight, and that the Americans considered that the nights were for dancing.

More realistically, the real problem with his line of thinking was that Japanese intelligence estimated perhaps 2,000 marines had landed, when there were actually more than 10,000 Americans dug in within the Lunga Point defensive perimeter. His force landed carrying light packs, 250 rounds of ammunition per man, and supplies for only seven days.

The Matanikau—Action on the Western Perimeter

In mid-August the medical services began administering a regimen of Atabrine tablets to treat the cases of malaria that were emerging. Scuttlebutt—the rumor mill—said that Atabrine made a man impotent. Because many of the men felt they'd rather be dead than impotent, the overworked corpsmen wound up watching to make sure the marines swallowed the pills. Of course, the Atabrine did not make the users impotent, as their eventual return to the civilized rear areas proved.

Although malaria would eventually take more marines out of combat than all the wounds, a more immediate problem assaulted the strength of the warriors. An acute form of dysentery, brought on by poor sanitation and consumption of untreated water, raged through the landing force.

The evident presence of Japanese combat troops moving about west of the Matanikau River demanded attention. Vandegrift weighed the value of limited offensive action against a force of unknown strength with the need to protect the airfield. By August 18th the situation appeared stable enough to permit the 5th Marines to deploy units for what became the first battle—little more than a skirmish— along the Matanikau.

The Matanikau River, draining from the interior to the sea, was a fairly substantial natural barrier. Japanese forces would find that landing reinforcements and supplies on the island west of the river was easier and safer compared to similar events east of the marine perimeter. Once the Americans crossed this line, they were truly operating in the miasmic jungle sliced with uncountable ravines and ridges that confounded the movement of both adversaries.

Captain Lyman D. Spurlock's L Company led the way on August 18th by advancing 1,000 yards inland to make their crossing of the Matanikau. This unit was to cross the river the next morning and move north to the sea along the west bank to envelop the enemy in a pocket. Ten Japanese were killed before the marines reached their jump-off point and dug in for the night.

In a coordinated movement, Captain Hawkins's Company B would attack across the sandbar at the mouth of the Matanikau to close the trap. Captain Bert W. Hardy's Company I was to be moved by boat to the west of Kokumbona to cut off any Japanese who escaped the trap.

An artillery barrage from the 11th Marines greeted the Japanese in the area on the morning of the 19th, and Spurlock's unit crossed the river and discovered that the jungle was as difficult an enemy as the Japanese. Moving even a company of men in the rain forest was an exhausting exercise—four hours were required to move his column one mile. Coordination between units simply did not exist. Radio voice communications failed completely, as would be the case again and again.

Navy Corpsman Laing and his associates were suddenly overwhelmed with casualties. He was moving forward with a heavy machine gun patrol as it wound through the jungle valley when a Japanese mortar barrage erupted on the trail. It was clear that the marines would have to withdraw or be wiped out. Laing attached himself to a group of walking wounded, withdrawing from the firefight, screened by four riflemen and a BAR man. He helped the staggering and reeling, torn and bloodied fighters toward the rear through the tangled brush up and down the steep and muddy slopes.

"I realized that the shock, fear, and outrage that I felt," wrote Laing later, "did not even come close to the agony and the courage of these maimed marine comrades of mine."

Spurlock wheeled his company northward against fierce resistance from the west, and they made slow and steady progress as they hacked their way though the dense, grasping undergrowth. Finally, about 2:00 P.M., Company L deployed around Matanikau village, and heard the Japanese shouts and chanted cries of "banzai," a howl the marines now knew to be a prelude to all-out attack, much like the vaunted American "Rebel Yell." This psychological "pumping up" preceded the first daylight banzai charge against U.S. forces in the Pacific. As an omen of the future, the heavy hot lead laid in at close range from the American guns was more than a match for bravery and the cold steel of Japanese bayonets. A couple of hours later, after the marines routed the remaining defenders in the village, they counted sixty-five dead Japanese at a cost of four Americans killed in action and eleven wounded. Small arms fire from a dominating ridge ripped into the struggling marines, killing platoon leader Lieutenant George H. Mead, Jr., heir to the Mead paper fortune. The company executive officer who took over the platoon was also killed in the action.

Boats carrying Company I departed Kukum at 4:30 A.M. and drew rifle and machine gun fire from the beach. Salvos from enemy destroyers, departing after the night's bombardment of the Lunga perimeter, made no hits. After a brisk action in the village of Kokumbona, the defending Japanese fell back into the abutting hills. After this small success, the company-sized force was back in Kukum at 5:00 P.M., losing only one dead in the process. Lieutenant Takahashi, newly arrived on the island, later boasted that his leadership caused the marines to be driven back into the sea, and claimed the capture of three landing boats and a machine gun.

These skirmishes, contributing little to the final success of the campaign, provided information and revealed serious tactical control problems. Although it was evident that complicated and coordinated efforts were difficult in this terrain, the lessons weren't fully understood. Both sides were much too inclined to rely on traditional tactics despite the obvious limitations imposed by the terrible terrain. The complicated and intricate Japanese maneuvers—which looked so good on paper—compounded with their overweening refusal to accept delays wreaked by unforgiving natural obstacles, would prove to be disastrous.

Cactus Air Force Sets Up Shop—August 20

Thirteen days after the Marines splashed ashore on Guadalcanal, the Cactus Air Force (CAF)—all the air arms who flew off of Henderson Field, regardless of service—was ready for business. In the afternoon, twelve Marine SBD dive bombers of VMSB-232, led by flight leader Major Richard D. Mangrum, landed to a highly emotionally charged reception by the beleaguered Marine garrison. Soon after came nineteen Marine Wildcat fighters of VMF-223 under Captain John L. Smith, from Lexington, Oklahoma, all from the escort carrier *Long Island*, a converted freighter. Eight of the Wildcats assigned to VMF-223 were from VMF-212, still on Efate, in the New Hebrides. Captain Loren D. "Doc" Everton led this contingent, with "Tex" Hamilton on his wing. Launched from about 200 miles southeast of Guadalcanal, the first planes of the famed Cactus Air Force flew in, and together with the ground crews, some of whom had already arrived, set up base in the area of the Pagoda, a landmark the Japanese had left behind.

Smith, a tough disciplinarian, had joined the Marines in 1936 and served two years as an artillery officer before he moved on to flight training. He drove his Wildcat aviators hard but set a high personal standard for himself as well, for he knew superb personal effort was needed to match the Japanese pilots flying the superior Zekes. So when a flight of Betties was reported heading for Guadalcanal the next day, Smith took four Wildcats up to 14,000 feet over Savo, and caught sight of an unsuspecting escort of six Zekes a few hundred feet higher.

He raced head-on, guns blazing, toward one who chickened out, and when the Zeke swung out of the way, Smith traced a path of cannon fire along its exposed belly. When two of the enemy teamed up and came after him, he dived away into a cloud. Stressing smart flying and discipline, by the 29th he had shot down five Japanese planes to become the CAF's first ace.

The appearance of the planes brought tears to the eyes of many gaunt, battle-hardened troops, who almost believed that they had been written off and abandoned. Vandegrift admitted the sight left him a little choked up. One marine said, "I just looked up and grinned till I felt the mud crack on my whiskers. It looked damned good to see something American circling in the sky over the airfield."

Soon the Navy R4D (C-47) twin-engine transports of Marine Air Group 25 began flying in supplies. Usually 3,000-pound loads, a ton and a half—not nearly enough to sustain the men on the island—were brought in daily, weather permitting. They could evacuate as many as sixteen badly wounded or critically ill stretcher-laden casualties per trip.

Yet few could anticipate the grueling demands on the pilots and crews. Soon it was acknowledged that about thirty days was the realistic limit pilots could fly and retain their physical and psychological proficiencies. Of the first group of dive bomber pilots to fly combat from Henderson Field, only one was able to board the evacuation transport plane under his own power.

"Cactus" was the radio calling code name assigned to Henderson's air operations, in the same way that "Watchtower" was the code name for the invasion of Guadalcanal. This small air contingent—the Cactus Air Force (CAF)—was badly needed, and the newly arrived pilots did not have to wait long for action. While these flyers were not directly involved that night in the first phase of the bloody confrontation at Alligator Creek on the small perimeter, they proved their value early the next day.

In the Spotlight

Sir Jacob Vouza, Melanesian Hero

The stubborn courage of the Coastwatchers and some of the former native constabulary on Guadalcanal is best exemplified by Sergeant Major Jacob Vouza. Although retired after twenty-five years of service in the local native constabulary, on August 15 he accompanied Captain Martin Clemens, an official of the Royal Australian government, in volunteering their services to the marines. Their sudden appearance out of the bush startled the marines as they crossed into the perimeter.

Probably the toughest man ever to walk on Guadalcanal, Vouza was absolutely fearless. His first impulse when the Japanese landing force came ashore on June 29, 1942 was to place them under arrest. Clemens convinced him that it would be best to wait until the Americans arrived. At the time Vouza had never heard of Japan or the United States.

Vouza, a longtime member of the native police, was chief of Clemens's scouts. Vouza was a tall, husky, and tough man who was known to sometimes take the law into his own hands and throw his weight around. Though there were some initial misgivings, he was allowed to join the patrol group. It is well he did, for he had come to despise the Japanese, referred to by the locals as "the new white men." His intimate knowledge of the island was desperately needed for intelligence gathering.

On one scouting patrol he was captured by troops of the Ichiki Force, who were moving into a position to attack the eastern end of the marine perimeter along Alligator Creek. Ishimoto, supposedly an itinerant Japanese carpenter who had dwelt on the island for years and who was now wearing a Japanese officer's uniform, identified Vouza, who was found to be carrying a small American flag given to him by some marines as a safe-conduct pass through the lines. The spy, now happily among his own countrymen, gladly helped in the torture and interrogation of Vouza to obtain information about the marine strength and positions. Tied to a tree for questioning, the stoic Melanesian was slapped, badly beaten, and stabbed seven times with bayonets for refusing to answer their questions. In a final parting gesture, his throat was slashed with a sword and he was left for dead.

But he didn't die. In the gathering darkness Vouza recovered consciousness, chewed free of his grass rope bonds and ultimately struggled about twenty miles back to the marine lines in the pitch black night, the last three miles on his hands and knees because of his loss of blood. He arrived back at the perimeter, where the marines were dug in behind a single strand of barbed wire along the stagnant creek, in time to warn of the impending attack.

Grievously wounded, and with Clemens holding his hand, Vouza related his observation of the size of the Japanese force and its equipment. Before he collapsed, believing he was dying, he dictated a good-bye message to his wife. Rushed to the field hospital, he was given large transfusions of blood. The doctor who sewed up Vouza's throat reported that as soon as the operation was finished, the island police officer asked for something to eat. In an astounding recovery, he was back on his feet in two weeks and ready for more patrols.

For his heroic resistance, he was later awarded the United States Silver Star and the George Medal, the highest award for bravery that a British civilian can win. Later he was knighted by the British government. Perhaps in the greatest reward of all, Vandegrift appointed Vouza a Sergeant Major in the USMC, thereby entitling him to wear the marine uniform on ceremonial occasions, along with an engraved marine sword. He was ninety-two when he died in 1984, the most respected man on the island, and immensely proud of his dress blues to the end.

While the loyalty and willingness of the natives of the island to help was seldom in question after the marines had landed, many had assisted the Japanese to one degree or another after their occupation of the island. So far as the natives were concerned, one outside governing authority had replaced another, so it was politic to back the winner. Yet, by the time the Allies did return, the brutal Japanese behavior and humiliation directed toward the native population had destroyed much of the good will and cooperation the Melanesians might have given.

Forced labor, the wanton looting and destruction of the natives' carefully tended gardens cleared out of the jungle, and the ruthless ferocity of the invaders soon turned the natives against them. No one can provide an estimate of how many Japanese troops wandering in the jungle were killed by the inhabitants, but it must have been a considerable number. As they fled the area of the American landing that fateful August day in 1942, numerous Japanese were believed to have been slaughtered by enraged and vengeful Melanesians.

After the war, the Solomon Islands gained their independence and self-rule. Vouza was accorded great respect and admiration for his bravery, and held in high esteem by his fellow islanders.

CHAPTER 6

AUGUST 21–22 BATTLE OF ALLIGATOR CREEK: THE FIGHT ON THE TENARU

Marine patrols and the remarkable efforts of local inhabitants like Vouza had established that the Japanese Ichiki Force was moving toward Alligator Creek. The enemy had chosen to force a crossing under the cover of dark over the sandbar closing off the mouth of the creek—a brackish tropical backwater, opening to the sea only at the highest tides—hoping to push through, fan out, and capture Henderson Field about a mile beyond.

The first Japanese flares lit up the assault area in an eerie green glow that cast weird shadows in the coconut grove, following mortar shells falling on the marine positions along the west bank of Alligator Creek about 2:00 A.M. This was not the nearby Tenaru River (nor the Ilu), as it was mistakenly marked on the rudimentary maps available. Whether called the Battle of Alligator Creek, or the Tenaru, as it was known for years, this was the first full-scale battle for the increasingly hungry, sick, and weary marines.

Just such an attack was expected, and the soldiers of Lieutenant Colonel Edwin A. Pollock's 2nd Battalion, 1st Marines were positioned from the spit to about 1,000 yards inland along the creek. A little earlier he had called his observation posts back in when the unmistakable sounds of enemy movement were heard. Antitank guns with an extra supply of 37-mm cannister and machine guns covered the sandbar. Two platoons of the 1st Special Weapons Battalion and a platoon of Company G, 2nd Battalion, 1st Marines were dug in covering the sand bar. The defenders in their positions, including machine gun pits, were as concerned about the presence of deadly crocodiles as they were about the Japanese.

"Now let the bastards come," shouted one of the sweaty, dirty, and bone-tired defenders. They were as ready as they could be with what they had.

Sergeant George Herbert, from Weapons Company, 5th Marines, had placed his section of 37-mm antitank guns on the spit. Packed closely in an attack formation, their fixed bayonets waving, 200 screaming and yelling veteran Japanese infantrymen of the Ichiki Force tried to charge across the narrow sand spit, which was about fifteen feet long where it met the Sealark Channel. Herbert's guns fired cannister shot at point blank range until their barrels glowed red in the dark, tearing gaping holes in the attacking ranks, and destroying the maniacal onslaught.

"The Japs got so close that some of the dead lay within feet of our guns. Some were so ripped up they...they didn't look like humans anymore. They damned near overran us."

Medium and heavy machine guns and other automatic weapons were fired from pits about 10 feet square by 5 feet deep along the water's edge that had been dug during the day's oppressive heat and humidity. These pits were buttressed with sandbags and coconut logs, and protected and supported by marines equipped with 1903 .30-caliber Springfield rifles or Browning Automatic Rifles (BARs).

One of these defenders was Private 1st Class Robert Stiles, just behind the main line. One of his buddies in a nearby foxhole had impaled a Japanese soldier on his bayonet. In the morning Stiles found him mesmerized at the sight of the dead soldier. "When he saw me, he got real embarrassed. Something really smelled and it wasn't the dead Nip. You guessed it...Chuck had crapped in his pants. He got up, sighed, and cleaned himself up. You know, I never heard of Chuck being petrified again."

Many of the Japanese who made it across the creek got caught up on the single strand of barbed wire that had been "appropriated" from the coconut plantation and became easy targets for heavy and deadly marine machine gun fire. Some managed to blow holes through the wire (which they hadn't known about) with bangalore torpedoes, and reach the marine positions before finally being driven back after ferocious hand-to-hand fighting.

When the Japanese made their banzai charge—a "tactically dramatic" gesture—across the sand spit that steamy night, Private Joe Wadsworth opened fire with his BAR, killing a number of attackers before his gun jammed. (The sweltering humidity and dirt was not kind to personal weapons.) Looking around, he grabbed up a Springfield and resumed firing with the old marine standby until the Japanese had closed in around him. Then he went after them with his bayonet. Struck by a bullet and knocked down in the melee, he survived, and later refused medical evacuation until those he considered more seriously wounded had been cared for.

"That's Hell's Point. That's where the Japs tried their crossing," Captain James F. Sherman, from Somerville, Massachusetts, related later. "Some of our men moved up onto the point to get a better field of fire, and the Japs put up flares that were as bright as daylight. We lost some people in there. But, we stopped the Japs."

In some spots unprotected by wire, a few Japanese got through long enough to overrun some positions before being hurled back. Corporal Dean Wilson's BAR jammed as three Japanese rushed his foxhole. One leaped into the foxhole as Wilson grabbed his machete and slashed his attacker's midsection and left him dying. Jumping from his foxhole, the sweaty and dirty Wilson engaged the other two and hacked them to death.

There were a terrible few minutes while screaming and shouting marine and Japanese warriors engaged in ferocious close combat using fists, knives, rifle butts, and bayonets. Lieutenant Colonel Edwin A. Pollock had to send in a reserve platoon to close up the breakthrough. The carnage was sickening, but faced with the option of life or death, the tired and filthy marines in the foxholes soon overcame the revulsion of the dead, and of the shattered, dying, and screaming bodies piling up around them.

"Hold your fire!—1st Battalion coming through!" came the shout as fresh marines joined the fight. They had crossed upriver, to the south and right of the battered and weary 2nd Battalion, and were intent on rolling the Japanese up toward the sea. Ichiki's unit was finished as a fighting force.

Toward the end of the night attack, Lieutenant Maurice Ahearn was seriously wounded. Corpsman Richard Garrett sprinted to where he lay and shielded the man's body with his own. He was also wounded, yet managed to drag himself and his "patient" to safety and the nearest aid station.

At dawn on the 21st, when it became evident the position had held, Vandegrift sent a reserve battalion from the inland right flank to cross the river and sweep the area to the ocean. Some Japanese soldiers in rudimentary defensive emplacements panicked and tried to escape into the sea as marine tanks—engines roaring and whining from the continual starting, twisting, and stopping, their cannons firing cannister shot and machine guns blazing—overran enemy foxholes and machine guns. Highly effective in the relatively open Lunga plain, the tanks swept the east bank of the creek, crushing and tearing apart living, dead, and dying Japanese under their grinding treads. Few survived the slaughter, and some who did tried to swim around behind the marine lines to lob grenades at the defenders. Others fled along the coast eastward toward their landing point, and became easy targets for strafing runs by the newly arrived fighters and dive bombers.

An estimated 800 elite Japanese infantrymen were killed in the ghastly battle, with many of the mangled bodies—twisted grotesquely from agonized deaths—slowly being covered with sand at the mouth of the river. American losses in the battle were reported to be thirty-four dead and seventy-two wounded.

All day the fighting continued, although at nowhere near the intensity of the first attack. "We heard the crack of their guns, and bullets ricocheting among the trees. Our artillery was still ranging on the Jap positions on the far side of the Tenaru. And the Japs were throwing rifle grenades over to our side," reported Richard Tregaskis, combat correspondent at the scene. "We could see one of the bursts ahead, a spray of dirt rising where the explosive hit. Occasionally we heard the bursts of sharp-sounding Jap machine gun fire; the light .25 calibers."

Corporal Raymond A. Negus, from Peabody, Massachusetts, was wounded in both arms, the abdomen, and the left thigh just after the American enveloping movement moved out. Two buddies got him onto a stretcher, but then he clambered off, yelling at them to take cover from the devastating Japanese mortar, rifle, and machine gun fire ripping the area. Without assistance, despite his severe wounds, he crawled alone to a safer spot.

This particular battle merely emphasized what the Raider Battalion had discovered in their first day fighting on Tulagi. The highly disciplined and determined troops of Japan's finest light infantry could be defeated by the heavier weapons possessed by the equally disciplined marines. Imperial Japanese soldiers were steeped in the code of Bushido, which dictated a soldier's life...and death. The American equivalent was, "Death Before Dishonor," which to the Japanese simply meant *No Surrender*.

"Later that day I took a walk out toward the sandbar and, from then on, I knew I was truly at war," recalled Captain Bill Hawkins. "Christ Almighty, what a sight! The Japanese are truly much shorter than we are as it is, and dead men always appear smaller than they really are. They looked like contorted rag dolls. With that brutally fierce sun, they'd already started to puff and swell. The stench was beginning to sweep the whole area. My God, what a gruesome sight!"

Most of the Japanese who were captured during this campaign—and throughout the war—were either too badly wounded to kill themselves or unconscious from concussions. One significant consequence of the idea that surrender was not to be thought of is that there had been no military instruction as to what a captured man could or could not say. Japanese prisoners could, and often did, pass along critical military information to the Americans, without worrying that they had violated any military law or moral code. If they did not return to their units, they were already considered dead.

The marines discovered the hard way in the aftermath of the brutal battle that many wounded Japanese skulked among their dead comrades, waiting until an unsuspecting marine ventured close, to rise up and shoot or toss a grenade at him. This meant one thing: when moving among "dead" Japanese, use one more bullet to make sure they were really dead and not alive and lying in ambush.

Ichiki and the remaining survivors straggled back to their landing point, where the now thoroughly disgraced colonel burned the regimental flags rather than let them fall into the hands of the marines. Some historians claim he then committed suicide, while others assert he had been killed in the fighting. In a final irony forever unknown to the impetuous Ichiki, who had disobeyed the orders to wait for the remainder of his regiment to arrive before launching his attack—they did not arrive in time to have been of any help that night. The ships bringing them to Guadalcanal and glory had been turned back by the American Navy.

In any event, it is likely that an attack by the entire regiment would have failed as miserably as that of the first Ichiki Force had failed. The job of wresting the island back from the Americans demanded close coordination and planning between rival Imperial Army and Navy, a problem that was never solved. The jealous infighting at the Japanese high command level was even more counterproductive than that at the American high command level.

In the Spotlight

Albert "Al" Schmid

When Albert A. Schmid heard the news of the Japanese attack on Pearl Harbor he at first thought it was a big joke. For a day or two he did not realize how much the event had affected him. On December 9th he told his girlfriend Ruth Hartley that he had gone to the Philadelphia Customs House and enlisted in the Marines. He reported on January 5th for transportation to the boot training facility at Parris Island, South Carolina.

After advanced training at New River, North Carolina, on his short leave, he bought an engagement ring for Ruth. When he boarded the troop transport *George F. Elliott* for a destination unknown, he had been assigned to the 11th Machine Gun Squad, Company H, 2nd Battalion, 1st Marine Regiment of the 1st Marine Division.

Al was born in 1920 to Mr. and Mrs. Adolph E. Schmid, and when his mother later died he was on his own, working at odd jobs until 1940 when he became an apprentice at Dodge Steel Company in Philadelphia. If anyone had told the young man—who didn't even know where Pearl Harbor was located—that within a couple of years he would be wading ashore in an armed invasion of an unknown island in the South Pacific, he would have told them they were crazy.

Like all the other marines around him, he was surprised at the initial lack of resistance but felt sure hot action would soon ensue. Two weeks later, at about 2:00 A.M. on August 21, 1942, came the expected counterattack by a portion of Colonel Kiyono Ichiki's elite regiment. Aware of the Japanese intentions, marines of the 2nd Battalion were moved into positions along Alligator Creek, believed at the time to be the Tenaru River.

Schmid, along with Corporal Leroy Diamond, and Private 1st Class John Rivers, a Native American, had set up their .30-caliber water-cooled machine gun in a firing pit reinforced with logs and sandbags on the west side of the creek. Across fifty yards of stagnant backwater Schmid saw the enemy approaching. "It looked like a herd of cattle coming down to drink," Schmid later recalled. Rivers, manning the gun, opened fire and broke up that group. Then the Japanese focused on his position, trying to knock out the gun. Bullets were kicking up the mud and chipping splinters off the logs.

The marine machine gun about a hundred yards upstream was knocked out, and gunner Rivers was killed by about a dozen bullets in his face and head. In death his fingers froze on the trigger and he fired another 200 rounds at the attackers. Schmid shoved the dead man from the gun and took over the firing, with Diamond doing the reloading. Suddenly Diamond was hit hard in the arm and could no longer reload, but he could spot targets and direct Schmid's firing and signal him when to reload. Diamond watched the ammo belt, and when it got low he'd punch Schmid on the arm, and Schmid would fire another burst, yank open the receiver, insert a new belt of ammo and resume his deadly firing.

Its water jacket punctured by rifle fire, the machine gun overheated, but continued to work, and for four hours Schmid kept up his savage fire. One Japanese soldier managed to climb past the piled up bodies and toss a grenade into the gun emplacement. "My helmet was knocked off. Something hit me in the face," he recalled. He had been wounded in the eyes, left shoulder, arm, and hand.

"They got me in the eyes," he yelled to Diamond. Schmid pulled his .45 automatic pistol from his holster.

"Don't do it, Smitty! Don't shoot yourself!" Diamond yelled back.

"Hell, don't worry about that," replied Schmid. "I'm going to get the first Jap that tries to come in here!"

"But you can't see!"

"Just tell me which way he's coming from and I'll get him," swore Schmid.

Both men were wounded and all but helpless as dawn came. A sniper across the way had a good firing angle, which prompted Schmid to get back on the machine gun, and with Diamond yelling the direction in his ear, he fired toward the sniper's position. Another marine, Private 1st Class Whitey Jacobs, managed to crawl through the heavy fire and into their hole. He worked to stop their bleeding and bandage their wounds prior to their being evacuated.

Marine records credit Schmid, Diamond, and Rivers with at least 200 kills that terrible and steaming few hours on Guadalcanal. For their determined and desperate action that night, both Schmid and Diamond were awarded the Navy Cross. But for Schmid the worst was yet to come. Arriving at the naval hospital in San Diego on October 20, 1942, he endured a series of operations to remove shrapnel and other fragments from his face and eyes. One eye had been destroyed, and the other seriously damaged.

"When I came back, I was the most disgusted man you ever saw. I didn't want to bother to do anything. I could see people looking away from my ugly scars. They wouldn't want to associate with me. I even told my girl it was all over." His girl didn't accept that, and in April 1943 they were married. In June 1944 Albert A. Schmid, Jr. was born.

After he married, he was invited to attend war bond rallies, made hospital visits, and appeared at charity events. A book, *Al Schmid—Marine*, by Roger Butterfield, was published and became the basis for the highly successful movie Pride of the Marines produced in 1944 by Warner Brothers Studio.

"I wanted to help the boys, and at the same time I was helping myself," explained Schmid. "I got used to people again." In time he recovered some sight in the remaining eye, and became an avid ham radio operator. He also loved to fish. Once he brought in a 130-pound tarpon while fishing off Florida's coast.

Schmid died of bone cancer December 2, 1982 in St. Petersburg, Florida, where he moved to be near the Bay Pines Veterans' Hospital after his discharge from the Marines in 1944. Schmid was buried at Arlington National Cemetery with full military honors befitting an American hero.

The first element of the Army Air Force 67th Fighter Squadron—flying P-400s, or Aircobras—arrived on Guadalcanal on August 22nd. The P-400 was the export version of the P-39 that was used in England and Russia. Compared to the Wildcat and the Japanese Zero, it lacked speed and maneuverability, and did not even have an oxygen supply to allow it to climb to normal combat altitudes. Derisively, pilots often called it a P-40 with a Zero on its tail.

This group of army pilots and crews landed at Nouméa, New Caledonia and wrestled the still-crated planes to the squadron's base up in the rain-swept hills, and discovered various parts of forty-five P-400s and two P-39Fs. Lacking even a single technical manual, the ground crews—who had never seen the planes before—and the pilots had to figure out how to put them together from scratch and then fly them. Only two pilots had ever flown a P-39. The squadron moved to Guadalcanal by flying 277 nautical miles from New Caledonia to Efate, another 153 nautical miles to Espiritu Santo, and then, using supplementary gas tanks, they flew to Henderson Field guided by a B-17. This was a remarkable feat for pilots who had never flown long distances over water before. The slow and clumsy Aircobra was all they had, and they used it. Eventually, the "klunker" proved of great value when its relatively powerful weaponry was used in close support missions for the land forces.

Marine Food

"We eat two meals a day with a Marine artillery unit.... The meals are small and the rations short," reported 67th Squadron member Richard Ferguson. "A lot of supplies were lost during the landing or didn't get ashore and we are eating mostly captured food—Jap rice that is full of weevils in the morning and Jap rice with weevils and some kind of canned fruit mixed in with it in the afternoon. Or is it the other way around? Our Marine cook is a comic. He says, 'Don't skim off the weevils; they are very high in protein.' If we don't get some more U.S. forces here and more supplies on the island, we could be goners."

Sometimes they were served portions of dehydrated potatoes that tasted like wallpaper paste, powdered eggs that didn't taste like anything they'd known before, and that ubiquitous hodgepodge of meat, the notoriously monotonous Spam. Actually, Spam was a great source of concentrated energy, but with one terrible side effect for the aviators. Pilots climbing to fighting altitude at 5,000 to 20,000 feet suffered from the buildup of excruciatingly painful intestinal gas.

Scouting 250 miles southeast of Guadalcanal on August 20, Kawanishi flying boats spotted "two carriers." One was *Long Island* and the other the fleet carrier *Wasp*. The Japanese had suspected American carrier activity in the area but had been unable to confirm it. The following morning the 11th Japanese Air Fleet sent a strike force of twenty-six Betties escorted by thirteen Zeroes to attack *Wasp*. Failing to find the enticing target, the Betties returned home while the Zeroes headed for Guadalcanal to pick a fight. At a little after noon, four Wildcats of VMF-223 led by Captain John L. Smith encountered the Zeroes over Savo. After the fight the Japanese reported they had been met by at least thirteen fighters. Neither side lost a plane in this air action, although Smith was credited with a victory on the testimony of ground observers who thought they saw a Zeke plunge into the sea.

The intruders put rounds into all four Wildcats, and Technical Sergeant John D. Lindsey made a remarkable "dead-stick" landing of his F4F on Henderson. Never to fly again, this plane was hauled off to provide the cornerstone for the "bone heap" that would serve as a source of supply parts throughout the campaign. The mere fact that all the Wildcats returned was a boost to sagging morale.

The sighting of a small American convoy bringing supplies to Guadalcanal prompted Mikawa to dispatch the destroyers *Kawakaze* and *Yunagi* to seek out and destroy the small detail, consisting of cargo ships *Fomalhaut* and *Althena*, escorted by destroyers *Blue*, *Henley*, and *Helm*. Bad weather forced *Yunagi* to turn back, but *Kawakaze* bulled its way on. As Richard B. Frank summarized in his definitive *Guadalcanal*, "Once again, Japanese eyes excelled American radar." Just as *Blue* made both radar and sonar contact at 3:55 A.M. and began lining up her guns and torpedoes on *Kawakaze*, a torpedo from a spread fired by the intrepid intruder blew away *Blue*'s stern, tore loose the steering gear, and froze her propellers. Nine Americans were killed in the blast and twenty-one wounded. *Kawakaze*, having done her job, and not wanting to tangle with the three warships, sped away from the scene. *Henley* stayed alongside *Blue* until dawn, when it was seen that *Blue* was still afloat.

Japanese Fleet Baits a Trap

Vice Admiral Chuichi Nagumo formed the *Kido Butai*—a massive armada—at Truk around the aircraft carriers *Zuikaku* and *Shokaku* to draw out the American fleet, fall upon it with a superior force, and destroy the enemy's capacity to support and reinforce Guadalcanal. Nagumo had also commanded many of the same carriers and support ships in the sneak attack on Pearl Harbor. Rounding out the strong arms were two battleships, three cruisers, and thirteen destroyers. The *Kido Butai* was led by a patrol screen of six submarines. Six other submarines were deployed to the southwest of Santa Cruz Island, and four groups of three each patrolled to the south and west of the fleet.

A diversionary group consisting of the old light carrier *Ryujo*—commanded by Captain Tadao Kato—a heavy cruiser, two destroyers, and a seaplane tender was sent forward as bait. One destroyer was *Amatsukaze*, commanded by Captain Tameichi Hara. Flying bombers off *Ryujo* to attack Henderson Field was a psychological ploy intended to coax the American carriers into exposing themselves.

With four transports and four destroyers, Rear Admiral Tanaka was to rush in under the cover of the big guns, and unload 1,500 additional troops to buttress Ichiki's assault (its destruction was still not known to Imperial Headquarters). The destroyers were to bombard marine positions on Guadalcanal while men, equipment, and supplies were landed. This reinforcement group had sailed from Rabaul on August 19.

The accumulated intelligence reports from Coastwatchers and patrol planes, as well as messages intercepted by eavesdropping stations, were evaluated and forwarded, along with suggestions from Pearl Harbor. This prompted Ghormley to order Fletcher's Task Force 61 to intercept the enemy fleet moving on Guadalcanal. TF 61 had the three carriers *Enterprise*, *Saratoga*, and *Wasp*, seven cruisers, and eighteen destroyers.

Ghormley, an intelligent and dedicated admiral, who had long believed that the Guadalcanal operation was doomed to fail, was beset by a multitude of problems beyond his capacity to handle. His indecisiveness, as he increasingly isolated himself from his staff, worried King and Nimitz. One serious problem—a run-in with organized labor—

highlighted his ineffectiveness. The crews of sixty merchant ships at Nouméa, loaded with rations for the starving marines fighting for their lives on Guadalcanal, refused to sail unless the relatively few members of the civilian crews were given exorbitant pay for overtime and service in the dangerous combat zone. The obscene demands of Joe Hill, the maritime union leader, were rejected, but at the same time the many marines all but stranded on the Canal were suffering.

At dawn on August 23 the U.S. Task Force was less than 150 miles east of Guadalcanal off Malaita Island, in a perfect position to block the Japanese. Later that morning a PBY sighted Tanaka's five destroyers and four transports coming down from the north toward the island. At 1 P.M. this small contingent reversed course and sailed north, out of aircraft range. Five hours later Vice Admiral Nobutake Kondo's diversionary force, still undiscovered 40 miles to the east of the transports, also reversed course. Tanaka's move convinced Fletcher that no major engagement was likely to take place for two or three days, so he ordered *Wasp* south for refueling. Detaching a third of his force when there was a real possibility of an engagement was partially a result of poor intelligence from Pearl Harbor indicating that the main Japanese contingent was near Truk, and partially due to his reluctance to possibly lose an aircraft carrier. The presence of the Japanese carriers had not been verified. For a few critical hours neither the Americans nor the Japanese fleets knew where the other was located.

CHAPTER 7

AUGUST 23–24
BATTLE OF THE EASTERN SOLOMONS

The Japanese Navy devised a ruse to draw out and destroy the American flattops in an effort to gain full mastery of the waters around Guadalcanal. The old and small Japanese aircraft carrier *Ryujo* was sent out as sacrificial bait on August 24 ahead of the main force to tempt TF 61. Just before dawn the diversionary group swung back south, while the main force lurked out of sight, waiting for Fletcher to strike and thereby reveal the location of his carriers.

At 9:05 A.M. an American patrol plane discovered *Ryujo* and its small protective force once again heading for Guadalcanal, 280 miles northwest of TF 61. Fletcher hesitated, waiting for more information, until 1:30 in the afternoon, when the two fleets had closed to under 135 miles of separation. When American radar detected blips representing fifteen fighters and six bombers taking off from the Japanese carrier and heading toward Henderson Field and its slender air arm of nineteen Wildcat fighters, twelve Dauntless SBDs, and fourteen Army P-400s, Fletcher ordered the attack.

Surprisingly, *Ryujo* failed to position fighters on its deck for combat air protection. Commander Hara signaled the carrier with a message for his naval academy friend, Commander Hisakichi Kishi, the carrier's executive officer. "Fully realizing my impertinence, am forced to advise you of my impression. Your flight operations are far short of expectations. What is the matter?"

"Deeply appreciate your admonition. We shall do better and count on your cooperation," replied Kishi. Just as seven fighters were rolled in to takeoff positions, the American air strike arrived overhead.

Within fifteen minutes *Saratoga* launched thirty SBDs and eight TBF Avenger torpedo planes led by Commander N.D. Felt to attack *Ryujo*. Two hours later the dive bombers took positions at 14,000 feet and began their assault. A 1,000-pound bomb scored on the carrier. Six Douglas Devastators slipped in at 200 feet and launched torpedoes. The hapless carrier was hit with at least four bombs, and a torpedo tore a hole in its hull. Shortly *Ryujo* was dead in the water, listing 20 degrees to starboard. The sacrificed carrier slipped beneath the waves at 8:00 that evening.

The torrid day was stunningly and deceptively beautiful. Large billowing clouds blown into fantastic castles and mountains by high winds covered half the sky, and provided excellent cover for a hundred deadly aircraft. Dive bombers could conceal themselves among the intermittent cloud cover to almost their dive path points before being spotted by nervous antiaircraft crews. The ocean sparkled brilliantly in the late afternoon sun, often blinding the anxious lookouts, who knew the enemy was coming. The men had been at their battle stations for hours, sweating and broiling in the hot tropical sun, which sent working temperatures in closed compartments to over 100 degrees. Simply touching the fiery hot metal plates of the deck and superstructure could cause painful burns.

Ryujo was sinking, but the ruse had worked. The *Kido Butai* had located the American carriers. Within an hour, based on sightings of the large Japanese force, Fletcher realized that he had been taken in, but his efforts to divert the first attack force toward the main threat came to naught because of quirky radio atmospheric conditions. The Japanese launched a large dive bomber attack on the discovered American carriers.

The two separate carrier groups were operating in conjunction with each other about ten miles apart. Each group was formed into a tight defensive circle about two miles across. They closed on each other as the battle progressed. At 4:29 the Japanese attack group was about twenty miles away from "*Big E*" *(Enterprise)*.

Enterprise, accelerating to 27 knots, was buttoned up at general quarters, all guns manned. The August tropical heat was stifling. Men like Machinist's Mate W.E. Fluitt took preventive measures, such as draining the ship's aviation gas lines and pumping them full of carbon dioxide. The carrier's CAP (Combat Air Patrol) stacked fifty-one Wildcat fighters in three layers to intercept the attackers. When about twenty-five Val dive bombers penetrated the screen to close on and attack the carrier, several American dive bombers and torpedo planes joined the fighters to protect the ships. Direction of the fighter cover was hampered by pilots' inconsequential chitchat filling the air and blocking the combat channel.

Ensign Donald Runyon was one of those Wildcat pilots who succeeded in attacking the dive bombers. Roaring down out of the sun, he opened fire and exploded a Val. Repeating his approach, he shot down two more Vals and a Zeke. Still, a few dive bombers did get through the fighters and heavy exploding flak and attacked *Enterprise*.

The plunging bombers were timed by Captain Arthur C. Davis at 7-second intervals as they began their 70-degree dives. They released their bombs at 1,500 feet in a well executed and determined onslaught. At exactly 5:14 P.M. a bomb penetrated through five decks and exploded in the chief petty officer's quarters, killing thirty-five men instantly. Two instantaneous-fuse bombs ripped holes in the wooden flight deck and wiped out many 5-inch gun mounts. In one starboard 5-inch gun mount the crew was killed by the concussion and then roasted by the horrendous fires. The dead looked like a macabre sculpture of nonhuman objects placed in normal positions around the gun. Photographer's Mate 2nd Class Robert F. Read, filming the attack, recorded a bomb exploding on the deck. Seconds later a second bomb hit 15 feet away, killing Read and thirty-eight more sailors. As the trained and disciplined damage control teams rushed to their desperate work, another bomb blew a 10-foot-wide hole near the Number 2 Elevator.

Damage control parties turned to and began their heroic efforts to save the ship, struggling to get *Big E* ready to land its CAP after the attack was repulsed. Seaman Henry Dunn made his way through the fires in the aviation metal shop and pulled two injured men to safety. Heat from the fires along with the high tropical temperatures was almost unbearable, but Chief Shipfitter Jim Brewer spotted the source of the fires for the firefighters until he passed out. Farther below decks, Carpenter W.L. Reames struggled desperately to build a cofferdam stuffed with mattresses that would hold back the water until the pumps were working again.

Down in the engine room the men staggered in 170-degree heat to do their work. To make sure the ship had sufficient operating power to run the elevators, antiaircraft guns, electronic equipment, and steering, these men worked until they dropped in a stupor from exhaustion. Sometimes, after only a brief rest, they struggled back into the suffocating heat to do whatever they could do to save the ship. This kind of heroic dedication was something even Lieutenant Commander Herschel A. Smith, assistant damage control officer, could have hardly expected, much less taught.

A few Japanese dive bombers broke through the air screen and headed for the new battleship *North Carolina*. With its massive array of antiaircraft batteries, this recent arrival in the South Pacific shot down or drove off 14 dive bombers. The ship suffered minimal damage from several near misses, which poured as much as a foot and a half of water across some areas of the deck. By 4:47 the attacks had ended.

Raging fires that melted steel had to be brought under control. About an hour later the flight deck had been patched sufficiently to allow *Big E* to resume landing its aircraft. After the planes had landed, unexpected damage to the big ship's steering engine brought it to a full stop, jamming the rudder. Men trying to fix the problem passed out in the heat, which had increased to about 200 degrees. Seaman William Marcoux clambered to the engine, turned a valve, engaged a clutch, and threw the first of two switches before unconsciousness claimed him. With the rudder jammed, the hurt ship moved in large circles and almost rammed the destroyer *Balch* before superhuman efforts on the part of a few sailors saved the day. Chief Machinist's Mate William A. Smith, thirty years in the Navy, and Machinist's Mate 1st Class Cecil Robinson put on emergency breathing gear and plunged into the suffocating oven to restore control.

Enterprise regained its steering just as the second large Japanese aerial attack group headed for the two U.S. carriers. With *Big E* in serious trouble, the brunt of the attack would have fallen on *Saratoga*, and the two American carriers would probably have been lost. Due to a navigational and communications mix-up, however, the Japanese attack group missed the vulnerable Task Force by about 50 miles. Fortunately, the Americans weren't the only sailors to have operational problems that day.

Saratoga was spared any damaging attacks. In anticipation of the second attack, which didn't come, Lieutenant Harold H. Larsen led five TBFs and two SBDs off the ship to counterattack the Japanese fleet. Attacking alone, they badly damaged *Chitose* of the Advanced Force without any losses, and by 7:30 were back aboard *Saratoga*.

On the Japanese side *Ryujo* continued to blaze. Hara hoped the ship could be saved, but the damage was too massive, so he ordered his *Amatsukaze* in close to remove the wounded and the rest of the crew, about 300 in all. Commander Hara came face-to-face with Captain Kato, last to leave his sinking carrier. "Please accept my thanks on behalf of my men," he told the destroyer captain. When Hara asked about his friend Kishi, Kato's haggard face wrinkled in sorrow. Kishi had died in the battle.

Envisioning a night fight with his only remaining carrier, Fletcher wisely decided to retire south from the battle zone. Nagumo's armada, keyed up and ready for a battle to destroy the rest of TF 61, pursued the Americans until 8:30 P.M. before giving up the chase. The enthusiastic Imperial Navy pilots claimed to have sunk three carriers, including *Hornet*—which was not even in the battle—five cruisers, and four destroyers. While this battle can be counted as a marginal American victory, the results were inconclusive except in one critical area. The Japanese air arm lost seventy planes and most of the crews, contrasted to seventeen American aircraft shot down. Slowly but surely the cream of the elite and highly trained Japanese naval aviators, whom many critics and historians considered the best in the world when the war began, was being drained away. U.S. Navy dive bombers and fighters flew off from the damaged *Big E* and joined Marine and Army combat planes in the Cactus Air Force.

Meanwhile, Rear Admiral Tanaka was ordered to move the transports on to Guadalcanal and cover the unloading by having his destroyers shell the marine positions in the Lunga perimeter. Having been ordered alternately to advance and withdraw, his force belatedly headed for the island. He then ordered Captain Shiro Yasutake to take the destroyers *Mutsuki*, *Yayoi*, and *Mochizuki* forward to bombard Henderson Field while the transports tried to catch up.

Arriving at midnight, this formation made an unproductive sweep searching for ships, then, in the early morning hours of the 25th, they tried to find the airfield. A desultory and poorly aimed bombardment killed two marines and wounded three, but did little damage to the facilities. Yasutake considered his bombardment chore a failure, but did alert the fleet to the presence of patrolling American aircraft. The Combined Fleet ignored the warning and kept the transports on course.

Tanaka's transport group was discovered at 2:33 A.M. by a PBY patrol, and its contact report placing the group about 180 miles up the Slot reached the field at 4:30. Yasutake's destroyers rejoined the group at 7:40, by which time eight SBDs and eight F4Us were already airborne, first searching for the carrier *Ryujo*, which had already slipped under the waves of the Pacific. The Wildcats were running low on fuel and turned back, but the dive bombers took a different route back and at 8:08 came up on the Japanese transports.

Five dive bombers went after Tanaka's flagship, the light cruiser *Jintsu*, and three headed for the largest transport, *Kinryu Maru*. The Japanese mistakenly identified the planes as friendly, and there was no air cover or antiaircraft fire. The first bombs dropped narrowly missed, until 2nd Lieutenant Lawrence Baldinus's 500-pound bomb penetrated between the two forward guns of *Jintsu* and exploded below decks, destroying the radio room and causing heavy casualties. On the bridge Tanaka was knocked unconscious and came to in heavy smoke from the fires raging below. He had to transfer his flag to the destroyer *Kagero*.

Ensign Christian Fink, from *Big E*'s Flight 300, placed his bomb onto *Kinryu Maru*, setting off a fire that quickly swept over the cargo of supplies and ammunition. In blithe disregard of a high-altitude attack by three Army B-17s, which were not known to ever hit ships, the destroyer *Mutsuki* had stopped in the water next to *Kinryu Maru* to rescue survivors. Much to the astonishment of both sides, a bomb from a B-17 hit the ship, destroyed the engine room and sank the destroyer before the unbelieving eyes of its commander.

Major Mangrum, discovering his bomb had not released, returned to the transports alone, this time releasing the bomb to score a near-miss on *Boston Maru*. He noted that the transport force was withdrawing to the northwest away from the Canal. Tanaka returned to Faisi Harbor, in the Shortlands, and the shattered transport was scuttled at 10:53. The Japanese resupply mission had failed.

In anticipation of another attack on the convoy, the American airmen returned to refuel and rearm. But at 11:00 the Coastwatchers warned of twenty-one bombers approaching Guadalcanal. While all but three planes were able to take off, the Wildcats did not have sufficient time to gain fighting altitude. The Japanese bombers, accompanied by twelve Zekes, managed to place forty bombs near the field operations center, killing four men and wounding five. The field and the dispersal area suffered little damage.

The Imperial Navy's two-pronged *Kido Butai* not only failed to destroy the American carriers and large ships, but their slow-moving reinforcement convoy to the Canal fizzled as well. Another way of resupplying Japanese troops would have to be found. While the Americans surely won the Battle of the Eastern Solomons, the victory did not turn the tide of battle on Guadalcanal.

"Doc" Everton of VMF-223, who took off as wingman for now Major Marion Carl, had a field day with Japanese bombers over Malaita, shooting down three Betties. Regarding his first kill in combat, Everton related, "All my hours in the air seemed to do me no good; all that practice in making smooth passes was thrown away. I had buck fever.... Instead of waiting for a good shot, I opened up at 400 yards." But he moved in closer on the second pass, avoiding the fixed machine gun in the tail of the bomber, and the top turret with its limited field of fire. He shortened his range and put bullets into the gas tank, flaming the bomber. He'd hit it at 23,000 feet, and at 20,000 feet it fell apart into a shower of flaming parts.

"What made me feel good was not the thought of those Japs with smoke choking them and the fire jumping in their faces. Their number was up, and of course they knew it, but a pilot doesn't let himself think about that. He shoots at the plane, not the men in it...the count is only on the planes."

The flight lost Lieutenant Roy A. Corry, Jr. when the pilot ran into fire from a rear gunner. Closing back up on the bombers, Everton fired a line of tracers into the pilot's compartment. The plane nosed down and crashed into the ocean. When the bombers spread out, Smith contacted Everton to coordinate. He attacked from one end while Everton came from the other. Smith shot down one, and Everton got his third victory of the day. He got a "probable"—smoking it, but not seeing it actually crash—as his low fuel situation forced him to turn back to Henderson Field.

The CAF flyers were devastating the Japanese bombers being sent to "Death Island," or the "Island of No Return." Sometimes the bomber losses on a raid were so heavy they would not be able to launch another attack for two or three days.

Marine reconnaissance in force encountered Japanese opposition west of Matanikau on the 27th and returned to the perimeter the next day. The Japanese were there, fairly well dug-in and organized, but the frustrated Vandegrift did not have the manpower to mount an offensive capable of dislodging them or driving them away.

One of the scout-snipers, Private 1st Class Robert Stiles, was called on by Colonel McKelvy to go over to the area where a patrolling company was being harassed by a Japanese sniper. By the time he arrived, a couple of marines had been wounded. Stiles moved into the kunai grass, which offered a great view of the treetops, and soon spotted a likely location. He waited, then saw a movement, then a head and a rifle emerged. One shot from Stiles's rifle and the sniper toppled dead from the tree. When Stiles moved up and opened the sniper's shirt to search the body for papers, he discovered it was a woman! Killing a woman in these circumstances didn't bother Stiles, because she was shooting at marines with the intent to kill them.

During the day nine more P-400s of the 67th Fighter Squadron arrived. The grind of constant air battles continued to use up pilots and planes at an alarming rate. Flight support groups struggled valiantly against both nature and the enemy to keep the planes flying.

On the 28th the first echelon of four Japanese destroyers attempting to bring in 3,500 troops failed. Marine dive bombers blew up the *Asagiri* and damaged *Shirakumo* and *Yugiri*. Five destroyers from the Shortlands managed to land some 1,000 Japanese troops near Taivu Point the next day.

Nineteen Wildcats of Major Robert E. Galer's VMF-224 and twelve SBDs of Major Leo R. Smith's VMSB-231 flew in to join the Cactus Air Force on the 30th. This was the remainder of MAG-23 (Marine Air Group), commanded by Colonel William J. Wallace. The survivors of the first-segment VMF-212 under Everton were relieved and sent back to Efate. These reinforcements were timely, because only five flyable Wildcats were on hand at the end of the previous day.

A busy day began for the CAF and the 67th Fighter Squadron after midnight of August 30. The SBDs had been sent to look for enemy ships and the army pilots were on continuous alert until dawn, when they began their regular duties. This consisted of flying combat air patrol over four American destroyers at Tulagi Island. The usual enemy raid was expected at about noon—"Tojo Time," because of the regularity of the air raids. The Coastwatchers had reported twenty-two single-engine planes coming through Buka Passage, between Buka and Bougainville Islands. At 11:30 A.M. the CAP came in to be refueled and serviced.

The Japanese would not send in Zekes alone, so the incoming aircraft probably included dive bombers heading for the ships at Tulagi. Eight F4Fs and eleven P-400s were scrambled to meet the expected attack. Seven P-400s cruised in the towering cumulus at 14,000 feet to engage the enemy before they started their dives, while four patrolled over Tulagi hoping to hit the dive bombers as they pulled out. The F4Fs were at a higher altitude.

The seven P-400s had been cruising for about thirty minutes. The pilots—already feeling the lack of oxygen—were attacked by six Zekes that had dived down around a cloud and climbed up to take the P-400s from behind and below. Major John L. Smith roared down with his F4Fs to join the melee, ordering his men to pick a target and stay with it. In less than a minute his Wildcats had flamed four of the Zekes, which the American pilots had taken by surprise. Smith himself shot down one Zeke. Then he found another trying to hide in the clouds, and blew it out of the sky as well.

The Oklahoman Smith and his wingman discovered another Zeke moving across in front of them, and a stream of machine gun and cannon fire from Smith's guns stitched the enemy fighter. With smoke and flames pouring from its engine, the Zeke jerked up, then fell in a long graceful arc to crash into the sea. Trying to descend through the dense clouds when the weather closed in, Smith lost track of his wingman. At 800 feet he came out of the clouds to find two Zekes crossing his path. A fiery blast from his six guns staggered one of them, and Smith watched it disappear into the jungle. That day he had shot down four Japanese aircraft, which helped make up for the losses of the army P-400s.

When the weather closed down to 1,000 feet over the sea, with less than a quarter mile visibility, the four-plane patrol started back to Henderson Field. As they emerged from the rain squall, the P-400s' formation was torn apart by the attack of a half dozen Zekes. Two army pilots, Lieutenants R.E. Wythes and R.E. Chilson, were lost.

Altogether four P-400s were shot down. Two pilots managed to bail out and later make their way to back to Henderson Field on foot. Five of the seven planes that did return had been badly damaged and were now out of commission. Against these losses, the 67th was credited with four kills, and the marines got fourteen of the raiders.

At 3:00 P.M., seventeen F4Fs and a dozen SBDs, escorted by two B-17s, arrived at Guadalcanal. Thirty minutes later, with eighteen planes on the ground, the Japanese dive bombers came again. Surprisingly, they ignored the parked places and went for the shipping. They caught the destroyer *Blue* a half mile offshore and sank her. The destroyer transport *Burrows* ran aground on Tulagi. Mother Nature stepped in at around 4:15 to add two earthquakes to the commotion.

That evening the Tokyo Express again steamed in to bombard Henderson Field. After only four days of operations at full strength, only three of the original fourteen P-400s remained fit to fly on September 1st. The air battle of the 30th proved that P-400s were ineffective when used as interceptors. The 67th knew the dreadful limitations of its planes, and reports of the action convinced General Harmon. No army or marine aircraft then extant was truly effective against the Zeke. The P-400 pilots were skilled and courageous, as Major Smith, commander of VMF-223, later testified. Harmon began looking for a way to improve the planes' performance. Since .50-caliber bullets could nearly disintegrate the Zekes, replacing the 37-mm cannon with either a .50-caliber machine gun or a 20-mm cannon would lighten the weight and make it easier to handle.

On the 31st the fighter group mysteriously lost three planes and two pilots after they scrambled in response to a false alarm. The Japanese couldn't mount an attack that day because of foul weather. Missing in action was 2nd Lieutenant Richard R. Amerine, from Lawrence, Kansas, and two other newcomers. Remarkably, because of the attrition of pilots and planes, the Marine, Navy, and Army pilots were cooperating unreservedly to provide air cover over Guadalcanal. Often mixed units under the command of the best leader—regardless of service affiliation—would rise up to handle whatever chore was needed at the time. Their only purpose was to fly and fight.

The 3rd Defense Battalion arrived with radar equipment and 5-inch coastal guns to buttress the Lunga defenses in late August. Ten days of hard manual labor were required to move the two coastal batteries into their positions on the beach—the normal trailers and sleds required to move the weapons had not been brought along. When the guns did get into action, their 5-inch shells were relatively ineffective against the Japanese ships that came down to bombard the beachhead.

The possibility of a Japanese amphibious landing in force—an assault on the Lunga beaches—was the foremost fear of the local commanders. This would be a "black flag" condition, in contrast to the "red flag" situation, when air raids and surface bombardment were imminent. Few men on Guadalcanal were optimistic enough to think that a landing in force at that time could be repelled. The fear of an enemy counterlanding continued until the Japanese finally withdrew months later.

A few antiaircraft guns were brought in and were operating in early September. Until the radar was improved to where the guns could be automatically and accurately trained, they were fired manually. The beachhead was too small to be able to use the searchlight batteries effectively, but they would have had a positive psychological effect on the defense if for no other reason than their presence. Their effectiveness greatly increased as the perimeter was expanded and more guns were brought in.

Torpedo Junction

When Commander Minoru Yokota raised the periscope of his *I-25* on the morning of the 31st he saw a sight every submariner on patrol dreamed about. He saw an aircraft carrier and a battleship escorted by cruisers and destroyers patrolling approximately 260 miles southeast of Guadalcanal. Moving into position, approaching closely to the destroyer screen, at about 7:45 A.M. he launched a full spread of six torpedoes toward *Saratoga*. Two of the undersea missiles struck home, inflicting enough damage to knock the hapless carrier out of combat until the end of November.

At nearly the same moment her torpedoes were released, the *I-25* was spotted by the destroyer *MacDonough*, which scrapped over the sub's superstructure as it crash-dived, and dropped depth charges, which failed to explode. Some anxious torpedoman had neglected to set the charges. For twelve hours the submarine evaded efforts by the American destroyers to sink her. Yokota then reported back that the American antisubmarine tactics were poor, encouraging other Japanese submarines to attempt to penetrate the screens of large task forces. In the long run, this led to the destruction of a number of submarines.

"Admiral Fletcher, flying his flag on her at the time, was now relieved, and during the rest of the war received commands more commensurate with his abilities." This restrained but terse comment by the noted naval historian Samuel Eliot Morison summed up the opinions of many who had watched Fletcher's actions with far less than enthusiastic admiration. They thought he had long ago lost the daring and competitive edge required of a reliable fleet commander. (Morison's often caustic criticism of inept and downright stupid commanders is a worthwhile feature of his authoritative volumes describing naval operations in World War II.)

Eight Japanese destroyers brought in and landed Kawaguchi and 1,200 men of his assault force during the night of August 31–September 1 in preparation to oust the marines from Henderson Field. He would move in from the east, while one of his regiments, brought in by barges, would move in from the west. The Japanese high command still estimated the number of Americans on Guadalcanal at roughly 2,000 men—far below the actual count.

WWII Snapshot—September, 1942

South America—Brazil joins the Allies on August 22 by declaring war on Germany and Italy. This move placed Brazil's navy under the operational control of the U.S. Navy and denies use of the country's harbors and waterways to the enemy.

North America—On the 8th a small Japanese airplane, launched from a submarine, drops incendiary bombs near Brookings, Oregon, setting off a forest fire.

German submarines lay naval mines in the Atlantic off Charleston, South Carolina. The "Wolfpacks"—the synchronized operations of several U-boats working together against a single convoy—continue to sink Allied merchant ships within sight of the East Coast. The magnitude of Allied shipping losses is appalling. Only recently has Admiral King reluctantly agreed that there is a much higher degree of safety when the ships travel in convoys. He did not want to assign his fighting ships as escorts for merchant vessels—essentially a defensive maneuver.

In one Wolfpack attack, on Convoy ON 127, nine ships and the escorting Canadian destroyer *Ottawa* are sunk, without the loss of a single submarine. Between June and November the average monthly loss is 500,000 tons of shipping.

Southern Russia—Thousands of miles away the Nazi juggernaut, led by the German 6th Army, is approaching the industrial city of Stalingrad on the Volga River, gateway to the great oil fields of the Caucasus Mountains area. Hitler wants to capture Stalingrad, not because it was necessary for his immediate needs, but because it is the Soviet Union's Premier's namesake. He issues the order that the city be destroyed, all males are to be killed, and all the women are to be shipped off to an unspecified destination. Stalin decides to hold the city at all costs. In response to the pleas of Stalin, Allied forces are being assembled in England and America for the invasion of Morocco and Algeria, in North Africa, behind the German forces.

Egypt—General Erwin Rommel's Afrika Corps, with crack German and Italian tank units leading, is barely fifty miles from Alexandria. The loss of Egypt would close the Suez Canal to Allied shipping and seriously disrupt the Allied capability to wage war around the globe. There appears to be no way to avert disaster with the men, supplies, and equipment available. The ANZAC units, which have been withdrawn to Australia to protect their homeland, are soon engaged against the Japanese in Papua on the large New Guinea island mass.

Germany—For the first time in the war, British bombers attack the city of Düsseldorf. They use the 2-ton bombs known as blockbusters.

Southwest Pacific—On Papua, Australian troops—under the overall command of General Douglas MacArthur—barely arrive in force before the Japanese invade on August 26. For days they fight to repulse a large counterattack at Milne Bay, a loathesome but vital jungle stronghold at the eastern tip of New Guinea that possesses a grand natural harbor capable of sheltering the largest of ships. Using the superior heavy firepower of their machine guns and larger-caliber rifles, the Aussies defeat a force reinforced by about 800 men of the Japanese Special Landing Force. Both the Australian and the Japanese forces suffer heavy losses in the night fighting, handicapped by torrential rains and gooey mud. The Australians hang on to gain victory in a desperate and bitter battle, forcing a Japanese withdrawal.

So far as Guadalcanal is concerned, there simply is not enough manpower, equipment, or supplies for the United States to adequately reinforce the South Pacific island nobody had heard of a month ago, much less the Allied troops of the Southwest Pacific area fighting on Papua. These Pacific sideshows are minor irritants compared to the large European land and sea battles engaging hundreds of thousands of fighting men.

Along Papua's Kokoda Trail—which crosses the Owen Stanley Mountains from Japanese-occupied Buna to Australian-held Port Moresby—the battered Aussie 2/14th Battalion and 39th Battalion are forced to withdraw from Isurava toward Aola. The primitive and narrow trail, swamped with heavy rains, winds upward through dense jungles and across the steep treacherous mountains. The path the Japanese have chosen to reach and capture Port Moresby is not much of a route. In many places only one or two men can walk abreast. The commanding officer of the 2/14th is killed in the fighting. The 1/16th Battalion then moves up from the reserve and takes the lead. But the 21st Brigade forces have become severely depleted and on September 2 are withdrawn to Templeton's Crossing and relieved a few days later by the 2/27th Battalion.

The 21st Brigade has been heavily engaged for nearly a week. Most of the time they have been unable to brew a mug of tea, much less get hot meals. Sleeping in the open, sweltering in the daytime, and freezing at night, they are constantly soaked from the rains and their feet are shriveled and pulpy from the dampness. Taking out the wounded is extraordinarily difficult as there are never enough stretcher bearers to move the casualties back over the congested and rugged trail.

Small groups of survivors of the battle-worn Australian 21st Brigade, which have been savaged in the fighting at Ioribaiwa, begin drifting toward the rear and Port Moresby. The men of this brigade came from the Middle East suntanned and cheerful in mid-August, but are now shrunken and pale from their experiences in the great rain forest.

A Captain Buckler leads his tattered force off the track between Isurava and Aola and into the wilderness. He leaves the rest of his party behind while he strikes out looking for food and a way back. He has to cross the high mountains and traverse the mist-shrouded 9,100-foot pinnacle known as "Ghost Mountain," an area the natives avoid because they think it is haunted. Alone now, he and a native boy endure icy winds as they make the trek across silent moss-clad forests. Finally they reach the Port Moresby area, where he stumbles upon some of the first American GIs to set foot on Papua.

This is a reconnaissance party from Easy Company, 126th Infantry Regiment, 32nd Infantry Division seeking another track across the great mountain divide to flank the Japanese on the Kokoda Trail. The patrol is told that no white man has crossed the Owen Stanleys there since 1917. The anticipated crossing by the 2nd Battalion of the 126th is a desperation move by MacArthur back in Brisbane "to get things moving" on Papua. He thinks American troops will do much better than the Australians in driving back the Japanese. He appears to have ignored the fact that the Diggers, the Australian infantry, are defending their country from invasion.

The general believes that the Australian force outnumbers the enemy force, not because it is true—it is not—but rather because he wishes it to be true. This kind of myopic vision is to plague the Allies, and even more so the Japanese, for the next few months. MacArthur, with his eyes set on Buna, still does not know nor does he appear concerned that his Allied units face the superior numbers of crack Japanese Army units of Major General Horii's elite jungle fighters of his South Seas Detachment.

The alternate route looks good on the maps. But neither General MacArthur nor General Sir Thomas Blamey, commanding the Allied Land Forces, back in Brisbane, has seen the terrain or has any idea of the difficulties inherent in jungle fighting, much less the near impossible task of moving troops across such a forbidding primeval barrier. This sets the stage for the most useless and difficult movement of the entire war—crossing over the mountains on the Kapa Kapa Track.

The Allied commanders, however, begin to realize that if the Japanese are successful in defeating either the Australian forces on Papua, or the American forces on Guadalcanal, both will be lost. MacArthur thinks the only possibility for victory lies in New Guinea, as he thinks the Allied efforts on Guadalcanal are hopeless. Moreover, the increasingly tense and morose commanding general needs a clear-cut victory by his troops, a fact that moves him to push his unprepared forces into bloody situations. The MacArthur who emerges in 1943 would never consider such a move.

Chapter 8

The Desperate September Ordeal

Just as actors in classic Greek tragedy events move toward their predestined course, so the actors in this drama, however courageous and selfless, were powerless to change the result.

—S.L.A. Marshall

"Neither side at that point [as of September 1] had the right composition of forces," stated the Japanese submarine commander Zenji Orita, in *I-Boat Captain* in 1976. "On shore our troops could fight only a holding battle, until enough reinforcements arrived to make possible a mass attack on Henderson Field. This crude airstrip was the key to the overall campaign. Whoever would hold and exploit it would control both the island chain and the surrounding seas."

The Japanese 17th Army and Major General Kawaguchi planned Operation Ka—a massive, coordinated attack in early September to overrun and capture Henderson Field. His plans were in such complete detail they indicated the exact spot where on September 13th he would personally accept the American surrender of Guadalcanal from the American commander, Major General Archer Vandegrift! With this in mind, he also took along a fresh dress uniform. With 6,000 fresh men—including the remaining 2nd Battalion of the ill-fated Ichiki's 28th Infantry, the 124th Infantry under Colonel Akinosuku Oka, and the 2nd Battalion, 4th Infantry, and attached artillery, engineers, communications, and antitank gunners—he fielded a force fully capable of destroying the marine beachhead. What he ignored were the natural geographical difficulties inherent in moving troops through the jungle and into position once they had arrived, and the internal command conflicts within the Imperial staff.

Japanese intelligence consistently failed to realize that there were far more marines on the beachhead than their estimates indicated. Equally elusive to the thinking of the high command was that they merely had to *deny the use* of Henderson Field to the enemy by effectively employing artillery on land and naval bombardment from the sea. Without their invaluable air support, the American capability to fight would have been eliminated. The Japanese didn't have to actually assault and capture the airfield; all they had to do was make flight operations impossible. This kind of thinking, of course, was contrary to the arrogant pride of the Imperial forces.

Kawaguchi had his own troop movement ideas, and objected to being transported to the island on Tanaka's destroyers. He wanted the troops and equipment from Rabaul moved by barges to Taivu Point to the east of the Marine perimeter, where the Ichiki Force had previously landed. Kawaguchi had previously used barges with great success and chose to ignore the navy's more recent adverse experiences in transporting men and materiel across areas within range of American planes. Reluctantly Tanaka agreed, and when the heavily loaded barges approached Guadalcanal, they were promptly attacked and sunk or driven off by the makeshift but still feisty CAF.

Planes from Henderson mounted continuous attacks on Japanese barges trying to bring in Colonel Oka's eastern unit, the 124th Infantry. Oka was ordered by Kawaguchi to transport 1,000 men in a barge convoy along the southern edge of the Solomons and land them at Taivu Point east of the airstrip. The 17th Army authorized the move but didn't feel that the movement had much chance of success. For whatever reason, Oka moved the convoy along the *northern* edge and landed *west* of the Lunga perimeter.

This barge convoy had been spotted and attacked on the 3rd by a morning patrol of eleven SBDs from Henderson Field. That afternoon, seven SBDs, accompanied by two Wildcats, again strafed the hapless barges. This attack was resumed again the next morning by thirteen SBDs led by Major Dick Mangrum. Despite the efforts of the Japanese to conceal the barges during the daylight hours, about a third of the barges were damaged and required repair before moving on.

An hour after dark on September 3rd, seven jeeps raced up to the southern end of Henderson Field, turning their headlights onto the field to provide the minimum illumination to allow the late arrival of an Army DC-3. The plane roared in barely above the heads of the jeep drivers to land on the battered field. The transport rolled to a stop at the Pagoda for Brigadier General Roy S. Geiger, head man of the 1st Marine Aircraft Wing, to step onto the Canal. The abrupt, hard-nosed Geiger was first and foremost an aviator, who preferred to sit in an aircraft cockpit rather than an office chair.

Now the stern, often ruthless, white-haired leader (of the same cut of men who had led the Roman Legions) came in determined to get the maximum effort and usage from every man, piece of equipment, and moment in the day. Geiger was much like his old friend, 1st Marine Division Commander Archer Vandegrift, in that he could not conceive of leaving the initiative up to the enemy. So when the Japanese barges bringing Kawaguchi's troops were discovered coming down the Slot, Geiger sent in his SBDs in local waters, and then sent the bombers further up the Slot looking for more targets.

Colonel Oka's small force finally departed San Jorge Island off of the southeast end of Santa Isabel at 9:30 P.M. on September 4th for the long and dangerous final leg of the trip to Kamimbo Bay, just west of Cape Esperance on the northwest coast of Guadalcanal. Spray from the rough seas, accompanied by bad leaks from bullet holes delivered earlier by the American planes, soon necessitated serious bailing by the soaked Japanese infantrymen. The churning seas scattered the barges from each other. As the troops tried to keep the barges together, many badly strained engines began to falter, causing the boats to lose headway.

The estimated time of arrival of 5 A.M. September 5th on Guadalcanal passed as the barges—still out of sight of their landfall—continued the struggle to survive. About an hour later, the desperate troops saw the looming mountaintops of their destination on the horizon. By 7:40, when the first boat scraped bottom on Guadalcanal, the fifteen-barge convoy had been attacked first by two P-400s, led by Captain Dale Brannon, then shortly after by a flight of six Wildcats. Major Takamatsu Etsuo, commander of the 2nd battalion, 124th Infantry, in one of the lead boats, led the barrage of small arms fire against the attacking planes, and before he was killed managed to shoot down one Wildcat. Some Japanese infantrymen, tired of cringing close to the wooden hulls of the open boats, leaped from the barges into neck-deep water to escape the deadly rain of machine gun fire falling from the sky.

Only 150 infantrymen of the original 1,000 could at first be accounted for. The air attacks had scattered the force along the coast, and it took nearly a week to locate and reassemble the survivors of the risky venture that Rear Admiral Tanaka had so seriously discouraged. While fewer than 100 of the now widely scattered troops had been killed, hundreds more of the lost and wounded Japanese would not be available to take part in Kawaguchi's attack on Henderson Field.

Fomalhaut and three other American destroyer transports (APDs) brought in and unloaded critically needed supplies on September 3rd. The next day the APDs *Gregory* and *Little* ferried two companies of the Raiders to Savo, where the presence of enemy troops had been reported. The Raiders discovered newly dug graves for the Japanese troops who hadn't survived the barge passage across Iron Bottom Sound. The natives who had buried these Japanese corpses—just as they had buried American dead from previous actions—would continue to bury the dead of both sides while the incredible fight they couldn't even begin to understand continued to swirl around them.

The APDs returned the exhausted Raiders—weary from clambering up, over, and down the sides of Savo looking for live enemies—to the marine perimeter. Then they remained on patrol off Lunga Point because it was too late to cross Sealark and drop anchor in Tulagi Harbor overnight as they usually did. At about 1:00 A.M. the ship's radar discovered three Japanese destroyers that had just left the resupply drop and were heading to a position from which to administer the usual nightly bombardment.

Gregory and *Little* chose to make a surprise attack on the destroyer force—a bluff to force them to depart the area. A Catalina flying boat on patrol over the scene spotted flashes from the bombardment and dropped illumination flares that revealed the presence of the American ships, which immediately came under heavy fire. Salvo after salvo of Japanese shells ripped into the converted old WWI destroyers, now stripped of most of their armament. Some initial survivors who jumped overboard were killed as the Japanese swung in close to blast the burning and sinking hulks. The final survivors were plucked from the water by landing craft after the sun rose.

War correspondent Dick Tregaskis reported being shaken awake at about 9 P.M.—not by the usual naval shelling, but by an earthquake! The effect was much like someone had grabbed one end of his cot and was shaking it to wake him. These tremors are fairly common in the Solomons, but their occurrence just then caused many of the desperately tired marines to wonder what the Japanese had come up with this time.

On Sunday, September 6th, the marine pilot Lieutenant Amerine—who had parachuted from his shot-up fighter when the oxygen system and then his engine failed a week earlier and landed near Cape Esperance—finally made it back to the marine lines. He was exhausted, thin, and hungry, having existed on red ants and snails for food during his ordeal. Having studied entomology (the study of insects), he'd known which were edible. During his harrowing trip back to safety, he'd managed to evade most of the enemy, but had killed a man he found sleeping along the trail by bashing his head with a rock, then taken the victim's pistol and shoes. Later he had killed an enemy soldier with the butt of the pistol, and had shot another in order to safely return to his own lines.

Pilots of the CAF were flying eight to ten hours a day under combat and grueling weather conditions. Most nights they were kept awake by Japanese ships shelling the area. The haggard flyers quickly became physically and mentally weary and began losing concentration—a deadly situation. Although they lost about twenty-five percent of their aircraft weekly, replacement planes and pilots helped keep the force in the air. Recovered wrecks and planes destroyed on the ground were cannibalized for parts by badly overworked ground crews. The rain, the terrible heat and humidity, and the constant pressure combined to drag down everyone managing to stay alive on Guadalcanal.

Admiral Ghormley finally announced on September 7th the formation of Navy Task Force 64, composed of three cruisers and six or seven destroyers, for screening missions off Guadalcanal. Admiral King thought TF 64 was a good month late in its activation. This belated development was only one of several that caused concern about Ghormley's decisiveness in those early days of the war. On Ghormley's behalf it must be said that he had been assigned almost impossible tasks without the wherewithal to ensure success. Now there was serious talk of abandoning the Guadalcanal venture, with the result that morale and confidence in his leadership plummeted to a serious low point.

The Marine force was losing its keen fighting edge. The primary Marine mission had been a fast, hard-hitting shock assault to seize a beachhead, after which the Army would come in and conduct longer-range operations. Now involved in a situation alien to their basic doctrine, mere survival became the driving force. Sick and exhausted men on the verge of starving don't continue fighting because of patriotism or pursuit of some holy, higher cause. American fighting men expect support when they go into battle. Ammunition, food, medicine, and equipment were not being brought in for the marines, while in their eyes the enemy's reinforcement was moving freely. The sad truth was that things were actually worse than they seemed.

After weeks on the island the clothing the men wore was beginning to rot and fall apart. The gaunt defenders fought and suffered wounds while clad in indescribably filthy and tattered fatigues. Some felt that only the dried sweat caked in the uniforms kept them from falling completely apart. Skivvies (underwear) were a long forgotten luxury. Few of the men wore socks, which soon rotted or were thrown away as being too vile for even a ragged marine to wear.

Through all this, the marines still had a sense of humor, which included kidding the other units. They told the story that some native Melanesians out in the boondocks were mopping up Japanese stragglers. After wiping out one party, they discovered a goat the enemy had brought along. They studied it for a time, and then went to their chief to decide whether they should kill it or not.

"What manner of beast is it?" asked the chief.

"Oh, he's very strange, majesty. He has fierce eyes, long horns, a shaggy beard, will eat anything, and stinks like hell!"

"Spare him," the chief immediately ruled. "Don't kill him. He's what the Americans call a Seabee."

Native scouts reported the landing by two to three thousand Japanese troops in the Tasimboko area on Taivu Point. Marine intelligence discounted that figure, thinking Clemens's scouts didn't know how to count. Somehow the division "brains" conjured up the idea that even the few Japanese at Tasimboko were half-starved and poorly equipped remnants of earlier infiltrators with arms for only "two out of ten." Again intelligence data, despite evidence to the contrary, was being massaged to produce conclusions intelligence wanted to hear, not to represent what actually existed. Pleased with this optimistic appraisal—if it should happen to be true—Vandegrift prudently ordered Lieutenant Colonel Merritt "Red Mike" Edson to move his Raiders to the area and take a look around.

The weary men of Edson's newly combined elite but depleted Raider and Parachute Battalions were moved to a ridge about 1,000 yards north of Henderson Field—a quiet area, so they were told. These experienced but now short-handed units, which had seen the first sustained hot action of the campaign on Tulagi on the very first day of the invasion, needed a rest.

A significant change was slowly evolving in the thinking of both high commands. Whatever lingering doubts there may have been about the use of air power in troop support were fast being erased. Because possession and operation of Henderson Field was the critical key to the control of Guadalcanal, it became the central point about which all other actions revolved. That airfield was the reason the Americans had landed in the first place. Possession of the airfield had become the focus of the almost continuous Japanese air, sea, and land efforts, shifting their attention away from the nearly successful campaign to capture Port Moresby. There the Japanese drives had been badly blunted, and their fresh troops arriving at Rabaul were diverted for a massive effort to drive the marines off Guadalcanal. This once unknown island, which had gained sudden fame and notoriety throughout the world, was becoming the principal objective of Japanese activity in the South Pacific.

To flesh out gaps in the 1st Raider Battalion, the 1st Parachute Battalion was attached, bringing Edson's force to 849 officers and men. The destroyer transports *McKean* and *Manly*, along with two former tuna boats now commissioned into the Navy, YP *346* and YP *298*, were designated to take the raiding force to their landing area—3,000 yards behind the enemy—on the 8th. The YP vessels—called Yippies from their designation as "yacht patrol" boats—were as often as not, converted fishing trawlers from the west coast under their previously civilian captains and owners. This assortment of small ships and boats couldn't carry the entire reconstituted battalion in one trip, leaving part of the attacking force to be moved up later.

By about 6 P.M. on the 7th, in a heavy rain, the troops were loaded and ready to go. Lieutenant Colonel Griffith and the correspondent Tregaskis were loaded onto an auxiliary transport, itself a former west coast tuna fishing boat. The raiders would go ashore east of the small village of Tasimboko and then double back to raid the village. The 5:20 A.M. landing on the 8th was to be preceded by a naval shelling, as well as a strafing and bombing air attack.

Marines Raid Tasimboko

Just as the marines began to scramble into their landing boats Tuesday the 8th, a small American convoy steamed by on its way to another part of Guadalcanal. In the still pitch dark at 5:30 A.M. the Raiders, having expected to have to shoot their way ashore, were surprised at the lack of resistance when they hit the beach. The Japanese had seen the wakes from an apparently large group of ships lapping up onto the beach, and from that evidence decided a massive assault was under way and retreated into the jungle to prepared positions.

Moving toward the village, the marines found several 37-mm field pieces, ammunition, and field packs. More packs were then discovered, along with life preservers, shoes, and entrenching tools scattered in disorder among the newly dug foxholes and slit trenches. Led by Edson, the marines moved cautiously forward through the underbrush around a small pond and forded a river through water up to their waists. They found more newly prepared and carefully camouflaged foxholes amidst caches of food and ammunition. It was just after 8 A.M. when they made their first contact with enemy troops.

On the beach a row of Japanese landing boats were lying on the sand, and a group of brown-uniformed soldiers were observing the American approach. Major Floyd W. Nickerson from Spokane, Washington ordered the machine guns brought forward and gave the "open fire" command. Possibly 300 Japanese fighters responded with rifle and light machine gun fire. Mortars from both sides joined in the battle, and soon light artillery was in action against the marines. The firing tapered off as marines began knocking out some of the gun positions, and the Japanese attempted to move around the Raiders. Kawaguchi, advised of the landing, ordered what was essentially a rear guard action to handle the marines. His main body of troops was already hacking their way through the jungle, headed for the airfield. Nothing was going to stop that movement.

Marine aircraft again strafed the village. Moving through a jungle brake, the Raiders found a large stash of medical supplies. The supply caches grew more numerous, and included crates of canned meat, fish, and sacks of crackers. They discovered well maintained equipment and supplies, which indicated the Japanese had landed recently—and in force.

The fighting picked up again, with 75-mm field pieces blasting away amidst the flat crack of .25-caliber rifle and machine gun fire. "At the time I was squatting in a thick jungle brake—a tangle of vines and dwarf trees—but the crash of the firing so close was scary, despite the good cover," recalled Tregaskis. "Each time the gun went off, one felt the blast of hot air from the muzzle, and twigs rattled down from the trees above. But we knew we were safer here than back where the shells were falling."

In the torrential rain, the water flooding the ground, the fierce fighting continued. The Raiders were beginning to suspect they had taken on more than they could handle. Edson called for naval gunfire support. A group of destroyers steamed in close to the beach to rain shells on Tasimboko.

By around 11:00 the battle and the rain began to let up. The sky was clearing and the sun emerged. The remainder of the battalion, including the Parachutists, were coming ashore by 11:30, but they were no longer needed. At 12:30 the Raiders entered Tasimboko, where they discovered large supplies of rice and other foods, more than 500,000 rounds of rifle, machine gun, and artillery ammunition, which they destroyed. Also destroyed was Kawaguchi's new radio station. The medical supplies were taken back to the Lunga perimeter, along with substantial quantities of British cigarettes. Not surprisingly, quantities of Japanese sake and beer also made the return trip. Captured records and documents were brought back and turned over to the intelligence section. Positive evidence of the recent landing of fresh troops in force by the Japanese convinced Marine intelligence that the native scouts really did know how to count.

Despite the heavy skirmishing, only two marines were killed and six wounded. The Japanese losses included twenty-seven dead. On the bodies of some of the dead Japanese were found photos of Javanese women, American tommy guns, and ammo marked with Dutch labels. Some of the troops had obviously seen action in the Dutch East Indies, and possibly Malaysia. By 5:00 P.M. the raiders were on their way back to their lines.

On September 8, Geiger and the CAF were in trouble. Eight of his planes crashed while trying to take off from the usually muddy and frequently bombarded Henderson Field. Through arduous work of the ground crews, two of the planes were restored to flying condition, which is more than can be said about the nearly exhausted and worn out pilots. The remaining planes were permanently retired to the boneyard to be cannibalized for replacement parts to keep the others flying. By the 10th Geiger had only eleven Wildcats left of the thirty-eight that had been flown in since operations began about three weeks previously. The P-400s were doing a marvelous job in close combat support, but the most critical need was for high-altitude fighters to take on the bombers and their escorting Zekes.

The Japanese supply caches indicated a big attack was going to be made soon. But when and where? Edson figured, correctly, that the most likely target for the newly arrived Japanese troops was the quiet ridge where his Raiders were now resting, and which led directly into the perimeter toward Henderson Field. It has been said that Edson was a hard, grim man, and that when his lips smiled, the smile could not be seen in his eyes. He had nothing to smile about at this particular moment.

Vandegrift was kept well informed about the movement of the Japanese in the jungle and knew right where they were. The native scouts were doing a magnificent job of observation and reporting. Unable to mount an attack to break up the intruders, the anxious marines had to sit and wait until the enemy made its move.

On September 10 the native scouts reported that Kawaguchi's column was less than five miles from the perimeter. On the same day the Joint Chiefs of Staff in Washington requested that Vice Admiral Ghormley hand over a reinforced regiment of "experienced amphibious troops" with their supply and transport ships to General MacArthur in Australia. When the request reached a justifiably enraged Rear Admiral Turner, he replied that the only experienced troops were fighting for their lives on Guadalcanal! He added that instead of reducing their already precarious strength, the marines urgently needed reinforcements. Doubtless, the irascible and frequently outspoken Turner used more colorful and less diplomatic language to emphasize his point. Needless to say, a worried MacArthur did not get the marines he asked for, although he probably thought he needed them to support his movements on the north coast of Papua to aid the Australians trying to turn back the Japanese advance over the Kokoda Trail. Perhaps he made these unrealistic requests simply to forestall similar requests to him to supply troops and supplies to help relieve Guadalcanal.

Vice Admiral Fletcher, after *Saratoga* was sent to the rear for extensive repairs, did not wish to have his highly trained carrier air units broken up and wasted on Guadalcanal. Regardless, Nimitz finally transferred all the carrier aircraft he could spare to Ghormley, who with surprising alacrity on the 11th ordered twenty-four Wildcat fighters of Lieutenant Commander LeRoy C. Simpler's Fighting Five to be flown from Espiritu Santo to the combat zone. Accompanying this group were eight more Wildcats of Lieutenant Colonel Harold F. "Indian Joe" Bauer's VMF-212 led by Major Frederick R. Payne.

Arriving at Henderson Field at 4:20 in the afternoon of the 12th—warmly welcomed and immediately readied for action—were twelve SBDs of VS-3, led by Lieutenant Commander Louis J. Kirn, and six TBF torpedo bombers led by Lieutenant Larsen, all from *Saratoga*. The next day the new pilots were up in the air with some of the "old-timers" to break up a forty-two-airplane enemy attack aimed at the exposed ridge. Betties plastered parts of the field and the ridge with high explosives and incendiary bombs. The defenders shot down twelve bombers and three fighters at the loss of one American who died trying to make an emergency landing. In just three days the CAF had been reinforced with sixty additional planes. The bad news was that on one day, the 12th, Rear Admiral Yamagata brought in twice that number to his air bases on Vunakanau and Lakunai, near Rabaul on New Britain.

The usual night shelling by the Tokyo Express was aimed at the ridge, not at Henderson Field as expected. The next day twenty-six Betties, escorted by eight Zekes, plastered the target area with 500-pound bombs and antipersonnel "daisy cutters"—bombs designed to explode into hundreds of fragments. Marines who took what cover their foxholes did offer survived the onslaught. Despite shouts of "hit the dirt" and "stay down, you fools," too many who panicked and tried to run were cut down by the hail of shrapnel, which more often inflicted multiple ripping wounds rather than delivering a single killing blast.

The men on the ridge suffered casualties because they had not dug in properly, still assuming this was a rest area. Badly wounded men had to be evacuated from the line, weakening an already precarious defense. Eleven Raiders were killed, and seventeen others were wounded.

"Some goddamn rest area!" shouted one corporal. "Yeah, some goddamn rest area," someone else agreed. The men of the new composite battalion began to understand that they were facing real trouble. The Raiders were supposed to be relieved by the 2nd Battalion, Fifth Marines on the 12th.

Meanwhile, Kawaguchi was having his own problems. The main difficulty was the jungle itself. In order to move his columns safely into position—to prevent their destruction by fighters and dive bombers from Henderson Field—his soldiers were forced to traverse the appalling Guadalcanal rain forest at night.

Despite the shouts of the officers and colorful ridicule screamed by NCOs, movement was nearly impossible over the heartbreakingly steep and muddy ridges, where men were barely able to pull themselves up one side by clutching and crawling over exposed roots and then slither back down into the ravine on the other side. It proved impossible to move the artillery and ammunition forward, carried on the backs of the faltering, profusely sweating, ever thirsty and hungry overburdened troops. Big guns and shells to support the attack had to be discarded and left behind. Yet they struggled on, racked with dysentery from drinking river water, burning with malaria, and eating their rations of dried fish, crackers, and hard candy. Some jungle birds learned to mimic simple Japanese phrases. From the high rain forest branches parrots mimicked, "*Oi, Jotohei!*" ("Hey, Private 1st Class!") and "*Hikoki!*" ("Enemy planes!"). Even when the words were screamed by parrots, the warning "*Hikoki!*" sent Japanese troops crawling for cover.

Even before he had landed on the island, Kawaguchi had grave misgivings about having to make a night attack. "No matter what the War College says, it's extremely difficult to take an enemy position by night assault. There were a few cases in the Russo-Japanese War but they were only small-scale actions. If we succeed here, it will be a wonder in the military history of the world." This he confided to Gen Nishino, a Japanese war correspondent who accompanied the operation.

Kawaguchi had begun to suspect that much more than "divine spirit" would be needed for success once the attack was launched. Lacking coordination and communications between his separated forces once deep in the jungle—in the oppressive humidity, Japanese radios didn't work any better than those of the marines—and unable to bring his heavy weapons, he was increasingly worried about his chances for success. No one back at the remote headquarters in Rabaul seemed aware of the horrible hardships imposed by the jungle itself. Since his main radio center had already been captured by the marines at Tasimboko, he had no way to let his other units know where he was or when he would attack.

"We will take the enemy airfield by surprise," Kawaguchi told his rain-drenched staff as they prepared for the attack. "As you know, gentlemen, the Americans have been strongly reinforced with men and supplies. Perhaps they are stronger than we are. Above all, their air force cannot be underestimated. Our troops must also overcome difficult terrain problems before we even reach the enemy lines. We are obviously facing an unprecedented battle. And so, gentlemen, you and I cannot hope to see each other again after the fight. This is the time for us to dedicate our lives to the Emperor." The fatal flaw in Kawaguchi's thinking, which undermined the attack, was that he did not believe his brigade faced a force strong enough to repel his brigade.

CHAPTER 9

SEPTEMBER 12 AND 13 BATTLE OF EDSON'S RIDGE

"Come on, you sons of bitches—do you want to live forever?"

—Gunnery Sergeant Daniel Daly, USMC
Belleau Wood, June 1918

Kawaguchi finally had three battalions of his 35th Infantry Brigade moving toward its assembly area south of Henderson Field. A fourth unit didn't have as far to travel. The Kuma Battalion, remnants of Ichiki's failed expedition, was to attack the airfield from farther east across the Tenaru River below where the Ichiki Force had been slaughtered. Colonel Oka was still struggling to gather his widely dispersed force for its scheduled attack from west of the Matanikau. He advised Kawaguchi that he would not be ready on the night of the 12th and asked for a postponement, but it was refused. Kawaguchi may have had 6,217 able-bodied men available, according to Japanese records, but he didn't actually know how many would be in position to take part in the attack. (In a similar situation, American marines or GIs would not have been ordered to begin an attack without the assurance the entire force was in place and ready to attack.)

Kawaguchi had been advised to reconnoiter the target area first to determine whether more troops and supplies were needed to make a successful attack. The general chose to ignore an essential basic of warfare—combat information patrols—because he didn't think the area was heavily defended. Never mind that the Tasimboko raid had revealed the presence of his force, now floundering through the jungle, and that the marines knew he was coming.

Had he taken the time to send out patrols, he would have certainly discovered his approaches were defended by experienced combat troops. Moreover, the exhausting ordeal of moving 3,500 men through the rain, mud, and pestilential heat without decent maps had left his troops spread all through the jungle. Just before kicking off his attack, Kawaguchi discovered that his brigade's main force of three battalions—more than 2,500 men—would have to get over a large ridge to capture Henderson Field.

The large, irregular-shaped ridge, which the Japanese equated to a centipede, pointed like a broad knife at the heart of the prized airstrip. Bald on top, heavy brush and skin-slicing kunai grass grew in the low areas, and there was pure jungle on the end farthest from the airstrip. Still, the prickly and proud Kawaguchi saw no reason to delay. Nothing—especially not a handful of spineless, emaciated, and exhausted marines—could prevent his gaining a plump and glorious victory.

Raiders and Paras Man the Line

Private Jim McCarson, the North Carolina mountain boy who had lied about his age, had been relieved as an ambulance driver and reassigned to the Raiders as a machine gunner four days earlier for disciplinary reasons. Convinced for weeks that he would not get off the Canal alive, he felt his time had come. While the underage marine worked in the rear helping to handle the wounded at the inadequate hospital, he was appalled at the horrible conditions endured by the suffering men. The badly wounded with little hope of recovery were left exposed in the endless rain, unprotected from the swarm of mosquitoes and flies attracted to this charnel house.

"One hopelessly wounded man, a big strong man once but now in terrible pain, would look at me each time I came by. Each time he begged me to shoot him." McCarson recalls. "He knew he was dying, but couldn't kill himself. I couldn't do it then, but now? I don't know that I wouldn't do what he asked."

When the medical officers arranged for the construction of an officers' mess and some beds where they could rest in comfort—using the mosquito netting denied to the wounded and dying—the then sixteen-year-old North Carolina mountain boy got some explosives and blew it up.

In being assigned to the Raiders, "the most terrifying thing for me was being assigned to the Cossack positions—listening posts. That's where two or three men would have to go four or five hundred yards ahead of the front line. Sitting there back-to-back we could hear everything. Even the crickets sounded like sirens." He was back at his light machine gun position on the ridge when the probing attack came, and saw and heard the guns and the flash of exploding shells, the shooting and wild screams. Like his new buddies, he had no idea what was happening, only that they were scared as hell.

Underage Enlistments

The seeming epidemic of underage enlistments in the Army, Navy, and Marines could be attributed to the sudden and widespread surge of patriotism after the December 7, 1941 attack on Pearl Harbor—except for the fact that many had already entered the service in peacetime. The usual requirement was that the enlistee be 18 years of age, with the exception that parents could give signed permission for a 17-year-old to enter the armed forces. No one seems to have shown much concern about how many forged a parent's signature and even a birth certificate in order to qualify. In remote rural areas, records were skimpy at best and often nonexistent. Army, Navy, and Marine recruiters were not known to probe too deeply into an aspirant's qualifications in back-country areas when they had quotas to fill.

Jim McCarson was fifteen when he enlisted in a small town in the North Carolina mountains. He was nearly turned down—not because of his age, but because he was just shy of the minimum weight. The recruiter suggested that when he went for his physical he should stuff himself with bananas and water before stepping on the scales. On Guadalcanal he was only one of a number of underage marines.

Serving on almost every ship in the many battles in and around the area were 16- and 17-year-olds who had lied to get into uniform. This writer's orphan father lied to get into the Navy in the early 1920s, at age seventeen, to get off a southern Alabama farm and away from a tyrannical guardian. Attending—much less graduating from—high school was an impossible dream. He was farm-strong and intelligent, and his most difficult adjustment to Navy life was having to wear shoes every day. After thirty years' service he retired with the rank of Lieutenant Commander. As hard as the service was in those early days, it was still easier than the dreary dawn to dusk every day of the year laboring on a farm.

Without doubt the prime motivation for many of these young men was just to get away from the marginal existence that otherwise was almost impossible for them to escape. The difficulties of having enough food to eat and clothes to wear were aggravated during the deep depression years of the 1930s. In the service a young man ate regularly, was provided with clothing and a place to sleep, and with luck, could learn a trade. One young man from the mountains of Georgia joined the Army and sent most of his meager private's pay back home to help his sharecropper parents and family feed and clothe themselves. Without doubt he loved his country and flag for giving him the opportunity to be able to help his folks.

The quest for adventure was another motivation that cannot be discounted. McCarson had seen the posters proclaiming that the Marines were the first to fight. "Join the Navy and see the World" was an irresistible lure for many others who had never even visited the next county. In 1940, when the United States began the explosive expansion of its armed forces—most notably the Army—many underage youngsters saw the opportunity and grabbed it. Not a few town constables and county sheriffs offered many restless, hot-blooded minor offenders the alternative of jail time or enlistment in one of the services. The theory was that if these youngsters were going to fight, then a community should send them to someplace where their aggression was appreciated.

One orphan boy from near Greenville, Texas got a neighbor to sign his enlistment papers so he could join the Army and help support his destitute family. Even then, only the Army was remotely interested in this scrawny farm boy who looked younger than he was, and they made a great effort to keep him in a service unit behind the lines. But his fiery Irish temper could not be denied, and he went ashore at the invasion of Sicily as a rifleman. Near the end of the war, having seen combat in Italy, France, and Germany—and just shy of his 21st birthday—Audie Murphy had received every American medal for bravery, numerous foreign awards, and been given a battlefield commission, achieving the rank of 1st lieutenant prior to his presentation with the Medal of Honor.

Food—consisting of soggy rice and distasteful dehydrated potatoes—and a last issue of ammunition was handed out. To strengthen the line, men with temperatures as high as 104 degrees were released by the dispensary and returned to duty. By the time dark fell on the 12th, the new combined Raider and Parachutist force of about 840 men had barely finished stringing barbed wire—appropriated from less threatened positions, in front of their exposed southern front—and digging foxholes. The boundary line ran down the ridge, placing the Raiders to the west and Parachutists to the east. The Parachutist Company B was situated at the southern fringe of the ridge into the edge of the jungle and backed up by Companies C and A in echelon. Company B of the Raiders were to their right on the western slope, up against the rain forest. Company C filled in the area between Company B and the Lunga River. Cutting through Company C's position was a long shallow lagoon paralleling the ridge, ending in an impassable swamp. One platoon of Company C abutted Company B, while the other two platoons defended the area between the lagoon and the river.

Adding to the drama was the fact that Vandegrift's headquarters had just been newly moved to the northern approach to the ridge where it flattened out toward the airfield. Companies A, D, and E (heavy weapons) held positions along the ridge, frequently fragmented by the encroaching jungle, back of the thin main line crossing the ridge. Strong points with mutually supporting fields of fire had to do instead of a continuous line. On a hill and behind the main line and just east of the Lunga the 1st Pioneer Battalion established a strong point. The 1st Amphibious Tractor Battalion covered the rear of Edson's battalion to the west, and the 1st Engineers Battalion to the east.

About 100 yards south of Vandegrift's new command post, the men of Edson's meager reserve company dug in the communications switchboard. Captain William D. Stevenson's phone men manned this rudimentary command post and ran telephone wire back to Division. Expecting an attack, but still not knowing when, Edson met with his company commanders to plan a full-scale patrol of the area the next day, hoping to disrupt Japanese movements. As the meeting broke up they heard the distinctive engine sounds of Japanese scout plane "Louie the Louse"—the detested colleague of "Washing Machine Charley"—who began dropping flares, which lit up the ridge area. Japanese warships opened fire at 9:30 P.M., but most of their shells fell back near the airfield.

The growing sounds of rifle and machine gun fire, punctuated by mortar and grenade blasts, signaled the beginning of a firefight. Frenzied Japanese troops shouting "Banzai!" and screaming "Maline you die!"—in quite understandable English—charged from the shelter of the inky jungle.

Kawaguchi's carefully drawn plans for a coordinated attack to kick off at 8:00 P.M. had fallen apart when Oka's regiment and the Kuma Battalion failed to reach their starting positions. Nearing the ridge, his late-arriving battalions lost their sense of direction in the night and began running into each other. At about 1:00 A.M. on the 13th, Japanese troops, believed to be part of III/124 (III Battalion, 124th Regiment), pushed into the space between the lagoon and the ridge and fell on Company C of the Raiders, for a time cutting them off from the rest of the defending force. Several listening posts manned by dutiful and frightened marines were swept away in the first rush. Company B's right platoon was forced to curl back to protect its parent. Seven marines were lost in the fight, but the company was not hit again that night.

Company B's single platoon in the swampy area east of the lagoon was cut off and surrounded for a while, but men from Company A came to their rescue. Gunnery Sergeant Harry F. Ericson was one of those who fought his way through the attackers. During the fight, he was wounded and treated by Company B Corpsman Laing. Ericson, who later won a Silver Star and was killed in action on New Georgia, had to be evacuated to Australia.

As Edson had said earlier, "this was no motley of Japs." These were experienced combat troops who proceeded to fan out once they had passed by a Marine position, and began cutting firing lanes so they could concentrate and better control their rifle and machine gun fire. Attackers and defenders were fighting among each other in the eerie lightness provided by flares and exploding artillery shells. Although they had separated a platoon from Company B, the Japanese were too busy trying to destroy isolated small groups or individuals to exploit what could have been an opening for a breakthrough. Kawaguchi and his troops had not expected such intense resistance.

When Edson tried to telephone one platoon and tell them to disengage, the reply was, "Our situation here, Colonel Edson, is excellent. Thank you, sir." No marine ever spoke like that, so he knew the phone line had been tapped. So he called on a corporal who had a voice like a bullhorn to deliver the message.

"'Red Mike' says it's OK to pull back!" the NCO's voice roared over the sounds of battle. The platoon then pulled back, keeping the fighting line intact.

More shrieking Japanese, with their fixed bayonets glittering from the light of the bright flares, moved through the gap and toward the west flank of the ridge. Marine artillery cut a swath in their ranks, as mortar shells plummeted into the swarming mass, which continued to attack the machine gun and rifle positions. Scared nearly out of their wits, the marines fought like demons. During the intense fighting, two corpsmen had to amputate the shattered arm of one Raider with only a pen knife. This emergency operation saved the badly wounded man's life. One of the corpsmen was killed in the battle later that night.

American machine gunners had been taught to fire short, well regulated bursts in order to conserve ammunition and keep from burning out the barrels of the guns. That night the guns fired continuously at the surging attackers. There were too many targets—the Japanese kept swarming forward. Special asbestos gloves had been issued to handle the hot barrels when changing them, but there wasn't time for that. Many marine gunners didn't know they had suffered badly burned hands until after the fighting died down.

To the Raiders it didn't seem possible that the Japanese could keep attacking into their heavy gunfire. This wasn't a futile banzai attack like the small ones on Tulagi or at Alligator Creek—this was the main thrust of an effort to overrun and destroy the Raiders. This was a battle like no one could have envisioned. Even the Raiders would not have pressed an attack that incurred such heavy losses.

Floundering in the waterlogged jungle and devastated by intense high-arcing 105-mm artillery fire from the 11th Marines barely beyond the Raiders' own positions, the Japanese had to withdraw. Kawaguchi, soaked and muddy, screaming and furiously trying to unsnarl the monumental foul-up, still didn't know where his battalions were. He later reported that "because of the devilish jungle, the brigade was scattered all over and completely beyond control. In my whole life I have never felt so helpless." His earlier misgivings about a night attack were proving to be true.

At 10:00 P.M. Colonel Oka, able to muster only two companies rather than the two battalions of his 124th Regiment he was supposed to have, was still too far off to the west to get into the action. One prong of the "coordinated" three-prong attack was missing. The plan—which looked so good on paper—could not be fulfilled because of the treacherous jungle. Japanese records found after the war revealed that this ragged and chaotic but firmly pressed attack was supposed to have been the actual main attack to capture Henderson Field, and not merely a feeling out of the Raider positions, as some have suggested. Kawaguchi, seething because of the chaos, was forced to pull his units back into the jungle and try to reorganize and prepare his force to resume the attack the next night.

Confusion at Japanese HQ

Lacking radio contact, the Japanese 17th Army HQ on Rabaul was not certain that the first attack had taken place, much less that it had been repulsed. They simply *assumed* that Kawaguchi's brigade had succeeded in capturing the airfield. They had men and supplies loaded on ships waiting to complete the occupation of Guadalcanal. Yet, before sending in a large fleet of planes to land on Henderson Field, two patrol planes, escorted by nine Zekes, were sent down to determine the success of the attack. Even when the CAF rose up to intercept the group and shot down four Zekes—indicating that the marines were alive and well—the Japanese were still not convinced Kawaguchi's attack had failed.

Twenty-six Betties and twelve Zekes sortied for their usual daily raid, and—still confused as to the actual status of Henderson Field—decided to drop their bombs on Taivu Point, which they thought was still in American hands. After unloading their bombs on their own soldiers, who had moved back into the village, the fighters swooped down for a vicious strafing attack. There are no records detailing the casualties.

Rear Admirals Turner and John S. McCain, South Pacific Air Commander, flew in to confer with Vandegrift. Carrying a written message, Turner brought some bad news. Back in Nouméa, the fatigued and increasingly pessimistic Ghormley had concluded that because he could no longer adequately supply and reinforce Guadalcanal the operation would fail, although he was not giving up hope. Turner was more optimistic. He said he could get the 7th Marines to the island safely and promised to bring them in.

Then Turner, in his characteristic superior fashion, began offering his own views about the ground tactics that should apply to the new troops. Suddenly it seemed that the admiral thought he was a general as well. Vandegrift said politely that he would consider Turner's suggestions, then firmly asked that the new regiment be landed at Lunga Point, within the perimeter. Still, it would have been interesting to lock Rear Admiral Turner and General MacArthur together in the same room to discuss tactics and command until they reached an agreement.

In an interview with correspondents, Turner said that the Marines would remain on the island although "things will get worse before they get better." When the sounds of battle began a few hundred yards away on the night of the 12th, Turner was skeptical, thinking this might be a display staged for his benefit to encourage his cooperation. As the naval bombardment from IJN destroyers led by *Sendai* whistled overhead to crash on the ridge, he no longer entertained doubts about the seriousness of the situation.

After Turner departed, Vandegrift confided the contents of the message to Brigadier General Geiger—friend and air deputy—and explained his intention to stay on Guadalcanal "come hell or high water." If they couldn't hold where they were, he would take his men into the hills. Geiger then assured him, "Archer, if we can't use the planes back in the hills we'll fly them out, but whatever happens, I'm staying here with you."

The haggard marines, barely clinging to the desolate island, satisfied they had done their defined job in seizing the beachhead, felt they should have been relieved by the Army weeks ago. This they blamed not on the Army, but on the U.S. Navy. Almost to a man, they were convinced their parent service, especially Fletcher, had deserted them.

Still, something was happening on the island that was incomprehensible to Admirals Ghormley, Nimitz, and King, as well as other commanders far from the scene. These exhausted raggedy-ass marines, poorly supplied, underfed, and seemingly ignored, refused to think of giving up the island. They might die on Guadalcanal, but they were not about to hand it over to the Japanese. These hardy men understood that the enemy might be able to drive them into the sea, but they would not tuck their tails between their legs and run away.

Eighteen Wildcats (F4Fs) from *Hornet* and *Wasp*, along with twelve SBDs and six TBFs from *Saratoga*, arrived during the day on the 13th at Henderson Field, despite the confusion created by the attack on the nearby ridge. The once again reinforced CAF conducted bombing and strafing runs on the area where the Japanese troops were thought to be, in support of Edson's attempted advance. Edson tried to organize a patrol in force during daylight on Sunday the 13th to break up the enemy assembly areas, but heavy resistance forced him to cancel that plan. Instead, he changed his position by drawing back along the ridge, closer to the airfield.

Meanwhile, Back on the Ridge

Badly mauled in the fight the night before, Company C was pulled back from the front and placed on the high knob. Company A and what was left of Company D were assigned to defend the crest on the right flank of the big knob. There weren't enough able-bodied men on hand to defend the positions of the night before. Glassy-eyed men mumbled their words and moved along in the mechanical high-stepping gait common to thoroughly exhausted men, as they found new positions for their heavier weapons, brought up boxes of ammo and hand grenades, and crawled back into their fighting holes.

In pulling his troops back, Edson created a trap that Kawaguchi had no choice but to walk into. The Japanese commander was compelled to lead his men over a more open area after emerging from the jungle and onto the ridge itself—an area pre-targeted and registered by the increasingly effective marine artillery and mortar crews.

In the new alignment, along 1,000 yards anchored on the south slope of the big knob, only 400 soldiers were available. The 250 Parachutists, who had not been hit the night before, were dug in on the eastern slope. Units of platoon size were placed at intervals along the main line of resistance (MLR). The only clear fields of fire were in the center. Even these fire zones were ragged because of the abrupt slopes and gullies, which broke up the defensive area.

At 9:00 P.M. "Louie the Louse" circled over Kukum and cut off his wheezing engine to coast in and drop a high-powered parachute flare over Henderson Field. That flare was answered by a red flare from the jungle, which signaled two battalions—about 2,000 fired-up, screaming soldiers of Nippon—to begin the first attack up the slopes toward the center and right of the ridge. They yelled *"Banzai!"* and attacked. Then they added the ultimate threat—"Maline you die!"

"You'll eat shit first, you bastards!" whooped a marine in return, at the top of his voice.

They first hit Company B, Raiders, now holding the position from which Company C had been withdrawn. Company B was forced to pull back when another attack column moved through an opening to the west, cutting off B's right platoon. Only sixty men of the company were available to fall back when the order came to withdraw. The hard-hit company fell back about 250 yards, positioned adjacent to Company C. There was now a 200-yard-wide gap through which the Japanese were pouring, attempting to get up on the ridge and out of the jungle. Bedlam seemed the rule for both forces as the bitter fight progressed under the shimmering light thrown out by calcium flares.

Despite withering Raider fire, the Japanese keep coming. This onslaught forced Edson's line backward into a horseshoe shape. An hour after the first attack began, the Imperial soldiers seemed to pause to reassemble. Taking advantage of the lull, Corporal Walter Burak, Edson's runner, crawled to the rear to find and bring forward some communications wire, which he then spliced to connect the battalion message center to the division command post. The senior staff, having heard only the cacophonous sounds of the battle, were anxious for news.

At 10:00 Edson informed the division operations officer that his force had been reduced to about 300 men still able to fight. Other men, cut off from the main line, continued to fight and fire on the Japanese from totally unexpected positions. Kawaguchi's forces on the ridge increased in number against the dwindling number of marine forces despite the destruction that mangled his Imperial soldiers.

Once again a red flare was fired, and at 10:30 a fresh wave of Japanese troops poured forward out of the darkness of the jungle following an intense mortar barrage on Company B of the Parachutists. This second attack was met by a blistering barrage of 105-mm artillery fire from twelve guns of Colonel Hayden Price's battalion of the 11th Marines. The guns were firing at such a high angle of fire, at ranges as short as 1,600 yards, that the artillerymen had to dig pits underneath the breech blocks to handle the recoil. The battalion fired off 1,992 rounds, some falling as close as 200 yards to the defending lines. There were no defensive troops between the guns and the combined Raider-Parachutist positions.

By now Major Charles Nees, assistant operations officer of the 11th Marines, a 33-year-old reservist seeing his first action, had moved forward into the thin lines as a forward artillery observer. He was soon joined by Private 1st Class Tom Watson, a clerk with the unit's Headquarters Battery, who seemed to have a gift for calling in artillery fire. Watson proved his value over and over during the long night, and the next morning he was promoted to 2nd Lieutenant.

Private 1st Class Jerry R. Gillard, a sturdy, heavy-set boy from Winter Garden, Florida, had his ambulance up on the ridge to pick up a couple of wounded marines. As dark fell and the Japanese began to attack, he wasn't able to leave the ridge. A sergeant recruited him to help, gave him several crates of smoke grenades and orders to keep throwing them. "I spent the rest of the night tossing those smoke grenades off the ridge, creating a helluva lot of smoke," he recalled later.

In the morning four wounded marines were loaded into the three-quarter-ton truck he used as an ambulance, and two assistants jumped on. Heading back Gillard discovered the Japanese had set up a machine gun nest on a hairpin curve. They opened fire on the truck. "I put my head down on the floorboard where I could look down and see the tracks through the crack next to the steering column...they were so deep they were like railroad tracks...I accelerated using my hand [on the pedal]. Part of the steering wheel was shot and I lost the two guys [killed by enemy fire]." After making it past the road block, Gillard was forced to halt the ambulance for an air raid while he got the wounded men to safety in bomb craters. After the all-clear, he reloaded the wounded men and delivered them to a medical detachment near the airfield.

Each new Japanese attack wave was initiated with a red flare fired into the air, followed by more attacking swarms. Of course, the marine observers, quickly realizing the flare's purpose, used it as an aiming point for their artillery and mortar fire. The assaulting troops took heavy losses as the exploding shells cut them down.

The heaviest weight of the new attack fell on Company B, Parachutists. The commander, Captain Harry L. Torgerson—"the mad bomber of Gavutu"—was angered when someone panicked and yelled, "Fall back!," but he had to confirm the order as the now shattered unit had already begun the untimely and unauthorized withdrawal. The slashing artillery barrage against the Japanese made possible the disorganized American unit's retreat. As they scurried back, Major Kenneth D. Bailey stepped forward to stop the near rout—which would have meant total defeat. It took every inch of his commanding presence and a colorful but angry fusillade of choice traditional marine epithets and curses to stop the flood of near stuporous men to the rear.

At this critical juncture only 300 marines held the knoll, the battered gateway to Henderson Field. The fiery and aggressive Torgerson was given command of what was left of the 1st Parachute Battalion when the previous commander folded. Most of the Paras did not fold. Sergeant Keith Perkins was crawling and creeping in the dark, seeking additional ammo for his two–machine gun section. When the crews of those guns were put out of action, he took over the firing—until he was killed. The fierce captain reorganized his Companies B and C and led them in a counterattack that took them back and abreast of Paras Company A.

The defensive artillery fire was called in closer and closer to the horseshoe, but the waves of Japanese kept coming. Advancing while being shelled by artillery is one of the worst possible experiences any man can endure. Artillery fire and exploding shells are brutal and lethal. The explosions blow men apart—severing legs and arms from the body—but do not always kill. The actual blasts burn like furnaces, charring exposed areas such as faces and arms. The shrapnel—often super-hot torn and jagged shards, chunks, and slivers of steel—tear into soft flesh and organs, slicing arteries and veins. The maimed who survive the blasts and shredding become wounded casualties who demand treatment or else involve others in helping them back to safety. One wounded man alone can take two or more unharmed helpers out of action.

Lieutenant Commander E.P. McLarney and his overworked eight corpsmen operated on the critically wounded under ponchos rigged into a tent using flashlights to see what they were doing. In these primitive and harsh conditions they dressed wounds, applied tourniquets to limbs fragmented by lead and steel fragments, and administered plasma transfusions. By the morning of the 14th they had worked forty-eight hours without a break for rest or food, ignoring the bullets whizzing in the air and the explosions of mortars and grenades nearby. Still, try as they might, they couldn't keep up with the influx of dozens of wounded. The entire crew was recommended for the Navy Cross.

In the early hours of the heartbreaking clash Pharmacist's Mate Laing heard the imperative call of "Corpsman!" As he crawled forward over marine and enemy dead, a badly wounded Japanese soldier grabbed his bayonet and ran it through Laing's right leg. A nearby marine rose up and blasted the assailant's chest to pieces. The corpsman pulled out the bayonet, plastered his leg with sulfa powder, and briefly wondered why there was not more bleeding as he slapped on a makeshift bandage before crawling on to help the marine who had called for help. He found the man had been shot in both arms and in the thigh, and—out of battle dressings—Laing ripped off the wounded man's pantleg and used it for bandages.

Private 1st Class Jimmy Corzine spotted four Japanese setting up a machine gun on a knob near where he was fighting. Making sure his bayonet was properly fitted, he attacked the enemy position alone, bayonetting the man about to fire the gun. As he tried to kill the others with rifle fire, he himself was killed. Around him, Japanese trying to avoid the furious fire and explosions jumped into foxholes with marines, who promptly tossed them out dead or alive.

By 2:00 A.M. the blazing light of the flares showed that the Japanese had advanced to within sight of the precious airfield. They also unleashed a flood of mortar fire that once again cut the marines' telephone line back to Division, which was so desperately needed to call in more artillery. Linesmen working busily under the deadly grazing fire managed to run in new wire and reestablish communications.

At about 3:00 the desperate call for more machine gun ammunition and grenades got through, which resulted in a resupply being rushed forward. Major Bailey again took charge and, crawling through the heavy fire lashing across the embattled ridge, delivered the goods to wherever they were needed. A bullet punctured his helmet and grazed his scalp. His pugnacious leadership during that bloody night earned him the Medal of Honor.

But it was "Red Mike" Edson—up on the lines with the stunned, scared, and hurting marines—who kept the defense together. Though many of his men called him a "glory hound," he fought like a demon from hell. Through his determined presence, in his command post scant yards behind the firing line, he grabbed the few men staggering to the rear and sent them back to their fighting positions.

"Get back to where you came from. The only thing they've got that you haven't is guts!" rasped Edson. The ferocious melee eased off a little, but now his haggard defenders had been driven back to the final knob on the ridge. At around 4:00 reinforcements in the form of companies from the 2nd Battalion, 5th Marines began moving into the vulnerable line. Private 1st Class A.F. Arnold and Jimmy Corzine, and Sergeant Daniel Hudson, won the Navy Cross that night.

The Japanese, however, would not be stopped easily. From where I was, before you ever saw them, you heard the hollering and screaming as they broke up the ridge. I thought that was the end," Private Jim McCarson recalled years later. "When you did see them they had their weapons over their heads—you could see the tracer bullets cutting into some of them before they lowered their durn rifles. You only know what's going on in this little space in front of you, and left and right of you. You try to protect your space, and from what I remember I've wondered many a time that if had they come over that ridge shooting and firing, as some of them were, that they couldn't have overrun us. You can believe that they came awfully close as it was.

"There were so many of them that came over that ridge compared to what we had strung out there you could shoot two and there would be six more. It didn't last but a few minutes like that, ten or fifteen minutes, but they just kept coming in waves." McCarson's Company C was defending near the top of the knob from which Edson was directing the defense.

"Two Japs had gotten close, about ten yards, and it was terrifying. I thought for sure then that we were gone. To this day, unless God had his hand on us, considering how many of them came over that ridge I don't how we stopped them.

"I'll always believe that they had some kind of dope or something that got them all fired up, more than just human willpower. You'd see the tracers go through them half a dozen times—one had to have been hit six or eight times—he'd go down and get back up again," McCarson marveled, shaking his head in disbelief. "You didn't bother wasting bullets on the ones you knew was gonna die, but you'd look up and see he had crawled fifty yards closer. He'd been bound to have been full of bullets, and I saw some of them crawl when they should have been dead. They were hard to kill.

"One had crawled within ten feet, and he died on his own with his whole stomach stringing out behind him. He was dragging his intestines behind him but he'd crawl on a little bit and stop. We'd check him because he might have had a grenade, then all of sudden he just gave it up and died. In the back of your mind you knew that others were coming and you didn't want to waste no bullets." McCarson was telling his story for the first time, more than fifty years after the battle.

"If you were with the machine guns, they gave you asbestos gloves to change the barrels. Somehow in the excitement I lost mine, but I thought my friend Paul had his. That morning on Bloody Ridge when the doggone machine gun got hot, I yelled 'change the barrel!' When he reached down with his wrench in one hand and grabbed the barrel with the other, you could hear the meat frying. Didn't bother him one bit, he was so darned scared. He didn't even realize he was being burnt.

"The first line and second line of guns were staggered to set up a cross fire for more firepower, but the second line wasn't sitting back there waiting—they were firing too. I saw some Japs that actually got in between the guns so you would have to say they had passed the first line. When you are firing free guns you swing wherever there's targets, but that day you didn't have to do no looking, everywhere you looked there was Japs coming.

"God knows the bullets that must have been fired that day. When it finally ended I had only a quarter of a belt left, that's all there was. It was all gone and after that it would have been 'Katie bar the door'—if there had been any more of them...ugggh.

"They were tough," mused McCarson softly, "they were really tough."

During the horrifying, long, and seemingly endless night, the unbelievably courageous Japanese troops launched about twelve attacks against the thin American lines, each new group blending in with those already advancing. Each succeeding attack was a little less fierce and determined than the last, but still they kept shrieking threats while rising from the jungle and surging up the ridge. Nishino, the war correspondent from Tokyo, joined a charge with 800 men led by Kawaguchi himself. They charged forward in the dark—directly into an area registered by American artillery. With machine gun bullets ripping through the bush, the ground shook like an earthquake that toppled trees and spewed red-hot shrapnel in all directions. His men were dying as Kawaguchi kept the attack moving. He could not turn back.

A badly wounded man ran up to Nishino and clutched his leg with one arm, pleading for his mother and a drink of water. The man's other arm had been blasted off. Nishino shook his empty canteen and put the damp spout to the dry lips of the soldier, who gulped, smiled in gratitude, and died.

Just before dawn Nishino was hurled through the air by an explosion from a mortar shell. After he regained consciousness the war correspondent vaguely remembered his brief somersault, like seeing himself floating in a slow-motion movie. From his prone position he could barely see the end of Henderson Field's runway in the distance, less than half a mile away. Knowing that the attack had been ground to bits by marine guns, Nishino crawled back to the questionable safety of the jungle.

The 7th Company, II/4 battled through to reach the northeast side of the ridge. It was then Major Tumura who ordered his 6th Company to break through. Despite losses of half the company, its bloody and wounded commander led roughly sixty men through the line to reach the west end of Fighter One, where they overran a small section of Company C, 1st Engineer Battalion. These men rallied, and with help from Company D and the HQ Company blunted and destroyed the penetration.

Far off to the left and east of the ridge, the Kuma Battalion of the Kawaguchi Force finally attacked the right flank of the 3rd Battalion, 1st Marines, commanded by Lieutenant Colonel William J. McKelvy, Jr. A night-long battle ensued, but the Japanese were unable to push past to the airfield. Repulsed in their attack near the Tenaru River, if they had properly scouted the marine defensive line they would have discovered the marines' unprotected flank and an open lane directly to Fighter One and Henderson Field. If this revenge-driven second echelon of the Ichiki Force had sideslipped only a few yards to their left, they could have probably ensured a Japanese victory. In their obedient and rigorous adherence to orders—a fatal weakness imposed by higher commanders—units such as the Kuma Battalion frequently failed to exploit openings that would have worked to their advantage.

The Japanese launched one last assault at dawn, which was cut apart by the 37-mm nose cannons, machine guns, and bombs of three of Captain Dale Brannon's Army P-400s flying low in close air-ground support, about twenty feet above the marines' heads. The enemy fired into the low-flying aircraft, forcing two of them to have to make "dead-stick" landings back at Henderson Field. The Aircobras attacked in the same area and at the same time that marine artillery was still killing and butchering the enemy.

In the morning six marine tanks without infantry support moved in to attack the isolated Kuma Battalion. Two were stopped by antitank fire, while a third plunged down a 30-foot drop into the Tenaru, killing the four crewmen. Then another took a hit from the antitank gun, and a fifth was stopped by a wrecked truck about 50 yards from the intrepid Japanese gunners. The crew of this tank clambered out and hurried back to the safety of their lines. The sixth tank returned intact, but the attack was a total failure. Ironically, the Kuma forces caused no more serious trouble, though they fought sporadically until they withdrew on the 16th.

Incredibly—and inexplicably—the III Battalion, 124th Infantry that had led the previous night's assault never got back into the fight on the night of the 13th. There is little doubt that if this unit had moved into the attack, the Raiders and Paras could not have prevented a breakthrough and the loss of Henderson Field. The invaders came within a razor's edge of success as it was. The Japanese Army and Navy, still prepared and ready to rush in reinforcements, were finally informed that Kawaguchi's attack had failed. Had he and his commanders resorted to a little deception, such as a diversionary attack from one direction and a full-scale main attack on a flank, or sideslipping when the opportunity presented itself, Edson's Ridge—originally called Bloody Ridge—might have been overrun and the Americans forced to give up the still tenuous battle for Guadalcanal. (The designation of Edson's Ridge applies specifically to Guadalcanal, as the marines have fought for other Bloody Ridges in various wars.)

The Kawaguchi Force was finished as an effective fighting unit. While a few hundred troops of his II/4 managed to join the Kuma Battalion in a retreat to Koli Point, the bulk of his surviving soldiers headed from Kokumbona along a miserable trail that wound past the southern slopes of Mount Austen and up along the Matanikau. Having expected to dine on captured American rations, they were now out of food. Without "even one grain of rice" for sustenance, the hungry men ate betel nuts, weeds and grass, and sometimes coconuts. Those more able killed fish with grenades to secure a small meal.

Nearly every soldier was employed in carrying the wounded back—four or five in a single litter—in a five-day struggle along jungle ridges and streams on a horrifying trail of death. Wounded men on the swaying and jolting litters died from their untreated wounds. Those seriously wounded who could not be carried by their exhausted comrades were left to die. With no medical care for the wounded, nor food or water for the retreat, the wasted stragglers became a rabble. Many were forever lost in the jungle, while a few wandered into Japanese or American lines weeks and months later.

Oka's regiment attacked the afternoon of the 14th, a day too late to help the assault on the ridge and in belated support of Kawaguchi's horribly mauled and retreating force. This attack was driven off by the defending 3rd Battalion, 5th Marines, inflicting even more casualties in the abject effort to capture Henderson Field. The astounding bungling of leaders in the jungle, and the breakdown in communications, when combined with an impossibly complicated assault plan that demanded precise movement and coordination, were the prime causes for the defeat of the Kawaguchi Force.

WASP Lost at Torpedo Junction

At dawn on September 14th, as the Battle for Edson's Ridge wound down, fresh reinforcements—consisting of the 7th Marines, part of the 5th Defense Battalion, and the 1st Battalion, 11th Marine Artillery with 75-mm pack howitzers aboard six transports—departed Espiritu Santo. These transports, escorted by three cruisers, destroyers, and minesweepers, were screened by the larger Task Force 65, sailing about 100 miles away. The Task Force was formed up around the only two operational carriers in the Pacific, *Wasp* and *Hornet*, the battleship *North Carolina*, seven cruisers, and thirteen destroyers.

Commander Takaichi Kinashi—commanding the submarine *I-19* on its patrol line in the area that gained infamy as "Torpedo Junction"—slipped his boat in close to the formation of 23 American ships. The protective screen of warships had drawn attention away from the vulnerable transports. Aiming at the nearby *Wasp*, he launched a spread of six Long Lance torpedoes.

After having sent her planes up, *Wasp* had returned to the patrol course at 2:45 P.M. when three torpedoes ripped into her starboard side. The aircraft on deck, with full gas tanks and loaded with bombs, were tossed into the air like toys by the concurrent explosions. Because the water mains had been broken in the blast, the gasoline-fueled fires that erupted raged out of control. Then a massive explosion shook the ship, flipping and knocking men off their feet. Rear Admiral Leigh Noyes was blown out onto the signal bridge, his clothes afire. Heroic efforts to save the ship were doomed, and at 3:20 the order to abandon ship was given. Four hours later torpedoes from the escort destroyer *Lansdowne* sent *Wasp* to the bottom. Casualties were 193 dead and 366 wounded. Only the twenty-five CAP aircraft launched from the Wasp were recovered.

The remaining three torpedoes missed the carrier, but one went on to blow a huge hole in *North Carolina*, and another opened up the bow of the destroyer *O'Brien*. The new battleship, which avoided disaster because of her redesigned damage control compartmentation, made it back to Pearl Harbor for repairs, but sixty days later the hastily patched up destroyer split in two and sank off Samoa.

Kinashi added to his fame by sinking or damaging three American warships with one spread of six torpedoes! Because of his previous exploits in sinking six ships off Malaysia and in the Indian Ocean, the commander was already acknowledged as Japan's top submarine officer. While the American submarine skippers were no less brave and determined, they did not have torpedoes comparable to the Long Lance until late in 1943—nearly a year later.

This exploit left only the carrier *Hornet* and its 75 planes available in the Pacific to confront *Zuikaku, Shokaku, Zuido, Taiyo, Junyo, Hiyo, Unyo,* and *Shoho*. This was a vastly superior force of eight operational Japanese aircraft carriers—with more than 360 planes—that could have been used to overwhelm the American fleet.

"We still had such superiority in forces that it seems almost unbelievable now that the chance to race down on Guadalcanal with overpowering strength was not seized," commented Captain Orita after the war. "A swift and overwhelming blow could have been struck at Guadalcanal at any time between September 15 and October 1. There would have been absolutely no way for the Americans to counter it." The caution of the Japanese naval high command after the loss at Midway, and the slowness of the Army commanders to take the American presence on Guadalcanal seriously, contributed to the failure to take advantage of this never-to-be-repeated opportunity.

Since the Battle of the Eastern Solomons both sides had concentrated on reinforcing their positions on Guadalcanal. An almost absurd situation had evolved: the U.S. controlled the sea from dawn until dusk, and the Japanese had mastery from dusk until dawn. During the day the Americans ran in supply cargoes, and at night the big ships steamed out of the area seeking the safety of the high seas, while the smaller craft took cover in the waters off Tulagi. After darkness fell, the Tokyo Express roared down the Slot with freight- and troop-carrying destroyers to replenish their positions. After the unloading was taken care of, the big ships would swing over by Lunga and bombard the airfield, then depart for the haven of Rabaul. This situation existed partly because the CAF was unable to mount night operations.

Any attempt by either side to change the arrangement inevitably provoked a bloody battle. The destruction and disabling of three important American ships at Torpedo Junction did not cancel the critical mission of moving reinforcements to the Canal. On September 18th the Americans decided to land a six-transport convoy moving the 7th Marines from Samoa, where they had been training to reinforce the garrison on Guadalcanal. Admirals Nimitz and Turner understood that without prompt and substantial reinforcements for Vandegrift, any kind of concentrated effort by the Japanese would shove the Americans off the island.

At dawn on the 18th the six transports carrying the 4,262 men of the 7th Marines sliced through the waters of Sealark Channel toward the Lunga perimeter to land the regiment—including guns, vehicles, and supplies—in twelve hours. Destroyers *Monssen* and *MacDonough* shelled enemy positions on Guadalcanal to cover the unloading, while the attack transport *Bellatrix* and two destroyer transports unloaded aviation gasoline for the CAF.

Troops crowded the decks, escaping their oven-like sleeping compartments for a breath of the fresh morning air and their first look at the famous island. Soon they swarmed down the cargo nets slung over the sides of their transports and into the bobbing landing craft and headed for shore.

All the regiments of the 1st Marine Division were together at last. Now there were 19,251 men on Guadalcanal and 3,260 on Tulagi—nine battalions of infantry, a weakened Raider Battalion, a special weapons battalion, four battalions of artillery, and two companies of light tanks. Engineers, pioneers, tractor units, and other auxiliary units were on hand to support the fighters.

Vandegrift was elated until he saw the regiment's commander step ashore dressed in a spiffy clean uniform, low cut shoes and silk hose. The Colonel, James C. Webb, was to be on his way back home within a few days, which surprised no one. Webb must have been disturbed by the appearance of the gaunt, unshaven men shambling about the perimeter in filthy, tattered remnants of uniforms. This officer's insensitivity to the reality of combat was more than offset by the presence of the battalion commanders, Lieutenants Colonel E.J. Smith, Herman Hanneken, and the incomparable Lewis "Chesty" Puller, the Marine Corps legend.

Most of the hungry, ailing, and filthy men ashore agreed that the "first team" had arrived. Any kind of fresh reinforcements boosted the general morale, particularly in the aftermath of holding Edson's Ridge. The aviation gasoline, ammunition, and supplies they brought along—the first major result of Turner's promise to give all the help he could—was heartily welcomed.

Puller, commander of the 1st Battalion, ordered his men to dig in about 500 yards away from the beach in the coconut grove. The men, nearly exhausted and suffering from the heat after their day-long effort to move and disperse their supplies inland, could hardly eat their dinner, and many fell asleep on the ground instead of preparing their foxholes.

Soon after midnight their stuporous sleep was interrupted by planes droning over the area, dropping flares. But the threat came from the sea—not from the air—as Japanese ships began the usual bombardment. Amid the cacophony of exploding shells and the screams of wounded men, the newcomers suddenly gained the strength to dig their holes. Three men of the 1st Battalion were killed and twelve were wounded in their baptism of naval gunfire.

In the Spotlight

Lewis Burwell "Chesty" Puller

By the time Lewis Puller landed on Guadalcanal, he had proven himself as a gifted and highly competent combat leader during campaigns in Haiti and Nicaragua. For his bravery in Nicaragua he had been awarded the Navy Cross. Although he was only about 5 feet 10 inches tall, and on the slender side, his military bearing—with chest thrust forward under his firm jaw—made him an imposing, seemingly larger man. "Chesty" was a great fighting leader, descended from a line of proud Virginians who had fought for the Confederacy. His grandfather had been killed in action during a charge against the Yankees while riding with Jeb Stuart's cavalry.

Born at West Point, in Tidewater Virginia, on June 26, 1898, he left after his first year at VMI to enlist in the Marine Corps when World War I broke out. He was commissioned as a second lieutenant just before the fighting in France ended. After his release from the Corps, having served only two weeks as a lieutenant, he headed for Haiti to join the constabulary, where he served under Vandegrift, and alongside Herman Hanneken. Puller was the quintessential warrior, and the thought of returning to civilian life never crossed his mind.

In Haiti he quickly proved to be a determined, resourceful officer who could be depended on to get the job done. His brave leadership quickly impressed his native troops, whose families often accompanied the men on the campaigns. A baby born to one of the women on the trail was proudly named after his godfather, Leftenant Puller François. In February 1924 he once again became a second lieutenant in the USMC, and was assigned to the Marine Barracks, at the Portsmouth, Virginia Navy Yard.

He was at Pensacola for flight training for five months, before he was found not to be suitable aviator material. Despite failing to get his wings—a minor blow to his pride—he was one of the first to recognize the importance of the intimate connection between ground warfare and close air support.

In 1926, on leave from the Marine Barracks at Pearl Harbor, he met Virginia Evans, whom he didn't see again for nearly eleven years. But he didn't forget her and he wrote to her regularly. He warned her that he was in the service to stay. When a native bandit uprising broke out in Nicaragua, he bombarded headquarters with requests to be sent there—a fact that surprised no one who knew him.

After his usual exemplary services in that besieged republic, he was promoted to 1st Lieutenant in October 1929. In Nicaragua's rugged jungle terrain, he learned more about setting ambushes, makeshift land mines, and troop movements under adverse climatic conditions—knowledge that he could call upon later in the South Pacific. Because of his success in five fights against superior enemies, "Chesty" was recommended for the Navy Cross—the first of five he would receive. After five years in the jungles, he was assigned to the Army Infantry School at Fort Benning, Georgia, over the protests of many Nicaraguans who didn't want their hero to leave.

Returning to Nicaragua after completing the Infantry School, he immediately returned to the elemental and vicious combat that characterized the fighting there. In a short time he was awarded his second Navy Cross for bravery under fire. He left Central America in January 1933, and in February he was assigned to China duty. There he came in contact with the Japanese and their training methods, and realized they would be formidable enemies in war.

From China he wrote to Virginia Evans, "...even if you do marry me and make me a happy man, even then, if I hear the beat of the drum, I must leave you. I want you to know that." His promotion to captain was dated July, 1935, and he was soon back in the States as an instructor in the Marine Basic School in Philadelphia.

Lew Walt, who later became a general, said, "Being under Puller in Basic School did more for me than anything I experienced until I got to Guadalcanal. He taught us the use of terrain like a master, how to use the tiniest bit of cover to our advantage. Ground form really meant something when he explained it. He taught us to use the bayonet, with all the tricks of close-in fighting. You couldn't mistake it, he knew the stuff cold."

Virginia married her persistent suitor on November 13, 1937. Marriage seemed to soften him for a few months, but soon he again became "Chesty" in all its rigorous meaning. They were ordered to China in May 1940 and Puller was promoted to major and assigned to the 4th Marines. His daughter, Virginia Mac, was born there but was soon shipped home with her mother. Remaining behind, Puller had his first confrontation with Japanese troops, who entered the neutral International Zone to seize 200 Chinese. The Japanese commander retired from the Zone without his prisoners.

In August 1941 he was assigned commander of the 1st Battalion, 7th Marines at the recently opened New River, North Carolina Marine Training Base. The United States was beginning to train for war. He took his men to live and train in the wilds, insisting they were field marines, not barracks marines.

At home on leave with his family on December 7th, he promptly returned to New River, where the already rigorous training was stepped up in tempo. On April 5th, 1942 the 7th Marines boarded ships for their trip to Samoa. The hard, unrelenting training there under Puller had them as ready for combat as they could be without facing enemy gunfire.

After arriving on Guadalcanal, his battalion was sent out on patrols toward Mount Austen and along the Matanikau River. In one confused action, his unit was caught in a trap on a beach without him. He managed to board a nearby supporting destroyer and began issuing orders to make sure they were relieved. In a later Matanikau action he was badly wounded, but continued to command the unit for another twenty-four hours until the fight was over. For this he won another Navy Cross.

He participated in the heavy fighting at Peleliu with another battalion, and continued to train first-class combat troops between actions. Years later, as commander of the 1st Marines in Korea, he led them in the fighting to recapture Seoul in 1950 and in the desperate fighting a few months later in the frigid cold near the Chosin Reservoir.

Frequently outspoken, and never pretending to be anything other than a field marine, he found his opportunities for advancement limited. He did become commander of the 2nd Marine Division at Camp Lejeune, and retired as a Lieutenant General. Puller was probably the most decorated Marine in history, and won five Navy Crosses—but he never did win the Medal of Honor that so many of his supporters sincerely believed he should have been awarded.

Matanikau—Patrol in Force

When daylight came on the 20th, Vandegrift ordered Puller to take his men into the jungle west of the Lunga River on their first large-scale patrol. A file of more than 800 men entered the steaming jungle early in the afternoon—their first experience over such malignant terrain. The force floundered, and movement began to break down as units got separated and then lost. Yet Puller pressed forward, looking for the enemy, leading at the front of his men. The marines had grimly held on to the beachhead for weeks with little hope of relief. By now they were familiar with the stench of unburied enemy dead, and the disturbing and frightening loss of close buddies.

Combat wounds continued to claim men. On the 22nd, during a patrol, Captain Jack Stafford had his face and neck splattered with shrapnel from a rifle grenade he was attempting to fire. Lieutenant Colonel Puller saw the officer strangling on his own blood, and raced over to help. He reached in Stafford's mouth, grabbed the man's tongue, pulled it out, and pinned it to the wounded man's jacket. That saved Stafford's life.

Machine gunner Bill Rust, 5th Marines Operations Section, was ordered by Edson, now a full colonel and the new commander of the 5th Marines, to explore and map the trail that the larger part of Kawaguchi's crippled 35th Brigade—survivors of the fight at Edson's Ridge—had cut to reach Point Cruz. To accomplish this task, he would work with Puller's 1st Battalion, now trying to follow the ragged month-old trail—something that suited Rust just fine.

The Second Matanikau

The plan for Puller's 1st Battalion on the 24th was to push into the area between the Matanikau River and Kokumbona on the coast after skirting Mount Austen, where they met heavy Japanese opposition in the afternoon. Rust and his scouts had moved forward, and he had crossed a small creek when from 100 yards ahead he discovered no one was with him. The marines had stopped to have a drink and fill their canteens. After a suitable demonstration of his mastery of salty profanity, the point detail resumed their march. Meanwhile, looking for a bivouac area, Captain Regan Fuller, a University of Virginia alumnus from Washington, DC, was on the point late in the day behind Corporal Turner when they stumbled upon and surprised two Japanese guarding the camp for fifty of their countrymen. Rust's patrol near the stream had come under fire and was forced to fall back to the main body.

"The Old Man bobbed up behind us almost as soon as the shots sounded, and when it slacked off he began to eat some rice from the Jap pot," Fuller remembered later. "A machine gun bullet knocked the bowl from his hand and sent it flying. We were caught in some cross fire, pretty wicked on the open slopes." A runner near Puller was shot through the throat, killing him.

Captain Chester Cockrell got his Company B into position with the encouragement of Puller's curses, forming a skirmish line that began moving forward. The company ran into a brisk firefight, and started taking casualties from snipers armed with machine guns. In the close quarters action, Puller killed three Japanese with his .45-caliber pistol, including a major, from whom he retrieved a dress sword.

Earlier, Puller had chewed out Cockrell to get him moving—a necessity he later regretted when he found out Cockrell had been killed in the action. The marines counted seven dead and twenty-five wounded—eighteen of them stretcher cases. More than thirty Japanese bodies were found in the area. When the reinforcements from the 2nd Battalion, 5th Marines came up on the morning of the 25th, Major Otho Rogers was ordered to take A and B companies and the stretcher-borne wounded back to safety. They had to struggle through the treacherous terrain on their return to the perimeter.

Puller continued his advance, moving down the east bank of the Matanikau toward the beach, guided by Rust, who knew the way because of his previous patrols. He reached the coast on the 26th as planned, where he drew intense fire from enemy positions on the ridges west of the river. An attempt by the 2nd Battalion, 5th Marines, to cross was beaten back.

That night headquarters ordered Puller's C Company and the 2nd Battalion, 5th Marines to hold their positions. The Raiders would move upstream to get behind the Japanese. Edson would take command and Puller would act as executive officer. Because of poor communications between units from division headquarters, this arrangement was not made clear, which further added to the confusion of the small unit leaders. Few seemed to have any idea of what to do and when to do it. Chaos was in the making.

At this time the Raiders, like the other battalions, were involved in patrols searching for Japanese assembly points in the area near the Matanikau. Even if Vandegrift didn't have sufficient forces to mount a decisive offensive, he could unleash the fury of del Valle's artillery. The enemy assembly points had to be found and the positions pinpointed for his guns to be effective.

"The thing I dreaded more than anything else in the world—and was more afraid of—was patrols," recounts Private McCarson. "We'd send out a thirteen man patrol, to hunt for men lost on a previous patrol. Then we started losing the last two men at the rear of the patrol, so some patrols made the last man walk backwards, take turns, to keep from getting knocked off. The Japs would hide in shelters with a lid on it and let a patrol go by, and then they'd lift that lid up and pop the last man.

"We were on patrol one time looking for two bodies, knowing that two men were shot the day before and two more are gonna be shot today" recounted the young Raider. "We didn't see any sign of the bodies, but all of a sudden we walked out into this little clearing and discovered a body hanging by its ankles—that's one of the things I try not to think about when it comes to my mind. This was a marine, but he had been shredded like a coconut. I don't know how they did it but it must have been with bayonets. That was an absolutely horrible sight. Up until that day I don't think I would have committed an atrocity, but after I saw that I think I would probably have done anything, whatever opportunity I had. He was from the 5th Regiment—we found his dogtags lying on the ground— and I'm sure that he'd been out on patrol. We didn't try to take his body back."

Patrolling was a continuous daily activity. They usually went out in squads of perhaps a dozen men—as described by McCarson—or in company or battalion strength like the patrol led by Puller. The men went out lightly armed—with enough ammo to fight their way out of an ambush—carrying one canteen of water. They moved slowly, spaced well apart, flanking both sides of a trail. Many covered no more than one agonizing mile in a day in looking for the hidden enemy.

One company ran into an ambush by men of Colonel Oka's command near the Lunga south of the perimeter. In an instant they were pinned down from well concealed machine gun fire. The Japanese taunted the men, asking them to "Come here, please." Private Jack Morrison was shot in the chest, and fell into the underbrush with his feet stuck out across the trail. When the company fought its way out, he was left behind. Near him another marine moaning from the pain was bayoneted and killed by one of the Japanese. A few yards away lay an unhurt marine, Private 1st Class Harry Dunn, who was playing dead. The Japanese continued to search around the area, stripping souvenirs from the dead, talking and laughing among themselves. After dark Morrison was startled awake from unconsciousness by Dunn, who then tried to find some water, but all the canteens had been taken by the ambushers.

Dunn pulled Morrison off the trail and into a thicket and tried to bind the man's wounds. When Morrison's shirt became blood-soaked, Dunn threw it away. When he could not move close to the Lunga, where the Japanese were camped, he returned to Morrison. They stayed in the thicket through that night and the next day, with flies, ants, and other creepy crawly things using them as food. When their terrible thirst could no longer be tolerated the next night, Dunn dragged his buddy to the river for their first drink of water in two days. They hoped the Japanese would be gone.

Worried about crocodiles, Dunn dragged the seriously wounded man—who sometimes cried out in pain—on his back alongside the river, now and then passing out from exhaustion, always waking up and crawling on again. When they reached the perimeter the next morning the still bleeding Morrison was gently lifted from Dunn's back, placed in a jeep, and rushed back to the airfield and evacuated. Dunn, who had passed out from exhaustion, recovered in the Guadalcanal hospital.

Sunday, September 27th, became a day of deadly blunders, as garbled messages and misinterpreted orders created mistakes and then compounded the confusion. Edson had his force at the mouth of the Matanikau, from which Lieutenant Colonel Sam Griffith led the Raiders upstream along the east bank. The CAF dropped bombs on the far shore, but the expected artillery barrage never came. This coastal force did not attack, but stayed where it was.

"Some of my men thought their hand grenades were too heavy. They tossed them aside when no one was looking," commented Platoon Sergeant H. R. Strong. "Later they would have given six months' pay for one hand grenade."

Believing that the Raiders had crossed the river as planned, and now needed reinforcements to trap the enemy, headquarters instructed the men Puller had sent back the night before to move down the coast in Higgins Boats and land behind the Japanese. The Raiders ran into fierce opposition, in which Griffith was wounded and executive officer Major Bailey—a Medal of Honor winner—was killed. The force had been stopped from making the crossing. Puller wasn't aware of this order involving his men until he saw the boats carrying the impromptu force passing by beyond the surf line. He tried to flag them down to join them.

Major Otho Rogers had been ordered to lead Companies A and B and part of D to the west of Point Cruz and force the Japanese toward the mouth of the Matanikau and into the guns of the 2nd Battalion, 5th Marines, who had failed to occupy their blocking position. Rogers's force was cut off and badly roughed up by the Japanese soon after landing and moving a few hundred yards inland. The small, placid reservist was killed in the fighting, blown apart by the explosion of a mortar shell that hit almost directly between his feet.

Cut off, with their radio gone and in need of help, the marines used white T-shirts to spell out the word H-E-L-P on an open patch of ground. A patrolling American dive bomber spotted their message, and the situation was reported to Edson's HQ. Puller boarded *Ballard*, an old destroyer turned seaplane tender, to rush to the scene and oversee the rescue of the trapped force. From the beach Sergeant Robert Raysbrook, remembering his semaphore code, repeatedly stood exposed and in the open and wig-wagged his signal flags to direct fire from *Ballard*'s 5-inch guns that held the Japanese back. Raysbrook was one of two men in that action to be awarded the Medal of Honor.

Captain Regan Fuller took over and directed his men back to the beach. Platoon Sergeant Anthony Malanowski assured Fuller, "I'll handle the rear." He picked up a discarded BAR, laid it across a log and wriggled into the sand. Some retreating marines said they heard the rattle of the BAR, but Malanowski was never seen again.

Puller signaled the flotilla of Higgins Boats that had put the marines ashore to move in and take them off again. Signalman 1st Class Douglas A. Munro, U.S. Coast Guard, was in charge of the boats. After ordering the other nine boats to circle offshore, he took his own boat in to reconnoiter the scene. Even with Japanese machine gun fire slapping his boat while taking on thirty wounded marines, Munro deliberately placed his boat in a position to draw enemy fire away from the other boats as they made their runs to the beach. The Japanese were determined to prevent evacuation of the force and destroy it on the beach.

While the able-bodied marines held off the advancing Japanese, the landing boats took on the survivors and wounded. More marines were wounded as they fought their way to the boats. Captain Fuller had to use his pistol to compel several of the coxswains to remain long enough to pick up some stragglers. On the other hand, a brave Munro spotted one of his boats that had grounded on the jagged coral, the crew working desperately to rock it off. He ordered his boat alongside, tossed a line to the stranded vessel, and pulled it free and into deeper water.

A Japanese machine gun was set up on the beach and took the boats under fire. Two of Munro's crew were hit. He and another crewman, signalman Raymond Evans, manned their boat's machine guns, and in the exchange of gunfire Munro's bullets silenced the Japanese gun. When the firing ended Evans turned to his longtime friend to find him slumped down at the base of his gun mount.

As Evans knelt by his friend, Munro opened his eyes and in a voice so weak Evans had to bend over to hear, asked, "Did we get them all off?"

On hearing Evans answer "Yes," Munro smiled, and died. Through his brave leadership 500 marines had been saved to fight another day. Munro is the only Coast Guardsman ever to earn the Medal of Honor.

Born in Vancouver, British Columbia, on October 11, 1919, Douglas Munro grew up in Cle Elum, Washington. After a year at Central Washington University, he enlisted in the Coast Guard in 1939. Munro's mother Edith accepted her son's posthumous Medal of Honor from President Roosevelt on May 24, 1943, then enlisted in the Coast Guard and served two years as an officer.

From start to finish the Second Matanikau Operation had been fouled up beyond recovery, doomed to failure. Communication between units was scanty at best, and the chain of command was confused and ineffective. The mistake of ordering Puller's disorganized battalion to make a beach landing under Major Otho Rogers cost about eighty men killed or wounded. Nothing had been gained for the Americans. The victory in this skirmish belonged completely to the Japanese. Overall American losses for The Second Matanikau were 67 killed and 125 wounded. For once Japanese losses were considerably less, one of their few bright spots during the long campaign.

The marine planners had fallen victim to the same overconfidence that had brought such devastation and destruction to the enemy. They thought they could easily conduct a complex and coordinated action in the snarled and treacherous jungle without knowing where they were going. Yielding to the compulsion to conduct offensive moves—any kind of offensive action—they failed to send out patrols to determine enemy strength and positions.

Colonel Edson, ever an aggressor, never developed a clear picture of the overall objective. Instead, he split his forces in a disjointed manner, sending them hither and thither. Few on the scene had any idea of who was commanding what unit or what each unit was supposed to be doing. The illusion of doing something concealed the real problem of accepting the expedient to "try this, and if that doesn't work, then we'll try something else." That the lives and bodies of marines were at stake in this comedy of errors did not seem to be considered in the equation.

Lessons Learned

"We have learned from the Nips to make the standup covered spider hole," said 2nd Lieutenant H.M. Davis, 5th Marines. The spider hole is a camouflaged foxhole deep enough for a man to stand in, and provides excellent cover for an ambush.

Commenting on the harsh lessons learned in jungle fighting, Platoon Sergeant C. M. Feagin said, "We are learning the hard way to move quietly in the jungle.... I have been fired at many times by snipers and haven't seen one yet."

A fact that quickly became evident is that troops new to jungle fighting needed at least a few days of orientation before they settled down and went into combat. They needed to be told what to expect. "Get used to the weird noises at night," advised Corporal E. J. Byurne, Company L, 5th Marines. "This jungle is not still at night. The land crabs and lizards make a hell of a noise rustling on leaves. And there is a bird here that sounds like a man banging two blocks of wood together. There is another bird that makes a noise like a dog barking."

"Red Mike" Edson later made some cogent observations on what was needed. "If I had to train my regiment over again, I would stress small group training and the training of the individual even more than we did when we were in training.

"We need the rifle grenade, or a weapon to fill the gap between the hand grenade and the mortar. We need to dig the Nip out of his hole under the banyan trees.

"We need the knee mortar badly. The name 'knee mortar' is a misnomer. It is not fired from the knee. One of my men tried this and broke his leg. The following reasons are in its favor:

"1. It is a one-man weapon.

"2. A man can carry ten rounds on his person *besides* his weapon.

"3. It has a high rate of fire.

"4. It gives the Platoon Commander a weapon of this type which is immediately available to him.

"5. This mortar uses the Jap all-purpose hand grenade—ranges from 50 yards to 650, I believe.

"The Japs have three (3) of these mortars in a Mortar Squad in each Rifle Platoon. They have two ammunition carriers per mortar."

Edson went on to say, "The Japanese night attacks, of course, have limited objectives; and sometimes withdrawing after dark as much as fifty yards will fool them and they won't know where you are." This tactic was based on the knowledge that the Japanese followed their orders explicitly. When faced with a situation not covered by orders, they would withdraw. Along these lines he strongly suggested that the commanders "Discontinue the use of tracers for night firing. They give away your position." Further, "Both our riflemen and machine gunners must be taught to shoot low."

Major Lew Walt, commander, 2nd Battalion, 5th Marines, added an urgent warning about the fighting Japanese soldier. "I can report officially to you that we had 9 men killed in one company in the last assault! 4 [sic] of these men were killed by a wounded sniper who had three holes in him. He was laying in thick brush 15 yards from my CP [Command Post]. He was camouflaged and had been passed over for dead. You have to KILL to put them out."

Partially compensating for the fiasco of the Second Matanikau Operation, on the same day the CAF shot down nine Japanese aircraft out of fifty-three attacking the perimeter. Little damage was inflicted by the attackers. In heavy air raids on the 28th, the Japanese lost twenty-three bombers and one fighter out of a force of sixty-two planes.

The CAF reported no loss of aircraft in combat. Pilots of Nippon were suffering serious losses far in excess of damages inflicted on the defenders.

"Bombers and fighters headed yours"—a typically terse warning from the Coastwatchers—gave the weary CAF pilots and ground crews sufficient time to get fighters off the ground and up to an altitude where they could attack the invaders. Yet, because of the bomb-holed, patched, and muddy runways, noncombat losses incurred during take-offs and landings were high. The growing boneyard of crashed or too badly damaged aircraft that couldn't be repaired and returned to service grew almost daily. Even the more optimistic members of the ground crews—who preferred to think of this scrapyard as a "spare parts depot," who had vowed to use everything but the bullet holes—were worried that replacements wouldn't arrive in time to do any good.

The Japanese continued to suffer high losses. In addition to the pilots and planes actually lost in combat, damaged planes and those that simply ran out of gas on the long return trip ditched in the sea or made crash landings on nearby islands. Numerous pilots and crews were rescued to fly another day. By the end of September, Captain Marion Carl had sixteen confirmed kills, and Major Galer was credited with eleven. When Wildcat fighter pilot Major John L. Smith departed the Canal, he was the Marines' leading ace with nineteen confirmed kills. On February 24, 1943, President Roosevelt personally awarded Smith the Medal of Honor.

WWII Snapshot—October 1942

Egypt—Field Marshal Erwin Rommel, exhausted from the continuing stalemate at El Alamein, visits Rastenburg, in Germany, to brief the Führer. The Desert Fox is physically and mentally worn out, and his army is in little better shape. The RAF is dominating the skies and is savaging his road convoys. Supplies must be moved at night over the only surfaced road in North Africa, which is disintegrating.

The Italians have promised 3,000 workmen to maintain the Coast Road. They never arrive. The only "assistance" Rommel gets from his pleas to Benito Mussolini is a speech: "You have done the impossible before, Field Marshal. We are all sure you will do it again."

Rommel does not bother to argue with Hermann Goering's assertion that the Luftwaffe rules the Egyptian air at this point, but does mention the heavy aid the Americans are supplying to the British 8th Army.

"Quite impossible!" Goering says. "Nothing but latrine rumors! All the Americans can make are razor blades and Frigidaires!"

Hitler promises to send Siebel Ferries (which are proving resilient against air and torpedo attacks) to Egypt, a "heavy-mortar brigade with 500 tubes, as well as 40 of Germany's newest and awesome Tiger tanks, to be followed soon by several assault gun units." Rommel is dismayed by the cavalier dismissal of his complaints.

On the 10th the Luftwaffe begins a 10-day air assault on the British-held island of Malta. More than 600 German planes take part.

Southern Russia—At Stalingrad Luftwaffe supply officers are running out of bombs with which to attack the Soviets, so ground crews also load the Junkers 88 bomb bays with pieces of metal, plows, tractor wheels, and empty cans to use as shrapnel. Yet, the Luftwaffe continue to attack, and knock out five of the six enemy cargo ferries.

Despite the hammering, General Vassili Chuikov, the Soviet commander in the mangled city, is slightly optimistic even though he has only 54,000 men left to defend the key city. In less than a month his army has lost more than 80,000 men killed, wounded, or missing. The German air attacks seem less coordinated and slower. Major General Khryukin's air force goes into action and Lagg-3 and Yak-1 fighter pilots find out what their British cousins already know: Ju 87 Stukas are pretty easy targets. Things aren't much better for the Germans on the ground.

"We have fought during 15 days for a single house," writes a German officer, "with mortars, grenades, machine guns, and bayonets. Already by the third day fifty-four German corpses are strewn in the cellars, on the landings, and the staircases. By now the fighting front is often a corridor between burnt-out rooms, or the thin ceiling between two floors. From storey to storey, faces black with sweat, we bombard each other with grenades in the middle of explosions, clouds of dust and smoke, heaps of mortar, floods of blood, fragments of furniture and human beings."

Stalingrad has endured eighty days and nights of unceasing hand-to-hand struggles. Distances are no longer measured by meters, but by corpses. Stalingrad is no longer a city, and by day the ruins are covered by an enormous cloud of burning, blinding smoke—a vast furnace lit by reflections from the flames. "Animals flee this hell; the hardest stones can not bear it for long; only men endure."

Soviet reserves are deployed behind Chuikov's 62nd Army, as Moscow hedges its bets on its ability to hold. Movement of fresh men, ammunition, and supplies into the city and evacuation of the wounded back to the west bank of the Volga is becoming extremely difficult.

On October 2nd the German 6th Army unleashes a terrifying artillery barrage followed by an attack in the industrial zone around the Red October Factory, on the city's north side. Shells blow up and ignite supposedly empty fuel tanks and hundreds die in the conflagration that sweeps toward the Volga. The attack, which involves determined and horrifying fighting by both sides, is inconclusive. The Germans fail to drive out the Soviets, who have been seriously weakened.

The German drive further south to capture the Caucasus oil fields is stopped by the Red Army.

Germany—On the 3rd, at Peenemunde, the A4—a 12-ton rocket capable of carrying a one-ton warhead 200 miles—is launched. One of Germany's "awesome secret weapons" is now a reality.

During the last week of September, at Auschwitz, Poland, 4,000 Jews die in the gas chambers. In these camps able-bodied men are assigned to forced labor, and the more attractive women are consigned to army brothels.

Southwest Pacific—Major General Horii has been ordered to withdraw his troops from the Kokoda Trail on Papua, New Guinea because his senior commanders at Rabaul have reached the conclusion that General MacArthur intends to conduct an amphibious assault around Milne Bay and in the Buna area. Horii is appalled to have to give up his advances, which have taken him within sight of Port Moresby, and reluctantly bows to his orders. At Myola, the most difficult spot on the trail, he mandates the construction of a heavily fortified position on the heights of the treacherous ravine to cover his withdrawal.

On October 4th, when the Japanese withdrawal is well under way, MacArthur and his staff journey up the Owen Stanley Range "as far as he could go," which is to the starting point of the Kokoda Trail. Two days later the vanguard of the American force to cross the mountains starts up the Kapa Kapa Track. After one day on the trail they are shaken by the sudden appearance of the thirty-five survivors of Captain Buckler's company. The emaciated, ashen, and filthy Diggers, caked with blood, look like ghosts—a sight that causes the native bearers to run away.

From that point on, the trek gets worse. Often they are forced by the rough terrain to crawl forward on their hands and knees, and to cling to vines and roots when they rest to keep them from sliding down the mountainside. The main body, which follows a few days later, endures five straight days and nights of heavy rain. It later lets up raining only in the afternoon and at night.

They have to cross raging streams that carry men away, and frequently sink into mud up to their knees. The terribly sick and hurt can not be evacuated to the rear and are forced to keep up. Many pray for the release of death. By the time they emerge from the mountains on the 28th, still far from Buna, they are nearly finished as a fighting force.

CHAPTER 10

LIMITED OFFENSIVE ACTION ON THE MATANIKAU

If I were king, the worst punishment I could inflict on my enemies would be to banish them to the Solomons.

—Jack London

The first three days of October brought more intensive Japanese air raids down from Rabaul. Vice Admiral Seizo Yamagata had gathered almost 200 planes in the 26th Air Flotilla, half of them Zekes, and announced he would use them to flatten Henderson Field.

The 2nd of September was a rough day for the CAF, which had serious difficulties getting its planes up in sufficient time to break up the increased air attacks. Marine Wildcat pilot Major Galer—who had run his string of victories up to eleven enemy aircraft destroyed—was himself shot down. He managed to parachute from his battered plane and was soon picked up, ready to fly again. After more attacks the next day, the Japanese hadn't eliminated the CAF, and with the intrusion of a spate of bad weather, there was a seven-day lull in the Japanese air attacks. Marine Major Leonard "Duke" Davis brought 20 more Wildcats to the Canal.

Lieutenant General Masao Maruyama, commanding the 2nd Division (the famed Sendai Division—the Emperor's Own) of the 17th Army, landed safely at Tassafaronga on October 3rd at 8:00 P.M. After establishing his headquarters on the Mamura River the next day, he discovered that 2,000 of the 9,000 men who had preceded him had already been killed, and some 5,000 others were too weak to use in his new offensive. Many members of the once proud units no longer had any equipment to fight with. Although Kawaguchi, again on the Canal, had been ordered to occupy portions of the east bank of the Matanikau River, he had not done so because of the desperate circumstances of his surviving troops.

Maruyama posted his 29th Infantry, commanded by Colonel Masajiro Furimiya, on the coast between the Matanikau and the Poha Rivers, and placed the 16th Infantry between the Poha and Mamura Rivers. Kawaguchi's exhausted 124th Infantry was moved far to the west to guard the coast near Tassafaronga Point. It was the possible presence of this force—by no means verified—that concerned Vandegrift.

October 7—Third Battle of the Matanikau

The new American attack plan was based on the belief that the Japanese had already moved into positions along the west bank of the mouth of the Matanikau preparatory to another large-scale attack on the airfield. Five of his ten available infantry battalions with supporting sniper-scouts, artillery, and air support—larger than the first group sent in a couple of weeks previously—would be involved. Vandegrift hoped to seize Kokumbona, and possibly establish a garrison there to curtail enemy movements in the area. Two battalions of Edson's 5th Marines would lead an attack at the mouth of the river to make the enemy think that was the main thrust, while the forces under Colonel Whaling crossed to the west about 1,800–2,000 yards upstream, and wheeled north to push the Japanese into a pocket. Hanneken would follow with a second group, and Puller, with a third group even farther upriver, would also wheel right to get behind the Japanese and trap and destroy them. Each successive unit would push on three or four hundred yards past the other before cutting back toward the sea. Another force was ready to move by sea, in Higgins Boats, and land behind the enemy to close the pocket, if needed.

The success of the new attack depended heavily on Edson's diversion at the river mouth. The advance was delayed as the marines spent precious time filling their canteens from a water trailer that had been trucked in from the rear. Those marines had already hiked ten miles in sweltering strength-sapping heat just to reach this position, so they needed water badly. At 10:15 A.M. the advance guard of the 3rd Battalion, 5th Marines was stopped by machine gun fire half a mile short of the river. By noon the Japanese began falling back to previously prepared positions. With the enemy engaged at the river mouth, the 2nd Battalion, 5th Marines moved to the left of the 3rd Battalion and quickly reached the river. Whaling's group, including the 3rd Battalion, 2nd Marines—accompanied by the scout-snipers along with two battalions of the 7th Marines, now under the command of Colonel Amor Leroy Sims—would cross the river north of the 5th Marines, who turned south heading for their jump-off point. Once there, they were to dig in for the night preparatory to their attack in the morning.

"Few Americans have ever heard of the Matanikau River, to say nothing of its Third Battle," reported John Hersey, in his stirring memoir *Into the Valley*. "The river is a light brown stream winding through a jungle valley about five miles west of Henderson Field. When I arrived on Guadalcanal, our forces did not hold positions out to the Matanikau. The Japs were moving up in some strength, evidently to try to establish their bridgehead—the first in a series of heavy moves against our camp. It became imperative for our troops to push to the river and force the enemy back beyond it, before it was too late."

Hersey's vivid images of worn and weary marines in yet another ordinary combat situation accurately portrayed the ragged columns of young malaria-ridden soldiers dragging their way through the stinking and verdant green hell of a jungle.

The first artillery barrage—outgoing 75-mm and 105-mm shells—broke the stillness of the morning as the men got in position to move out. At 8:30 the column started to move forward along the rugged trail. The 7th Marines under Colonel Sims started off about eight miles from the Matanikau, but the difficulty of the terrain would force a march of at least fifteen miles before contact.

Warned to keep a sharp eye out for snipers, the troops—accompanied by Hersey—began moving forward along a trail winding through the jungle and occasionally opening into clearings. At about 3:15 P.M. the column reached the top of a broad and fairly high ridge overlooking more jungle, only to discover they didn't know where they were. They were befuddled by a maze of interlocking ridges across the line of march, and thwarted by the dense undergrowth in the ravines.

In the distance ahead, Whaling's force came under fire from snipers, machine guns, and mortars. The approach of night soon curtailed the forward motion. Soon the walking wounded began struggling their way back, up over a steep slope, into the new bivouac. At about 6:15 P.M. it was almost completely dark and rain was expected. As near to the equator as Guadalcanal is, the tropical days and nights are of about equal length.

Cascading rains swept the area on the 8th and turned the soft ground along the river into an ankle-deep swamp, forcing Vandegrift to postpone the attack for twenty-four hours. During that time artillery and systematic mortar barrages fell on the Japanese positions across the river's mouth from Edson. Apparently by 6:30 P.M. the bombardment goaded the Japanese into trying to escape their trap. That hapless unit ran into the Raiders' position, and in furious hand-to-hand fighting that lasted forty-five minutes the small force was decimated. Fifty-nine Japanese bodies testified to the ferocity of the fighting.

Battle surgeons and corpsmen worked through the night under ponchos rigged to hide the flashlight beams to treat the twenty-two wounded Raiders. Of less than 100 Raiders in the fight, twelve were killed. This firefight was the last for the badly depleted Raiders on Guadalcanal.

When the Whaling group resumed the attack the next morning, it went smoothly as planned. His 3rd Battalion, 2nd Marines crossed the ford known as "The Jap Bridge," wheeled right and advanced along a ridge line to the sea, meeting no resistance. Lieutenant Colonel Hanneken's battalion of the 7th Marines pushed on for about 200 yards to the west after crossing the ford, then attacked to the north. Last in line, Lieutenant Colonel Puller's battalion of the 7th Marines pushed on beyond Hanneken's force, then also turned north for their attack toward Point Cruz. Crossing over the steep and muddy ridges and ravines, which ran north and south, was difficult and slowed the advance. Once the units swung northward, the going was much easier and resulted in faster forward movement.

Puller's group was the only big unit to run into resistance. His flankers, moving in the jungle brush along the ravine, discovered a large group of Japanese in bivouac. He immediately called in artillery fire, and within minutes 105-mm shells from the 11th Marines erupted in the encampment. Japanese troops who ran for the cover of the opposite ridge from their concealment in the jungle ran into a fusillade of mortar and machine gun fire, which drove them back into the path of the horrifying shellfire. When Puller's battalion withdrew from this valley of death, more than 700 corpses of the Japanese 3rd Battalion, 4th Infantry littered the jungle. In this encounter—which wrecked the Japanese 4th Division—the Marines lost fewer than 200 men killed and wounded.

At this point Vandegrift unexpectedly ordered the surprisingly successful operation terminated and called the Whaling force back to the Lunga perimeter. The 5th Marines were ordered to hold and improve their newly won positions at the mouth of the Matanikau. Maruyama's forces had been driven back roughly two miles from the outlet of the river, losing key offensive positions and sites for "Pistol Pete's" artillery bombardment of Henderson Field. The reduction of enemy artillery fire on the airfield had been one of Vandegrift's objectives in this limited offensive.

The timing of the new U.S. attack, however, had more fortuitous benefits than the destruction of a large Japanese force. Among the Japanese documents found in the cauldron of a crater was a new order. It read:

> "From now on, the occupying of Guadalcanal Island is under the observation of the whole world. Do not expect to return, not even one man, if the occupation is not successful. Everyone must remember the honor of the Emperor, fear no enemy, yield to no material matter, show the strong points of steel or of rocks, and advance valiantly and ferociously. Hit the enemy opponents so hard they will not be able to get up again."

Another document that delighted the ragged American rabble who continued to fight the Japanese into the ground was a fanciful report of supposed marine atrocities.

> "The Americans on this island are not ordinary troops, but Marines, a special force recruited from jails and insane asylums for blood lust. There is no honorable death to prisoners, their arms are cut off, they are staked on the airfield, and run over by steam rollers."

There were atrocities committed by both sides. One—the case of a marine who had been hung upside down and bayoneted and hacked to death—was meant to strike fear into American hearts. It had the result of steeling those hearts with the thought that no death was too gruesome for their implacable enemy. Had the marines known of the "medical experiments" taking place on the island, where a few Japanese doctors operated without anesthesia on living subjects—removing parts of the victim's body, including internal organs such as the liver—it is difficult to visualize what the consequences would have been. One Japanese officer who witnessed such an experiment later wrote in his diary that it was a most informative demonstration.

New Japanese Threat

General Hyakutake, accompanied by Kawaguchi and Colonels Norio Konuma and Masanobu Tsuji, waded ashore at Tassafaronga Point at midnight on October 9th. The 17th Army artillery commander, Major General Tadashi Sumiyoshi, landed with them. Their party encountered ragged and terribly emaciated survivors of the Ichiki and Kawaguchi units, who offered to help unload the supplies, including bags of rice. At breakfast time, in a new headquarters positioned five miles west of the Matanikau, Hyakutake was informed that most of the rice had been "liberated" by the helpers!

"Along the coast near Hyakutake's headquarters the last survivors of the Battle of Bloody Ridge were stumbling out of the jungle." wrote Toland. "Their ribs protruded.

Their black hair had turned a dirty drown and could be pulled out in patches. Their eyebrows and eyelashes were dropping off and their teeth were loose. For almost three weeks no one had had a bowel movement, and their bodies were so starved for salt that the sea water tasted sweet. The water brought on a painful urge to evacuate, but they were too weak. They had to help each other with fingers. The relief was indescribable."

One wretched survivor of Kawaguchi's retreat through the jungle, a private who was now recuperating near Tassafaronga, wrote in his diary of his agonizing ordeal. "Rations are gone and our clothing is in rags. I wonder how long this will last and pray it will soon be over. It makes me feel like a little bird in the rain. I am lonesome and think of my native village."

When Hyakutake learned of the extent of damage inflicted on his troops by the Marine victory on the Matanikau, especially the loss of 700 men of the 4th Infantry's 3rd Battalion, a different battle plan had to be devised. The surprising *seishin*—courageous fighting spirit—of the marines was now recognized and had to be taken into account. A straightforward drive along the coast and across the river was scrapped, and a new plan to attack Henderson Field from the rear was quickly devised. The 2nd Division forced its way through the mantrap of a jungle to behind Mount Austen. This peak was not a continuous height, but rather an interlocking network of rising ridges and deep crevasses.

The major attack by Lieutenant General Maruyama's Sendai Division would begin after the artillery laid down a barrage from the west bank on American positions, by a regimental-sized diversion at that spot a few hours before the division moved to the main attack. The central attack from the south would be a two-pronged assault. Major General Yomio Nasu would lead the main body and approach between Bloody Ridge and the Lunga River. Kawaguchi would lead the right wing east of Bloody Ridge—over much the same formidably rugged ground he'd seen before and now justifiably dreaded. He had just returned from a meeting of Army and Navy commanders in Rabaul where he had related the extraordinary difficulties inherent in forcing passage through jungle that was little more than a sinkhole for men and equipment. His unpleasant report was largely ignored, and the manipulative and scheming Tsuji considered him an ineffective loser trying to justify his lack of success in capturing Edson's Ridge and Henderson Field.

Colonel Matsumoto, the Sendai's intelligence officer, went over aerial photographs with the engineers in preparation for cutting the new trail. Not able to see beneath the solid cover of the jungle, he decided there would be no undue difficulty in completing the essential supply line. Matsumoto had been interrogating captured Americans about Marine positions, but despite being tortured they had refused to talk, which surprised him greatly. They were then beheaded—a death bestowed on honorable warriors. Colonel Masajiro Furimiya, 29th Infantry commander, secretly admired the fortitude of the captives.

The outcome would depend largely upon the timely arrival of artillery and ammunition to cover troop movements along the almost completed fifteen-mile-long "Maruyama Road." Swinging out from behind Mount Austen north along the Lunga at a point near the airfield, the passage out of the thick jungle had been hacked out by Japanese Army Engineers using only hand tools in the month-long effort. They had to cut through arm-thick vines and fell huge trees to clear the way, and they used some of the logs to span the marshes. Primitive bridges were constructed of thick vines for footholds and smaller vines for handholds lashed together in precarious spans to help the men cross the deeper and more treacherous ravines.

A U.S. transport group carrying the 164th Infantry Regiment, Americal Division, left Nouméa on October 9th covered by three forces: the Task Force around *Hornet* under Rear Admiral L.W. Murray; the battleship *Washington* led by Rear Admiral Willis A. "Ching" Lee; and a cruiser group under Rear Admiral Norman Scott.

An attack force of thirty-five Betties escorted by thirty Zekes raided the field on the 8th. Eight Betties and four Zekes were destroyed—a high price for the Japanese to pay for only minimal damage to the airfield.

The Japanese planes had distracted the CAF's attention away from transports bringing more men, supplies, and equipment for Maruyama's grand new attack. Coastwatcher Martin Clemens presented a detailed and accurate count of the numbers of troops and weapons so far landed to the skeptical marines. Many of the native scouting force—at great risk to their lives—had "volunteered" to help the Japanese unload their transports.

This was "an actual count, and not an estimate!" Clemens insisted fiercely, reacting to the skepticism toward the remarkable intelligence gathered on the new Japanese buildup. Their information, obtained on the scene, was entirely accurate. In his frustration, he must have wondered if the opinionated Marine intelligence section back in their bunkers had learned anything about the capabilities of his small but audacious group since the Ichiki attack back in August.

Natives scouts located a Japanese radio outpost in the village of Gurabusu, about 30 miles east of the perimeter. The equivalent of a couple of companies of survivors of failed actions in the area had concentrated at Koilotumaria, five miles closer to the perimeter. The 1st Battalion, 2nd Marines from Tulagi, led by Lieutenant Colonel Robert E. Hill, was assigned the task of seeking out and destroying these concentrations.

Four officers and 430 men aboard eight Higgins Boats towed by two YP boats headed for Aola at 3:30 P.M. on the 9th. When one Higgins Boat came apart from excess strain, three sailors, one marine officer, and fourteen of his men drowned. The rest kept going, but with coordination lost the others straggled in from 1:00 A.M. through noon of the 10th. Hill promptly moved A and B Companies out for an overnight approach to Koilotumaria.

At dawn on the 11th, Captain Richard Y. Stafford's Company B caught the Japanese at Gurabusu sleeping and by 8:30 killed thirty-two men. During the brief skirmish Stafford was killed and two Japanese escaped into the jungle. The body of Ishimoto, the spy-shipwright who had tortured Vouza in August, was identified by natives. As a key officer in the Japanese occupation, he had tried to gain the allegiance of the natives of Guadalcanal. His often brutal verbal and physical personal assaults in the name of the Japanese Empire had not won many converts. A collection of Roman Catholic artifacts, including vestments, altar cloths, chalice, and pattens from the Ruavatu mission were recovered. A chalice was being used as an ashtray. Back in late August he had summoned two priests and two nuns from the mission, made them prisoners, and then had them murdered on September 3rd.

Delayed by the difficult terrain, Hill's force did not arrive at Koilotumaria until late afternoon. The village was all but deserted, for when the Japanese had heard the gunfire from Gurabusu, most ran south into the jungle. Three of the enemy who remained were killed, with one marine dead and one wounded. The battalion arrived back at Tulagi on October 12th.

Attempts to clean out the isolated pockets of stragglers in the east were to continue, although these units alone posed no serious threat to the Marine perimeter. There was always the chance—despite the shift of most operations to the area west of Henderson Field—that Japanese reinforcements would find these pockets of men and incorporate them into a larger assault force.

Chapter 11

October 11–12
Battle of Cape Esperance

It now appears that we are unable to control the sea in the Guadalcanal area. Thus our supply of the positions will only be done at great expense to us. The situation is not hopeless, but it certainly is critical.

—Admiral Chester W. Nimitz

The four Patrol-Torpedo (PT) boats of Squadron 3 were moving into their new station at Government Wharf on Tulagi Island, thirty miles across Sealark Channel from Guadalcanal. The original Squadron 3, commanded by the legendary John Bulkeley, had been wiped out in the early Philippine Islands actions. These PT boats were substantially improved over the models available at the beginning of the war. This was the first combat exposure for most of the crew. The boats had been towed into the area from the New Hebrides, their arrival greeted with derisive chants from the big ship sailors: "Rub-a-dub-dub, five gobs in a tub!"

On October 9th, Marine Captain Joseph J. Foss landed at Guadalcanal as executive officer of VMF-121. Major John Smith and the remnants of VMF-223 departed the Canal three days later. Smith would take part in a war-bond selling tour and morale-building rallies that showed off America's heroes, after which he was assigned to train hundreds of other John Smiths.

The 164th Infantry—a reinforced regiment of the Americal Division, commanded by Colonel Bryant E. Moore—was aboard two large transports nearing Guadalcanal escorted by eight destroyers under Rear Admiral Turner. Task Force 64, a four-cruiser group with a five-destroyer screen under Rear Admiral Norman Scott—whom historian Samuel Eliot Morison called, "a young and brilliant flag officer"—was assigned to run interference and keep the Japanese away from the troop convoy.

Rear Admiral Aritomo Goto was leading a bombardment group with the heavy cruisers *Aoba*, *Furutaka*, and *Kinugasa* of Cruiser Division Six, escorted by two destroyers, *Fubuki* and *Hatsuyuki*. Their mission was to plaster Henderson Field and destroy the CAF with 8-inch shells retrofitted with antiaircraft timed fuses designed to burst above the field and shower the surface with shell fragments. This group had managed to approach Guadalcanal almost undetected, as they had selected a course outside the Slot, and did not expect to engage American ships.

The separate Reinforcement Group was composed of the destroyers *Asagumo*, *Natsugumo*, *Yamagumo*, *Murakamo*, *Shirayuki*, and *Akizuki*, and the seaplane tenders *Nisshin* and *Chitose*. The tenders were carrying 280 soldiers, some heavy artillery, howitzers, and antiaircraft guns with ammunition and equipment. Five of the six destroyers were ferrying fresh troops to Tassafaronga. These two groups of the Tokyo Express came at night. The Japanese were so convinced that the Americans would shun a night engagement that they sent in the Reinforcement Group hours before the Bombardment Group. After all, eight Allied cruisers and three destroyers had been sunk in night encounters, without any losses for the Japanese.

Scott's Task Force 64 had the heavy cruisers *San Francisco* (his flagship) and *Salt Lake City*, light cruisers *Boise* and *Helena*, with the destroyers *Farenholt*, *Duncan*, and *Laffey* leading, *Buchanan* and *McCalla* following, steaming in a column north of Guadalcanal's Cape Esperance. They did not really know the Japanese were coming. Still, the men—weary from the strain of months at sea—were as ready as they could be. On *San Francisco* gun trainer Boatswain's Mate 2nd Class Vance Carter was always fully dressed and never without his lifejacket and belt knife. Like most of his shipmates, he slept on the steel decks near his battle station, fearful of being trapped in his own bunk below decks.

Scout planes were launched from *San Francisco* and *Boise*, but when *Salt Lake City* attempted to launch hers, the plane burst into flames from her own flares and was shoved overboard. The plane burning in the water could be seen fifty miles to the north by Goto's sailors, but he dismissed the idea that American ships were in the area because he simply did not expect to find any.

A scout plane reported sighting one large and two small vessels off Guadalcanal six miles from Savo, but Scott didn't think this was the force he was looking for. It was just before midnight when they intercepted the Japanese bombardment fleet. Radar aboard *Helena* made first contact with Goto's force coming out of a series of rain squalls at 11:25 P.M., locating the enemy ships at 27,700 yards and coming from the northwest at 35 knots. At 11:23 Scott ordered the column to make a reverse course change, which would place the Japanese to starboard of the column now steaming to the southwest. In a misunderstanding of orders for the column to come about, the leading destroyers split away during the turn. For a few crucial moments Goto thought that these American destroyers—spotted off his port bow, and jockeying for a torpedo run to protect the turning column—were his own Japanese Reinforcement Group appearing where they shouldn't be.

San Francisco's fire control radar found the Japanese column only 5,000 yards distant. From some station on *Helena* came the report that the oncoming enemy ships were now visible to the naked eye—which meant they were much too close. An impatient ensign asked urgently, "What are we going to do? Board them?"

Admiral Scott had issued orders that any of his ships could open fire once a target had been positively identified without having to ask for permission to do so. Captain Gilbert Hoover on *Helena*, concerned about the position of the American destroyers, queried Scott over the TBS for a clarification. However, before a clear answer could be received, Hoover knew the ships he had sighted were Japanese and that the time had come to engage the enemy. He gave the order for *Helena* to open fire.

At 11:46 P.M. the fifteen guns of *Helena*'s main battery shattered the darkness of the night with flame and the rumbling of shells. This first screeching salvo of 8-inch, 6-inch, and 5-inch shells tore through the superstructure of *Aoba*, mortally wounding Goto and killing others on the flag bridge. Goto thought it was his own ships firing on him, and as he lay dying cursed the "stupid bastard" who had done the damage. Almost immediately shells fired from other ships—notably *Boise*, about 4,500 yards away—demolished two 8-inch turrets and the main battery director. The big guns of the Tokyo Express began returning fire. Goto ordered his ships to cease fire and turn right, a movement that allowed them to unlimber all their guns. The churning water from the turns allowed the Americans to mass their fire on each Japanese ship as it advanced.

In reversing the direction of his column of ships at the northern end of his patrol area, Scott had managed to "cross the T" of the Japanese. In this classic and highly desired naval maneuver, his column of ships was able to bring all guns to bear, from his starboard, against the approaching Japanese column, who could employ only their forward guns. After his first salvos were fired, Scott thought his ships were firing at each other and ordered a momentary cease-fire. Fortunately, some of his ships ignored the order, because they were certain they were blasting Japanese ships. At 11:51 Scott again ordered all his ships to resume firing. The destroyer *Laffey* swung in behind the cruisers as the destroyers *Farenholt* and *Duncan* sailed between the opposing cruisers.

On *San Francisco*, which had become the lead ship, Captain Charles "Doc" McMorris's lookouts spotted a ship paralleling their course, switched on their searchlights and identified *Fubuki*. The already trained guns opened up with a merciless barrage that shattered the Japanese destroyer. She broke apart and went to the bottom at just before midnight. The gunfire from Scott's ships then turned on the fleeing cruisers—*Aoba* with *Furutaka* directly behind trying to protect the mangled flagship—inflicting more damage. Watching the effects of the shells wrecking the latter from his telescope in Turret Number 2 on *San Francisco*, Boatswain's Mate Carter felt a surprising sense of sadness at seeing the enemy ship being reduced to a flaming pile of junk.

But the cruiser *Kinugasa* remained in the fight, booming a salvo from 8,000 yards. Her 8-inch shells straddled *Boise*, which swung about on a hard right rudder to avoid torpedoes. *Farenholt* absorbed two friendly hits that holed her port side just above the waterline, and forced the abandonment of her Number One Fire Room. Before being let off the hook, *Boise* picked up *Aoba* with her searchlights, which *Kinugasa* promptly shot out, followed by accurate gunfire that poured shell after shell into *Boise*. One shell, at ten minutes after midnight, jammed the Number 1 Gun, starting a smoky fire that caused its abandonment. Eleven gunners had reached the main deck when another 8-inch shell penetrated and exploded in the main magazine between Turrets 1 and 2, igniting the exposed powder into a flaming gas that roared through all forward areas and burned nearly one hundred men to death. *Salt Lake City* moved in between the battling ships and drove off *Kinugasa*.

Just after midnight the heavy shooting was over, but the battle for survival on some of the ships was just beginning. The desperately hurt *Furutaka* managed to crawl twenty-two miles northwest of Savo before she slipped forever beneath the waves. The mangled *Aoba* managed to escape the seething cauldron off Cape Esperance, but was forced to return to Japan for repairs. The intact and unhurt destroyer *Hatsuyuki* and the lightly damaged *Kinugasa* sped off to the north.

The destroyer *Duncan*, after taking hits from both sides, was abandoned a couple of hours later. Scott detached *McCalla* to pick up swimmers—the survivors—and nearly all were found and rescued. *Duncan* could not be saved and had to be scuttled late in the afternoon. *Boise* was ablaze, as her damage control and firefighting teams struggled to save their ship. With the help of the seawater that had rushed in through holes in her hull and flooded the magazines, the fires were put out and *Boise* made it back to Nouméa for repairs. The lightly damaged *Salt Lake City* had taken a hit that temporarily knocked out her power, but sailed to safety on her own.

Shortly after dawn of the 12th, SBD scouts of VS-71 caught up with the destroyer *Murakumo* at 8:20 as she was running north, but they failed to stop her. On her decks were packed together survivors of *Fubuki* and *Furutaka*. A second air strike of seven VS-71s and a VMSB-141 under Lieutenant Commander Kirn, along with six TBFs of VT-8 under Lieutenant H.H. Larsen, again found *Murakumo* and *Shirayuki* and resumed the attack. The dive bombers scored another near miss and the fourteen escorting Wildcats of VMF-121 and VMF-224 strafed the fleeing destroyers 170 miles from Guadalcanal. A third attack—highlighted by a torpedo hit from one of the TBFs from Torpedo-8—stopped *Murakumo*, forcing hundreds of sailors into the water. She had to be scuttled that evening. In the afternoon the destroyer *Natsugumo* had joined *Shirayuki* to pick up survivors when American SBDs led by Lieutenant Commander John Eldridge attacked. This time the Americans got a direct hit on *Natsugumo*—followed by two near misses from other SBDs—that caused her to sink about half an hour later. (A "near miss"—at perhaps twenty to thirty yards—could bend the steel hull, pop the rivets and separate the hull plates, and shower a ship with bomb fragments.)

In this battle one Japanese light cruiser and three destroyers were sunk by Scott's blocking force. For the first time in these deadly waters, the Americans had inflicted the heavier damage to the Japanese in a head-on battle. In retrospect, Scott's victory was due more to preparedness than flawless planning. His men and ships were ready for a fight, while those under Goto were not. Historian Richard B. Frank points out the sobering fact that the cruiser *Furutaka* was the largest Japanese warship sunk during a surface ship action in the Solomons area in 1942 and 1943. Counting the two enemy destroyers sunk by the CAF, the Americans were the clear victors. On the downside, the Japanese reinforcement group got through without opposition and landed tanks, artillery, ammunition, food, and troops that materially increased the Japanese 17th Army's strength on Guadalcanal. Yet Scott's force had distracted the IJN away from his reason for being there—a large American reinforcement of Guadalcanal. No Japanese ships appeared the night of the 12th.

Army's 164th Infantry Arrives

On the clear and bright morning of October 13th Turner and his transports sailed safely into Sealark Channel, dropped anchor off Lunga Point, and landed the Army's 164th Infantry Regiment and its equipment. Waiting on the beach to board those same ships when they left Guadalcanal were the haggard and battered tough "old" men of the 1st Raider Battalion.

Included in this needed infusion of strength were 210 ground personnel of the 1st Marine Air Wing. Probably the most important items to be found on the beach that day were several hundred cases of candy bars brought in by the Army. By 9:00 that Tuesday morning every marine with half a reason had sneaked through the shadowy coconut trees and down to the beach to begin trading his "authentic" souvenirs for candy. A samurai sword could be exchanged for three dozen large Hershey bars, and a Japanese "meatball" battle flag fetched a dozen. Candy bars were an indisputable luxury on the island, whereas additional enemy souvenirs could easily be picked up any old time. On display at this impromptu bazaar were Japanese rifles, helmets, pistols, sabers, and even officer's map cases.

The resourceful marines produced excellent copies of battle flags when the supply of originals ran low. To panels of silk cut from slightly used parachutes it was easy to add the meatball from supplies of red ink. Captured rubber stamps were used to add the Japanese characters, usually mottoes and divine exhortations.

"Flags were always good for trading," recalls Lieutenant J.G. "Ken" Morgan, the misplaced dentist. "But later one officer, who could read Japanese, pointed out that many were fakes. Seems the rubber stamped characters often meant something like 'file copy' or 'please handle soon' or some other office instruction."

Morgan was given a souvenir he never parted with. Soon after the landing some marines looked up the young Navy dental officer and presented him with a beautifully encased set of Japanese dental instruments designed for use in the field. They had found it in the piles of enemy equipment left behind. He never found out just how effective the enemy's dental service was, but admitted that they did have nice tools to work with.

The weary Marine presence was bolstered by the three thousand men of the 164th National Guardsmen from the Dakotas. With them they brought in their forty-four jeeps, twenty 1/2-ton and seventeen 1-1/2-ton trucks, sixteen British Bren gun carriers, twelve 27-mm guns, five units of fire, seventy days' rations, sixty days' supplies, and tentage, ammunition, and standard supplies for the marines, all unloaded by noon. This unit was, on the average, ten years older than the marines they were reinforcing. Within the next couple of nights they probably aged even faster.

The Army had barely arrived and moved their equipment inland when without warning about twenty-seven Betties heavily escorted by Zekes attacked Henderson Field and the new "Fighter One" supplemental airstrip, about 2,000 yards long, located a little more than a mile to the east. They cratered both fields with 500-pound bombs dropped from 30,000 feet, and set fire to 5,000 gallons of precious aviation gas. All of CAF's forty-two Wildcats got off the ground, but were unable to climb to combat altitude until too late. Only one Betty and one Zeke were shot down.

The Japanese had now discovered the supplemental strip, which had been roughed out in early September. The Seabees had hacked down an area of 8- to 10-foot-tall sage grass with machetes to about 18 inches. They rolled down the grass and filled in depressions to create a rough landing strip. Farther up the Slot, Coastwatchers Read and Mason were unable to send an alert because they were being chased by the Japanese, and the new radar unit was temporarily out of action.

Caught napping, the CAF scrambled desperately to get fighters off the field and into the air while some parked planes were destroyed on the ground. Later that day, at about 1:30, a second surprise Japanese raid hit the field as aircraft were being refueled and rearmed, inflicting serious damage. Trying to get a fighter into the air while dodging bomb craters and strafing Zekes is extremely difficult.

The only American to shoot down an enemy plane that day was VMF-121 Marine Captain Joe Foss, who, coincidentally, hailed from near Sioux Falls, South Dakota, the same region as the newly arrived soldiers. In the fight, the green division leader's Wildcat was shot up. He was forced to make a dead-stick landing at full speed, and piled up at the end of the runway. He climbed unaided from the wreck and was driven back to his tent. Embarrassed by the episode, he quickly proceeded to learn the needed lessons about aerial combat. Foss became one of America's foremost aces, the first aviator in WWII to match the record of twenty-six kills set by Captain Eddie Rickenbacker in WWI. He was awarded the Medal of Honor for his achievements.

By now the Japanese had hauled their big 150-mm howitzers into position and "Pistol Pete" began preparations for the painstaking registration of the guns. Located to the west of the perimeter, they were far enough away to be safe from the 11th Marine counterbattery fire. The howitzers were a more potent and continuous threat than the enemy airplanes or ships could be. A few well placed shells could drive off the men working on the airfield, cease fire, wait until they tried to return to repairing the damage, and pump in more shells.

The Tokyo Express brought down the battleships *Kongo* and *Haruna*, which lit up the sweltering night of October 13–14 with high-intensity flares. The huge 14-inch shells fired by the two battleships—in the most concentrated, terrifying, and destructive bombardment of the entire campaign, which the Japanese equated to the firing of a thousand field guns—caused the ground to erupt, shake, and tremble like a prolonged earthquake. Marines, pilots, and soldiers shivered in abject terror in their foxholes, as their positions were shattered by detonations from more than 900 rounds of high-explosive and armor-piercing 14-inch shells. The barrage killed and wounded many of the totally helpless, rattled defenders, who were unable to hit back. Some of the hardiest and bravest of men when fighting the Japanese face-to-face—but who were in this case unable to handle the fear created that night by this unseen enemy—actually went insane.

Seabee Shipfitter 1st Class Dune Gillis remembered that between the shelling and the rain that terrible night Guadalcanal "was one helluva mess. Those big 14-inch babies would come whistling in, go off, and you'd rattle around in your foxhole like a ping-pong ball." In a lull between shellings, he heard a cry for help from nearby. He and his buddy, Shipfitter 1st Class Howard L. Osborn, from Dearborn, Michigan, dashed to a hole where eight other Seabees had been buried by a close hit. They had gotten five of the men out of the debris when the shelling resumed, and their five helpers ran back to their holes.

"Osborn and I were kind of crazy, but I'll always remember what he said: 'I'm still with yuh, Dune.'

"This was all located in a coconut grove, and trees were every which way, and dirt and mud scattered all over...we used our helmets and our hands. The shelling was scaring the hell out of us, but by this time we were working too fast to care." One man was stuck up to his armpits and another, Carpenter's Mate 1st Class Wayman M. Carlisle, from Morning View, Kentucky, was buried up to his neck, his head barely showing. They dug him out while the shells were still ravaging the area. One man was recovered dead, most likely killed by the concussion. For this stunning effort under heavy fire, both Dune Gillis and Howard Osborn were awarded the Silver Star.

The perimeter was in shambles, debris scattered all over the area. Damage to the airfield from the shelling was devastating, and thirty-four of thirty-nine SBDs were destroyed or knocked out of commission. Sixteen of forty Wildcats were destroyed, and another twenty-four were damaged by direct hits from the scything shrapnel or by the fierce fires burning out of control. Forty-eight aircraft in all were destroyed. Huge craters had been blown in the runway and adjacent work area, with some large segments of the steel Marston matting landing several hundred yards away. Nearly all of the aviation gasoline supply on the Canal had been ignited, and the roiling flames and voluminous choking smoke made it difficult to see or breathe.

Seabee Commander Blundon later related, "We found 100 Seabees could repair the damage of a 500-pound bomb-hit on an airstrip in forty minutes, including the replacing of the Marston mat. In other words, forty minutes after that bomb exploded, you couldn't tell the airstrip had ever been hit. But we needed all of this speed and more. In twenty-four hours on October 13 and 14, fifty-three bombs and shells hit the Henderson airstrip! During one hour on the 14th we filled thirteen bomb craters while our planes circled around overhead waiting to land. We got no food during that period because our cooks were all busy passing up the steel plank. There were not enough shovels to go around, so some of our men used their helmets to scoop up earth and carry it to the bomb craters."

The newly arrived VMSB-141 suffered appalling human losses: its squadron commander, executive officer, and flight officer were all killed in the deadly shelling. It was relegated to a battered and depleted force before the squadron learned enough about operations to become effective.

Private 1st Class Warner Pyne, P Battery, 5th Battalion, 11th Marines, from Pelham Manor, New York, enlisted at age seventeen and was waiting to be called up before Pearl Harbor was attacked. He was in the command post when the shelling began, but one of the men cracked up and Pyne scrambled to another hole about a half mile away. During the night that command post took a direct hit, killing everyone who had remained there.

"I mean, that's all she wrote, nothing! The nine men at the post were all blown out of town," he later related. "The place where I had been [minutes before] was obliterated."

No one slept well on the island that night or the next. Sealark Channel was coming to be known as "Sleepless Lagoon." When the massive shells began exploding and shaking the ground tens of thousands of berserk rats were driven from their nests. They scurried all over the area and into the holes occupied by the terrified men, who had to fight them off, screaming at this new outrage.

"Anybody who says a naval bombardment ain't worse than any artillery shelling is absolutely crazy," said one marine. One shell made a direct hit on a bunker near the galley, killing almost everyone taking shelter there. "We tried to dig the men out but we saw it wasn't any use." Within a couple of nights another 2,000 rounds of 14-inch shells tore into and blasted the airfield and landing beach.

A sense of black humor came through in the most critical of times. One story has it that a group of marines were cowering in a bunker for protection from the huge shells, when one asked, "D'ya think if I lit up a cigarette right now, I'd give away our position?"

Another marine, frightened by the bombardment, dashed into the trees seeking concealment. He brushed up against something hard and unyielding—and cool. He hugged the object all through the night, satisfied that he was safe. In the morning, shaking his head in utter disbelief, he discovered that he had been embracing a 50-gallon barrel of high-octane aviation fuel, and realized that the penetration of the container by a single flaming piece of shrapnel would have ignited the fuel.

Time of Crisis

Under the cover of another nerve-wracking bombardment the next night, under the personal supervision of Mikawa on *Chokai* and *Kinugasa*, more Imperial troops came ashore west of the battered perimeter. The Henderson Field area took hits from 752 8-inch shells. If the Japanese High Command at Truk and Rabaul had taken time to digest their intelligence reports, which had determined the desperate panic and emotional vulnerability of the American defenders in the aftermath of the massive naval bombardments, a few more nights of such terror would have likely forced the giving up of the Canal that the deaths of thousands of Imperial foot soldiers had failed to achieve. When the combined minds of the Japanese Army and Navy belatedly reached that conclusion a month later, the time for easy victory had passed.

As if the morale of the suffering defenders was not bad enough at dawn on October 15th, they looked out onto the channel to see Japanese transports blithely unloading troops and supplies off Tassafaronga Point as if the Americans weren't even there! Support ships and planes were covering the bustling activity.

The flying distance from the field to the transports was 10 miles, but getting planes in the air off of the badly damaged field wouldn't be easy. When an angry General Roy Geiger was informed that there was no gasoline left on the airfield, he shouted, "Then, by God, find some!" Surprisingly, 400 drums of gasoline were retrieved from widely spread holes where they had been stored for safety, including the one that had provided a "safe shelter" for a lucky marine. A rough map listing the locations of the stashed fuel was actually at Geiger's headquarters, where the general, noted for his disdain of paperwork, had misplaced it.

This fortuitous hoard—plus every drop of gas that could be drained from wrecked planes—kept the fighters and dive bombers flying all day, raining death and destruction on the transports and driving off the air cover while shooting down twelve bombers and five Zeroes. American losses were three dive bombers and four fighters. From Guadalcanal the call for more aviation gas went out, and soon whatever transport was available in the South Pacific was flying in more fuel and bombs.

The volume and intensity of new Japanese activity prompted Vandegrift to inform Vice Admiral Ghormley that the Marine Expeditionary Force urgently needed maximum air and surface support if there was to be any hope of holding the island. Ghormley then warned Admiral Nimitz that the Japanese had initiated an all-out offensive and that his U.S. forces were totally inadequate to stop it.

This crucial situation had developed partly from the bitter interservice rivalry between the Navy/Marine forces employed on Guadalcanal and the forces available to

General MacArthur. The Air Force units controlled by MacArthur in the Southwest Pacific Command were denied to the beleaguered forces on Guadalcanal. MacArthur considered Guadalcanal a lost cause.

Now there was talk in Washington of giving up Guadalcanal. The American public was just learning some of the details about the humiliating and disastrous American losses in the Battle of Savo, which had taken place more than two months ago. Newspapers all over the nation were expressing grave doubts about the faltering campaign. The Joint Chiefs of Staff continued to assert that the priority destination for military production was the Atlantic and Europe. Army Air Force General "Hap" Arnold, back in Washington, DC, stymied Admiral King's requests for more high-altitude fighters, namely P-38 Lightnings. He was convinced the Navy didn't know how to fight a modern war with their own ships, much less with airpower. He knew the Navy was in trouble at Guadalcanal, but was certain that what they needed most of all were "leaders who know and understand modern warfare; men who are aggressive and not afraid to fight with their ships." A nice thought—when what was needed most at that moment were combat airplanes to support the island and protect the fleets from deadly Japanese air raids.

The reason Admiral King and the Navy sent the Marines to Guadalcanal in the first place was to stop the Japanese construction of an airfield to support their Imperial Fleet. While they recognized that the Japanese intended to use the airfield for that purpose, the Navy and Marines so far had not been able to develop Henderson Field as a major air base in order to control the air around Guadalcanal.

In reality, Henderson Field could not be developed as a major base as long as the field forces on Guadalcanal were fighting just to hang on to what they already had. To think of expanding an airfield that was constantly exposed to air attacks and warship bombardments was wishful thinking.

"Fear, horror, fatigue, anxiety: that was Guadalcanal for the navy as well as for the fliers, marines and army troops," observed Ronald H. Spector, naval historian. Until an unqualified commitment was made by the Joint Chiefs of Staff in Washington to take Guadalcanal and hold it, those conditions would continue to plague the men serving there.

Early in the morning, at 2:00 A.M., the PT boat sailors at Sesapi on Tulagi awakened to heavy naval gunfire reverberating across the channel. Once again the Tokyo Express had ventured down the Slot to bombard Henderson Field. Lieutenant Commander Alan Montgomery, Squadron 3 leader, rousted all hands into action, and soon the boats were manned and racing into harm's way. Montgomery ordered the boats deployed into attack formation. The crews knew where the enemy was; they could see the flashes from the Japanese guns.

Like mosquitoes, the small boats swarmed toward their target. Lieutenant John M. Searles, from Leonia, New Jersey, a Princeton graduate, was captain of PT *60*, in which squadron commander Montgomery rode. Following in his wake was PT *39*, skippered by Lieutenant Robert L. Searles, John's younger brother, also a Princeton grad.

Somehow the boats became separated and Bob Searles realized that PT *39* was racing toward the enemy alone. The lookouts spotted the outline of what appeared to be a light cruiser against the sporadic fire from ships and shore. Slowing PT *39* to ten knots, the boat loosed a pair of torpedoes from 400 yards, revved up the engines and charged in to fire the remaining two torpedoes from roughly 200 yards. As they spun away to clear the area, the intense heat from the fiery explosion at the cruiser's midships swept over them.

PT *60* was stalking a possible Japanese cruiser engaged in shelling Henderson Field. Just as they were about to launch their first two torpedoes, the boat was pinpointed in the intense beam of a destroyer's searchlight, and they came under fire from another destroyer. PT *60* continued its attack, firing two "fish" from less than 300 yards. As the boat veered away, Chief Machinist's Mate H.M. Ramsdell observed two explosions on the cruiser, which despite serious damage began firing and landed a shell close enough to solidly rock the small boat.

Suddenly the boat was caught between two searchlights and came under heavy Japanese fire from several destroyers. PT *60* was nearly lifted out of the water by a shell exploding about twenty-five yards away. The boat laid smoke to mask its course, and dropped a couple of depth charges to discourage pursuit as it put a safe distance between it and the enemy.

Then, creeping along off Sandfly Passage, at Florida Island's western tip, PT *60* ran aground on a coral reef. It was a desperate few minutes while the patrolling Japanese destroyer passed by without spotting the stranded boat. The plywood PTs were no match in a head-on fight with heavily armed and armored warships, and depended solely on surprise to get in close enough to release their torpedoes. So when it was time for these courageous sailors to run and hide, it was time to run and hide!

The naval forces had to improvise tactics and create doctrine as they went along, the same as the land forces slugging it out on Guadalcanal proper. There was no book or manual dictating this kind of toe-to-toe back alley combat. The small and vulnerable PT boat force adapted an Old West tactic that had been pioneered by the U.S. Cavalry to counter American Indian war parties. Scouts—one or two boats—would sortie each night to the entrance channels off Savo to lay in wait and watch for the arrival of the Tokyo Express. When they sounded the alert, the main boat force held in the rear would move out to attack the Japanese columns.

During midafternoon of the 15th Major Jack Cram, Brigadier General Roy Geiger's aide, on an "emergency supply run" from the New Hebrides—bringing two torpedoes—landed the general's assigned Catalina amphibian "Blue Goose" on Henderson Field. The fish were for the Navy's Torpedo Eight, but Cram insisted he was entitled to one of them. A young ensign flyer who was finished flying for the day said he could have both of them. The ground crew rigged mounts on the plane so that all he had to do was pull toggle switches to release the deadly warheads.

Cram took a long low approach to the Kokumbona target area, escorted by a single Wildcat. Flying though flak thrown up by Japanese destroyers that shook both pilot and plane, Cram tenaciously held to his course and released both torpedoes, one of which exploded into a beached transport, breaking her back. He turned the slow balky plane back for Henderson—with three Zekes swarming behind him. Antiaircraft fire and the patrolling Wildcats drove off two enemy fighters as Cram tried to land the now damaged and thoroughly perforated "Blue Goose."

He was coming in too fast to put down on Henderson Field, so he aimed at Fighter One. A Zeke followed him in, ready for the kill, when 1st Lieutenant Roger Haberman of VMF-121, his Wildcat smoking from damage and his wheels down for landing, swung over and shot the Zeke off Cram's tail. The big lumbering Catalina pancaked onto the strip, digging furrows in its wake. Despite nearly a hundred shrapnel and bullet holes, Cram and his crew climbed out of the patrol plane unhurt.

When Geiger heard of the exploit and came out and examined his battered personal aircraft, he roared, "Goddammit, Cram! I ought to court-martial you for the deliberate destruction of government property." The air chief returned to his office and wrote out a recommendation to award a Navy Cross to Major "Mad Jack" Cram.

The destroyer *Meredith* was sunk towing in a barge of gasoline and bombs for the CAF. The submarine *Amberjack* slipped in through the blockade to deliver 9,000 gallons of gasoline, while a small supply was ferried in by air. Fuel, bombs, and ammunition came through in dribs and drabs, at the expense of more food.

During the night of the 15th the Japanese cruisers *Myoko* and *Maya*, personally commanded by Admiral Kondo, fired 1,500 8-inch shells into U.S. positions from ranges of 8,000 to 10,000 yards. The barrage was far short of that inflicted on "The Night," but the casualty list grew, and shell fragments ripped into the parked planes. By dawn fifteen Wildcats had been wrecked. The CAF had only twenty-seven aircraft of all kinds left, and half of those needed to be repaired.

In the afternoon help began arriving in the form of drummed gasoline, spare parts, and more men for the maintenance crews, brought in by air transport from New Caledonia. Lieutenant Colonel Harold Bauer brought in the nineteen Wildcats of his VMF-212 late in the afternoon. The field was under "Condition Yellow." A Japanese attack group was on its way. Without reporting to Geiger, Bauer urged the ground crew to refuel a section of his fighters and got them off the ground, less than 60 minutes after his arrival. When Bauer and his section returned an hour later, he personally had shot down four Betties. His wingman enthusiastically summarized the feat in a few words, "The Chief stitched four of the bastards from end to end."

On the 16th planes from *Hornet* raided Rekata Bay at Santa Isabel and destroyed twelve Japanese seaplanes. Afterward they raided enemy positions on Guadalcanal. The next day the destroyers *Aaron Ward* and *Lardner* bombarded Japanese positions west of Kokumbona with 2,000 5-inch shells.

For the first time Admiral Nimitz made a public announcement that the situation at Guadalcanal was critical. Back in the States, a task force assembled around the battleship *Indiana* was ordered to the South Pacific. The Joint Chiefs of Staff committed the Army's

25th Infantry Division to the area, but not specifically to Guadalcanal. Fifty additional fighters, more B-17s, submarines, supplies, and equipment were authorized for movement to the South Pacific. The question was whether this buildup of forces would arrive in time to do any good. Ghormley did not think that it would. He thought it was a waste of men and materiel that could be better used at a later date.

The "Fighting Admiral" Takes Command

In Washington, the Joint Chiefs of Staff were jolted by a message from President Roosevelt: "My anxiety about the Southwest Pacific is to make sure that every possible weapon gets into that area to hold Guadalcanal." That "suggestion" from the American Commander-in-Chief was an order that quickly solved the many problems of moving men, ships, and aircraft to the combat zone, regardless of European priorities.

The Joint Chiefs of Staff, with King's concurrence, had already made a start: on the 16th of October they appointed Vice Admiral William F. Halsey—nicknamed "Bull" by reporters for his well known aggressive leadership, proven time and again in the early days of the war—to replace Vice Admiral Ghormley as Commander of the South Pacific Theater of Operations. Because of the tardy reports now reaching the public, many Americans incorrectly assumed that Ghormley was being sacked for the Navy failure at Savo. But it was his leadership that was in question—during his tenure of command he had never once visited Guadalcanal, and he had not sent any of his senior staff to the Canal to get a firsthand impression of the operation. The job he had been given was actually, at that point of the war, beyond the capability of most of his peers. His bad luck was to be in the wrong job, at the wrong place, at the wrong time.

At a meeting at his new headquarters on Nouméa, 900 miles from Guadalcanal, Halsey assembled his principal commanders: Generals Vandegrift and Harmon, and Admiral Turner. Vandegrift told him that the Americans could hold Guadalcanal if they could get the necessary supplies. Without any equivocation, Halsey promised to send him everything he needed to stay on the island. Fresh troops and materiel were streaming into the Pacific, and Halsey was determined to deliver them to where they were most needed. He told Vandegrift, "Go on back. I'll promise you everything I've got." It's a service axiom that a new broom sweeps clean. Halsey had brought along a huge broom and was about to kick up a lot of dust.

Additional reinforcements were headed for Guadalcanal, and barely in time. On the 20th the Japanese established a new fighter strip on Buin, Bougainville. Thirty Zeke fighters would operate from there, considerably shortening the flying distance to Guadalcanal. Now they would have more time over the island to support the long-range bombers from Rabaul.

No Holds Barred

Regarding the deep and abiding contempt in which the Japanese were held by the Americans living and fighting on the Canal, the veteran marine infantryman E.N. Sledge wrote in his book, *With the Old Breed*, "They were a fanatical enemy; that is to say, they believed in their cause with an intensity little understood by many postwar Americans—and possibly many Japanese as well.

"This collective attitude, Marine and Japanese, resulted in savage, ferocious fighting with no holds barred. This was not the dispassionate killing seen on other fronts or in other wars. This was a brutish, primitive hatred, as characteristic of the horror of war in the Pacific as the palm trees and the islands. To comprehend what the troops endured then and there, one must take into full account this aspect of the nature of the Marines' war."

Eight Japanese destroyers led by the light cruiser *Yura* sank a tugboat and a seaplane tender off Tulagi on the 25th, then came under a concentrated bombing attack from the CAF. *Yura* was badly battered by the buzzing dive bombers, and was later sunk by its own forces. One destroyer was damaged.

Twenty-seven Japanese planes were downed in the Guadalcanal area. Much like the RAF during the Battle of Britain, a handful of driven, tired, and courageous flyers were keeping the enemy at bay. The attrition rate of CAF pilots from debilitating illnesses and the sheer physical demands of keeping the planes flying under the most miserable and relentless conditions rendered many of them unfit for further combat once they were relieved—if they survived. Most of the pilots and air and ground crews who fought on did so at a mindless, primitive gut level instinct beyond explanation and understanding, until they dropped in their tracks, died, or at long last were relieved and ordered away.

Across the channel another group of pesky PT boats arrived at Tulagi. The combat effectiveness of the MTBs (Motor Torpedo Boats) was limited because of the inferior torpedoes they fired at enemy ships, not by the sailors manning them. At the same time, they were a distinct thorn in the side of Japanese shipping. The harassing attacks by the MTB crews had to be fought off, diverting some attention and response from the primary mission of engaging enemy warships.

President Coolidge, ferrying elements of the Army's 172nd Infantry, 43rd Division to the island, was inadvertently sunk trying to navigate through the American minefield designed to protect Espiritu Santo. A few soldiers were killed and all the regiment's equipment was lost. At times like this the commanders on Guadalcanal had to shake their heads in wonder that they still possessed the manpower, resources, and capability to fight the Japanese.

The U.S. Navy faced enormous obstacles in finding enough shipping to move men and supplies in the South Pacific, even without the great demands imposed by Guadalcanal. The losses of warships alone were depressing, and civilian morale would have suffered had the news been known at home. Admiral King advised his officers to say nothing to the press when queried about losses and shortages until the fighting was over, and then just tell them who won.

CHAPTER 12

OCTOBER 21–26
BATTLE OF THE MATANIKAU RIVER: THE LAST BATTLE FOR HENDERSON FIELD

The late October Battle of the Matanikau River is a misnomer that remains today. It should, more logically, be called The Battle for Henderson Field. The capture of the airfield was the primary Japanese objective, and the sole reason for the battle. A large Japanese fleet had been assembled to bring in reinforcements to occupy the field, and a large air fleet was waiting to fly in immediately once the field had been secured. While the first attack in this battle, a diversion, took place at the mouth of the Matanikau, the main fight took place south of Henderson Field and adjacent to Edson's Ridge. The later, smaller fights of this battle to the east and west were also aimed at the airfield. Many historians have wondered why this most influential battle on the Canal wasn't honored with a more appropriate name.

Lieutenant General Maruyama was still moving his Sendai Division on October 21 into his designated attack position south of Henderson Field as one part of a synchronized three-pronged attack. Creeping and crawling through the hilly, muddy, and pestilential jungle as far as his force had advanced had been a battle in itself. The critical—and quite unrealistic—timetable for the decisive attack had been wrecked. Moving large bodies of troops through the horrendous jungle was a truly nightmarish endeavor faced by both sides during the campaign.

Since it was painfully obvious that the floundering forces could not be ready to attack as the 17th Army commander Lieutenant General Hyakutake had planned, Maruyama was forced to postpone the attack for 48 hours. This delay was more irritating than crucial, since the marines had no inkling that a major attack was being staged in the Mount Austen area to the south of their perimeter. Vandegrift had surmised that a large attack was coming, but that it would come from along the beach across the mouth of the Matanikau. The Japanese had landed and moved into that area an array of eight 150-mm howitzers and smaller-caliber cannon, which soon began firing on Henderson Field, often with delayed-fuse shells from the larger guns that burst under the runway. This forced American flight operations to be shifted to the smaller Fighter One Field. Del Valle's usually confident artillerymen could not locate the new guns to destroy them with counterbattery fire. They did not have the sound and flash ranging section needed to spot the well concealed guns, so the CAF was unable to pinpoint the enemy battery locations.

All the Sendai Division's artillery and heavy weapons had to be wrestled up and down the steep banks of the muddy, vine-clogged ravines along Maruyama's trail. The already heavily laden riflemen were also ordered to carry the artillery and mortar ammunition.

The artillery ultimately had to be abandoned along the way in the jungle, taking away the major weapon that could have made the difference between success or failure. Maruyama felt that even without the guns he had the manpower to overwhelm the thin American lines.

The near total breakdown in Japanese communications left Major General Sumiyoshi uninformed of the second postponement. Sumiyoshi, in a coma from malaria, never received the message. On the 23rd, thinking the attack was proceeding right on schedule, Colonel Oka's 124th Infantry, less its 3rd Battalion, was to strike down the Matanikau toward Colonel Nakagama's 4th Infantry area at the river mouth. Again, as had happened a few weeks earlier, Oka had difficulty assembling his battalions in time for the attack. At dusk Nakagama's tank element spearheaded the attack from the west behind a barrage of his big guns, along the Matanikau River. The nine lightly armored 15-ton Type 97 tanks clanked and creaked along the coastal track. The first was destroyed by 37-mm antitank guns manned by such men as Sergeant George Herbert. The second ground across the sandbar, flattened the barbed wire and eliminated a machine gun position. When it raised up on a stump near Private Joseph D.R. Champagne's foxhole, he deftly placed a grenade in the drive wheel mechanism. This damaged the tread, causing it to slew away toward the surf, where it was promptly destroyed by a 75-mm half-track-mounted gun.

Not a single Japanese tank got across the river. The two accompanying infantry battalions in the assault were promptly shredded and repulsed by concentrations of shellfire from the marine artillery already zeroed in on the attack route. By midnight the area was quiet. At the end of the bloody night, it was discovered that del Valle's artillery had expended almost the entire supply of 75-mm and 105-mm shells on the island. More than 6,000 rounds of artillery and mortar shells had been used to crush the attack. Marine losses totaled two dead and eleven wounded, while the Japanese suffered grievous losses. An emergency request was sent to Nouméa to rush in more artillery shells.

Although Sumiyoshi's attack failed miserably, it diverted the marines' attention away from the south and to the mouth of the Matanikau. Vandegrift thought the coastal road at the outlet of the river was the logical attack route. That is the area the Japanese tanks and artillery barrage had come from. One Marine battalion was moved from the inland flank of Henderson Field—the primary target of the main thrust—leaving only the 1st Battalion, 7th Marines, under "Chesty" Puller, to defend the 4,000-yard southern line protecting the perimeter. To the left of his battalion were the fresh and "unblooded" Army troops of Colonel Moore's 164th Infantry.

Heavy rains continued to make Henderson Field a morass of mud, but some Wildcats could usually scramble into the air to meet Japanese air attacks. On the 23rd a handful of pilots rose up to meet sixteen enemy bombers escorted by twenty Zekes. Captain Joe Foss shot down four of the Zekes. One Betty was shot down in the attack and three others were trailing smoke as they struggled back toward Rabaul. Most often, Japanese aircraft leaving the Guadalcanal area shot up or smoking from damage were presumed to have been lost, though they were not credited to any individual pilots.

During the daylight hours of the 24th, Maruyama had established his command post south of the "Centipede-Shaped Heights" known to the marines as Edson's Ridge. At noon he announced that the division had reached the rear flank of the enemy in absolute secrecy, and that he intended to exterminate that enemy in one blow. The right and left wings would attack at 5:00 P.M. But a long Japanese column had been spotted moving down a heavily wooded ravine. Further, late in the afternoon, a startling piece of information was passed back to U.S. division headquarters. A marine had spotted a Japanese officer with binoculars studying the terrain around Edson's Ridge. Another marine, a scout-sniper, had observed the smoke from cook fires in a camp back up the Lunga. It was too late to alter the Marine and Army defenses, but the defenders now knew for sure they were in for another night fight along the southern flank.

The Japanese troops began to move forward into the attack positions at 3:00 P.M. but were thwarted by a torrential, cascading rain that swamped the ground and knocked out communications. In the deluge battalions lost companies, companies could not find platoons, and squads got lost. Each step was an ordeal in the treacherous mud, and in some places the nearly exhausted riflemen waded through waist-deep bogs. Disorder and confusion reigned when the jump-off time came, and critical minutes were spent trying to reorganize the force. Fuming at the delay, Maruyama ordered the left wing to attack even though the right wing was not yet in position. At just after midnight Colonel Furimiya, commander of the 29th Infantry of the left wing, fired a flare as the signal for the 1st Battalion to begin the attack. Visibility dropped once again when clouds blocked off the moon and the rains poured down.

Puller's 1st Battalion of 700 men had to cover a 2,500-yard sector from west of the Lunga east of Edson's Ridge, a front usually manned by a regiment. That equates to one man every three and a half yards, but the marines operated in at least two-man teams. On this night one platoon from each rifle company—reinforced by machine guns—was placed in the improved positions around the legendary ridge left by Hanneken's battalion. Puller walked the entire length of the line to check each position's field of fire and make suggestions where necessary. Still, there were far too many gaps.

A marine outpost about 3,000 yards to the front, held by Sergeant Ralph Briggs, Jr., Port Edwards, Wisconsin and a platoon of forty-six men, reported to Puller hearing the passage of about a battalion of Nasu's east wing heading for the perimeter. Puller, who had protested the regimental order sending the platoon out so far ahead, insisted, "They're going to sacrifice those men—that's all. We don't need any bait on the hook.... It's foolishness to throw away that platoon." Briggs, told to come back in by Puller, began withdrawing westward toward the position held by 2nd Battalion, 164th Infantry south of Alligator Creek, and then through to the sea.

Briggs and his men had several frightening narrow escapes. "We gained cover in the woods, where it was cold as hell and the Japs seemed to be all around us. We could hear them jabbering and walking so close that one Jap stepped on a marine's bayonet and another stepped on the helmet of a man hit by fire." When they again tried to escape the trap they were in, they came under Japanese mortar and machine gun fire. One selfless marine, Private Robert Potter, leapt to his feet and scampered back and forth to draw the enemy fire, yelling to his buddies to run for the lines. Potter was killed. Only three others from the outpost failed to make it back. Captain Regan Fuller, Company A, thought that the Silver Stars won that night by company commanders should have gone to Ralph Briggs and Robert Potter of the outpost.

Probably the first Japanese unit to make contact that night, about 10:00, was Colonel Shoji's 1st Battalion, 230th Infantry (I/230) of the right wing, which had wandered off course and was trying to get back into the proper attack position. This unit did not engage to any great extent, but it did precipitate the false report to the 17th Army by Colonel Matsumoto that they had broken through and captured the airfield, a misinterpretation that may have been the result of his suffering from a bad case of malaria.

The III/29, which had passed Briggs's marines, was headed for the barbed wire in front of Puller's Company A. Puller ordered his men to hold their fire until the outpost had time to clear out, ordering that "If the bastards break through, use the bayonet."

Just after midnight on the 25th Major General Nasu's first wave of III/29—Captain Jiro Katsumata's 11th Company—quietly crawled forward and began cutting through the wire. Inexplicably, one of his men, in an exhausted stupor, stood up and began walking to the left. Another screamed out a war cry, which the others quickly picked up—a chant that got the full attention of the marines. The American machine guns and mortars began firing, catching the lead company entangled in the wire in front of Company A at about 1:00 A.M. Most of the attackers, slowed by the inky dark and pouring rain, were killed.

The 9th Company—supposed to be following in line—veered far to the left and at about 1:15 began screaming and yelling as they charged directly into the two heavy machine gun sections attached to Company C and directed by Sergeant "Manila John" Basilone, of Buffalo, New York. In the fierce frontal attack, the Japanese blasted his guns with grenades and mortar fire, putting one out of action and leaving only two men able to carry on. Under continual fire Basilone moved an extra gun into position, placed it in action, and then repaired another and manned it himself. With one gun cradled in his arms he stopped a screaming banzai attack, and when reinforcements came up at dawn nearly a hundred sprawled enemy of the 9th Company lay dead around his outpost. This was just the start, for few marines have ever experienced such a terrible and frantic ordeal as the dark-complexioned and handsome Basilone did that night—and lived to tell about it.

"Manila John's" guns were near the company center, placed with a decline to the front. Soon the hill was covered with bodies, and when the fury of that attack abated, he sent men down to push aside the corpses to once again clear his field of fire. Still the attack waves came, about once an hour, each more vicious than the one before and lasting about 15 minutes. Basilone scampered barefooted so he could move quickly through the mud in his trousers with a .45-caliber automatic pistol strapped on his hips, back to the battalion command post during lulls in the fighting to report the guns in trouble. He then returned to the front lugging spare parts, and most important of all, several 14-pound ammunition belts.

Once near the Company A area, Basilone reported to Fuller that his water-cooled guns were beginning to burn out from the continuous firing and that his men were urinating in the gun jackets to keep them cool enough to fire. The killing or wounding of his gun crews left him short-handed, so he set up several guns, then rolled and ran from one to the other firing each in turn to confuse the enemy. Once he shouldered a heavy, completely assembled machine gun and trotted through the mud to an exposed position, leading a handful of riflemen to turn back the enemy. This night's action won "Manila John" the Medal of Honor.

Fuller's Company A had its hands full, and was pretty well set for the assault. In addition to his riflemen he had a heavy machine gun section with four .50-caliber and six .30-caliber guns, two 37-mm antitank guns, a 60-mm mortar, and eighteen BARs. The half dozen old World War I vintage Lewis machine guns often jammed. In helping to protect his position, 600 mortar rounds were fired at the attackers, until the weapon glowed red-hot. When daylight came, the mouth of the mortar tube barely showed above the mud.

Despite the waves of Japanese who crashed against his hail of fire that night, the wire had not been broken. But the real miracle was that not one man in his company was lost in the bitter fighting that left the enemy stacked like cordwood. His 37-mm antitank gun had been brought to bear on a group of Japanese massing at the edge of the field and fired three rounds of cannister shot. The group, a weapons company with machine guns, rifles, mines, and dynamite, was found the next morning with the dead lying half atop each other in near perfect formation.

Puller requested del Valle to give his battalion everything the artillery could put in the air. The artillery chief promised he would, but said he didn't know what would happen when they ran out of ammunition. Puller replied: "If we don't need it now, we'll never need it. If they can get through here tonight, there won't be a tomorrow." The fighting was taking place to the east of Edson's Ridge, along some of the same ground that had hamstrung Major General Kawaguchi's earlier attack by his 35th Infantry Brigade on the ridge. Kawaguchi's protests against the three-pronged attack and his deplorable difficulties in moving the right wing into position led to doubts about his fighting spirit and his summary relief by Colonel Shoji.

Puller's calls to the regiment for help were shrugged off, and he shouted angrily, "Regiment is not convinced we are facing a major attack!" Colonel Sims, commanding the 7th Marines, did not come out to see for himself, nor did he send anyone to see what all the fuss was about. All the time Puller was with his men on or near the front line directing the action. His disregard for danger and his stirring bravery under heavy fire earned him a second gold star for his Navy Cross—his third citation. Finally he got through to Colonel Julian Frisbie, the regimental executive officer, and convinced him of the critical need for help. His battalion was now down to about 500 men and were in danger of being overrun.

By 2:00 on that horrendous night the predicament of the 1st Battalion, 7th Marines had become so bad that the fresh soldiers of Lieutenant Colonel Robert Hall's 3rd Battalion, 164th Infantry were led forward from regiment by Father Keough, a Navy Chaplain who knew where the line was, and were placed in small groups to fight side by side with the marines. The marines quickly discovered that these feisty army infantrymen sharing their sloshy mudholes—armed with the new Garand M-1 rifles—had brought an ability and readiness to fight, along with a wonderful supply of candy bars!

The mixed force worked well together the remainder of the night, and repulsed two or three more attacks before dawn. Lieutenant Colonel Hall thanked Puller for breaking in his men, as not one had ever seen action. Puller later admitted that these soldiers were almost as good as marines. No longer would the soldiers in this outfit be called "doggies."

The persistent Colonel Furimiya—accompanied by only nine officers and men—penetrated deeply into the marine front carrying the regimental colors of the 29th Infantry. His small group held out behind American lines for 48 hours before being eliminated. Only one man managed to escape. In the end, Furimiya committed hara-kiri. When morning dawned, more than one thousand Japanese bodies lay along the American battle line, as well as in and around small strong points. Two hundred and fifty dead Japanese were found inside the marine lines during the day. Fewer than two hundred Americans had been lost.

Hyakutake had relayed to Rabaul the erroneous message stating that the airfield had been captured by his glorious forces. The shame he would face in telling his superiors that he had not in fact captured the airfield increased his determination to regroup and resume the attack. He could not ignore that fact that the leader of the 29th Infantry had taken the flag of the Rising Sun deep into enemy lines.

Dugout Sunday

As the sun began its inexorable rise that Sunday morning the sickening sweet odor of decomposing bodies thickened in the area. The main attack was yet to come, and fresh troops were moved in to strengthen the defensive line. Additional artillery batteries were moved into position to reinforce the single battery that had supported the action that night. The weary defenders restrung wire and dug new fighting positions. Over in the vicinity of Edson's Ridge, Maruyama issued new orders for his main attack.

Puller first estimated that his under-strength battalion had been attacked by a regiment of about 2,000 men. Captured documents later revealed that there had been nearly twice that number. The appalling attacks that had resulted in the deaths of so many Japanese soldiers had been made by three regiments—the 16th, 29th, and the 230th—and the remnants of Kawaguchi's 35th Infantry Brigade. In this equivalent of a Japanese division, two regiments together had carried off 500 battle casualties on stretchers.

The Japanese morning artillery harassment of Henderson Field, transformed into a sea of mud by rains that had hampered the attack, prevented the CAF from getting off the ground to challenge the Zekes moving in from Rabaul and Buin to strafe and destroy the grounded Wildcats.

At Tulagi, the old destroyers *Trevor* and *Zane* had unloaded torpedoes, high-test gasoline, oil, and ammunition for the four PT boats they had hauled in the night before. The Yippie *284*—a converted fishing trawler—and the tugboat *Seminole* headed out for Kukum on the routine daily freight run. At 9:52 A.M. lookouts on *Trevor* disclosed three Japanese destroyers racing past Savo into Sealark Channel. These enemy ships, carrying the Koli Detachment to an unloading point east of the perimeter, had been sent in by Vice Admiral Mikawa upon receiving the erroneous "banzai" message indicating Henderson Field was in Japanese hands.

The two American destroyers, no match for the enemy guns, made a run at 26 knots for the open sea. Fifteen minutes after they had gotten under way, they were spotted and taken under fire. A Japanese shell destroyed *Trevor*'s aft gun turret, killing three sailors and wounding nine. Just as the fleeing ships were about to be blown out of the water, three Wildcats that had taken off despite the mud on Fighter One dived down to the attack, driving the Japanese destroyers back to the west.

In trying to evade the fusillade of armor-piercing and incendiary machine gun fire from the fighter planes, the enemy ships inadvertently rammed the tug *Seminole*, which sank in two minutes as its cargo of aviation gas exploded into flames. A 5-inch coastal gun near Lunga Point scored at hit on the fast-withdrawing destroyers, while more Wildcats—now accompanied by SBDs—roared in to score two direct bomb hits and strafe the enemy decks, ravaging the Koli Detachment.

A fire support force for the reinforcement force—made up of the light cruiser *Yura* and five destroyers—had been sighted off Florida Island heading for Indispensable Strait. SBDs from the CAF plunged downward on *Yura* at 12:55 P.M. Lieutenant Commander Eldridge planted a 500-pound bomb on the cruiser's forecastle that tore through the deck and blew off a piece of her bow. Struggling to escape to open waters north of Santa Isabel, *Yura* endured three more dive bomber attacks, which left her burning and listing to one side. She was sunk by a torpedo from the destroyer *Yudachi*, while the damaged destroyer *Akizuki* made its escape.

The American submarine *Amberjack*—loaded with 9,000 gallons of aviation gasoline and 200 100-pound bombs—witnessed this skirmish through its periscope. It had to remain submerged while patiently waiting to deliver its crucial cargo. No doubt the skipper cursed this missed opportunity to attack Japanese warships, but their current mission was more important. She had to wait 24 hours before it was safe to deliver its load of goodies for the CAF.

In the early afternoon of the 25th, after the field had dried out sufficiently to get more planes up, sixteen Betties and twenty-seven Zekes raided the perimeter. Seventeen Zekes were shot down, and four more were credited to Captain Foss, giving him a remarkable total of eight kills in three days of flying! Four Betties crashed into Sealark and one crashed on land within a mile of the airfield. Anyone who could find a reason to do so visited the fallen Betty. An attack by Aichi dive bombers later in the afternoon had a great time blasting the wrecked planes in the boneyard. Disturbed by the events of the day, and recognizing that Henderson Field remained in Marine hands, Mikawa withdrew his fleet to safer waters to wait for the opportunity for a conclusive victory later.

Because of the diversions occupying his enemy's attention, Maruyama had the time to reorganize his remaining two wings for the "final death-defying attack" on the night of the 25th–26th. During this lull in the line the American Army and Marine units separated and took up adjacent positions in the defensive line. Puller's battalion took responsibility for the western 1,400 yards, and Hall's battalion took the eastern 1,100 yards. All the Allied forces on the island were alerted to the possibility of a Japanese amphibious landing.

At 8:00 P.M. the few guns of the Sendai Division's artillery bombarded the new enemy positions for an hour. This was followed by several small attacks of perhaps thirty to two hundred men, on the American Army positions, until midnight. A massive attack, mounted by the Japanese 16th Infantry and supported by heavy weapons fire, was then unleashed against the section held by Hall's 3/164, the American left flank. Platoon Sergeant Millard A. Tate, Galatia, Illinois, said, "They'd blow that damn bugle and over the hill they'd come.... We fired our rifles so much we thought they'd never work again." After the fight, "...our bulldozer would come out and cover up their dead. If they would have had our leaders they might have won the war, the poor bastards."

Soon elements of the 2nd Battalion, 164th Infantry became involved, as the enemy surged even further east. The invaders were trying to force their way along a trail that was the boundary between the Army units, but two 37-mm guns of the 7th Marines Weapons Company covering the entry to the trail used cannister shot to savage the area, killing more than 250 Japanese attackers. A few managed to filter through the seam in the lines, but were stopped and then hunted down and killed by the weapons company and one company of the 3rd Battalion, 2nd Marines.

Maruyama's powerful engine was running out of steam. Major General Nasu was killed leading a charge. Colonel Hiroyasu of the 16th Infantry was killed by flying steel shards, along with four battalion commanders who also fell in the massacre. Half the officers in the Sendai Division were killed or wounded in the two-night battle.

Colonel Oka, who seemed to remain a bridesmaid to disaster, was still breaking trail and struggling to get into position while the big attack begun the previous night south of Henderson Field was being mauled. Although totally confused by the terrain, he had not ordered a reconnaissance of his area. A day late and a dollar short, as usual, Oka's force at last attacked in the early morning hours of the 26th. Following a preparatory artillery barrage, the Japanese troops surged forward toward the positions of Company F of Hanneken's 2/7. The machine gun section, under Sergeant Mitchell Paige, from Pennsylvania, was ordered to establish a defensive position on a previously unoccupied ridge near the Matanikau River, about five miles west of Henderson Field. While under enemy artillery fire, Paige moved his thirty-three men to protect the southern flank from a position at the top of a hill that sloped down toward the jungle's edge. They were exposed on three sides and they felt like they were "out on a diving board."

It was pitch dark and raining, and the marines were forced to crawl and feel their way through the terrain. "The next morning, I looked around and wondered why in the world anyone would pick a spot like this to defend," Paige recalled. The reason: an enemy penetration here would have given the Japanese a clear shot at the airfield.

On October 25th, huddling in their rain-soaked foxholes atop the ridge, Paige and his men heard noises from the jungle below their position. He looked over the ridge and saw tiny lights in the jungle from the enemy preparing for the attack. "Just as sure as anything, the enemy came out of the jungle, armed with machine guns and knee mortars, and they began climbing the hill toward my men. It was pitch black by now and we waited until they got to within a few feet of us....there were hundreds of them. When they slammed into my men, it was like a tornado hit."

A few of the enemy made it through the lines and engaged Paige's men in fierce hand-to-hand combat. At the center of the line, Paige and his marines beat back their attackers. That first wave faltered and slipped back into the jungle. The Americans had held the line, but eight were wounded or dead.

Paige had just removed the jammed cartridge from an inoperative machine gun and fed in a new belt of ammunition when the enemy opened fire and hit his gun. The blast knocked Paige backward and destroyed the gun. Miraculously, he was unharmed. Moments later the second wave of enemy troops came up the slope, and every marine in Paige's platoon became a casualty. Company F, protecting Paige's left, were soon forced back over the crest of the ridge. Now alone and under fire, Paige slithered from gun to gun in an effort to stop the enemy soldiers creeping up the hill.

Some Japanese soldiers moved behind Paige and were ready to overwhelm the post when he "swung a machine gun around and hit them with a burst." Not one made it past the ridge. Paige said later he didn't have time to think about being completely alone on the hill, but he held that line for nearly four hours, with a bayonet scar, a bullet wound, and a shrapnel wound as remembrances.

At dawn Paige saw hundreds of bodies, and an enemy infantryman crawling toward one of the American machine guns. Ignoring the gunfire and grenades that exploded around him, he grabbed the gun and discovered that it was empty. Down the slope, he saw that a Japanese soldier had set up his machine gun into position only a few dozen yards away and was preparing to fire as Paige struggled to load his gun. Loading and arming the water-cooled machine gun required that the bolt be pulled back twice, and he had pulled the handle back for the first time just as the enemy soldier squeezed his trigger. "I struggled to lean forward, to grab the bolt handle and load my weapon. But I couldn't overcome the force...holding me back."

Still unable to move, he heard the chatter of the enemy gun and felt the heat from the stream of bullets as they passed under his chin in the sweltering air. Finally, when the enemy gun ran out of ammunition, Paige pulled the bolt and quickly swung the gun around to the left, killing the enemy soldier.

Early on the morning of October 26, two dozen marines arrived, and Paige removed his eighty-pound machine gun from its tripod and cradled it in his arms. Yelling to the reinforcements to fix bayonets and follow him, he charged down the hill, where they fought in hand-to-hand combat to drive the Japanese back. After the fierce skirmish, Paige staggered up the hill and looked at the body of the machine gunner that he had faced off with earlier. "Why him and not me?" Paige asked himself. "I just sat there."

In an action similar to that of Basilone the night before, Paige's individual and heroic performance also won for him the Medal of Honor. Despite Paige's machine gun fire and the skillful, accurate American mortar fire dropped on them as they moved up through a muddy ravine, elements of the Japanese III/4 managed to drive Company F survivors off the hill at 5:00 A.M. After gaining this toehold in Hanneken's area, the Japanese unit was bloodily ousted with the help of a thrown-together "provisional" force of cooks, bandsmen, and runners led by Major Odell M. Conoley, the battalion executive officer—part of a counterattack launched at 5:40. Scuttlebutt had it that one Japanese officer had been killed by a pancake hurled in anger that one of the cooks had brought along!

Elements of Company G, joined by two platoons from Company C, 5th Marines, and accompanied by Paige—who reclaimed three marine machine guns and the five brought up by the enemy—also moved back up the ridge before the Japanese could get dug in and drove them back with a shower of grenades. By 6:00 the ridge was once again secure. Ninety-eight enemy corpses were counted on the ridge, and another two hundred lay dead in the ravine. Blood trails left by the fleeing wounded led south into the jungle.

The new Japanese attacks had failed, a fact Maruyama recognized with agonized reluctance. At 8:00 he notified the 17th Army and his remaining troops that he was halting the Battle for Henderson Field. By this time, Major Samuel B. Griffith later wrote, "The commander of the Division had not a single reserve left; no food was to be had nor any expected...even if all died fighting, it would have been impossible to tear the enemy positions. No hope was left." All that the brave Japanese survivors had to look forward to was another brutal, punishing retreat in the jungle sinkhole. Those who made it back to safety were reduced to eating tree bark and roots, scrounging for berries and other edibles, chewing their rifle slings, and drinking fetid water from stagnant pools.

The American defenders were not quite sure the fighting was over, for they had to fight off a few additional jabs at their lines. The historian Richard Frank asserts that these were efforts by the Sendai Division to remove wounded soldiers and recover the 29th Regiment's colors, which had been carried forward by Colonel Furimiya.

Once again a massive and determined attack to shatter and penetrate the U.S. lines and capture Henderson Field was beaten back. During the entire campaign for possession of Guadalcanal, this was the largest, bloodiest, and most ferocious clash of Japanese and American forces.

Estimates of Japanese losses for these two nights of bitter fighting approached 3,500. Numerous wounded, trying to make their way back the way they had come, perished in the appalling and deadly jungle. Never again could the Japanese hope they could drive off their despised enemy.

This land attack was supposed to be coordinated with the movement of a massive Japanese naval strike force that would immediately move in transports, planes, and additional men once Henderson Field had been wrested from American hands. Fortunately for the defending marines and GIs, the Japanese high command's complex plans for land attacks, which looked so good on paper, were almost impossible to achieve because of the miserable jungle. Often it seemed that the jungle was the real opponent, and that the Americans and Japanese were minor characters.

The problems of the Imperial forces were further complicated by American knowledge of the status of the Japanese fleet, which had moved down from Truk and Rabaul to support the occupation of Guadalcanal. Halsey's intelligence units had accurately revealed the size and destination of the enemy fleet.

Chapter 13

October 26
Battle of the Santa Cruz Islands

"STRIKE—REPEAT—STRIKE," came the terse message from Comsopac Halsey at Nouméa radioed to Rear Admiral Thomas C. Kinkaid, flying his flag aboard *Enterprise*, on station again two months after being sent back to Pearl Harbor for repairs. While sweeping to the north near the Santa Cruz Islands just after midnight early on October 26, a PBY patrol made an incomplete report placing the enemy about 300 miles away. At 3:10 another PBY reported all the information needed to launch an attack against the Japanese, but its message failed to reach Kinkaid.

Japanese efforts to pound home the final simultaneous and crushing blows on the defenders of Guadalcanal were not having the desired effects. Lieutenant General Maruyama's infantry was attacking the thinly spread Marine lines south of the airfield, but was being bloodily repulsed. Vice Admiral Kondo had a large armada assembled to the northeast of Guadalcanal, ready to rush men and planes to the island as an occupying force as soon as he received word that the Americans had been defeated. That final word of an overwhelming victory was never to come. Instead, Kondo received a warning from the Combined Fleet that an American Navy task force was steaming toward him.

The Japanese main body—Carrier Division 1 with the heavy carriers *Shokaku*, *Zuikaku*, and the light carrier *Zuiho*—was seeking the American carriers. Rounding out the large fleet under Kondo was Carrier Division 2, based around *Junyo*. Yamamoto had ordered the Combined Fleet—with four carriers, four battleships, and ten cruisers, screened by a bevy of destroyers and submarines—to seek out and destroy the American fleet.

TF 61, under Kinkaid, was made up of two smaller task forces. It was comprised of TF 16, with *Enterprise*, the new battleship *South Dakota*, one heavy and one light cruiser, and eight destroyers—working in tandem with TF 17, with *Hornet*, two heavy and two light cruisers, and six destroyers. TF 61 was ordered to intercept the Japanese fleet, which was known to be in the area of Santa Cruz Island. The enemy's lineup possessed a significant advantage in ships, as well as being able to put 199 planes in the air flown by experienced first-rate pilots, against 126 American aircraft flown by a mixture of experienced and green pilots.

The Air Group Ten leader, Commander John Crommelin, with his sandy hair beginning to turn gray, gathered his aviators together in the wardroom. He told them they had been thoroughly trained to drop their bombs and make them count, and he expected them to do just that. He said they shouldn't worry about overwork because he would use them whenever necessary, over and over again, and that the better they were the better their chances of survival. He advised them to get some rest because in the morning they were going to go out and "knock those sons-of-bitches off the face of the earth!"

By daybreak the Japanese had seven float planes out looking for the American ships, followed soon after by thirteen Kates. Eight pairs of *Enterprise* SBDs went looking around at thirty-eight minutes before dawn. The day had started with broken cumulus clouds hanging at 1,500 to 2,000 feet with unlimited visibility above and below—the ideal condition for bombing attacks. At 6:30 one pair spotted Japanese Rear Admiral Abe's Vanguard Force—reportedly two battleships, one heavy cruiser, and seven destroyers—170 miles away and moving north at 20 knots.

At 7:50 Lieutenant Commander James R. "Bucky" Lee, the Scouting Ten leader, hit gold. His rear gunner and operator Chief I.A. Saunders tapped out the signal: "Two carriers and accompanying vessels, latitude 7 degrees, 5 minutes south, longitude 163 degrees, 38 minutes east." Nagumo's carriers were 200 miles away. After reporting his discovery, Lee and his wingman, both armed with 500-pound bombs, climbed to attack altitude. Before they could start their run, Zekes on CAP zoomed in and chased them away into the clouds, where they managed to hide and make their escape.

Two other scouts nearing the end of their unproductive sweep, Lieutenant Stockton Birney Strong and Ensign Charles B. Irvine, had heard Lee's report and decided to attack the carriers. They found them at about 8:30 and dived at the cruising *Zuiho* from 14,000 feet. Surprisingly, there was no antiaircraft fire from the carrier and the covering Zekes were out of position. One of the bombs—dropped from 1,500 feet—blew a 50-foot crater in the empty aft flight deck, destroyed three Zekes below, and knocked out the rear antiaircraft batteries. Only then did the Japanese fighters sweep in to intercept. Strong's rear gunner, Clarence Garlow, exploded one out of the sky, and Irvine's gunner, Williams, claimed another with his .30-caliber machine guns. Then, after reporting their successful attack, they executed the time-honored maneuver needed for survival against a superior, angered, and aroused force. "We got the hell out of there." Their planes had been hit, and with fuel running low, they barely made it back safely to the ship. When they spotted their carrier they had to make the landings on the first try, since they didn't have enough fuel left for a second try.

A smaller force—skippered by Lieutenant Commander James Flatley, who had won the Navy Cross—ran into a pack of Zekes about twenty minutes away from *Enterprise*. Lieutenant John Leppla, flying an SBD with his gunner, John Lika, who had won the Navy Cross at the Battle of the Coral Sea, was leading the dive bombers of his group. Checking on the formation, Flatley saw one of his torpedo bombers—flown by Lieutenant Commander John A. Collet—aflame and spinning toward the sea. Another TBF, the pilot either dead or unconscious, was also plunging downward. Four Wildcats of the other division had come over and were engaging the swarming Zekes. The covering Wildcats had not had time to gain the needed altitude to cope with the more maneuverable Zekes at their flying finest, and the 20-mm cannons and 7.7s were cutting a swath in the U.S. formation.

Ensign "Dusty" Rhodes's drop tank failed to release and enemy bullets quickly set it ablaze, while Chip Reding's engine cut out when he dropped his tank. As Reding spiraled downward with Rhodes covering, both their Wildcats suffered serious damage but stayed aloft. When Reding finally got his engine going and Rhodes's fire burned out, they flew their shot-up F4Fs back into the fray. Employing the now famous Thatch weave, they held off the attacking fighters.

Then at about 2,500 feet Rhodes's engine died, its bearings burned out and fused together, freezing his prop in place. As he tried to get his plane safely down, more enemy bullets severed his rudder pedal cables. He bailed out at under 500 feet (1,000 feet was considered the safe minimum) and hit the water in one piece. In his half-inflated life raft at about 165 miles north of Santa Cruz, nursing a small leg wound, he was grateful he was still alive, even after some friendly planes flew over without seeing him. He was aware the entire Japanese fleet was between him and his fleet.

Two strikes from *Hornet*—launched at 7:32 and led by Lieutenant Commander William J. "Gus" Widhelm—included fifteen SBDs and four Wildcats. Lieutenant Parker's six TBFs were flying low at 800 feet looking for the carriers. These attack aircraft had left the ship late in following up the contact report and with relatively little coordination. A second force of eight Wildcats, three SBDs, and eight TBFs were launched at 7:47 but did not join up with the other group.

Widhelm's dive bombers pressed on while his fighters fought off Zekes trying to get to the formation. When more Zekes showed up, a bullet parted Widhelm's oil line and he ditched his SBD. Before parting, and having seen the four enemy carriers, he gave the order, "Stay in formation, men." Now he and his rear gunner, seated in their life raft, had a ringside seat for the rest of the attack.

At about 9:30 his eleven remaining SBDs rolled over to dive on *Shokaku*. Attacking through a heavy veil of flak, they loosed their 1,000-pound bombs, which stitched a line the length of the carrier. Badly damaged from the bomb blasts, burning from stem to stern, *Shokaku* was out of the fight and would not return to line duty for nine months. *Zuikaku* and *Junyo* remained undamaged.

The Japanese counterstrikes from the severely damaged *Shokaku* were already headed for Kinkaid's carrier force. One group was led by Lieutenant Commander Shigeharu Murata, who had dropped torpedoes at Pearl Harbor and Midway. The other, with a similar lineup of twenty-two Vals, eighteen Nakajima torpedo planes and twenty-seven Zekes, was led by Lieutenant Commander Mamoru Seki.

Murata's force missed *Enterprise*, steaming through a light, warm rain, at about 10:00. But the enemy bombers headed for *Hornet*, the famed carrier that earlier had launched Colonel Doolittle's B-25s to attack Tokyo. Protective efforts were provided by Wildcat pilots from Fighting Ten, such as Lieutenant Stanley W. "Swede" Vejtasa, who shot down a Val. Others, helped by antiaircraft fire from the ship, tore into the diving run. Lieutenant Albert D. Pollack got in a salvo that burned the belly out of a dive bomber, splashing it. Ensign Donald "Flash" Gordon blew up a torpedo bomber about ten feet off the waves and a few hundred yards from the ship. Still, most of the bombers survived the heavy flak and air attacks. Murata's Vals made two direct hits and scored a near miss. A main turbine bearing was damaged, and fires killed and wounded some defending sailors.

At 9:10 Seki's contingent roared in on *Hornet*. Despite the flak being thrown up by the ships, four Wildcats from the CAP zoomed in to shoot down three bombers. One Japanese bomb tore a hole in the carrier's wooden flight deck. Seki himself, his plane badly damaged, intentionally dived at the carrier, ramming through three decks, where his bombs exploded. Two torpedoes ripped open her hull, and were soon followed by three more bombs that penetrated deeply. Then a flame-crippled torpedo plane pilot crashed forward of the bridge. Fortunately, the carrier had already launched fifty-four aircraft before it was hit.

Hornet stopped dead in the water, flames erupting from several locations. Her electrical power and communications had been knocked out. Effective damage control efforts nearly saved the ship. But at 3:15 P.M., in air strikes from *Zuikaku* and *Junyo*, a Japanese torpedo plane got through to blow a hole in the battered carrier that opened the aft engine room to the sea. Soon the ship was listing about 18 degrees to starboard. The decision had already been made to abandon ship before two additional bombs added meaningless damage.

A 11:00 radar on *Enterprise* picked up a large force of hostiles approaching at twenty-three miles. Here the ship's questionable fighter direction control failed in its purpose. It continually sent out useless and meaningless information, which thrust the onus of interception onto the CAP pilots.

Minutes after the first radar warning, Pollack and his three F4Fs noticed a destroyer stopped dead in the water, picking up a downed pilot. Then he spotted a wild torpedo heading for the ship. Knowing he didn't have time to radio a warning—not with the flight deck officer already dropping the ball—he attacked the torpedo from the air. Seeing him plunge toward the water, the destroyer opened fire at him as he was firing at the torpedo. Then the destroyer, *Porter*, which had just picked up the downed TBF crew of Lieutenant R.K. Battern and his gunner R.S. Holgrim from their life raft, saw the danger and was kicking up water with its propellers trying to get under way when the water-borne missile exploded hard amidships. The destroyer *Shaw* moved in to take off survivors, who had to watch the shattered *Porter* sent to the bottom by *Shaw*'s 5-inch guns.

Now, suddenly, *Big E*'s radar wasn't picking up the incoming attackers. At 11:15 the men aboard the flattop could see the gleaming and deadly Japanese dive bombers as they began their plunge toward the vessel, which was veering at full rudder to evade the assault. Guns from every ship circling *Big E* were throwing up a hail of flak.

Half the Japanese force failed to get through, but the remainder dropped their bombs, shaking the maneuvering ship with near misses. Then at 11:17 Crommelin, on the bridge in his helmet and life jacket, was heard to say, "I think that son-of-a-bitch is going to get us," just as a 500-pound bomb ripped through the forward overhang of the flight deck. Its time-delay fuse detonated the bomb in the air near the port bow, puncturing the side of the carrier with large fragments. SBD gunner Sam Davis Presley died in the rear seat when his plane was blown overboard by the explosion. Another parked SBD, loaded with a 500-pound bomb, caught fire and was frantically pushed over the side by Machinist Bill Fluitt and his shipmates.

Almost at the same time, another bomb struck the flight deck and broke in half just behind the forward elevator. One half exploded in the hangar deck, destroying seven planes, while the nose tore through two more decks to detonate in the officers' quarters, wiping out Repair Party Two and a medical dressing station. Forty-two men were dismembered or burned to death in the blast, which set fire to the clothing, bedding, and personal effects of the officers who usually slept there. Light, power, and communications were cut and the fire mains damaged.

From the sky the Japanese bombers slashed down to complete the kill, scoring near misses that drenched *Enterprise* with tons of seawater, knocking over sailors and throwing their guns off target. Then the defender's antiaircraft fire began taking its toll, sending the brave enemy pilots to join their ancestors. Then at 11:19 *Enterprise* took a torpedo that tumbled and dumped almost every man standing to the deck, as it vibrated the ship through an 18-inch cycle like the tremor of an earthquake. Another SBD was thrown overboard and yet another into a gun gallery. The blast had opened a fuel tank to the sea, leaving behind a trail of oil as the ship kept moving. By 11:20 the attack seemed to be over.

The propulsion machinery of *Big E* remained in good shape, and she managed a steady speed of 27 knots. Then at 11:44 fifteen torpedo planes headed in from both sides of the bow to nail the carrier whichever way she turned. This attack was supposed to have been coordinated with the dive bomber attack half an hour before—the same kind of two-fisted attack that had scourged *Hornet*. This new threat to the Americans from the Kates skimming over the surface ran into the full fury of the fleet's guns. Three Kates coming in from the starboard got off three torpedoes aimed amidships of *Big E*.

"Right full rudder," Captain Osborne B. Hardison ordered.

"Right full rudder, sir!" came the enthusiastic response of the quartermaster. The stern began sliding off to the left as the torpedoes came on. Kinkaid and Hardison stood side by side on the port wing of the bridge watching the grim scene. Then Hardison ordered the rudder amidships, straightening out the ship. The three well aimed fish, running straight and true at 40 knots, passed ten yards away from the port side. Since the deadly missiles missed, *Enterprise* was now headed for the destroyer *Smith*, already suffering damage to its forward gun turret from a crashing Kate. Despite the damage when the torpedo of the Kate baked off and blew up—causing flames to shoot up and back over the bridge and superstructure—*Smith* stayed on course at speed, her guns still firing at the attacking planes. After the huge carrier cleared away, *Smith* moved up behind *South Dakota*, whose churning wake quenched the fires.

Another torpedo sped by thirty yards away as once again Hardison came hard right and skidded safely away. Having turned his stern to the attackers to present a smaller target, Hardison and his crew watched another torpedo pass along the port side. The determined and courageous torpedo attack might have succeeded but for F4F pilot "Swede" Vejtasa, who had earlier shot down a Val, and Lieutenants Harris and Ruehlow and Ensign Leder, who moved in to intercept the torpedo planes closing in at 250 knots on *Big E*.

On the first pass Vejtasa and Harris each knocked down a Kate. Angry at the foul-up in fighter direction, Vejtasa was now driven by a cold fury. Setting his eye on a formation of three Kates, he systematically destroyed them. He then attacked another Kate, which evaded him only to be shot down by flak from the ships. It was this victim that crashed onto *Smith*. Finally, running low on ammunition, Vejtasa shot down his fifth Kate of the day as it scurried away after its drop. His vicious attacks broke up this new threat, causing three to jettison their fish and two others to be ineffective. In the attacks on *Big E*, Hardison had evaded a total of nine torpedoes, but it is doubtful he could have escaped eleven others turned aside by Vejtasa—who was credited with seven kills that day—and his fellow flyers.

When the furor died down, *Big E* was making 27 knots inside the protective guns of her task force screen. *South Dakota* maintained position of her starboard quarter as she had done so well during the fight. Every available gun was loaded and trained outward—they knew more enemy planes were headed their way. Aboard the scarred *Enterprise* damage crews struggled to patch up the ship so that returning American planes could be recovered, refueled, rearmed, and readied to get back into the uneven contest.

Below decks where the bombs had ignited was in shambles. In one ammunition handling room ten sailors were trapped, cut off from light and phone communications. The men were mostly cook and messmen whose battle station was now sealed off under eight feet of seawater and residue of chemical foam used in fighting the fires. Electrician's Mate Paul Petersen was in charge, and told his men to remain as still and quiet as possible to save air. Hysteria and panic—there was none—would have complicated an already dire situation.

When battle telephone lines were restored, Chief Forrest warned the trapped group: "For Christ's sake don't open that hatch.... We'll get you out, but it's going to take a little while."

Just before noon, Landing Safety Officer Lieutenant Robin Lindsey on *Enterprise* began waving in aircraft, a chancy operation because of the gaping hole created after the flight deck elevator jammed in the down position. Few planes had been recovered when twenty more dive bombers from Nagumo's carriers dropped suddenly from the broken clouds in 45-degree dives. The Vals were terribly vulnerable during their shallow dives and the fleet's antiaircraft units blew eight of them out of the air and turned most of the others away. Lindsey climbed into the rear seat of a parked SBD and fired off the last of that machine gun's ammo at the Vals. Massive waterspouts from near misses geysered into the air. A lone bomb glanced off the exposed starboard side during a hard starboard turn and exploded in the water about eight feet away and fifteen feet beneath the surface. Again the ship shuddered its full length, jamming the number one elevator in the up position.

The main radar antenna stopped working after the many bomb shocks and the strafing administered by the attacking planes. Lieutenant Brad Williams, the Navy's first radar officer, grabbed a heavy toolbox and climbed the antenna. Lashing himself to the grid so he could work with both hands, he was exposed to more strafing and falling debris from the antiaircraft fire. Swinging wildly each time the ship shuddered from a near miss or made a course change, he managed to repair the malfunction. The concussion from the shock of the last near miss left him deaf for weeks. When the antenna was up and running again, Williams, still lashed to the rotating grid, was taken for a wild ride before someone noticed his plight and helped get him down.

A fresh attack wave was detected seventeen and a half miles away at 17,000 feet. The American CAP was low on fuel and nearly out of ammunition, so the defense fell mainly to the ack-ack batteries. The young men manning the 20-mm and the new 40-mm Bofors guns were now veterans, and having settled down into coolly efficient gunners, kept the Vals away from *Big E. South Dakota*, still maintaining its position adjacent to the carrier, suffered a bomb blast directly on top of its forward turret at 11:29. More than fifty men inside the heavily armored turret were wounded, and two later died. A fragment seriously wounded Captain Gatch, and when the steering was shifted aft the battleship veered out of line and onto a collision course with *Enterprise*. Captain Hardison turned the carrier away in time to prevent the ramming.

The cruiser *San Juan* took a bomb that penetrated the hull before it detonated underneath the ship. The blast knocked out the circuit breakers to the steering mechanism and the ship was soon locked into a high-speed starboard turn. This forced the other ships to scatter to avoid being run down by the wildly circling cruiser until emergency repairs restored the damaged steering.

At 12:45 P.M. the carrier was once again landing aircraft. Many simply ran out of fuel before they could be recovered and had to be ditched. The empty fuel tanks added enough buoyancy to slow down the sinking of the downed planes, giving the crews ample time to escape. The nearby destroyers rescued a large number of flyers that afternoon. To alleviate the crowding caused by the recovery of planes from *Hornet* as well as *Enterprise*'s own, thirteen refueled SBDs were flown off to Espiritu Santo.

Below decks, shortly after 5:00, Chief Forrest notified the group trapped in the ammo handling room: "You guys can open that hatch now but there's still some water and crap on top of it. Open it fast and come out fast and you'll be OK." The men, soaked from standing waist deep in water in total darkness, did just that, their eyes blinking in the dim emergency lights.

At three minutes before 8:00 the men of *Enterprise* stood down from battle stations, as did the men of the other American ships.

In the dark 250 miles to the northwest, Dusty Rhodes was fighting for his life. He was precariously perched in his bullet-punctured life raft, which had to be continually patched and reinflated—to about three-quarters of its capacity—by lung power. The sharks he had feared had arrived, attracted by the bleeding from his leg wound. He had his .45 automatic out to kill them if they attacked. He made it through the long dreary night, and late the next afternoon he was at long last rescued—by a Japanese destroyer.

With *Hornet*'s survivors now aboard other ships, efforts by American forces to sink the crippled ship with torpedoes and gunfire did not do the job. About an hour before midnight two Japanese destroyers homed in on the burning hulk and finally sent her to the bottom with four torpedoes. Putting this great ship into its watery grave was a prolonged affair, as she did not seem to want to sink.

Still chafing for a fight despite the loss of a hundred planes, Kondo's force kept looking to draw the Americans into a surface battle. Wisely, Kinkaid chose to withdraw. The Japanese headed back for Truk, not because they lost their sea battle but because Maruyama's infantry had lost its fight on land. This was the last time Japanese carriers took part in a battle in support of Guadalcanal.

WWII Snapshot—November 1942

North America—On the 10th German submarines lay a minefield off the coast of New York. In this one month the rampaging U-boats sent 721,700 tons of Allied shipping—eighty-three vessels—to the bottom of the Atlantic.

The Allied Western Task Force—composed of 102 ships sailing in perfect autumn weather from Hampton Rhodes, Virginia, and British ports, and commanded by Rear Admiral H. Kent Hewitt—arrive safely off the Moroccan coast on November 7th. The German U-boat commander in the area believes the Allies mean to attack Dakar, further south, and posts his submarines near Madeira and the Azores.

Egypt—Since October 23rd the decisive battle of El Alamein—in the desert sands of Egypt near Alexandria—has been raging. Britain's 8th Army under General Bernard L. Montgomery launches a massive attack against the Germans and Italians beginning at 9:40 P.M. Four infantry divisions move out along a 6-mile-long front, including the 9th Australian and the 2nd New Zealand Divisions. This initial thrust covers a longer front when the tanks of the armored units move forward through the infantry. On October 24th, as the attack continues with furious fighting, the Desert Air Force flies 1,000 sorties, mostly in direct support of the ground forces.

The British lineup of men and equipment committed to this battle includes approximately 195,000 soldiers, 435 armored cars, 1,029 tanks (other than light), 908 field and medium guns, and 1,451 antitank guns. Montgomery has some manpower reserves, and can call on an additional 1,000 tanks if necessary.

The Axis forces, under Field Marshal Rommel, are comprised of 50,000 German soldiers along with 54,000 Italians, with 192 armored cars, 496 tanks, about 500 field guns, and about 800 antitank guns, of which 86 are the fearsome high-powered 88-mm variety. The Axis strength is diminishing, and often ships bringing reinforcements of men and especially gasoline are driven away or sunk en route. Axis reserves are nonexistent. Every available man is in the field.

It was not until November 2nd that the situation changes sufficiently in favor of the British that they can launch the final backbreaking assault, Operation Supercharge. The desert is littered with dead men and shattered tanks and other vehicles burning with fires that light up the night sky. Rapid advances come to a halt when confronted with the hundreds of thousands of land mines planted by the Axis forces.

The 9th Australian Infantry Division is considered the linchpin of the battle and once again proves to be superb fighting men. By the night of November 3–4 the back of the Axis defense is broken and Rommel is forced to retreat. Although the British are unable to pursue and destroy the battered Axis forces, Egypt is safe and the pressure is increasing daily on the now defensive Axis army.

Despite this defeat in the desert, Hitler does not believe his intention of capturing the Suez Canal has been thwarted. His intention is to drive into the Middle East and link up with his forces driving southward of Stalingrad in the western Ukraine. His plans suffer a further, more conclusive setback when the Allied forces make a landing on the shores of Morocco and Algeria.

North Africa—On the morning of November 8th, armed forces from the United States launch Operation Torch, the Second Front that the Allies promised to the Soviets to help draw off German forces enmeshed with Russian armies on Europe's Eastern Front. The large American amphibious invasion of Morocco and Tunisia in North Africa comes from the Atlantic Ocean to strike at Rommel's poorly protected rear, effectively sandwiching his forces, which are already beset by the British to the east.

Vichy French naval forces engage U.S. ships and carrier aircraft off Casablanca, Morocco. On the 10th the Vichy French forces in Oran, Algeria give up the fight, followed the next day by the Vichy French in Casablanca, Morocco, which results in the signing of an Allied-French armistice. Immediately Germany responds by occupying the remainder of France south to the Mediterranean Sea. Italian troops land on Corsica prior to moving to southern France. The free French (non-Vichy) fleet, under the command of Admiral Jean de Laborde, is scuttled in the harbor at Toulon, France, to keep the ships out of German hands.

A substantial portion of the men, ships, planes, and supplies amassed for this landing are those that were held back from the relief and reinforcement of Guadalcanal. The buildup of forces required for Operation Torch is the practical result of the Allied agreement that decreed "Europe first, then the Pacific."

Southern Russia—Far away, in the southern USSR, the German 6th Army is engaged in a frenzied battle fought house to house, room to room, and cellar to cellar in vicious fighting that fails to drive the Soviets out of Stalingrad. Oftentimes a handful of German troops on the first floor of a building, for example, might be stalemated and unable to move because of an equally small handful of Soviet troops on the second floor.

Battalions of soldiers fight battalions to a terrible death within the confines of a factory. Thousands of rotting corpses are left on the streets, in houses and factories—wherever they have fallen. Every savaged and wrecked house becomes a stronghold, sometimes a one-man fortress that prevents all enemy movement within a few yards of the small redoubt.

Weeks of brutal assaults by the Germans have failed to drive out the few hundred Soviets determined to stay in Stalingrad. The cost in human life and destruction is appalling. Yet the cataclysmic battle—which many on both sides consider a battle of egos between Hitler and Stalin—continues despite horrendous losses. As November comes, bringing the first frosts of the dreaded Russian winter, the Soviet command in the city has their supply line for men, ammunition, and food from the west bank all but severed as ice floes begin drifting down the Volga.

As the time the barbaric battle for the besieged city is reaching its climax, the Soviets are rushing several hundred thousand fresh troops, hundreds of their famed T-34 tanks, thousands of artillery pieces, and other necessary supplies of war into positions west of the Volga. These new armies are destined for Operation Uranus, a counterattack to cut off and encircle the Germans into a pocket from which they can not escape. German intelligence is fully aware of the buildup, but fails to take steps to strengthen the distrusted Romanian armies in the front lines to the north, and to buttress their own combat units south of the city. It appears the German juggernaut is running out of steam, and the high command can not decide what to do, not as long as Hitler demands that the troops remain in position at all costs.

On the 19th the Red Army launches its massive counterattack, preceded by an artillery bombardment named "Siren"—more than 3,500 guns and mortars opened up along a 14-mile front. The main assault is against the Romanian-held sector, and twenty-four hours later 65,000 Romanians are Soviet prisoners of war. Hungarian and Italian troops, as well as German forces, are driven back.

The Russian pincer movement closes south of Kalach on the 22nd, trapping more than a quarter-million Axis soldiers in a huge pocket. As a reaction to the military disaster, on the 27th Hitler assumes "personal command" of the German Army.

Southwest Pacific—MacArthur notifies General Blamey on October 21st that the Australian progress across the Kokoda Trail is "NOT, repeat, NOT satisfactory," and is upsetting his timetable to capture Buna. It is on that day that the Diggers run into the Japanese defensive fortress at Eora Creek, at Myola, on the Kokoda Trail. They are stuck there until October 28th when the 2/3rd Battalion outflanks and routes the isolated Japanese rear guard position.

While hurrying his main body back to Buna, Major General Horii is swept to his death while trying to cross the rushing Kumasi River. On November 2nd, the leading battalion of the Australian 25th Brigade reenters the embattled town of Kokoda and captures its airstrip, which solves the critical supply problem. On November 5th, the 2/2nd and 2/3rd Battalions of the 16th Brigade at nightfall are in relatively open country when they confront the last strongly defended Japanese positions before Buna at Oivi. A Japanese counterattack on November 6th is driven back. While the 16th Brigade keeps pressure on the Japanese, the 25th Brigade moves around to the southern flank to sever the Japanese communication lines. After days of fierce fighting, the Japanese defense around Gorari is overcome on November 9th, and the Gorari-to-Ilimo track is severed, isolating the nearly three-mile-long Japanese pocket at Oivi. Frantic Japanese efforts to break out of the trap on the 10th fail.

The ill-conceived Japanese campaign to capture Papua is disintegrating and the Japanese hope for victory in the Battle for Guadalcanal was increasingly in doubt. The Diggers—so lightly regarded by General MacArthur and his staff, but who are already recognized as great fighters in far-flung parts of the world—are quickly mastering the harrowing art of jungle warfare. They are learning, without orders or permission from the Australian High Command, to get off the track and up on the adjacent heights. The basic goal is to drive back the enemy, and the primitive man-to-man fighting requires innovative responses and flexibility of movement that defy a rigid chain of command. The Japanese troops are drastically restricted in their ability to react to unanticipated events by their inflexible discipline.

MacArthur's first amphibious operation—requiring the movement of men and supplies to the northern side of Papua—is transported by a makeshift flotilla of coastal trawlers. The target is Buna Station, once the seat of the Australian government. Allied troops are being moved into position. The American 32nd Division, a National Guard unit, leads the attack against that bastion. The Australian forces attack Gona and Sananda to the west along the coast.

The Japanese are reinforcing the area around Buna, including Sananda and Gona. Colonel Hiroshi Yamamoto takes command of the area, after bringing in fresh troops for the 14th Infantry and the 3rd Battalion, 229th Infantry. In this area, and along the eleven-mile front between Gona on the west and Cape Endaiadere three miles to the east, the Japanese have constructed hundreds of heavily reinforced, interlocking bunkers, carefully camouflaged to blend in with the natural terrain. Yamamoto sends about 800 troops, buttressed with experienced jungle fighters from Formosa, to Gona. At Sananda he places the bulk of his able-bodied force, including two mountain gun batteries. It is against this massive defensive fortress that the Allied forces move when the orders from General MacArthur come down.

Both the Americans and the Australians are primed and ready to get the impending battle over with. They think it will be short and sweet, believing the positions are "manned by a few sick Japs," according to intelligence provided by Major General George C. Kenny, Allied air commander. Kenny also asserts that tanks and artillery have no place in jungle warfare because his planes can better serve that purpose—a claim that, strangely, MacArthur accepts. To better oversee the upcoming action, MacArthur moves his headquarters from Brisbane to Port Moresby. It is not until much later that tanks and artillery, which turn the tide of the bloody struggle, are provided as ground support for the infantry.

When the Allies begin their attacks, they promptly run into a hornet's nest of bitter enemy opposition. The Japanese troops are determined to hold out until reinforced or relieved by other units that have been temporarily dispatched to deal with the problem of retaking Guadalcanal. Then they will resume the drive to capture Port Moresby. The Japanese high command at Rabaul has no intention of ending its campaign on Papua.

Chapter 14

Marines Barely Hanging onto the Canal

The situation for the Cactus Air Force was changing. On November 1st the first four SBDs of Major Joseph Sailor's VMSB-132 flew in to Henderson Field. This was part of Colonel William O. Brice's Marine Air Group 11, which was being brought in to bolster air operations. Ten pilots of VMF-112 arrived as passengers aboard an R4D the next day. On hand for their use were three airstrips. The original field now extended to 5,400 feet—more than a mile long—two thirds of which was covered with Marston matting. Nearby the more primitive grass-covered Fighter One boasted 4,600 feet of landing space that remained subject to mud or dust, depending on the weather. A new strip northwest of Henderson Field, Fighter Two, had been cut from the hardy terrain and graded. It was rough, but usable.

During a lull in operations caused by poor flying conditions and exhaustion on both sides, fresh new squadrons came in to replace units reduced by the exhausting demands of aerial combat, deaths, and wounds. Within a few days the surviving flyers of VB-6 and VF-71 ended their tours and rotated out. Bad as the conditions were for the ground troops, they were far worse for the aviators, who were ground down by the rigors of going into battle almost every day.

At this point the severely physically and emotionally fatigued Brigadier General Roy Geiger, as badly worn down as his pilots, was replaced by now Brigadier General Louis Woods. Ten years younger than the highly effective Geiger, the once kindly Woods had somehow been transformed into an aggressive, bloodthirsty leader. It was the right move at the right time for the embattled CAF. Although it was still unclear at the time, the kind of air war that raged around Guadalcanal was changing.

The Japanese were also making changes within their 11th Air Fleet. In one month this vaunted force had lost a third of its plane strength and too many exceptional pilots. Morale plummeted after the devastating land battle losses during October. The fifty-two planes of the R Area Air Force had been reduced to twenty-one, and the force was in the process of being rebuilt rather than patched up. Replacement aircraft were slow in coming, and the new air crews were noticeably less adept and less experienced.

Vandegrift now had 19,000 men on Guadalcanal. Robert Leckie, in *Challenge for the Pacific,* saw them—especially those who had been there from the beginning—this way: "They were shadow troops. Three months of uninterrupted ordeal such as no American troops had ever sustained, before or since, such as few soldiers in history have experienced, made them walking skeletons of parchment flesh and quivering nerve. They were the young ancients, the old-young, staring with a fixed thousand-yard stare out of eyes that were red-rimmed and sunken. Their bodies were taut rags of flesh stretched over sticks of bone. They had come to Guadalcanal muscular and high-spirited young men, but now each had lost at least twenty pounds, some had lost fifty, and their high fervor had ebbed and nearly flowed away. They were hanging on by habit only, fighting out of the rut of an old valor."

Another 4,000 with Brigadier General Rupertus on Tulagi weren't much better off. Most were convinced they had been abandoned by their country, and they were losing the resource that had carried them so far through this unfathomable nightmare—they were losing hope. While the marines were suffering and dying on this miserable, stinking island, the merchant seamen were demanding more pay to unload supplies.

Much like the Confederate Gray Wolves—the southern soldiers who fought while nearly starved, barefoot and dressed in tattered scraps of clothing in the snows of the last battles of our own Civil War—they simply existed from one firefight to the next. That was all they knew to do. Hardly able to move from the bone-wracking ravages of malaria, dysentery, festering fungal flesh rot, and other diseases, and on the very edge of starvation, they responded only to the sound of gunfire. Fighting and death was their only reality. They forged into small groups or clans who fought for each other. Some had survived so long in the same swampy filthy foxholes that they all but refused to move even fifty yards away. Their existence had been reduced to the simple non-thinking primitive instinct for survival.

Diseases Take Their Toll

A multitude of tropical illnesses ravaged both sides. The Japanese suffered worse than the Allies because they lacked medical services. Malaria, dengue fever, acute dysentery, elephantiasis, malnutrition, fungal infections, and other debilitating diseases caused far more casualties than battle wounds.

Most of the marines and GIs on Guadalcanal suffered from dysentery brought on by the terrible water and food. The worst cases suffered through twenty or thirty bowel movements a day, mostly liquids, causing body weight to drop drastically. Many of the men simply ripped the back seams out of their fatigues, because when an attack came, there was not always time to drop the pants. The pilots flying combat missions were not so lucky—they could not leave the cockpits when the belly-gripping pain wracked their bodies.

Malaria caused far more casualties than battle wounds. The parasites causing this disease were injected into the bloodstream by millions of disease-carrying mosquitoes. There was no effective way to control the infestation of mosquitoes, and there was precious little medicine available to treat or control the infection, and none to prevent it. The extraordinarily high fever accompanying the worst episodes often left a victim in a coma. Attacks of this debilitating disease often recurred years after its onset.

Perhaps the worst illness was brought on by dengue fever. Private Leckie said, "[I had malaria] nine times, and I had dengue, which is much worse—and I got that in a hospital. Dengue is called breakbone fever. It's as though your bones are in a vice and someone is turning the vice. You can't even take water. Your spleen becomes distended. You do nothing but vomit bile, so if you were in the jungle, you'd certainly die. But they had to feed you intravenously and maybe it's just as well that I got it in the hospital. But, yeah, the malaria doesn't compare to it."

Fungus infections and foot rot were common ailments. Living in the natural steam bath of heat and humidity, with incessant rain that left muddy water standing in the foxholes, caused foot rot. This affliction—the same as WWI's trench foot—caused the flesh underneath the boots to become withered and spongy. The men were compelled to remain in these dank foxholes for days at a time. Dry socks and boots might have solved that problem, but they were not available, nor was it possible to simply stay out of the muck. In time, patches of flesh rotted away or became infected and required medical treatment back at the hospital.

A new American advance across the Matanikau began on November 1st. In the wee morning hours from 2:00 to 6:00 A.M., A, C, and D Companies of the 1st Engineer Battalion put together three footbridges across the river under cover of Company E, 5th Marines, who had crossed earlier. Each 40-inch-wide bridge consisted of 2-inch by 4-inch wooden stringers tied to a frame secured to floating empty fuel drums.

Two battalions of the 2nd Marines were brought over from Tulagi to buttress Edson's rested 5th Marines. The 5th Marines led the attacks, supported inland by the reformed Whaling group, now composed of the Scout-Snipers attached to 3rd Battalion, 7th Marines. The 2nd Marines—less the third Battalion—were held in reserve. The objective was to drive the enemy back far enough to eliminate their artillery barrages against Henderson Field, and to close down the retreat of Japanese forces along the upper Lunga.

Howitzers of the 11th Marines, aided by the 5-inch guns of the 3rd Defense Battalion, went to work at daybreak pounding Japanese positions. The cruisers *San Francisco* and *Helena*, along with the destroyer *Sterett*, blasted targets west of Point Cruz. Joining in to descend on enemy artillery batteries were Aircobras and SBDs from Henderson Field. Nineteen B-17s from Espiritu Santo flew up and dropped 335 100-pound bombs on Kokumbona.

When the bombardment was lifted, two battalions of the 5th Marines easily crossed the new bridges, and by 7:00 they were deployed for the attack. Whaling's group, covering the left, had crossed the river further upstream. It was on the flat ground near the beach that the advancing 1st Battalion, 5th Marines, ran up against heavy opposition from a Japanese delaying rear guard. By 12:30 P.M. the adjacent 2nd Battalion, further inland and on higher ground, had pushed ahead and lost contact with the 1st, who were still engaged. Still, the enemy had been forced back enough for the engineers to construct a bridge for vehicles about 500 yards from the river mouth. When the first vehicles crossed the next afternoon, a new section of road had extended the old coast road.

Corporal Anthony Casamento of Company D, 1st Battalion, 5th Marines, Brooklyn, New York, was serving as the leader of a machine gun section along a ridge near the Matanikau River. He positioned his section to provide covering fire for two flanking units and to provide direct support for the main force of his company, which was behind him. During the fight all the members of his section were killed or severely wounded. Although Casamento suffered multiple grievous wounds, he continued to provide critical supporting fire after setting up, loading, and manning his machine gun. He single-handedly engaged and destroyed one machine gun emplacement to his front and took the other emplacement on the flank under fire, repeatedly repulsing multiple assaults by the enemy while protecting the flanks of the adjoining companies and holding his position until the main force arrived. The recommendation for the Medal of Honor was mishandled, and the medal wasn't presented to Casamento until 1980 by President Carter.

For the first time along the Matanikau, Americans were moving against an inferior enemy that was in bad condition—but still full of fight. Recognizing the threat to Kokumbona, the Japanese 17th Army sent Colonel Sugita to the new front with orders to stop the Marine advance at all costs—an action beyond the capabilities and resources of the depleted troops on hand. He gathered all the men he could find, including road construction workers, and tried to form an effective defense.

The attack to the west across the Matanikau continued on the 2nd with Edson committing his reserve 3rd Battalion to assist the 1st. The 2nd Battalion had advanced beyond Point Cruz, turned right toward Sealark Channel and moved into position west of the enemy, trapping the Japanese left in Santa Cruz between the forces of the 5th Marines. In the afternoon two battalions of the 2nd Marines passed to the left of the 5th to continue the push to the west, supported by destroyers shelling Japanese emplacements between Point Cruz and the mouth of the Umasami River.

To the east, after a forced march covering about 13 miles from the perimeter, Lieutenant Colonel Hanneken's 2nd Battalion, 7th Marines crossed the Metapona River and prepared new positions near Koli Point. That dark night in the rain, a Japanese cruiser escorting a transport and three destroyers landed about 1,500 troops of the 230th Infantry a mile east of Hanneken's new position. These troops, with supplies and ammunition for 2,000, were looking to join with survivors of the Shoji force and build an airfield near Koli Point. In the rain Marine communications failed and word of the Japanese landing could not be sent back to Division.

When the Japanese began moving west in the morning, they ran into the marines, who then came under mortar and artillery fire. To avoid being flanked from the southwest, the 2nd Battalion withdrew and took up stronger positions on the west bank of the Nalimbiu River. It wasn't until 2:45 in the afternoon that word of the Japanese presence finally arrived back at Division. The CAF struck at enemy positions but did not do much damage. The cruisers *San Francisco* and *Helena*, along with the destroyers *Sterett* and *Lansdowne*, moved over from the Kokumbona area to shell Koli Point. Colonel Amor Sims loaded his 1st Battalion, 7th Marines onto landing craft to reinforce his 2nd Battalion.

By the 4th, action in the vicinity of Kokumbona had lightened. The 164th Infantry, less one battalion, was moved to a position to block the enemy about 4,000 yards south of Koli Point. Brigadier General Edmund B. Sebree, assistant commander of the Americal

Division, would take charge of the area west of the Lunga. On this occasion he decided to accompany the 164th to gain experience with jungle combat. Brigadier General Rupertus, assistant division commander, now in charge of the area east of the Lunga, came in to take over the Koli Point operation.

The 1st Battalion, 7th reached Koli Point on the 4th along with Rupertus and its regimental headquarters. At 6:00 A.M. two battalions of the 164th—2/164 and 3/164—along with Company B, 8th Marines, marched toward the area seven miles from the Ilu line to help block the Japanese escape. At the same time the 2nd Raider Battalion, which had landed at Aola, was ordered to move overland toward the point and intercept any enemy forces moving eastward.

The prostrating heat of the snarled and swampy jungle and the saw-toothed kunai grass inland alternately delayed the 164th's progress. The soldiers, in full combat gear and carrying heavy weapons and ammunition, struggled through the thick morass and did not reach their assembly area on the Nalimbiu's west bank until noon, 3,500 yards (about two miles) south of Koli Point. The 2/164 then advanced north about 2,000 yards (more than one mile) along the west bank of the river against sparse opposition, but did not make contact with the 7th Marines until the next day.

American Transport Divisions Eight and Twelve of Turner's TF 65 landed 500 Seabees of the 14th Naval Construction Battalion (NCB) and 2,000 tons of supplies and equipment at Aola Bay on the 4th with the mission of building a new airstrip. Aola was about 30 straight-line miles—considerably more by sea—from the Lunga on the northeastern tip of Guadalcanal. The Seabees came in on the transports *Neville*, *Fomalhaut*, and *Heywood*. The 14th NCB accompanied the 100 sailors of ACORN-1, an advance base for land planes. The time for developing Guadalcanal into a major airbase seemed to have arrived.

Vandegrift's engineers and long-term resident on Guadalcanal Martin Clemens had warned the obstinate Turner—who chose to disregard advice he hadn't requested—that the swampy terrain of Aola was totally unsuitable for the construction of an airfield. Turner remained obsessed with the idea of establishing small pockets of Marine and Army troops to "mop up isolated enemy positions." A week later, after the Seabees had been able to make no progress in an area where ankle-deep water was the norm, the men and equipment were transferred to the newly secured Koli Point.

Companies C and E of the 2nd Marine Raider Battalion under Lieutenant Colonel Evans F. Carlson came ashore as the main body of the advance landing force. This unit had gained a measure of fame by their daring raid on Makin Island, which destroyed a Japanese radio station. The remainder of the 2nd Raiders didn't arrive on the Canal until December 12th.

Also coming ashore at Aola—a new unloading location designated by Turner—was the Army's 1st Battalion, 147th Infantry, under the command of Colonel W.B. Tuttle, artillery batteries for the Americal Division, as well as detachments of the 5th Marine Defense Battalion, and Marine antiaircraft batteries and 155-mm howitzers for coastal defense. All of these units had to be moved back to the Lunga perimeter.

On the morning of the 5th, Rupertus ordered the 3rd Battalion, 164th to cross the surging river and then swing north along the east bank to destroy the Japanese facing the

7th Marines at Koli Point. Two platoons of Company G were held by enemy machine guns, but artillery and mortar fire promptly silenced the opposition. The 2nd Battalion then withdrew to the river crossing and moved in behind the 3rd Battalion.

While the Army was hacking their way north through the tangled dense jungle on the 6th, the swollen and flooding Nalimbiu slowed the 7th Marine crossing to the east near the beach. A brief firefight broke out between the two Army battalions, who thought they had at last encountered the enemy. Their hope for a trap to clean out the Japanese units, possibly 3,000 men, failed to materialize, because the Japanese had escaped eastward, toward the oncoming 2nd Raiders. After joining up at Koli Point, the Marine and Army troops moved, against light opposition, to a position about a mile shy of the Metapona River's wide mouth. There they dug in on the night of November 7–8 to defend the beach against a threatened landing that never came. A search plane had spotted eleven destroyer transports of Tanaka's Tokyo Express heading for Guadalcanal. The next day the 2nd Battalion, 164th was attached to the 7th Marines as a reserve.

Most of the Seabees of the 14th NCB, back at the Lunga Plain, were used to extend and improve Henderson Field and Fighter One. A detachment was sent to Tulagi to work on the improvement of the base for Motor Torpedo Boat Squadrons 2 and 3, as well as on general harbor alterations.

The 8th Marines arrived on Guadalcanal, at the Lunga, on the same day, and were available for immediate deployment against the well established enemy to the west. This unit had just been released from the forces being hoarded for the seizure and occupation of Ndeni. Admirals Nimitz and Halsey finally decided no real advantage would be gained by taking Ndeni and canceled the operation, which Vandegrift had never been convinced was necessary.

Vice Admiral Halsey came to visit Guadalcanal. To Vandegrift his visit was "like a breath of fresh air." The new South Pacific Commander visited the men in the field, saw their awful physical condition, and promised to send more help. To round out his visit, a Japanese naval bombardment by a single destroyer from the Express awakened him during the night.

The eleven troop-laden Japanese destroyers landed 1,300 fresh men of the 38th Division on the 7th at Tassafaronga despite CAF attacks. A mixed group of seven SBDs of Major Sailor's VMSB-132, nine Aircobras of the Army's 67th, and three TBF torpedo bombers of VT-8—supported by twenty-one Marine Wildcats—had been sent to derail this run of the Tokyo Express. They inflicted moderate damage on two destroyers but did not prevent the landing of 80 percent of the troops and the subsequent evacuation of 497 wounded soldiers and sailors. In the sortie American pilots mixed with an assortment of ten IJN float planes screening the landing. Captain Joe Foss shot down three of them before he had to ditch his crippled Wildcat in the sea. He was rescued the next day, but was beginning to think that if he had many more Wildcats shot out from under him he might be designated a Japanese ace as well as an American ace.

The American cargo ship *Majaba*, approaching Lunga Point, was torpedoed by the Japanese submarine *I-20*, an attack witnessed by Martin Clemens returning from Aola. The badly damaged ship staggered for shore and was beached. Later it was patched up and eventually returned to service. When *Majaba* arrived at Lunga, they discovered that they had landed adjacent to a Long Lance that had run ashore and failed to explode. A bomb disposal team was already at work disarming and dismantling the deadly fish. The destroyer *Lansdowne* brought in more ammunition to the troops on the island.

Vandegrift, on the 9th, ordered most of the 164th Infantry and Company B, 8th Marines, back to the perimeter to be redeployed for another offensive near the Matanikau. Still in the Koli area, the 2nd Battalion, 164th extended its line farther inland along Gavaga Creek to seal off the Japanese. But the pocket had a hole in it. Company E of the 2/164th was committed to patch this hole, but during the night—with the help of nearby Company F on the other side of the creek—it was unable to stop the enemy breakout. On the 10th the hole still hadn't been stopped up and more of Shoji's regiment slipped through. Lieutenant Colonel Arthur C. Timboe, the 2nd's battalion commander, was relieved by Brigadier General Sebree for failing to close the gap. Still, 450 Japanese soldiers who did not get out died in the pocket when it was finally reduced.

Lieutenant Colonel Carlson's two companies of the 2nd Raider Battalion, marching from Aola, did not arrive at Koli Point in time to catch Colonel Shoji's troops. So they did the next best thing—they chased after the Japanese column as it circled around the Lunga perimeter in a march to join up with their forces in the west. Carlson's troops used unorthodox harassing tactics on the retreating column.

The Raiders, whose motto was *Gung Ho* (Chinese for "work together"), were guided through the jungle by Vouza's native scouts, who also carried the ammunition and rations that were periodically parachuted to the American force. Carlson's unseen main body of troops paralleled the route taken by the Japanese, while his combat patrols clung like shadows to the tail of the enemy column. Each time they made contact with a large body of the retreating force, the Raiders attacked. Then as Shoji rushed reinforcements to the skirmish, Carlson's men would quickly hit the enemy flanks with heavy rifle and mortar fire. Then just as quickly, they would disengage and once again vanish from sight. By the time Carlson's troops emerged from the jungle, the words *Gung Ho* had become a macho battle cry etched in Marine Corps lore.

Twelve times during the month-long trek in the bush this unique tactic—like wolves snapping at the edge of a herd of elk—had produced remarkable results. By the time Shoji's shattered group reeled into Kokumbona, they had lost 488 dead and scores of wounded at a cost of sixteen Raiders killed and eighteen wounded. The Japanese survivors no longer called the island Guadalcanal—they now used terms like *Ga Shima*, "Hunger Island," or, more appropriately, *Shih Shima*, "Death Island." When they at last reached the forces of the 17th Army, only about thirty of the surviving 700 to 800 stragglers were capable of fighting.

On the 9th, Rear Admiral Scott on *Atlanta*, with four destroyers, provided escort for three transports departing Espiritu Santo for Guadalcanal. American operations toward Kokumbona were renewed. Scott's force was sighted north of San Cristobal by a patrol plane launched from a Japanese submarine. The submarine *I-127* was sunk by the destroyer *Southard*.

Five Japanese destroyer transports had to fight off a PT boat attack during the night to bring in and land 600 men of the 38th Division led by Lieutenant General Sano.

Rear Admiral Scott's 62.4 Group arrived off Lunga Point on the 11th, sending in the destroyer *Fletcher* to make sure the area was clear of Japanese warships. In an earlier predawn launch, eight CAF Wildcats attacked Rekata Bay at Santa Isabel and strafed the Japanese base for float plane fighters and scouts. Led by Marine Captain Joe Foss, the aggressive and fiery ace, the fighters succeeded in temporarily shutting off the use of those enemy planes against the incoming ship convoys.

The three transports were greeted by a flotilla of worn and scruffy landing boats that had been left behind on August 8th. They began the rush to get as many men and as much materiel ashore as possible before the expected air attack from Rabaul roared in. Indeed, Vice Admiral Turner had warned this task force and TF 67: "In view of expected air attacks...it becomes highly essential to get troops, organizations, weapons, ammunition, and food ashore at the earliest possible moment."

The warning was timely, for news of the unusually early first air raid arrived at 9:05 A.M. The dozen Zekes and nine D3A Val dive bombers—usually armed with a 250-kg (550-lb) bomb and two smaller 60-kg (132-lb) bombs—had been launched from the Japanese light carrier *Hiyo*. This alert came shortly after one of the ships screening the transports reported a possible submarine contact.

Hurriedly the small boats headed for the relative safety of the shore as the convoy fleets dispersed to meet the raid. The cruiser *Atlanta* would be useful in this fight, as it was one of the newly designated and equipped antiaircraft cruisers in the South Pacific. The dive bombers, in the usual vee formation, were spotted coming in over Cape Esperance. At least eight Wildcats, with orders to get the bombers no matter what, were patrolling the area when the alert was sounded. Engaging the Zekes was to be avoided unless under direct attack. Eight more Wildcats clawed into the air from Henderson Field to reach the intercept altitude of 18,000 feet, and immediately ran into the Zekes.

Lieutenant Sam Folsom, scheduled to depart in a week with VMF-121, was quickly involved in a dogfight, but managed to get on the tail of a Val diving on the convoy. He poured a stream of bullets into the dive bomber and started it smoking before it disappeared into a cloud. He was convinced he had shot it down, but had to be content with a "probable" victory—which would have been his first. Marine pilot 2nd Lieutenant David Allen did shoot down a Zeke, but had his plane destroyed by another Zeke. He managed to bail out and was recovered by a landing boat and brought back to the beach.

At 9:40 the dive bombers were on their way down toward the evading ships. The transport *Zeilin*, scrambling around at 14 knots, was firing every antiaircraft gun it could bring to bear. *Betelgeuse*, veteran of many resupply runs to Guadalcanal, was barely missed by two 60-kg bombs, one of which exploded in the water only 20 feet away, with the other at about 40 feet, showering the ship with steel fragments.

Because of a near miss that scraped her starboard side and exploded underwater, *Zeilin* suffered steering damage that soon had her heading directly for *Betelgeuse*, which had to maneuver abruptly to avoid a collision. When the air raid ended, the transports resumed their position off Lunga and continued their unloading.

In the original combat air patrol alerted to intercept incoming Japanese aircraft headed for the transports was 2nd Lieutenant Thomas Henry Mann, Jr., from Sullivan, Indiana. When his group reached 18,000 feet, he spotted twelve Val dive bombers flying in a nice vee formation at about 12,000 feet, already beginning their runs on the ships. Mann shot down the last Val in the formation, then continuing on through he fired on the first or second in the bombing group, exploding it. Still in a dive, he followed a third Val down through 500 feet and shot it down, watching it fall into the sea. On the deck—that is, just above the water—he spun around on another bomber that had already dropped its bomb, got within 100 yards, and fired his guns until it exploded.

He was lining himself up on a fifth dive bomber, looking for a field day, when he suddenly spotted another one lining him up, its guns already firing. Damage to the engine and the wing took away any control of the Wildcat. As he was too close to the sea to bail out and was wounded in the left hand, arm, and leg with shrapnel, he rode it down. Crashing into the sea, he smashed his head on the gun sight, losing seven teeth in the impact. He managed to get out of the plane and inflate his life jacket. Figuring he was halfway between Savo and Florida Island, and fearing there might be Japanese on Savo, he began swimming toward Florida Island.

He swam from 9:30 in the morning until dusk fell, managing at last to make it to an islet about 200 to 300 yards around, and collapsed onto the beach. Two Melanesians found him, let him know they were friendly, and took him the rest of the way to Florida Island. There they treated his wounds with stone-age medical preparations, and made him rinse his mouth out with a vile tasting concoction that must have worked, for his mouth never became infected. They nurtured and fed him for seven days until he could travel, and on November 18 they put the wounded pilot aboard a large canoe and paddled him to Tulagi—45 miles and eight hours away—without stopping.

The twenty-two native canoeists chanted and sang Christian religious songs the entire trip. Mann arrived safely at Tulagi in a Japanese uniform taken from one of the Japanese the Melanesians had killed. They happily accepted his flight suit in exchange.

After medics removed seven pieces of shrapnel, he was evacuated to New Caledonia. After this harrowing escape and remarkable trip, one thing bothered him. "My wife was never notified that I was Missing in Action." he said. "The first she heard was when a letter she sent was returned with 'MIA' stamped on the envelope."

At 11:00 P.M. a new alert of "bombers on the way" was given. Once again, with klaxons sounding General Quarters, the ships moved into their defensive positions. At 11:03 one of the ships on antisubmarine duty reported a sonar contact and moved to drop depth charges. No positive contact was made. While the ships were scampering in their air defense formation, the Japanese bombers arrived, but this time they directed their attack on Henderson Field.

Among the fighter pilots who scrambled to intercept the new attack was 1st Lieutenant Haberman, who was already an ace with 5.5 kills. He managed to shoot down a Betty before his guns jammed up. He was wounded in his right arm, and took a bullet crease along his top right thigh.

Before noon, the transports returned to the task of unloading. As they finished, the damaged *Zeilin*—down ten feet at the stern from flooding—was ready to depart for

Espiritu Santo escorted by the destroyer *Lardner*, but left behind four of its ramped tank landing boats to lighten its load. The Lunga Boat Pool was elated to be able to add these well maintained vessels to their small fleet. The other two cargo ships took cover in the protected waters beyond the path taken by Japanese bombardment ships. Fortunately no enemy ships came down that night.

Intelligence and Reconnaissance

The alerts for approaching ships and aircraft came from a variety of sources. Many came from the Coastwatchers in their concealed lairs overlooking the Solomons "Slot," and were especially helpful as far as formations of aircraft coming down from Rabaul were concerned. These men often provided an accurate count and description of the kinds of ships headed for Guadalcanal.

Both sides regularly used submarines and long-range reconnaissance aircraft in areas beyond the sight of interested eyes. No intelligent fleet commander would move his ships without patrols nosing ahead. The Allies used Navy PBYs from Nouméa and Espiritu Santo, and Army B-17s from Australia or New Caledonia that flew long and often crushingly dull missions over set search pattern areas. Submarines were assigned definite patrol areas. Days and weeks might be spent without a sighting, and the crews had to deal with the enervating boredom. If a good target presented itself they could attack, but they first had to furnish information on the numbers and types of ships, their location, and the direction in which they were heading. It must be kept in mind that when a submarine or patrol plane broke radio silence and went on the air to send a sighting report, they often revealed their own presence to the enemy. Sometimes they had to fight whether it was to their advantage or not.

The primary mission of the aircraft was to find the enemy ships and report those sightings. Because of their slowness and vulnerability, many multi-engine patrol planes—which had to fly alone—were shot down when found, although they had no intention of attacking shipping. For these pilots, keeping a safe distance away and yet close enough for accurate observation was crucial. Cruisers and battleships often carried float planes to be used for reconnaissance and also as artillery and gunfire spotters. The Japanese employed these planes with great skill when a night battle was in the offing. Some, like "Washing Machine Charley" and "Louie the Louse," dropped flares to light up a bombardment target. Aircraft carriers kept patrol planes as well as a CAP in the air to detect any nearby enemy forces. Many of these aircraft—frequently pairs of the longer-range dive bombers or torpedo planes—would be armed with bombs or torpedoes for an attack, but would only use them after radioing back a spotting report. For all of these the primary mission was operational intelligence and reports, not combat.

Further, both the Americans and Japanese depended on what is called signals intelligence, or sigint. Radio intercept operators monitored the known frequencies and copied down messages sent between stations. By no means were all the messages decoded (cryptanalysis) in time to be of any use, but the call signs of the stations could often be relied upon to determine who was speaking to whom (traffic analysis, or TA). Even when call signs were suddenly changed, as they were from time to time, experienced eavesdroppers could identify the "hand" of an enemy operator—his unique rhythm or style of tapping out the Morse code signals—which was usually the same whatever call sign was used. Each ship, each unit, and each base had to have call signs to know they were being addressed. Obviously, any station or ship could overhear a message sent to anyone else—or by an enemy listening post. The third component of sigint was direction finding (DF), where two or more listening stations placed far apart could physically locate the transmission source while a message was being sent.

Efforts were made by intelligence units at higher levels to correlate all the bits and pieces of information into a meaningful whole in order to predict an enemy action or movement. Because many of the Japanese codes had been broken, the Americans often knew the composition of enemy forces, their leaders, and even their objectives. It was from a combination of contributions from all these sources—confirmation by more than one source provided the most useful information—that Vice Admiral Halsey knew that a large Japanese fleet was bearing down on Guadalcanal. Even though the Americans knew every detail of the fleet's intentions, the appearance of such a force could mean nothing but trouble for the beleaguered island of Guadalcanal. Halsey was determined that his ships would break up this movement before the Japanese could carry out their plans.

On the 12th Turner arrived off Lunga with four transports carrying the 1st and 2nd Battalions of the 182nd Infantry, and the 245th Field Artillery Battalion with its 105-mm howitzers—3,358 soldiers in all. The 4th Marine Replacement Battalion and a wealth of supplies were equally welcome additions. The transports were escorted by Task Force 67.4—four cruisers and eight destroyers under Rear Admiral Daniel J. Callaghan. The presence of the transport convoy off Lunga was reported by Lieutenant Commander Mitzi, a Japanese observer on the island. Armed with that information, Yamamoto was convinced that the ships would depart as usual by nightfall, and ordered Vice Admiral Abe's bombardment group—based on two battleships—to move down and destroy Henderson Field with a heavy concentration of their 14-inch shells. A similar bombardment had very nearly succeeded a month before. The Japanese knew they had to neutralize Guadalcanal's air operations if they were to successfully retake the island.

The same sighting report had been received by the 11th Air Fleet at Rabaul, which sent an air strike of sixteen Betties armed with torpedoes and thirty covering Zekes. A Coastwatcher announced that the Japanese air raid was on its way, and the American air fleet dispersed to fight off the attacking bombers and torpedo planes. Twenty Wildcats and eight Aircobras took to the air to repel the attack. When the Japanese attacked at 2:05 P.M., Turner handled his ships expertly and in such a way that no torpedoes hit home, and most of the vessels emerged unscathed.

San Francisco, Callaghan's flagship, was damaged when a shot-up Betty crashed into the secondary fire control station of the ship, just over the hangar area, knocking out the radar. The destruction included the 20-mm and 40-mm guns on that deck manned by the ship's aviation gang. Twenty-one sailors died—mostly from burns—and another twenty-eight were wounded. The destroyer *Buchanan* took a hit from a 5-inch shell that knocked out her torpedo tubes—a stray from the friendly antiaircraft fire thrown up to thwart the attacking Betties—killing five and wounding seven other men. Eleven Betties were splashed, along with one Zeke, at a cost of three Wildcats and one P-39.

When the eight-minute-long air raid ended, the convoy moved back into position off Lunga Point to complete the unloading of troops and artillery, and at about 6:00 P.M. headed out for Espiritu Santo. TF 67.4 remained in the channel to join up with Rear Admiral Norman Scott's TF 62.4 to intercept the Japanese bombardment group they knew was on its way. Callaghan, two weeks senior to Scott in rank, was to command the interception group.

Spirits were greatly lifted when Major Dale Brannon arrived at Henderson Field with eight new and often-requested eight P-38 Lightning fighters from Espiritu Santo. The twin-engine high-altitude Lockheed P-38 Lightning fighter was more than a match for the remarkable Zeke. The addition of these fighters, along with other last-minute arrivals, brought CAF's operational strength on November 13th up to seventy-seven planes. On hand were twenty Wildcats, eight Lightnings, eighteen P-39s, twenty-three SBDs, and eight Avenger torpedo bombers.

The Japanese Army and Navy planners at last had agreed to a total, coordinated operation to push the Americans off Guadalcanal. Following Abe's obliteration of Henderson Field, on Z-Day a field army counting 60,000 infantry troops would be landed to mount a massive and decisive offensive against the Lunga perimeter. The Japanese Navy would have to move about 30,000 more men, 300 artillery pieces, and 30,000 additional tons of supplies into place by mid-December. Logistics was the problem, thought Yamamoto, and the answer would be 150 round trips by his transports or more than 800 such trips by his destroyers. Total destruction of the airfield was absolutely necessary if this was to take place.

In the Spotlight

WILLIAM H. LAING

The Hospital Pharmacist's Mate is assigned to various Marine units as a combat corpsman—one of the many medical services provided by the U.S. Navy. By long-standing tradition, the doctors and surgeons who worked in the combat zone and behind the lines were all Navy men. When providing emergency medical treatment to the wounded during combat, the corpsmen—with red crosses painted on their helmets and brassards on their arms—were marines for all practical purposes. In the beginning corpsmen were not armed, but that was to change when it was found that the Japanese used the red crosses for targets.

Will Laing grew up in Shreveport, in northern Louisiana, where he finished high school after his war service. In mid-January 1942 he enlisted in the Navy while still a 17-year-old, forging his mother's signature on the consent form needed for young men under 18 years of age. After his boot camp in San Diego, California he was selected to be a hospital corpsman, which suited him fine, as he was hoping for a career in medicine, and to attend Tulane University in New Orleans.

He sailed for Guadalcanal as a Pharmacist's Mate 3rd Class on USS *George F. Elliott*, a converted freighter. He landed with Company A, 1st Battalion, 5th Marines, 1st Marine Division, about two hours behind schedule. A marine sergeant racing alongside him over Red Beach was shot through the head and killed by a sniper. Laing hurried over, but there was nothing he could do. By the time he left the Canal, he had seen so many dead men—American and Japanese—that he thought of the corpses only as a health hazard to the living.

Actually, Laing should not have even been in the service, and should not have served on Guadalcanal. He suffered from severe asthma and hay fever, which sometimes made him a casualty, especially in the extremely humid tropics. "Doc" Laing, as he was called by the marines—or "Tulane" to his close friends, who knew of his burning desire to attend medical school there—saw considerable action in the time he was in the Pacific before being discharged from the service in early 1943. For years after that he suffered from guilt because he had survived when so many others had died.

His first job was to select a site for a medical dressing station. Then he had to search through the cargo piling up on the beach for the medical supplies and hospital and aid station tents. Then as the 5th Marines began their advance inland, he handed out salt tablets to help prevent the men from passing out from the sweltering heat.

The next day he was moved to Tulagi, across Sealark Channel, where his services were in greater need—meaning that the corpsmen who had come ashore there were all dead or wounded. There he began treating the cuts and abrasions the men had incurred from the sharp coral outcroppings during the landing (infections from these untreated wounds could take a man out of action as easily as a bullet), as well as combat wounds. He heard that one of the corpsmen had been blown to pieces, and another wounded seriously enough to warrant evacuation. On the 12th he and his group were returned to Guadalcanal.

Soon malaria was spreading despite the administration of Atabrine, for many of the young marines thought it would make a man impotent. Laing was told, "A dead marine, maybe—but an impotent marine, never!" Atabrine, he related later, "turned every man on the 'Canal' as yellow as a Louisiana squash."

A gunnery sergeant told one of his point men, "I can't send you out on patrol. You're yellower than a Jap." Eventually the corpsmen had to stand at the head of the chow line every day to make sure the men swallowed their Atabrine tablet.

The marines were chafing for action, and on August 18th it came. "Doc" was assigned to Company L, 2nd Battalion, 5th Marines, which was to patrol along the Matanikau River. Two platoon leaders were killed and several other men wounded by machine gun fire. The next morning Laing was with a heavy machine gun patrol when it came under fierce enemy fire and was cut off. He soon had more wounded than he could handle. After another sleepless night in the vicious jungle, he managed to get his wounded to the rear. There he had one of his childhood buddies die in his arms.

He served in an aid station behind Alligator Creek the night of the 20th when the Ichiki Force was repulsed. A couple of weeks later he participated in the Raiders' raid on Tasimboko. There he found a group of Melanesian children who had been held prisoner, mistreated and starved by the Japanese. Treating their injuries, and then feeding the children while a fierce firefight took place around them, was one of his few gratifying moments during the Guadalcanal campaign.

Laing was wounded on Edson's Ridge while working in the open; he had to perform an amputation to save one Raider's life while the fighting raged around them. In addition to his leg wound, he suffered a serious asthma attack, and after the battle was assigned to duties behind the lines. Eventually his affliction forced Laing to be returned to the States and discharged from the Navy.

"Doc" Will Laing eventually settled in London, Ontario, teaching pathology in a medical school. He is an Anglican lay minister.

CHAPTER 15

NOVEMBER 13–15
THE NAVAL BATTLE OF GUADALCANAL

A powerful Tokyo Express consisting of two battleships, one cruiser, and fourteen destroyers under Vice Admiral Hiroaki Abe was approaching Guadalcanal to knock out Henderson Field and devastate the marines on Z-Day minus one. Following behind his bombardment force was a huge reinforcement force bringing men and supplies in preparation for a new and final offensive. Since Abe's sole mission was to annihilate the CAF, the field, and its support facilities, the 14-inch guns of his big battleships were armed with an ample supply of bombardment shells. What he did not want to do was to engage the Americans in a surface action.

Warned by air intelligence of the approach of the Japanese force, Rear Admiral Daniel J. "Uncle Dan" Callaghan and his Task Force 67.4, made up of two heavy and three light cruisers and eight destroyers—out to intercept the enemy on Thursday the 12th—were no match for the Japanese fleet. Lacking combat experience—and until a few weeks before serving as chief of staff to the overcautious Vice Admiral Ghormley—Callaghan was Turner's baffling choice to lead this force. He did not like being given the assignment and had made few plans or preparations to carry it out. The officers serving under him on this mission—such as the aggressive and proven leader Rear Admiral Norman Scott, the victor over the Japanese at Cape Esperance a month before—were concerned.

His alignment of his ships into a column and the placement of the vessels equipped with the latest radar technology was poor. The use of radar was still in its early days, and although the operators were well trained and confident, the senior officers commanding forces such as this one had no realistic understanding of its value. There simply hadn't been time to give them the proper indoctrination.

The destroyers *Cushing*, *Laffey*, *Sterett*, and *O'Bannon* led the cruisers *Atlanta*, *San Francisco*, *Portland*, *Helena*, and *Juneau*, followed by the destroyers *Aaron Ward*, *Barton*, *Monssen*, and *Fletcher*. The heavy cruiser *San Francisco*, chosen as Callaghan's flagship, did not have search radar. The best-equipped and most modern ship in the formation was the light cruiser *Helena*, commanded by Captain Gilbert Hoover. She had the only SG surface-search radar on the three light cruisers.

The difference between a light and heavy cruiser is solely one of armament—caliber and number of guns—not size nor speed of the ship. Two of the big ships, *Atlanta* and *Juneau*, were primarily antiaircraft weapons platforms designed to protect the carriers. Even with Scott, flying his flag on the cruiser *Atlanta*, there was no logical reason why these two ships should have been with this force.

Of the four destroyers in the vanguard, only the new *O'Bannon*—commanded by Commander Edwin N. Wilkerson—was equipped with the powerful SG surface-search radar. Why she was fourth in line, rather than first, is difficult to understand. The last in the thirteen-ship column was the modern, SG radar-equipped *Fletcher*, sister ship to *O'Bannon.*

The Japanese bombardment battleships, the old and slow *Hiei* and *Kirishima*, formerly designated as battle cruisers, were not now considered prime candidates for modern surface battles. Each ship had eight 14-inch guns besides fourteen single-mount 6-inch guns, eight antiaircraft 5-inch guns and twenty 25-mm antiaircraft guns. Japanese ships did not have radar, and still relied on the keen eyesight of lookouts. Only one cruiser, *Nagara*, flagship of Rear Admiral Susumu Kimura's destroyer squadron, was present to take part in the action. She had eight 24-inch torpedo tubes split into four pairs to fire the famed Long Lance weapons. Screening the formation were six destroyers—*Akatsuki*, *Ikazuchi*, *Inazuma*, *Amatsukaze*, *Yukikaze*, and *Teruzuki*. The latter was an antiaircraft vessel, for protective purposes.

Callaghan steered a collision course to intercept the onrushing Japanese, believing his fleet's chances of victory against the stronger fleet were nonexistent. The operating philosophy of the U.S. Navy was that when a confrontation was inevitable, you went with what you had. At this time and place that wasn't much, but that was all there was available. *Pensacola*, with her 8-inch main battery, had been detached that afternoon, and the two antiaircraft cruisers, which were totally out of place in a big ship surface action, were also sailing in the battle force.

Callaghan hoped to once again "cross the T," as Scott had done earlier in his battle off Cape Esperance, and bring all his big guns to bear on the enemy. Instead, the two forces collided head-on in Iron Bottom Sound at 1:50 A.M. and the ensuing battle took on all the aspects of a disorganized, catch-as-catch-can streetfight. The known movements and involvements of individual ships are reconstructed from the most reliable sources, as it is impossible to track the battle in the whole. Information on the participation of *Juneau* is sketchy, although some data recently developed credits this ship—which was sunk, with the loss of most of the crew—with greater action in the fight than previously acknowledged.

At 1:42 A.M. on the Friday the 13th (historian author Richard Frank has tried to reconcile the time differences to fit events, as the ship's clocks had not been synchronized) lookouts on *Cushing* sighted ahead what it believed to be three Japanese destroyers crossing from port to starboard. The enemy ships *Yudachi* and *Harusame*, 2,000 yards distant, simultaneously spotted the Americans as *Cushing* turned to port, ready to fire her torpedoes. Callaghan first approved launching the torpedoes, then quickly countered with "Stand by to open fire," and then ordered another course change.

First Night—The Free-for-All Fight

This plunged the closely aligned American ships into a deadly confusion, as the cruisers struggled to avoid running down the nearby destroyers. When they resumed a semblance of order, the task force was headed into the Japanese force. Callaghan, at 1:48, gave his questionable order for "Odd ships fire to starboard, even ships fire to port." This order failed to take into account that some ships had already acquired a target, but on the wrong side, and that others found no target at all. Abe was equally confused, from the sighting reports. At 1:48 his *Hiei* and the destroyer *Akatsuki* turned on their searchlights and caught *Atlanta*, commanded by Captain Jenkins, in brilliant cones of light. The first Japanese shells followed.

Suddenly the sky was ablaze with the muzzle blasts of the big guns, streams of red and white tracer bullets ripping through the darkness, and flares and star shells. High-explosive and armor-piercing shells exploded powder magazines and ruptured fuel lines to set off sweeping fires. Yellow fires sent heavy billows of dense smoke high over the swerving, twisting ships. To the witnesses on the beach it must have seemed like a scene from Dante's *Inferno*.

Atlanta was the first ship on either side to commence firing. Jenkins's main battery swung to port and fired at the source of the light at a range of only 1,600 yards. Then Jenkins realized the three Japanese destroyers were firing on *Atlanta* from the other side, and soon his aft guns were still shooting at *Hiei*, and his forward guns at the destroyers. Shells tore into and damaged one of the destroyers, probably *Akatsuki*, which fired its torpedoes. One exploded into *Atlanta*, along with shells from *Hiei* and *Akatsuki* that ripped into its superstructure. Lieutenant Stew Mordock, Scott's operations officer, who had thought he could feel the heat from the Japanese searchlights when they first snapped on, was on the port wing of the bridge when shells began hitting. A piece of shrapnel tore into his arm, and when he looked around, now in intense pain, he saw Scott collapse dead to the steel deck alongside three other staff officers. Only three of the thirteen enlisted men working on the bridge survived.

Buttoned up in battle stations, Lieutenant Commander Arthur Loeser, chief engineer, died instantly when a Japanese torpedo struck nearly amidships and exploded into the forward engine room, killing almost every man there along with a damage control team in the crew's mess overhead. The huge detonation shook the ship violently its entire length, lifting *Atlanta* out of the water and causing a massive reverberation as she settled back down. The blast in the engine room knocked out all power except that provided by an emergency diesel generator. Terrible sounds of metal buckling and tearing loose in the aftermath of the convulsion frightened Engineer's Mate 3rd Class Bill McKinney and Seaman 2nd Class Dan Curtin manning a damage control position four decks down. Within minutes the ship was afire aft and taking water through the holes blown by the torpedo. Losing her power, *Atlanta* drifted to the south and out of the action.

All hands who could do so turned to trying to save the fractured ship, a story rarely detailed in full. Watertight integrity—the sealing off of compartments to control the flooding—is key to these damage control efforts. Many times men were ordered to securely close, or "dog down," the clamps that will seal a hatch—even when they knew men were trying to get through to escape rising waters that would drown them. On *Atlanta* Machinist's Mate 1st Class Ross Hilton and another machinist deliberately disobeyed that order when they unbolted a hatch to let three men who would have certainly drowned escape. The water behind them was nearly up to the hatch level as they finally sealed it to prevent more serious problems. Hilton's compassion was misguided in this moment of crisis, although the three shipmates he saved would have certainly disagreed. As cruel as it seems, the death of a few men at times like this ensures the survival of many more, and quite possibly the ship itself. Situations like this depend on the moral courage of officers and NCOs to do what must be done. Too many men have died on land, at sea, and in the air when leaders abdicated their authority.

Never before and never again would a naval battle deteriorate into such a frantic melee, which one American officer characterized as "a barroom brawl after the lights had been shot out." Historians Richard Frank and Eric Hammel have tried to sort through the ensuing confusion, and they both admit it is unlikely anyone will ever fully understand what actually happened that night. Those at the scene—on both sides—saw only the tiny parts in which they were involved.

Leading the column, *Cushing*, under Lieutenant Commander Edward "Butch" Parker, who had combat experience against the Japanese, got off a torpedo and machine gun fire at the enemy battleship. Just as quickly, she took hits from the Japanese gunners, which tore apart her engineering section. Losing headway, the destroyer launched six torpedoes at *Hiei*, which was bearing down on her. Damage from ten significant hits silenced *Cushing*'s gun batteries, crippled her steering, and cut off her remaining power. With many sailors dead and wounded, and the ship unable to continue fighting, Parker gave the order to abandon ship.

Laffey had raced ahead toward *Hiei*, and had barely avoided being rammed by the big ship. Gunfire from her 5-inch batteries and machine guns killed Abe's chief of staff Captain Masakane Suzuki, but her torpedoes didn't have time to arm themselves before bouncing off harmlessly. After getting past *Hiei*, *Laffey* ran into three enemy destroyers, which laced her with gunfire. A torpedo blew off her stern up to the aft gun mount, and whipped the fantail of the ship fifteen feet out of the water. Sixteen-year-old Seaman 1st Class Rod Lambert, with a year in the Navy, felt the deck shimmy and shake. He got up to get out to the main deck, and had just spoken to a man there when the man simply disappeared, leaving only one shoe behind. The random extermination so affected the frightened youth that he simply passed out from shock.

Lieutenant Junior Grade Tom Evins crawled up the slanting deck and joined in the struggle to free a young sailor whose legs had been smashed and his body pinned by wreckage to the superhot deck, heated by raging fires directly below. The task of freeing him before he cooked to death seemed impossible. Up on the bridge engineering officer Lieutenant Eugene Barham advised the captain, Lieutenant Commander William E. Hank, that because of the extensive damage *Laffey* should be abandoned.

"I'm not going to abandon my ship," replied Hank. "You get us under way and I will get us out of here."

"Captain," said Barham, "we don't have any propellers. We just can't get this ship under way. May I have permission to put the boats and rafts in the water?" With that permission the engineer moved to prepare for leaving the ship. By the time he got to the main deck, Hank had finally ordered everyone to abandon ship. As they were going over the sides, *Nagara*, which had just sent *Cushing* to the bottom, loomed in sight and trained her guns on the totally helpless *Laffey*. Then, apparently deciding the battered destroyer was not worth the expenditure of more shells, *Nagara* moved away without firing a shot.

As the order was passed to leave the ship, two torpedomen working to free the young gunner in danger of being roasted yelled that they had gotten him loose! They got the boy onto a wire litter and loaded into a raft. The wounded Lambert emerged from unconsciousness hearing a cry for help. He espied a sailor missing several limbs, and unable to even look at the horrible sight he simply left, and was soon in the water.

As she went down into Iron Bottom Sound, *Laffey* exploded, and the huge fireball killed many men still aboard or already in the water, including the skipper. The young sailor who had been pulled from the wreckage and his two saviors had all gotten overboard, but were killed in the blast. Lambert was trapped in the suction created by the bow section going under. His life jacket raised the petrified youngster up through the undertow and back to the surface, where he floated and screamed in insane terror until he could scream no more—but he was still alive.

Sterett, third in line, with her guns pointed the wrong way, finally got them turned to starboard and fired off thirteen salvos at what was possibly *Nagara* 4,000 yards away. The first salvo were star shells, meant to light up the darkness. They lit up the enemy ship as they hit and erupted into showers of flaming sparks. She then took a hit that sliced the main steering control. As the ship struggled to steer with her engines and still fire at the enemy, *O'Bannon* steamed alongside, taking away *Sterett*'s line of fire.

Gunfire from Japanese ships to her port side damaged *Sterett*, one shell thwanging into her mainmast to knock out her radar and TBS (Talk Between Ships) antenna. Lieutenant "Cal" Calhoun, the gunnery officer—standing in the gun director a few yards away from that blast—took several shell fragments, and a piece of the mast was deflected by his padded helmet. The lucky officer later found twenty-three steel slivers had perforated his kapok life jacket. But *Sterett* kept on fighting and at 2:20 sighted an enemy destroyer about 1,000 yards away. The destroyer was pounded by shells from *Sterett*'s main batteries, and was reported to have been sunk. Less than ten minutes later—having lost twenty percent of the crew as casualties, and suffering from eleven direct hits (three from 14-inch bombardment shells) that took out the rear 5-inch guns, set fire to the powder, and forced the flooding of the magazines—the battered *Sterett* was taken out of the fight by its captain, Lieutenant Commander Jesse G. Coward.

Lead radarman Sonarman 3rd Class Roy Conn on *O'Bannon*, last of the four destroyers in the lead, had first made contact with the enemy at 1:30. As the ship maneuvered to avoid hitting or being run down by her slewing and twisting friends, lookouts on the bridge had a better view of the action than did Conn, trying to follow the movements on his radar. When a heavy cross fire fell on *Cushing* and *Laffey*, *O'Bannon* opened up on *Hiei*. When those two destroyers disappeared, *O'Bannon* was in the lead and 1,800 yards from the battleship, which seemed to be burning, at about 1:56, and which couldn't depress its guns enough to land hits on the destroyer. Steaming past the immediate battle and reporting five burning ships, *O'Bannon* reversed course.

"At 2:01 A.M., we maneuver to avoid hitting the sinking bow of the destroyer *Barton*," relates Signalman Ernest A. Herr—aboard *O'Bannon*—in his book *Horror at Guadalcanal*. "The *Barton* was originally well behind us but had managed to pass us as we maneuvered to avoid hitting ships ahead of us. Our crew throw life jackets to its sailors in the water who obviously were not expecting to be there since they have no life jackets. Unavoidably our ship plows though survivors as they thrash about trying to swim out of the way. At 2:03 A.M., the remains of the *Barton* exploded killing many more of the *Barton* crew and causing our ship to rise about a foot in the water. This disrupts communications in our main radio and knocks out our ship's power. Lucky for us, the engine room is able to restore power quickly but our top speed has been reduced to only twenty-eight knots.

"Our crew is not able to observe the ships behind us as well as those in front but we are getting their damage reports via radio contact from *Honolulu.* At my battle station in main radio, I am copying these Morse Code messages and calling them out as they come in. These messages are quickly relayed to the captain. Ordinarily these messages would be encoded but because of time limitations they are being sent in plain language. These messages report the extreme damage to the cruisers in our force. The *Atlanta* reports she is hit as 8-inch shells smash through its superstructure setting her afire the length of the ship killing Admiral Scott and all but one of his staff officers."

Behind the destroyers, *San Francisco* began firing salvos from its 8-inch guns at a destroyer, probably *Yudachi.* When other ships began firing on that destroyer, Captain Young ordered his guns shifted to a second destroyer, *Harusame*, which then changed its course. Apparently the American gunners failed to see the disabled *Atlanta* drift into its field of fire and sent two main gun salvos into its superstructure, killing Admiral Scott, along with many officers and men, and setting the ship afire. Traces of the green marking dye used by shells from *San Francisco* were later found in the shattered compartments and on the crippled gun mounts.

When Callaghan saw what was happening he ordered his flagship to cease firing—meaning on his own ships. Unfortunately the order was relayed to all the American ships—but luckily most commanders ignored the order. Callaghan, quickly trying to clarify his intent, gave the sketchy order: "We want the big ones! Get the big ones first!" That sounds great, but it was almost meaningless under the circumstances. Just then *San Francisco* and *Hiei*—only 2,500 yards apart—passed each other, and both opened fire. The enemy 14-inch bombardment shells exploded on *San Francisco* in a spectacular pyrotechnic display that sent huge sparks cascading through the night sky. Both ships were simultaneously targeted by other enemy ships. *San Francisco* was caught in a cross fire from *Nagara* and *Kirishima*. But it was *Hiei*'s smaller guns, firing standard shells, that scored hits on the bridge, killing Callaghan and all but one member of his staff. *San Francisco*'s captain, Cassin Young, was mortally wounded. The wheelman, Quartermaster 3rd Class Harry Higdon, was unscathed as shrapnel peppered Lieutenant Commander Bruce McCandless, the quartermaster. Most of the shrapnel was absorbed by his kapok life jacket. Then Higdon announced he had lost steering control, spinning the wheel uselessly for emphasis, and *San Francisco* swung out of line before steering was shifted to Battle-2 (the backup command station) by Lieutenant Commander Herbert E. Schonland. Then Battle-2 was destroyed. Sensing the ship was veering out of control again, Quartermaster 3rd Class Floyd Rogers in the armored conning tower just below the pilot house announced he was taking over control of the steering.

The death or serious wounding of senior officers topside thrust command upon McCandless. The damage control officer, Schonland—senior to McCandless and technically in command—was so busy trying to keep the ship afloat that he left and yielded the conn to the quartermaster. McCandless could have taken *San Francisco* out of the battle, as she had suffered forty-five shell hits: her guns were all but silenced, fires flared in at least twenty-five locations, and she had taken on a lot of seawater.

Able-bodied officers—who had been given morphine Syrettes to use if hospital corpsmen weren't available—went to work injecting the screaming wounded with the powerful painkiller. Wading through blood and severed limbs, one of them saw a victim with the top of his head blown off. Some wounded men, trying to reach the main deck, found themselves falling from ladders that had been severed, and suffered broken legs or arms from the impact of crashing onto the steel deck.

Several writers have indicated that McCandless—fearing that the other American ships didn't know the battering his new ship had taken—thought it would precipitate a general withdrawal if he took his ship out of the fight, and thus kept *San Francisco* headed west toward the enemy. Actually he was trying urgently to get his ship out of the battle despite the troubles with the steering and the colossal damage it had sustained. After a few further exchanges of gunfire, he finally got the ship turned around and headed east, along the shores of Guadalcanal, hoping *San Francisco* was finally out of danger.

For their decisive and prudent leadership in continuing to maneuver and fight *San Francisco*—and save the ship—after command was passed down to them, Lieutenant Commanders McCandless and Schonland won the Medal of Honor. The job they did that night—when the senior officers aboard were killed or too badly wounded to take over the battered ship—was extraordinary considering the wild and chaotic nature of the fight.

When the battle began, Captain DuBose of *Portland*, in his first night fight, received a contact report at 1:42. After completing a left turn to follow the ships ahead at 1:50, he found and opened up on the Japanese destroyer *Akatsuki*. Suddenly *Portland*, affectionately called the "Sweet Pea," fired off a nine-gun broadside that—combined with the mass of shells from other ships—greatly expedited the demolition and sinking of *Akatsuki*.

Portland began taking damage even as her guns blazed away, only to be silenced by Callaghan's order to cease fire. Then, when a target too good to miss was spotted, DuBose ignored the order to hold fire and ordered his guns back into action. They got off another full broadside when at about 2:00 *Portland* was hammered by a torpedo hit far aft on the starboard side, lifting both ship and sea upward. Tons of water and objects ripped loose in the explosion rained back down upon the ship like a monsoon. The hit snipped off the starboard propellers, and warped the adjacent hull plates to form an unwanted rudder that sent the cruiser circling to the right.

One sailor standing right above the blast was knocked off his feet and rolled up in a curl of steel plate. He suffered only a few scrapes and cuts in what was a miraculous survival, for many in the same area were killed instantly. Nearby gunners injured from the blast, some of them terribly wounded, remained at their guns. One marine gunner who survived was hit directly between the eyes by a single shell fragment that had already killed two of his buddies. Unbelievably, the impact knocked him unconscious, but didn't even bloody his face, although his face was swollen for several days afterward. Other men rushed around helping their shipmates by applying tourniquets to shattered limbs, staunching the flow of blood from gaping wounds, and getting them into whatever shelter was available.

At the end of her first full spiral, *Portland* fired off four salvos from the forward guns from 4,000 yards, registering hits on *Hiei*. She finally silenced her main battery in fear of hitting Americans in the confusion, and passed out of the battle.

When the command to open fire came, after eight long minutes of champing at the bit, *Helena* had already used her SG radar to train her guns on the most popular target of the night—the Japanese destroyer *Akatsuki.* Captain Gilbert Hoover, known as a willing fighter and leader, wished that Callaghan would receive his tracking reports directly rather than have them relayed over the TBS, which wasn't working properly. When *Akatsuki* switched on her searchlights and bathed Hoover's cruiser with high-intensity beams, every senior officer on the open bridge crouched or slipped into a shadow area. The captain shouted, "Open fire!" and *Helena* vibrated from stem to stern as all fifteen of her 6-inch guns bellowed fire and smoke into the night. Able to see other Japanese ships in the glare of the burning destroyer, Hoover later asserted that a blazing enemy ship was the ideal form of night illumination. A shell from that enemy ship knocked out one of *Helena*'s clocks at 1:48. Searching for a fresh target for her guns, *Portland* spotted *Amatsukaze* shooting at *San Francisco,* and blasted away with all available guns, holding up fire when *San Francisco* moved into the line of fire.

Amatsukaze was firing on *San Francisco*, its three dual 5-inch guns scoring hits from virtually point blank range. One of the 5-inch shells ricocheted off the American cruiser's teak deck about twenty-four inches in front of Seaman 1st Class Willie Boyce's shoes as he headed aft, the missile's momentum carrying it the over the port side—unexploded. He was incredulous at his brush with death. Commander Hara, the torpedo expert, catapulted his last four fish at *San Francisco* a few hundred yards away and heard them all hit home, harmlessly, because they had not had time to arm themselves. Frustrated at his stupidity, he cursed himself when his ship was shaken by a flurry of near misses that did not originate with *San Francisco,* but from another large ship bearing down on him.

"Douse the searchlight! Stop shelling! Spread the smokescreen!" he shouted rapidly, hands clutching the bridge railing. His destroyer had been spotted by *Helena,* which had raced up to help a friendly ship and now had *Amatsukaze*'s range. The cruiser's triple 6-inch guns were arcing shells at *Amatsukaze.* Two near misses stunned Hara and nearly tore his hands from the railing. American explosives had wrecked his gun directory overhead and the radio room below him. Then he discovered that because the hydraulic system had been disabled, steering was out, his guns were frozen in place, and the rudder was jammed into a right turn—even as shells continued to fall on his ship.

Helena—which had fired 125 6-inch rounds at *Amatsukaze* in about 90 seconds—now had to hold fire when *San Francisco* came between them. Hara's immediate problem now was to get his floating and burning junkpile out of these troubled waters.

In a shootout like this, keeping the guns firing—loaders had to lift and throw each 105-pound 6-inch projectile into the breech—was brutal work for the entire gun crew. It was in many ways a stunningly complex choreography of coordinated movements. In no more than six minutes *Helena*'s main battery fired 175 6-inch projectiles. She continued to unleash intermittent fire on the enemy even as she threaded her way through the confounding maze of ships. *Helena* herself suffered only light damage from five shell hits.

For a few minutes there was a lull in the big gunfight. As *Helena* passed by the troubled *Portland*, Butch Parker's destroyer *Cushing* was beating down fires and trying to restore power to guns and torpedo mounts while trying to stay afloat. Down in the magazine for Gun Mount Number 3, Seaman 1st Class Hugh O'Fallon realized the hoists were no longer working and the phones were out because of lack of power. Helping out in the adjacent powder room, he was astonished to realize that the ship's engines were silent, although muted sounds of the battle raging outside could be heard. He and the other men agreed it was time to move topside. One hatch could not be opened, but they found another passageway and reached the main deck.

The doleful glow of burning ships greeted their eyes. O'Fallon went to examine the jammed hatch they had sought to use, and found it covered with a stack of dead bodies that once had been the aft repair party. The Japanese light cruiser *Nagara* was circling a couple of thousand yards away, dumping shell after shell on *Cushing* in kind of a deadly target practice. Reluctantly but promptly, when it was clear there was nothing else he could do to save his crew, Parker ordered the ship abandoned.

Badly wounded, with a severed tendon in his left thigh, Yeoman 2nd Class Tom Foreman worked his agonizing way down to the main deck, where he first heard of the order to abandon ship. He asked a mess attendant to go into the water with him, but he said he couldn't swim and refused to go. O'Fallon and his mates tossed empty powder cans sealed with lids over the side, and jumped and started swimming, supported by the cans. The object was to get as far away from the ship as possible before she blew up. *Nagara* tired of the easy sport and sailed away.

Juneau was in the fight, and seven of her eight dual 5-inch guns blasted away at *Yudachi*, which was in danger of being blown out of the water by the automatic guns. Signalman 2nd Class Joseph Hartley saw a few 5-inch tracer rounds hit the destroyer's superstructure, while his ship took shell blasts behind the fighting bridge. During one of the confused turns, *Juneau* found *San Francisco* closing on her port side, and as she turned away she was smashed by one of four torpedoes launched by *Yudachi*. The explosion ripped through the port side into the forward fire room—killing the seventeen men there—and probably broke her keel. When she settled back down after being lifted by the blast, she rode lower than before and began listing to the port side. Central fire control was knocked out and her gunfire was sporadic. Some of it may have been aimed at *Helena*, with which she nearly collided. Her captain, Lyman K. Swenson, decided to take her out of the melee—with her keel broken she could literally fall apart at any moment—and across the troubled waters to Tulagi, where she could obtain some emergency repairs. As she limped away, several near misses from 14-inch shells from either *Hiei* or *Kirishima* threatened her precarious safety.

The four trailing American destroyers found themselves out of position in the early fighting. *Aaron Ward* fired ten salvos at *Hiei* from 7,000 yards, then had to check herself hard at 1:55 to avoid colliding with what was probably the Japanese destroyer *Yudachi*. A minute later two torpedoes passed underneath, followed by an explosion from *Barton*, which instantly sank. Setting a course for due north at 18 knots in the now clear sea at 1:59, *Aaron Ward* lined up her torpedoes on *Hiei*, but did not launch them when *San Francisco*, which seemed to be everywhere, moved close to the Imperial battleship.

Steering to avoid *Sterett*, Commander Orville F. Gregor on *Aaron Ward* rang up flank speed, checked with Chief Signalman Fred Hart about the identity of the nearby *Yudachi*, then gave the order to open fire—at the same instant as did *Sterett*, sparking off a huge fireball on the Japanese destroyer. A searchlight—probably from *Kirishima*—was probing for *Aaron Ward*, so Gregor had his guns aim for the light, and loosed the first of her four salvos just as the enemy opened fire. "Get those fucking shells up here faster!" yelled someone in Gun Mount Number 3. Pharmacist's Mate 1st Class Roland "Frenchy" Prevost didn't even have time to smile at the typical sailor's request when he heard a shell crash into the emergency radio room. He slung his first-aid pouch over his shoulder and darted to the damage site. Inside he found one man dead and the other, Radioman 1st Class George Haines, with a slash from shoulder to hip.

Doc Prevost immediately plunged the tip of a morphine Syrette into Haines's buttock, used gauze pads to help stop the bleeding, washed the wound with distilled water, sprinkled the cut with sulfa powder, taped the torn flesh together, and then stitched it closed. Finishing the bandaging, he helped the badly injured man stagger to a safe haven. Shells were still rending the ship and there was more work to be done.

Soon *Aaron Ward* was firing at enemy ships on both port and starboard sides. She withstood some hits from 14-inch bombardment rounds. After Doc Prevost got his patient to safety, he soon found himself searching a shattered antiaircraft gun mount. Feeling around in the pitch dark, he counted three dead, and discovered one man still alive. Inspecting Signal Man 2nd Class Melvin Griffin's maimed leg, knew he could not save the limb, but hoped he could keep the sailor from bleeding to death. He gave the man a couple of shots of morphine, applied a tourniquet amid the shells going off, and amputated the signalman's leg by the light of Japanese star shells. When Commander Gregor knew his ship had been spotted by another assailant—confirmed by a flurry of 14-inch and 6-inch shells falling around *Aaron Ward*—he ordered up flank speed and departed the area, followed by more shells but not by the enemy ships. In her brief action, his ship took nine direct hits—three of them 14-inch bombardment shells—which knocked out her fire control, radars, and steering control. Steering control went out at about 2:20, and Gregor resorted to steering with her engines. Then at about 2:40 she lost all power and coasted to a halt.

Seeing enemy searchlights and gunfire ahead, *Barton* joined in, trying to knock out the lights. At about 1:52 she loosed five torpedoes from her port mounts. Seven minutes after she opened fire, *Barton* had to stop to avoid a collision, and a Japanese torpedo smashed through to the forward fire room, followed by a second that took out the forward engine room. *Barton* cracked in two, erupting in a massive fiery explosion that sent her to the bottom, taking down three of every five men. Most of the pitifully few survivors thrown overboard were from the topside stations and gun mounts.

Commanded by Lieutenant Commander Charles E. McCombs, *Monssen* steamed nearby with her radars inoperable, looking for a target. This destroyer had shelled Guadalcanal on August 7th, the day of the American invasion. Since then she had fought off Japanese dive bombers attacking *Enterprise* at the Battle of the Eastern Solomons, and fought fire missions in direct support of the marines on the island. The torpedo officer, Ensign Robert Lassen, spotted *Hiei* about 4,000 yards to starboard and launched five torpedoes, all of which missed. Abruptly *Monssen* was forced to change course to avoid *Barton*, which was then hit by a torpedo that passed under *Monssen*'s aft control station. Several witnesses reported a furious fireball rising 300 to 500 feet high where *Barton* simply disappeared from sight!

After firing off her last five torpedoes, *Monssen* opened up her 5-inch guns on either the destroyer *Inazuma* or *Ikazuchi* about 4,000 yards ahead. Then the guns were suddenly shifted to a new target about 6,000 yards ahead that was firing at point blank range into an American ship. Numerous salvos were fired at the distant target and many hits were reported.

Lieutenant Junior Grade George Hamm, aft damage control officer, later related that he was suddenly overwhelmed by an inexplicable sense of doom. He sensed Japanese ships all around his ship, ready to commence firing. Until this time nothing had hit *Monssen.*

Almost simultaneously, thinking she was being exposed by the light of friendly star shells, McCombs switched on her recognition lights, which immediately attracted an avalanche of naval gunfire. While *Monssen*'s 20-mm gunners took aim at the searchlights that suddenly highlighted her, the destroyer took her first hit, a shell that smashed through Gun Mount Number 1's front shield and killed the entire gun crew. While McCombs tried to avoid torpedoes, two pair missed the ship. Incoming shells had severed the steam line in the forward fire room and ruptured the manifold in the aft fire room, releasing high-pressure steam that almost instantly cooked most of the men there—only Machinist's Mate 1st Class M.F. Wilson and Fireman 1st Class Joe Hughes emerged barely alive. This damage rendered the destroyer powerless.

Signalman 1st Class Jack Pease—on duty at the aft control station when it was wiped out—suffered numerous tiny fragment wounds, including one that entered over his left chest, cut along his rib cage and exited though his back. Moments later an explosion in the aft deckhouse below his feet lifted him right out of his shoes. The blast blistered both his feet and broke his right one. Now angered, he hobbled to a nearby 20-mm gun mount and asked for a chance to shoot back. The gunner, who had gone through boot camp with him, agreed, and helped strap him into the gunner's seat.

Thirty-seven hits set *Monssen* ablaze, turning her into a fiery wreck, and at about 2:20 her crew was forced to abandon the ship. The order was heard only as far as McCombs's voice could be heard, but word quickly got around. When the last man had jumped from the bridge, the captain followed suit, breaking both his shoulders when he hit the water.

Pease, who was still firing the big machine gun, decided he too should leave the ship. He helped another sailor cut loose a life raft, which they were getting overboard when he discovered his life belt would not inflate. He simply grabbed a life ring off the bulkhead and left the *Monssen.* Lieutenant Junior Grade Hamm—even after seeing all the death and destruction that had befallen his ship—was reluctant to leave. Only when convinced there was nothing he could do except to see that no men were left on the ship did he go overboard—the last officer to do so.

Bringing up the rear was *Fletcher,* which was totally confused by the hectic action, and had taken aim on *Akatsuki*. Seeing the Japanese destroyer was already inundated by heavy fire, *Fletcher* then trained her guns on what may have been *Inazuma*, then held up because of the cease fire order. That's when *Barton* blew up and disappeared. Firing at a succession of targets as she maneuvered through the accumulating litter of broken, burning ships, she tracked and fired a spread of five torpedoes at a ship that historian Richard Frank surmises might have been *Helena*. If so, *Helena* was lucky this time, as all missed.

The newly commissioned *Fletcher* was equipped with the new SG surface-search radar. Commanded by Commander William N. Cole—who appreciated the new tool—*Fletcher* was the last ship in Callaghan's column. Why she was not leading the column as she should have been remains a mystery to naval historians to this day, casting further doubt on Admiral Callaghan's combat command qualifications. During general quarters Cole had moved his executive officer, Lieutenant Commander Joseph C. Wylie, forward to the charthouse to interpret and immediately relay information from the radar display rather than assigning him to the usual exec's position aft.

Radar located and began tracking the enemy ships at about 1:30, and at 1:50 *Fletcher* was about to fire on *Akatsuki* when that destroyer drew the attention of so many other guns that *Fletcher* shifted her guns toward what may have been *Nagara*. Lookouts reported some hits before *Fletcher* ceased firing at 1:58 at Callaghan's order. A minute later, realizing that the Japanese had reached the rear guard, Cole decided to disregard the strange order and join the close-up fight. He ordered "make all possible speed," which sent his ship leaping forward, and they then had to make a hard swing to the left to avoid *Monssen*. Somehow a spread of four torpedoes missed her, and she had to maneuver to miss *Barton*.

As she locked onto a new target an American cruiser—most likely *Portland*—sailed into the line of fire, and *Fletcher* had to line up on one of the many other targets available. Racing along at 36 knots, her automatic guns shot at random ships as she weaved her way through the fracas and then passed beyond the awesome scene. Cole ordered a high-speed skidding turn, almost within her own length, and roared back along the edge of the battle with all her 5-inch guns thundering away at several enemy ships. "It looks like the Fourth of July out here," Cole reported to Lieutenant Commander Wylie. Alluding to the lethal altercation taking place around them, he mused, "Aren't you glad our wives don't know where we are tonight?" Although she steadfastly sailed in harm's way, *Fletcher* remained unhit and undamaged.

On the Japanese side the battle was as confused and disjointed as on the American side. Commander Hara's *Amatsukaze* raced around trying to get into the action and at 1:54 finally launched eight torpedoes from a range of about 3,000 yards at the rear ships in the American column. One almost certainly sank *Barton*. Five minutes later he fired off four torpedoes at what he thought was *Juneau*. Returning toward *Hiei*, he almost collided with *San Francisco*, and fired off four more torpedoes that failed to arm before hitting Callaghan's flagship. Captain Hara switched on his searchlights, which attracted the attention of *Helena*'s gunners, who landed thirty-seven hits and killed forty-three Japanese sailors in the action previously described.

Akatsuki, along with *Inazuma* and *Ikazuchi*, may have passed through the ships leading the American column. *Akatsuki* hit *Atlanta* hard, but her searchlights drew fire from at least five U.S. ships, igniting fires that attracted more gunfire. Salvo after salvo ripped into her and at last sent her to the bottom. *Inazuma* and *Ikazuchi* fired their guns and torpedoes but soon had to withdraw because of heavy damage.

Yudachi, of Destroyer Squadron 4, had a remarkable night. After crossing *Cushing*'s bow, she turned about and charged down the disorganized American column. At 1:55 she fired eight torpedoes at 1,500 yards, possibly scoring hits on *Portland* and *Juneau*. She nearly collided with *Aaron Ward*, and forced even more abrupt course changes on the Americans. Her rampage ended when she took a series of sustained hits that left her dead in the water at 2:26. The other Japanese destroyers roved back and forth rendering damage with their guns and torpedoes. *Murasame* launched seven torpedoes, claiming three hits on "a cruiser" at 2:04.

The battleship *Hiei*, easily the most recognizable target of the night, drew gunfire from almost every American vessel in the fight. By the end of the battle, she had taken eighty-five hits in her lighter armor and upper steel structure. Blazing fires attracted more shells, and the results added up to all antiaircraft guns being destroyed, radio and communications out of action, and secondary battery directors disabled. She sustained a hit in her duel with *San Francisco* that jammed her rudder and caused flooding of the steering machinery area. *Hiei*'s 6-inch guns also registered hits on her own destroyers *Asagumo*, *Murasame*, and *Samidare* as they raced by in the bedlam. With his flagship badly damaged and difficult to control, at 2:00 Abe permanently canceled his bombardment mission.

At 2:26 Captain Gilbert C. Hoover, on board the moderately damaged *Helena*, gave the order to break off the battle and retired, following *San Francisco*, which once again nearly collided with the badly hurt *Juneau*, as they and three destroyers steamed away from the floating junkyard. The cruiser *Atlanta*, and destroyers *Barton*, *Cushing*, *Laffey*, and *Monssen* joined the graveyard of ships in Iron Bottom Sound. They were joined there by two Japanese destroyers. The dark waters were lit by burning abandoned hulks that could be seen for forty miles.

Friendly and Unfriendly Fire

"Of the thirteen American ships entering the battle, only one, the destroyer *Fletcher*, can report no damage," remembered Signalman Ernest Herr. "Our ship [*O'Bannon*] sustains moderate damage but from friendly fire. One 8-inch shell fragment with *San Francisco*'s identifying die coloring landed between the legs of a torpedoman as he sat at his battle station on top of a torpedo launching tube. The fragment lodged itself in the torpedo tube without harming anyone. This shell probably bounced off of the Cruiser *Portland* which is directly in line between the *San Francisco* and the *O'Bannon*. Friendly fire from the *San Francisco* also hit the *Portland*. Unfortunately, friendly shells are just as nasty as unfriendly shells.

"This night battle...turns into a disaster for us as the Japanese force is able to sink one of our cruisers and put three other cruisers out of service for nearly a year. Of the thirteen heavy cruisers we have committed to the Guadalcanal area, all have been either sunk or badly damaged. This battle provides additional evidence to the fact that there appears no end to the supply of inept U.S. commanders that the American high command is able to field."

The battle was over but the shooting was not. At dawn *Hiei*'s aft turrets fired four salvos at the drifting *Aaron Ward* 14.5 miles away, finding the range just as planes from the CAF zoomed in and distracted her. *Portland* scored better on the already hard-hit *Yudachi* at 12,500 yards with five salvos. The sixth salvo caused an explosion in the destroyer's aft magazine that sent her to join the other brave ships at the bottom of Iron Bottom Sound.

Atlanta, burning and listing badly, was slowly drifting toward the Japanese-held portion of Guadalcanal. Despite the concerted efforts of Captain Jenkins and his crew, assisted by the tug *Bobolink*, the ship was abandoned and scuttled to the west of Lunga Point at 8:15 P.M.

When dawn lighted the sky over Iron Bottom Sound, a fleet of Higgins Boats and other craft were searching the waters for survivors, often directed by pilots of the patrol planes flying low over the terrible scene. Many of the swimmers, as well as those on rafts and in lifeboats, were so coated with oil and filth that identification was difficult. The first thought was to recover the American sailors. Japanese sailors did not want to be saved by the American boats and fought or resisted when such attempts were made. Most important of all, the boats had to get the wounded back to the safety of the Lunga perimeter. The ships that had taken part in the brawl were struggling to survive and were still targets for Japanese guns.

Once ashore, the wounded completely overwhelmed the still inadequate medical facilities ashore. Despite the enormous outpouring of care from the marines, who were not in much better shape, many sailors died before they could receive medical attention. The ragged and gaunt men taking part in the ground war on Guadalcanal scrounged around and came up with clothing for the sailors. Every available transport plane in the South Pacific took part in the seemingly endless evacuation of the badly wounded. For those who were able to move about, it took days to rid their bodies of the fuel oil they had soaked in or swallowed.

The Japanese battleship *Hiei* was so badly damaged in the fight that it couldn't keep up with the departing force, and Abe transferred to *Yukikaze* at 8:15. Twenty-three Zekes from *Junyo* and twelve from the 11th Air Fleet were sent in as cover. Air attacks from Henderson Field during the day on the 13th landed three bombs on the hapless battleship and registered at least four torpedo hits. With his ship still afloat at 3:30 in the afternoon and listing heavily, Abe decided it could not be saved and ordered it scuttled. At least 300 Japanese sailors on *Hiei* died in the battle and the following attacks. As it was going down, it took more hits from two torpedo planes.

Captain Gilbert Hoover ordered the retiring American ships—now off the southwest coast of San Cristobal, well away from Guadalcanal—to slow down shortly after 10:00 to transfer welding gear and specialists to the straining *Juneau*. When unidentified planes were spotted, the fleet dispersed into an antiaircraft defense formation. On finding the planes were American, he ordered the ships back into the antisubmarine formation and to steer a course for Nouméa, well to the south. Before this could be accomplished, however, the Japanese submarine *I-26*, captained by Commander Minoru Yokota, slipped in and at 1:00 P.M. fired a spread of torpedoes at close range. Two narrowly missed the bow of the intended target, *San Francisco*, which didn't even have time to swerve, and another missed *Helena*'s stern. A warhead that missed *San Francisco* slammed into *Juneau*'s port side amidships—apparently hitting a magazine—and set off a violent explosion that blew the ship apart. It simply disintegrated in a gigantic ball of smoke that roiled hundreds of feet into the air like a volcanic eruption.

No one who saw the blast—several went into shock—thought there could have been survivors. Large and small pieces of the ship flew through the air, raining down around the other vessels. One of her dual 5-inch gun mounts arched through the air and crashed into the water about 100 yards behind the faraway *Fletcher*. The explosion's concussion moved with such force that men aboard other ships thought they had been torpedoed.

About 683 sailors, including the five Sullivan brothers—George, Francis, Joseph, Madison, and Albert, from Waterloo, Iowa, serving together on the *Juneau*—died as a result of that unbelievable blast. From this time on, members of the same family were banned from serving together on the same warship. Despite the magnitude of the detonation, about 100 men—including George Sullivan and many others terribly wounded—survived the blast and got off the ship. For these men suddenly cast into the ocean, the nightmare was only beginning.

An officer on *Helena* stated, "There aren't any survivors!" Commander Cole was not sure, so he ordered *Fletcher* to right full rudder to move around to search for survivors. Instead, Captain Gilbert C. Hoover, commanding the small fleet of crippled ships, ordered his only destroyer *Fletcher* to search for the enemy submarine that had just annihilated an American cruiser. *Helena* was Hoover's only cruiser, damaged as she was, left in that area of the Pacific. No survivors from *Juneau* were seen in the water, and if he delayed departure from the danger zone any longer more of his remaining battered and torn ships might be lost in another torpedo attack, and thousands more sailors placed in dire jeopardy. To have not hurried away would have been a criminal abdication of a fleet commander's duty.

When Hoover arrived at Espiritu Santo on the 14th, he reported *Juneau*'s loss. Navy rescue planes began a wide search, but after taking down incorrect position reports they searched the wrong sector. For most of the shouting men in the water—screaming for help and struggling to stay afloat—the sudden departure of their sister ships would be a death sentence. The miserable wretches tried to swim or tread water in six inches of fuel oil that coated the surface near where their ship had gone down.

A communications foul-up prevented the notification of other ships that could have come to the rescue. Hoover adhered to the standard radio silence order. When a B-17 swooped down to check on the fuss, Hoover sent it a visual signal: "Ship down...send rescue." The plane flew off to Henderson Field, but failed to pass along the message. A few days later some passing B-17s dropped rubber rafts and supplies to aid the drifting swimmers but did not provide a position report that could have brought help. On the tenth day only ten sailors remained to be rescued. The last surviving Sullivan brother, George, died several days before the others were finally pulled from the sea. Only fourteen *Juneau* crew members, including four in a medical team that had been transferred off a few hours before the sinking, survived the heartbreaking disaster.

In the Spotlight

Juneau AND THE FIVE SULLIVAN BROTHERS LOST

Juneau was torpedoed and sunk in broad daylight on November 13, 1942. Aboard the antiaircraft cruiser were the five Sullivan brothers, from Waterloo, Iowa: George, Francis, Joseph, Madison, and Albert. The boys, of Catholic Irish descent, were all working at the Rath Packing Company, a large meat processing plant. The youngest, at twenty, Al, was married and the father of a one-year-old son. When war came in 1941, the brothers lived in a small house near the railroad with their mother and father, grandmother, and sister Genevieve, whom they adored. Even though their father had a good job as a freight conductor on the Illinois Central Railroad, the family had the same economic difficulties as many others in the Depression years of the 1930s. None of the boys cared for schooling, and went to work as soon as possible. The older boys, George and Frank, had both served a four-year enlistment in the Navy, but had been discharged in the summer of 1941.

All five had enlisted in the Navy on January 3, 1942, after hearing that their friend Bill Ball, of Fredericksburg, Iowa had been killed aboard the battleship *Arizona* at Pearl Harbor. Insistent on serving together on the same ship, they had to obtain special permission from the Navy Department. In February, after hurried boot training at Great Lakes, Illinois, the Sullivans reported aboard *Juneau*, a new 6,000-ton antiaircraft cruiser. There they met the four Rogers brothers, who had also wanted to be together on the same ship. A few weeks before the fateful Friday the 13th battle—by then aware of the potential for disaster—two of the Rogers brothers had moved to a different ship.

Their task force had escorted a convoy of transports into Sealark Channel and arrived early on November 12. The convoy had been attacked by Japanese torpedo planes, and *Juneau*'s concentrated antiaircraft fire had helped protect the transports. In fact, the only cruiser in the sea-to-air battle to suffer serious damage was *San Francisco*, Rear Admiral Callaghan's flagship.

In the donnybrook the night of Friday the 13th, *Juneau*'s bridge had been wrecked by gunfire from *Hiei* and *Nagara* that knocked out communications for a few minutes. Then, eight minutes after the battle began, a Long Lance torpedo from Commander Hara's *Amatsukaze* ripped through the thin armor plating and deep into the ship—which, as an antiaircraft cruiser, should not have been involved in a surface confrontation—and exploded in the port fire room. Apparently the keel was snapped, and the blast jammed the propellers. George Sullivan suffered back injuries when he was thrown against a bulkhead.

Equipped with light antiaircraft weapons, the largest being 5-inch guns, *Juneau* had a remarkable speed of thirty-two knots. Like her sister ship *Atlanta*, she was designed specifically to protect aircraft carriers, but she had fought as best she could without the large-caliber guns available on regular cruisers. Captain Lyman Knut Swenson had managed to take the badly mauled *Juneau*—with its steering crippled, down 11 feet by the bow and listing—out of the fight. By mid-morning she was clear of Guadalcanal and creeping along at eighteen knots in a small flotilla led by Captain Hoover, escaping toward Nouméa and safety.

Just after 11 A.M. aboard the cruiser *Helena*, Lieutenant William Jones, in the main battery control, stepped outside on deck to get some air. At almost the same moment on the nearby *Juneau*, Gunner's Mate 2nd Class Allen Clifton Heyn was set to relieve a shipmate on a 1.1-inch antiaircraft gun on the fantail. Heyn said to his shipmate, "Are you ready?" The sailor "just looked at me," Heyn said later, "with his mouth open. I didn't know what it was...everybody was just standing there and then [came] an explosion." Heyn was thrown against his gun mount, one foot painfully pinned by the gun shield. He grabbed a life jacket and took a deep breath as water closed over him. Miraculously the sheet of steel pinning his foot let go, and the panicked and gasping Heyn hurtled back to the surface.

On *Fletcher*, Cole and Wylie heard "the most tremendous explosion I could have ever imagined," Wylie said later. They dashed onto the bridge and looked aft, seeing an enormous ball of smoke and flame arising from *Juneau*. A 5-inch gun mount from the disintegrated ship came flying at *Fletcher*, which called for emergency flank speed and sounded the alarm bells. Wylie said to Cole, "My God—the welders must have touched off a magazine!"

Lieutenant Jones saw *Juneau* explode, and later compared it to pictures of an atomic bomb blast. As he tried to move to safety to avoid being hit by flying debris, he was blown against the bulkhead by the shockwave. In less than a minute *Juneau* had disappeared, hurling debris half a mile and leaving behind only a cloud of thick smoke.

Hoover's shrunken force headed south without taking the time to toss rafts over the side—there seemed no point in doing so. But Hoover was wrong, for about 150 of *Juneau*'s sailors, including Allen Heyn and George Sullivan, were bobbing in the water. George found his younger brother, Albert, in shock and clinging to a rope on one of the rafts. There was a report that Joseph was seen on another raft, but he was not found by George and was never seen again. Al disappeared during the night. Many of the survivors suffered severe burns and were struggling in the thick layer of oil. Those who had lost arms or legs mostly likely fell victim to the feeding frenzy of the swarming sharks.

Shaken from the disaster, and adrift, they were confident that help would soon be on the way. The survivors suffered from sunburn by day, and chill by night. The churning sea aggravated their wounds, and improperly secured food and water were lost. When the rations they did save ran out after three days, the men began to weaken and die. Heyn held on, together with signalman Lester Zook and George Sullivan, until one night, Sullivan, exhausted and delirious, undressed to take a bath and jumped from the raft into the sea, where he was instantly attacked by a shark. An officer struggled to maintain discipline, but went into a delirium himself, jumping out of the raft and swimming off into the shark-infested waters.

Seven days after *Juneau* sank, some survivors were spotted from the air completely by chance. The planes dropped rafts and sent in a sighting report, and two days later Heyn and Zook, along with eight other survivors, were finally rescued. Some 683 sailors had perished in one of war's most horrible ordeals. The two Rogers boys aboard were killed in the explosion.

Because of "national security" concerns, the Sullivan family did not receive official notification of their terrible loss until January 12, 1943. The grieved parents toured war plants and shipyards, urging workers to increase production, and gave solace to other families who had lost sons in battle. A new *Fletcher*-class destroyer—named USS *The Sullivans*—was launched by Mrs. Sullivan. One of the boy's uncles, 43-year-old Patrick Sullivan, served aboard her. Hollywood seized the opportunity to make a movie about the five brothers, with the added but erroneous drama of having *Juneau* sunk at night. The death of the five Sullivans in one battle stunned the nation, compelling a long overdue change in Navy regulations: brothers or members of the same family were no longer allowed to serve together on the same ship.

When Hoover led his battered fleet into Nouméa Harbor, the experienced, talented, and aggressive leader—one of the few to do things right that night—was straightaway relieved of command and sent back to the States in disgrace. The greatest charge was an emotional one, leveled by officers far removed from the scene: the abandonment of *Juneau*'s survivors. Admiral Halsey later admitted he acted precipitously in the matter, possibly due to the influence of his own chief of staff, who had hated Hoover since they had been classmates at Annapolis. A subsequent Naval board of inquiry exonerated Hoover of all charges, but the reputation and career of the best combat leader in the Friday the 13th fiasco had been destroyed.

Some writers, recounting that first night's action in the critical Naval Battle of Guadalcanal, have asserted that this was a well planned and stunning victory for the American fleet. Contrarily, is was nearly a total disaster because of the inept senior leadership of the American ships involved—and it would have been worse if the Japanese commander had been a little more aggressive. Ships of the American Navy took a terrible mauling that night at moderate cost to the enemy, and no one in the battered fleet that limped away to safety at Nouméa thought they had beaten the Japanese. Some find justification for claiming victory in the fact that a planned Japanese bombardment of Henderson Field and the Lunga Peninsula was turned away—but the Americans did not know that at the time. In retrospect Vice Admiral Halsey and Rear Admiral Turner should share the blame for sending an inexperienced and unprepared Callaghan into a fight on such short notice, especially when the experienced and successful Rear Admiral Scott was available.

Rear Admiral Scott was awarded the Medal of Honor posthumously, perhaps justifiably for his leadership at Cape Esperance as well as that on the night he was killed. The same award was given to Rear Admiral Callaghan, for reasons this writer and others cannot quite fathom. Possibly Turner and Halsey were making amends for sending the unprepared officer into battle—which is not a very good reason considering the many instances of outstanding bravery by men under his command who did not receive appropriate recognition. Ironically, when news of the admirals' deaths in battle reached the public they became heroes.

The loss of *Juneau* brought the total number of Americans killed in the action up to at least 1,439 men. It has been stated that the Japanese lost as many as 450 killed on *Hiei*, plus 552 aboard the other ships that engaged that night. The IJN emerged as clear-cut but not decisive victors in the Friday the 13th tactical battle. As important as the relative numbers of ships lost in assessing the long-term effects was the fact that Henderson Field and the Lunga beachhead were spared a mammoth bombardment that could have exposed the garrison to a massive combined land, sea, and air assault that Admiral Yamamoto had planned.

Vice Admiral Abe and Captain Masao Nishida, captain of *Hiei*, were summarily relieved and retired on their return from the slaughter of the American fleet. Admiral Yamamoto was compelled to reset Z-Day to the 14th. Admiral Kondo was ordered to take the two heavy cruisers *Atago* and *Takao* of his Division 4, with *Kirishima* and support vessels attached, and swoop down to Guadalcanal to bombard Henderson Field—the essential action that had been turned back the night before.

At 11:10 Halsey gave orders to Kinkaid to form a task force with *Enterprise* around Rear Admiral Willis A. "Ching" Lee's Task Force 64 with the battleships *Washington* and *South Dakota.* They were to block Japanese efforts to bombard the airfield and reinforce their troops. Even as *Enterprise* steamed north at 26 knots her forward elevator was jammed in the "up" position—no one dared to push the down button for fear of rendering the flight deck useless. Seabees and other engineers had remained aboard and worked around the clock to restore the still hurting carrier to its full operational capacity.

Halsey and his staff had serious misgivings about sending such large ships into the waters around Savo, but the need at Guadalcanal was too great to hold them back. In any event Lee's force was out of position and could not possibly reach Savo Island until 8:00 A.M. on November 14th. That night the Japanese had the full run of the surrounding waters to themselves.

At 1:30 A.M. on the 14th, a force consisting of the heavy cruisers *Suzuya* and *Maya*, light cruiser *Tenryu*, and three destroyers led by Rear Admiral Shoji Nishimura initiated a thirty-one-minute bombardment of Henderson Field—or what they thought was the field. The two big cruisers lofted 989 8-inch shells, causing scattered fires and explosions around Fighter One, destroying two Wildcats and one SBD and putting holes in another fifteen Wildcats. Nishimura's judgment that the airfield remained usable despite the heavy shelling was all too true. His force was set upon by two PT boats, to little avail. Nishimura's group rendezvoused with Mikawa's main body at 7:50 south of New Georgia.

Second Night

At just 12:45 in the dark tropical night Lieutenant Henry S. "Stilley" Taylor drove his boat, PT *60*, in the waters near the main route of the Tokyo Express. PT *47*, with Jack Searles, had left base together in a patrol but had become separated. The men on

47, clad in clinging wet, thin, and worn cotton uniforms, were shivering from the coldness induced by the continuous rain and stiff winds. The blowing salt spray in his face irritated Taylor's eyes and made it difficult to read the instrument panel. The crew kept a sharp eye out for underwater obstructions—such as unmarked coral reefs—that could open up the bottom of the wooden boat. The dual hazard of being dumped into the sea to drown or to confront hungry sharks was real and quite threatening.

White Japanese flares lit up the sky in the distance over Henderson Field, which meant the Tokyo Express was again on station shelling the island. The bright orange muzzle flashes from the big guns indicated the presence of cruisers, possibly even battleships. A pale eerie glow from the flares and muzzle blasts bathed the boat as it approached the bombardment force, making it easy to see.

Taylor ordered up full speed, which lifted the boat high in the water as it roared toward the enemy. PT *60* unleashed two torpedoes against what was identified as a Japanese destroyer, silhouetted against the flares, but scored no hits.

On the 14th five of Major Sailer's dive bombers from VMSB-132, six torpedo planes, and three TBFs each from VT-10 and VMSB-131—covered by eight Wildcats from *Enterprise* and Henderson Field—attacked Mikawa's retiring Tokyo Express at 8:30 near New Georgia, inflicting some damage. Planes from *Enterprise* were sent forward by Kinkaid and would operate from the island until the carrier was ready for full flight operations.

Two *Enterprise* scouts, Lieutenant Junior Grade Robert E. Gibson and Ensign R.M. Buchanan of VB-10, had spotted Mikawa's force at 8:15 and spent nearly another hour sending in continuous reports. Finally at 9:30 Gibson dove in to attack and placed his bomb into *Kinugasa* forward of the bridge and deep inside before it exploded. The blast killed Captain Sawa and his executive officer. Then a second pair of search planes found the retiring fleet. Ensign R.A. Hoogerwerf claimed a near miss, while his wingman Ensign P.M. Halloran missed *Maya* with his bomb, but crashed his plane, damaged by antiaircraft fire, about halfway down her port side, hurting her badly and killing thirty-seven of her deck crew.

A force of seventeen SBDs carrying 1,000-pound bombs—along with ten Wildcats launched earlier from *Enterprise*—under Lieutenant Commander James Lee had been listening to the scout reports. They found the Mikawa force about thirty miles west of Rendova Island at 10:45 and commenced their attack. They sunk the heavy cruiser *Kinugasa*—capsizing her along with 511 men—and damaged two other heavy cruisers, *Chokai* and *Isuzu*.

For the second time Rear Admiral Tanaka departed the Shortland Islands at 5:30 the night before with his twenty-three-ship troop convoy in high spirits, believing the bombardment force had knocked out Henderson Field. At 8:49 the morning of the 14th, his convoy was sighted by *Enterprise*'s Lieutenant Junior Grade M.D. Carmody and Lieutenant Junior Grade W.E. Johnson. Their attack at 9:08 failed and Johnson was shot down. When Japanese lookouts saw Lee's planes in the distance, Tanaka laid down protective smoke.

But at 12:50 Tanaka's luck ended when eighteen SBDs under Majors Sailer and Robert Richard, and seven TBFs of VT-10 led by Lieutenant Albert Coffin, selected their targets and flew in to attack. Japanese records later revealed that *Nagara Maru* had been punctured by two torpedoes, *Sado Maru* blasted by bombs, and *Canberra Maru* mortally damaged. Only the *Sado Maru* survived.

One attack after another ripped the convoy for seven tormenting hours. In the seething air battle each side suffered losses. Lieutenant Colonel Bauer destroyed a Zeke, was shot down, and was last seen alive and in the sea. An extensive search and rescue mission was launched, but he was never seen again. Five SBDs—all from *Enterprise*—and two Marine Wildcats were shot down, and thirteen of forty-five Zekes did not return to base, nine of them destroyed in combat.

Tanaka had sortied from the Shortlands with twenty-three ships, but after the air raids only nine remained near his flagship. Six had been sunk or abandoned. The remainder were picking up survivors, more than 4,800 of them. Astonishingly, only 450 men had been lost in the running fight. At 5:41 the Combined Fleet ordered him to continue to Guadalcanal. By 6:15 he had reformed the last four transports and the five remaining destroyers to once again head for the terrible island. He was soon rejoined by four of his assigned destroyers, which were so loaded with survivors plucked from the sea that they wouldn't be able to fight. Tanaka, ever the realist, surmised that prospects for his force and the Z-Day operation looked poor.

Kondo headed south with a strong naval force, while Lee sailed north. The two would soon collide in the Second Naval Battle of Guadalcanal, the night of November 14–15. In the afternoon Kondo had assembled the battleship *Kirishima* and the two heavy cruisers *Atago* and *Takao* to make up the firepower of the bombardment unit. Accompanying them were a screening unit under Rear Admiral Kimura commanding the light cruiser *Nagara* and six destroyers, and a sweeping unit of the light cruiser *Sendai* and three destroyers led by Rear Admiral Hashimoto, which would check out the area around Savo.

Lee wrestled with the problems at hand, one of which was that the enemy force he faced might include three battleships, eight or so cruisers, a dozen or more destroyers, and nine transports. Against this supposed might he had the battleships *Washington* and *South Dakota*, armed with 16-inch guns and accompanied by four destroyers: *Walke*, *Benham*, *Preston*, and *Gwin*. Six combat ships, none of which had worked together, were to face off with as many as twenty-three Japanese warships.

At about 10:00 P.M. Lee's task force was cruising in the area of Savo, big ship sailors feeling hemmed in by the sight of land in all directions. He tried to contact Guadalcanal, had a little difficulty establishing his identity, then was told there was no new information regarding the enemy ships. Then his force had to straighten out his identity with the skippers of three PT boats so they would not attack him.

The Japanese force was splitting into its three units about the same time, and almost immediately the eagle-eyed lookouts of the screening unit spotted the American ships just west of south. That force then maneuvered to draw the enemy from Kondo's bombardment group. When Lee started steaming due west, on a course that would intercept his ships, Kondo, thinking he was coming up against four destroyers and two cruisers, decided to join up the other two units to destroy the small force and then proceed to his bombardment task.

Washington's SG radar had picked up Hashimoto's ships at a range of 9 miles. At 11:12 she gained visual contact and trained her weapons on the approaching enemy ship, at which time Lee gave his permission to open fire when ready. At 11:17 *Washington*'s 16-inch main battery broke the quiet of the night with its first salvo, even as her 5-inch guns lit up the dark with star shells. *South Dakota*'s 16-inch guns hurled huge projectiles at the Japanese column. No hits were registered, but the enemy still didn't know the sizes of the guns shooting at them.

When the battleships checked their fire, *Walke* opened up on the destroyer *Ayanami*, which seemed determined to attack the entire American force. *Benham* joined in on the brave enemy ship. *Preston*'s lookouts had spotted *Nagara* coming around Savo and joined in with *Walke* and *Gwin* to take her under fire. The Japanese responded by launching torpedoes even as *Preston* was pummeled by shells that probably came from *Nagara*. She took hits that killed all the men in the two fire rooms, toppled the second smokestack, and ignited the contents of several torpedoes.

A Japanese heavy cruiser slipped unseen to the port side and from extremely close range sent a salvo of 8-inch rounds from its ten guns. At least three hits devastated *Preston*. One shell detonated in the aft engine room atop the generators, another between Gun Mount Number 3 and the aft control station, and a third destroyed Gun Mount Number 4. Machinist's Mate 2nd Class Gordon Klopf, the captain's talker (the man responsible for repeating the captain's orders over the ship's communications system), had his helmet and battle phones blown off in one of the explosions, took a sliver of steel in his leg, and was slammed into a bulkhead with such force that five of his ribs were broken. Flaming wreckage was all that remained of the ship aft of the second stack.

The captain, Commander Storme, with his ship settling by the stern, gave the order to abandon ship. Klopf had just stepped off into the water when the radar antenna rolled over on him and shoved him under the water. In a panic he tried to push free but passed out from the pain of his wound and the shock. When he regained consciousness a few seconds later, he was astounded to find himself floating in the water. *Preston* rolled over to the starboard and stood with her bow held in the air by a pocket of air for another ten minutes before sinking. A few minutes later Klopf dog-paddled over to help a man whose arm had been torn off, and in the struggle to swim free they were attacked by sharks. His companion disappeared suddenly, but Klopf kicked and splashed the water and drove off a shark that came at him. Forty-five percent of the crew—117 men, including Storme—died in the incident.

Walke reeled from multiple hits and then took a Japanese torpedo in her hull just forward of her bridge. This hit detonated her Number 2 Magazine, lifted the ship and pushed it to the left, and snapped off its bow. In Gun Mount 3 Coxswain Peter Trella, the gun captain, was knocked unconscious by the force from the blast. When he came to a moment later the mount was engulfed by tons of falling seawater and fuel oil. That's when he decided to leave, and went looking for his brother Paul, a Fireman 1st Class, who was discovered unhurt. Together they went over the side. With exploding ammo creating hell on deck, flames from end to end, and the ship rapidly going down, Commander Thomas Fraser passed the word to abandon her. Four rafts swung free but *Walke*'s depth charges—exploding as she sank—killed Fraser and many of his men, for a total of eighty dead.

As she passed the sinking *Walke*, *Benham* was struck by a torpedo, which took a chunk out of her bow and lifted her about 4 feet out of the water. She tilted to port, then swung back about 30 degrees to starboard, and finally righted herself. The quake that shook the ship was so violent that few if any were left standing. In an instant her speed fell from 27 knots to just 5 knots, a shock that contributed to the breaking of *Benham*'s back and left a crack across her main deck. Chief Torpedoman John Chapman was washed overboard by a deluge of settling water. The damages forced the ship to loop away to avoid more gunfire, and when she got back on course at 10 knots, she was out of the fight.

Only 300 yards back, two shells penetrated and exploded in *Gwin*'s aft engine room, starting fires that were soon extinguished. The concussion wrecked her torpedo mounts. As she passed the sinking *Preston*, both ships were rocked by a huge explosion, and debris from the stricken *Preston* landed on *Gwin*. *Gwin*'s guns continued to fire at a Japanese destroyer, but a minute later could find no targets.

Ayanami pressed within two miles of the American column and opened fire, which allowed *Washington* to see her for the first time and put shells into her that damaged her engineering plant, causing her to lose power and go dead in the water, with fires burning uncontrolled. *South Dakota* was not yet back in the fight, as at 11:30 a problem in the engine room had left her without electrical power. Without her radars she was groping in the dark, not knowing what was going on. She struggled forward past the burning destroyers, which were falling out of line, and electrical power was restored six minutes later.

Washington placed the stricken and burning destroyers to starboard for some concealment, dropping two life rafts for the *Walke* swimmers, while *South Dakota* put them to port, placing her in view of the Japanese ships. When her guns opened fire again, her rear turret firing dead astern set fire to three of her scout planes on the quarterdeck. The concussion of the next salvo, however, blew out the flames of one and knocked the other two overboard.

Lee's destroyers had done their duty of screening his battleships. At 11:48 he ordered the two survivors *Benham* and *Gwin* out of the battle. Meanwhile, having left the opening action to his other units, Kondo was trying to decide what to do since he suspected the presence of a second American force. His big mistake was to totally discount the very real presence of the two battleships. Then at 3:50 he decided it was time for him to shape a course for Henderson Field and conduct his bombardment. At three minutes before midnight he was once again warned of the American battleships but steadfastly refused to believe the reports.

Washington came to a new course just north of west at 11:35 just as its radar located and began tracking Kondo's bombardment group. *South Dakota*, sailing about a mile to the north, was still having problems with its radar, but when it came back on it showed an enemy unit less than three miles away. Kondo's lookouts saw *South Dakota* at 11:58, but the stubborn leader still wanted to think of it as a heavy cruiser. Lee's battleships were roughly 11 miles west of Savo, and the bombardment group sent out a spread of torpedoes from short range and at a perfect approach angle to *South Dakota*.

When midnight came on the 15th, *Atago*'s searchlights focused on *South Dakota*, revealing that the ship was indeed a battleship, and all Kondo's guns from 3.9-inch to 14-inch filled the sky with salvo after salvo of shells. A couple of minutes later the destroyer *Asagumo* fired off four more Long Lances. The Japanese thought several of the deadly water missiles had scored, but all had missed. The shells did not miss, however, and in a time span of about four minutes twenty-seven hits blasted and shook the battleship.

South Dakota's survival was not really threatened, but the rolling explosions took out communications and radar, demolished the radar pilot, killed numerous fire control men, and disabled the gun directors. All but impotent, the big ship's main battery got off only about five ineffective salvos. According to the later Japanese reports, though, the four starboard twin 5-inch guns landed some telling blows.

With all the enemy attention lavished on *South Dakota*, *Washington* had been overlooked. With searchlights blazing at *South Dakota*, followed by the blasts of every gun that could be brought to bear, *Washington* had no trouble finding the enemy ships. At the close range of 8,400 yards, her main battery's nine 16-inch and a pair of 5-inch guns sent shells flying toward *Kirishima*, engulfing her with sheets of seawater. About nine of the huge shells and forty or more 5-inch shells scored deadly hits, disabling the two main battery turrets, drilling holes below the waterline, setting off fires within the ship, and jamming her rudder. She was soon reduced to flaming rubble. The enemy battleship attempted to return fire and sent shells hurtling at *Washington*. Seaman 1st Class James K. Gammage, Searight, Alabama, on the bridge, described the noise of the shells passing by as sounding like big freight cars roaring past. "They scared the living daylights out of me!"

Japanese attention was still focused on *South Dakota*, which they thought they had destroyed and sunk. Gunfire raised water spouts on both sides of *Atago*, damaging her slightly, and did not hit *Takao* at all. Still, the enemy took the prudent gesture of shutting off all searchlights. *South Dakota* was beset with twenty-three major fires threatening to join into one stupendous conflagration. Commander A.E. Uehlinger, the executive officer, and five men stationed on Battle 2 were threatened when a shell sliced through a nearby steam line. At the moment it seemed they would be killed by either the flames, the scalding steam, or the suffocating smoke. Up on the bridge, at ten minutes after midnight, Captain Gatch decided to remove his shattered ship from the battle before it was completely destroyed.

Only the fast, potent, and well armored *Washington* was left to fight the swarming Japanese warships, and at 12:20 A.M. Lee took her back into the fray. Kondo retained the considerable offensive power of his torpedoes but could not find *Washington*. His units were widely dispersed and many of his guns were effectively out of the fight. The ever tenacious Tanaka detached two destroyers from his convoy to attack any enemy ships that came at his transports. Both sides were now maneuvering to carry home the attack, but did not reengage. A couple of Japanese ships fired torpedoes at *Washington*, with several passing uncomfortably close. At 12:32 Kondo canceled his bombardment, and at 1:04 ordered a general disengagement once his ships completed their current attacks. Some of his retiring ships found the floundering *Kirishima* barely under way and laboring for survival about 5 miles west of Savo. Seawater poured unabated through holes in her hull and the fires appeared beyond control. Her commander, Captain Sanji Iwabuchi, gave the order to abandon her and then shifted his crew—and the esteemed Emperor's portrait—to *Asagumo*. At 3:25 and 11 miles west of Savo, *Kirishima* rolled over and sank. Earlier, about 5 miles southeast of Savo, most of the crew of *Ayanami*—forty were dead or missing—were taken off by *Uranami*. After the ship went down, wracked with explosions, the skipper and about thirty others took a boat and landed on Guadalcanal.

The battered *South Dakota* and *Gwin* survived to reach Espiritu Santo, but *Benham*'s fractured hull and shortened bow presented too many difficulties for the ship to be saved.

It seemed only the paint was holding her together. At 3:30 *Gwin* moved alongside, and accompanied her until midafternoon when the seas roughened and *Benham* had to be abandoned. Gunfire from *Gwin* sank her, after the infamous American torpedoes failed to do the job. Perhaps the oddest fact is that despite her injuries, not one of *Benham*'s crew was killed that night and just nine were wounded.

Lee's task force sank *Kirishima* and a destroyer, while losing three destroyers and having *South Dakota* moderately damaged. The latter may have escaped destruction because the Japanese big guns were loaded with bombardment shells instead of the deadly armor-piercing variety, a likely result of Kondo's refusal to believe that American battleships were involved. The scheduled bombardment of Henderson Field was thwarted, derailing Yamamoto's Z-Day plans. Tanaka was forced to beach his four remaining transports, although 2,000 of the troops made it safely ashore. Most of the supplies were lost when air attacks and shore artillery set fire to the stranded ships.

The number of sailors killed on both sides was roughly equal: 242 American and at least 249 Japanese. The sinking of *Kirishima* made this a full-fledged victory for Lee's task force, resulting mainly because he adhered to his plan to let his destroyers screen the battleships. Lee attributed the winning edge to the successful employment of radar, rather than to experience, skill, and training, which the Japanese had in abundance.

When Tanaka at 3:30 announced his intention of beaching the remaining transports, Mikawa objected but was overruled by Yamamoto after receiving Kondo's assessment of the situation. The transports were run aground within sight of the happy floating survivors of *Walke* and *Preston*. Moreover, they were beached within a 15-mile range from Henderson Field.

At 5:55, Major Sailer and seven other SBDs began their dive toward two of the fat hulls beached near the Poha River, claiming three hits. Visiting pilots from *Enterprise* joined in the turkey shoot and claimed two hits. A VT-10 TBF scored another hit. On the 15th Captain Foss nailed down his twenty-third victory, but by that night he was suffering from such a violent attack of malaria that he had to be evacuated to Australia.

The planes returned again and again, augmented by 155-mm artillery fire from two guns of the newly arrived 244th Coast Artillery, and a pair of 3rd Defense Battalions's 5-inch guns. But it was the destroyer *Meade*, under Lieutenant Commander Raymond S. Lamb, that had the most spectacular results. The ship moved in close and for forty-two minutes her 5-inch shells set raging fires on three transports—one was already consumed in flames—then pounded the adjacent beaches with shells from both her 5-inch batteries and her 40-mm guns. After they were finished with their part in the target practice, *Meade* moved out to help recover American survivors of the sunk destroyers.

Boats from the beach were once again looking for and picking up survivors. Chief Torpedoman Chapman, who had been blown off *Benham*, was the only one from his ship to land on Guadalcanal. Coxswain Peter Trella and his brother Paul were rescued by *Meade*, as was Machinist's Mate 2nd Class Klopf, who was throwing up seawater and suffering from the agony of his wounds and injuries.

Two *Walke* survivors who were not picked up instead made it to shore well behind Japanese lines. Seaman Dale E. Land and Machinist's Mate Harold Taylor began their agonizing trek to reach the safety of the Lunga perimeter. Land had no shoes, which compelled them to move slowly. They recovered a Japanese rifle and ammunition and killed several enemy soldiers before Taylor was killed. When the nearly starved Land, cut and bruised, and delirious with a temperature of 106 degrees at last made it back to the Marine lines his uniform was almost unrecognizable. In time he recovered from his difficult ordeal.

"One time they told me to report to the airfield. I thought they'd found out how old I was and were going to finally send me home," reports Jim McCarson. He reported to a Navy lieutenant who told him he must know something about machine guns, so he figured that has to be the reason they sent for him. He flew an SBD dive bomber. "I'd never been in an airplane before."

"The first time we went up and made a dive, that was about the third day, my nose bled, I mean that whole cockpit was bloody. It felt like to me that somebody had driven a bulldozer into the back of my head when we pulled up out of a dive. I was tickled to death when we came back down. I told him that I had to go to the hospital and couldn't fly anymore.

"He told me a bloody nose wasn't that unusual, that I'd get used to it. But I didn't stay in that more than a couple of weeks. I really got sick. That's when the malaria hit me. I was almost glad to be sick. I'd never been in an airplane before and something like that just scared the shit out of me. I don't remember them giving us anything until I got the malaria, and I started getting Atabrine. I didn't go back to the line and didn't have to fly anymore because they were beginning to relieve us."

About the same time Private 1st Class Jerry R. Gillard, who had driven the ambulance in action on Edson's Ridge, had an unnerving experience. He too was suffering from illness and various infections. They were bad enough to cause a medical officer to offer him a seat on one of the outgoing evacuation transports. At the airfield, Gillard announced he had been on the Canal this long, that he had decided he could wait until the division was relieved. Another man took the available seat. As Gillard and the medical officer stood side by side watching the transport fly away they were stunned to see it blow up in midair, killing everyone aboard. Without speaking or looking at each other, they turned and walked away.

The gloom fostered in October was considerably brightened when the results of the naval battle were evaluated. Navy Secretary Frank Knox reversed his previous negative opinion about the Guadalcanal operation and announced that while there was more fighting ahead, "We can lick them. I don't qualify that." What historian Richard Frank calls the "Air–Naval Battle of Guadalcanal" was immediately perceived as a decisive American victory. American ships were now moving in men and supplies with little difficulty, while the Japanese had great difficulty reinforcing the island and suffered unsustainable ship losses.

The Americans had precious few fully operational ships of all descriptions left in the Pacific after the two-night naval battle. Halsey had taken a great risk in sending them in, and his decision to commit them to the defense of Guadalcanal was the fighting Admiral's finest hour. The two nights of The Naval Battle of Guadalcanal were without doubt the turning point of the Pacific war. After *Kirishima* was sent to the bottom on the heels of the loss of *Hiei*, the now hesitant Yamamoto and his Combined Fleet never again committed their big ships, including the big carriers, in a head-on fight with the Americans. The initiative completely and irretrievably passed to the U.S.

Captain Zenji Orita, the submarine commander, stated simply that after November 15th "Japan was to make no more major sea attacks on 'Death Island.' That day marked the actual turning point of the Pacific naval war (not the battle of Midway).... From November 15, 1942, Japan was purely on the defensive."

After reading the reports of the battle, Halsey turned to his staff, grinned broadly, and announced, "We've got the bastards licked!"

It was the presence of Henderson Field—home of the wild and woolly Cactus Air Force—on which Japanese actions had been based. Twice bombardment fleets were sent in to neutralize the airfield and open up the island to invasion, and twice they failed. The fleets were to have covered Tanaka's reinforcement transports, which were virtually destroyed by the CAF and aircraft from *Enterprise*, which the Japanese did not expect. The impact of the air strikes takes on a more remarkable importance when one considers that on the 13th the CAF had only thirty-one attack planes—twenty-three SBDs and eight TBFs—ready to send out against the Japanese. Air Group 10 from *Enterprise*—temporarily assigned to Henderson Field—more than doubled this attack force.

On the 16th heavy, oily smoke hung over the shimmering flames licking away at the blistered steel plates of the battered hulls forever beached around Tassafaronga. "Buzzard Patrols" from Henderson swooped in to pick at the bones and fire into the surrounding jungle. Occasionally their bombs or bullets hit ammunition or oil dumps, evoking violent explosions. Some troops and supplies had been put ashore by the Japanese Reinforcement Unit, but without relieving the pressure on Japanese troops still suffering on the island. Vandegrift felt the time was right to attack and liquidate the remnants of the 17th Army between his lines and the Poha River.

Land Attacks to the West

Under the command of Brigadier General Sebree, another advance west of the Matanikau River on the 18th moved out to seize a new line of departure between Point Cruz south to Hill 66—2,500 yards inland. Taking part in the attack was Hogan's 182nd Regiment less one battalion, Moore's 164th Regiment, Jeschke's 8th Marines, with Cates's 1st Marines in reserve. Earlier patrols, including one led personally by Sebree, had found that area free of the enemy.

But Hyakutake had not planned to withdraw his 17th Army from that very same line. The IJA had activated the 8th Area Army on Rabaul, under the command of Lieutenant General Hitoshi Imamura, for the possibility of helping out on Operation Ka. The Japanese Army Air Force would cooperate for the first time, since not a single Japanese Army airplane had taken part in attacks on Guadalcanal. Imamura, after studying the problem, anticipated he would need eight or nine weeks to prepare his force before heading for the Canal. Of the 10,000 officers and men of the Sendai Division that landed in October, less than 5,000 could be considered combat effective. Other units present were worse off, but were willing to continue the fight even though they no longer possessed an offensive capability.

Soldiers of Lieutenant Colonel Bernard B. Twombley's 2nd Battalion, 182nd Infantry stepped out carrying heavy packs and full loads of ammunition, in addition to rations and water, and crossed the footbridge in single file heading for Hill 66, the southern end of the anticipated line. His troops—who had come ashore only six days before—were devastated by the sweltering heat, and those who had not taken salt tablets passed out along a march that would have challenged even a superbly conditioned unit. Still, they reached the objective set by Brigadier General Sebree in the late afternoon and dug in for the night. Two men had been killed in a small patrol skirmish along the way.

On the morning of the 19th the 1st Battalion, 182nd Infantry crossed the river and reached the ridges about 100 yards east of Point Cruz. Between Lieutenant Colonel Francis F. MacGowan's force at the Point and Twombley's men on Hill 66 lay more than a mile of spiny ridges and undergrowth-choked ravines. Slowly they began moving toward each other to help fill in the gap. At first light on Friday the 20th the Japanese hit MacGowan's left flank, and within minutes a firefight erupted along 700 yards of front around the point. Sebree came forward and personally rallied his threatened part of the 1st Battalion along the beach. Despite initially mounting this counterattack, the Japanese began losing ground. Americans reached the beach west of Point Cruz, and sealed off the Japanese left there, but the advance was stopped by enemy artillery and mortar barrages.

The next morning 164th Infantry was committed to the intervening 700-yard gap, and had advanced about 40 yards before deadly rifle and machine gun fire from obstinate Japanese of the 1st Battalion, 228th Infantry brought them to a halt. Up near Point Cruz a combination of artillery, mortar, and small arms fire from well prepared positions stopped the Americans after an advance of 100 yards.

Sebree, just as stubborn about wanting to establish his line, brought up the 8th Marines the next day, the 23rd. He ordered the soldiers to fall back 300 yards while artillery pounded the contested area for thirty minutes with a heavy preparatory barrage. Jeschke's 8th Marines passed through the stalled Army forces, determined to show them how these things were done. But, as Marine Raider Griffith wrote later, they got rocked back on their heels. The two lead Marine battalions in column attacked through too narrow an approach that left no room for deployment, and the advance was smothered.

The Japanese soldiers of the 228th Infantry had apparently learned something about American tactics. They waited in their well constructed dugouts until the artillery let up, then came out to lay down heavy fire and grenades from their fighting positions. In the six-day struggle the 164th Infantry lost forty-seven men killed, the 182nd lost forty-five, and the 8th Marines lost forty. By November 25th less than 2,000 men of the 2,818—less 117 combat deaths—in the 164th who had landed on October 13th were fit for combat. On the 23rd Vandegrift suspended the operation and ordered his forces to dig in where they were and consider that line as the departure point for a move to the Poha. The enemy forces would face each other along this static line for more than six weeks.

An internal evaluation of Japanese Army strength on November 20th revealed that of 29,117 men landed on Guadalcanal since August 7th, only 18,295 remained with their units, with only 12,775 loosely considered fit for combat. Of the 2,376 IJN soldiers and construction workers brought in since the marine landing, only 550 were available. "Fit for combat" meant that the reasonably healthy few manned the patrols and attacks; those who couldn't walk manned the dugout fighting positions; and those who could hobble about one way or another prepared what few rations were available. Those rations were fast disappearing, and medical supplies for treatment of the ill and wounded were virtually nonexistent. The one thing in ample supply was the Japanese willingness to fight.

Thursday November 26th was Thanksgiving Day on Guadalcanal. While the 1st Marine Division ate the turkey and cranberry sauce that Halsey had made sure reached the still beleaguered island, they gave special thanks. They had received their marching orders to depart in early December for Australia. Coming in as replacement was the Army 25th Division, which MacArthur had "traded" in order to finally get the amphibious division he wanted. It would be many months before the badly worn and malaria-ridden division was once again combat effective. There had been more than 4,500 reported cases of malaria, with the fever cutoff point at 103 degrees. If a man's temperature was less than that, he was considered able to work, patrol, and fight—and, astoundingly, he did so.

Halsey received his fourth star on Thanksgiving Day, even as his fleet was gaining strength as ships reported back from repair docks. He ordered a task force under Kinkaid back to the waters around Guadalcanal, but Kinkaid yielded command to Rear Admiral Carleton H. Wright before reaching the island. Halsey probably should have given the new commander Wright a few days to become acquainted with his force before venturing forth.

A Japanese convoy reached Munda Point, New Georgia, on the 28th, where men and equipment were unloaded for the construction of a new airfield to station fighter aircraft closer to Guadalcanal. Their plans were to establish intermediate bases where small boats could find cover during the day and move supplies and men at night to Operation Ka. They desperately needed more aircraft in the fight and also an additional point for the recovery of planes short on fuel or badly damaged. However, the Japanese weren't the only ones interested in building a new airstrip. A day later Seabees, supported by the 3rd Battalion, 142nd Infantry Regiment and artillery, landed at Koli Point to construct a new American airfield.

Captain William Hawkins was transferred from the Canal to become a transport officer on *Alchiba*, a supply ship moving back and forth from Nouméa. While hauling a barge of supplies—including bombs and aviation gasoline—past Savo, the ship was torpedoed by Japanese midget sub *I-16* off Lunga Point that same day.

"Head her for shore," ordered the captain, Jim Freeman, an Alabamian. "Maybe we can beach her and not lose the cargo." The ship ran aground about fifty yards up on the beach, near where Hawkins had come ashore the first day. The crew managed to off-load the supplies the next day just before another submarine put a torpedo into the ship, ending its career. Hawkins, who had been compelled to abandon ship two days in a row, went back to Nouméa and was assigned to *McCawley*.

CHAPTER 16

NOVEMBER 30 NAVAL BATTLE OF TASSAFARONGA

There are no flowers
on a sailor's grave.

—German song

Back in Japan, the angry and frustrated General Tojo, incensed that the American Marines were still on Guadalcanal, demanded a decisive action to drive them off the island. That meant getting more men to the island, as well as supplying those already there. Of the more than 10,000 Japanese on Guadalcanal, most were suffering from a variety of illnesses and were on the verge of starvation.

On Rabaul, Rear Admiral Tanaka had devised a new technique to move a portion of the sixty-thousand combat-ready troops and supplies there to Guadalcanal to mount the offensive that would finally defeat the Americans. Using submarines to transport the sheer volume of needed reinforcements and supplies had been partially successful, but this method was still insufficient even for the simple survival of the men already there. Attempts to relieve the force by air proved to be an equally poor alternative, considering American air superiority. Launching a new massive offensive under the circumstances was impossible.

When the full-scale *Mogura* (mole) Operation—which would move slowly and hopefully out of sight—to resupply the troops on Guadalcanal was presented to the aggressive submarine captains, they were aghast, and vigorously opposed the idea. Captain Orita wrote of the verbal exchange that took place: "How can submarines carry out their foremost mission—attack—when we are forced into this stupid kind of work?"

"Word from Tokyo," replied Admiral Komatsu, "is that our Army troops under Lieutenant General Harukichi Hyakutake are starving on Guadalcanal. They used the last of their rations several days ago. More than one hundred men are dying from hunger daily. Many of the rest are eating grass. Very few men are fit for fighting. What are we to do, let our countrymen starve to death in the jungle? We must help them, no matter what sacrifices must be made in doing so!" That settled the matter.

Once the difficulties were smoothed out, each submarine managed to unload 20 to 30 tons of supplies nightly—about one day's supply of food for the isolated 17th Army. The Japanese Captain Orita said the subs could carry two days' supplies. The submarines would load up at Buin on Bougainville, then proceed on to Makino Point on Guadalcanal to unload at night.

The agonizing chore of moving those supplies by hand over land and through the jungles to where they were needed was a terrible demand to make on the overburdened men. On the 21st Major Nishiyama, acting commander of the 228th, noted that his only food for the last three or four days had been one dried plum. On the night of the 25th *I-17* succeeded in off-loading 11 tons of supplies. Earlier attempts had been harassed by American PT boats and aircraft.

Tanaka's solution was to pack basic food rations and medical supplies into large rubber-wrapped and waterproofed metal drums. His relief fleet would unload the drums into the sea about a mile offshore, to be picked up by boats and small craft from the beach. The drums, each with sufficient air trapped inside to provide for flotation, would be linked together with rope into a long chain that could be towed ashore. The concept was tested and found to be practical.

The first high-speed run would take place the night of November 30. Six destroyers carrying 200 to 240 drums each were loaded, taking up space at the expense of torpedoes, which were left behind. Commander Masami Ogura on the destroyer *Takanami* would stand guard to cover the unloading operation. Tanaka would be on the fully armed *Naganami*, his flagship. The schedule called for the small reinforcement unit to be off Tassafaronga and Doma Cove at precisely 11:30 P.M., when the unloading would begin. The reinforcement group consisted of eight destroyers, with six of them carrying the packed supply drums.

Contrary to some published reports, Tanaka's mission on the 30th was neither to evacuate nor land troops, but simply to resupply the basic necessities for Japanese soldiers already on Guadalcanal. His destroyer relief column was not hindered by the presence of cumbersome transports. Whatever happened, his force would be able to maneuver freely. In several accounts, the Americans were credited with the sinking of several transports. There were none in the battle zone that night.

"There is a great possibility of an encounter with the enemy tonight," said Tanaka in giving instructions to his ships as they approached Guadalcanal. "In such an event, utmost efforts will be made to destroy the enemy without regard for unloading supplies." Japanese aerial reconnaissance that afternoon had reported the presence of twelve American destroyers and nine transports in Sealark Channel.

Off Guadalcanal on the 30th, Task Force 67 was under the command of Rear Admiral Carleton H. Wright, aboard the heavy cruiser *Minneapolis*. Wright had relieved Kinkaid, who had been named the North Pacific Fleet Commander and given command of the cruiser force at Espiritu Santo only two days previously. The cruiser battle force passed through Lengo Channel at 11:00 P.M. on their way to intercept the Japanese supply and reinforcement at Tassafaronga. Rounding out this force were cruisers *New Orleans*, *Pensacola*, *Northampton*, and *Honolulu*, escorted by destroyers *Fletcher*, *Drayton*, *Maury*, *Perkins*, *Lamson*, and *Lardner*. The last two had been ordered to join TF 67 as the force approached the battle zone. They had no knowledge of the attack plan and were simply instructed to follow the cruisers.

Kinkaid's plan had divided TF 67 into three parts—one destroyer group and two cruiser groups. Each group was to be led by an SG radar-equipped ship scouting 10,000 yards ahead. When the enemy was detected by radar, Kinkaid intended for his destroyers to move in and launch a surprise torpedo attack. The cruisers would open up with their big guns at from 10,000 to 12,000 yards—five to six miles away—after the torpedoes had struck home. The cruiser float planes would look for the enemy force, and then drop flares at least a mile inland over the island to avoid lighting up their own ships. Wright adopted the plan with only a few minor changes.

According to Richard Frank's authoritative figures, the American fleet had thirty-seven 8-inch guns, fifteen 6-inch guns, and sixty-eight 5-inch guns—against only forty-six 5-inch guns for the Japanese. Only half the Japanese ships were carrying torpedoes. Moreover, the Americans knew where the Japanese force would be. By all standards, the Japanese force should have been easily blown out of the water.

At the same time Tanaka's force sailed by Savo and into Indispensable Strait, TF 67 entered the eastern end of Lengo Channel, forming into a column led by its destroyers steaming 4,000 yards (roughly 2 miles) ahead of the cruisers, with the ships spaced 1,000 yards apart. Here Wright departed from Kinkaid's original plan and chose not to deploy his SG radar-equipped pickets at the head of the column. With heavy clouds blocking the moonlight, night visibility was profoundly diminished to about two miles with American binoculars. The keen Japanese lookouts, with their night binoculars, could see out to about five miles.

Advised of the presence of American destroyers in Iron Bottom Sound, Tanaka ordered that if contact were made, the resupply mission would be aborted and his destroyers directed to destroy the enemy ships. With no moon, the night was totally dark. His lookouts reported the possible presence of enemy ships to the east at 9:12, a report quickly confirmed. At 9:16 Tanaka signaled: "All ships attack." Some of his destroyers dumped the cargo drums to prepare for the fight.

The American fleet was relying on its radar console operators, who had been glued to their screens for hours. Trying to make out the shapes of ships from the background clutter of Guadalcanal was painstaking and difficult work.

Still, at 11:08 radar on *Minneapolis* showed seven or eight vessels approaching. At 11:16 *Fletcher*'s radar revealed the Japanese at a range of 7,000 yards (about 4-1/2 miles) and the captain, Commander Cole, requested permission to launch his torpedoes. It was 11:20 before Wright authorized the firing of the ten torpedoes, which proved too late, as the original desirable angle of fire had altered. The following *Perkins* added eight more torpedoes. Simultaneously, Wright ordered his big guns to commence firing before the torpedoes had made their run, alerting the disciplined Japanese ships of the attack. None of the American explosive fish hit home.

Minneapolis fired its main batteries from 9,200 yards and *New Orleans* fired hers at 8,700 yards. Immediately all the big guns were belching flame and shot while the destroyers fired off star shells for illumination. Somehow most of this blitz was aimed at one destroyer, *Takanami*. She was closest and the fires that ignited had her lit up for all to see. When she began returning fire, launching her torpedoes, she drew more fire. In minutes, engulfed in flames, she slipped to a halt. The remainder of Tanaka's ships, virtually untouched, slipped out of the stream of gunfire, hugged Guadalcanal's dim shore, and prepared to launch their deadly torpedoes.

At 11:22 Tanaka's flagship *Naganami* fired her guns and began laying smoke. The destroyer *Suzukaze* released eight Long Lances. In the lead, Captain Sato made a remarkable decision to remain on course and steam by the American column. Once past, he turned his ships and slipped in close to the enemy. At 11:28 *Kuroshio* fired two torpedoes, followed a minute later by eight from *Oyashio.* Between 11:23 and 11:33 the Japanese put forty-four of their powerful fish into the water.

Minneapolis boomed off its ninth main battery salvo at 11:27, just as Wright decided to make a turn to face three enemy ships 6,000 yards away. Two of the torpedoes plowed into the forward half of *Minneapolis.* One ignited the aviation gasoline tanks forward of Turret 1, the second demolished Fire Room 2 and hurled tons of water and oil skyward that fell back and enveloped the ship. Two sailors were washed overboard. Somehow she got off two more main battery salvos before the power went out. Within minutes energetic damage control and firefighting efforts got her back to two degrees off vertical, but she was definitely out of the fight.

Moments later a Long Lance found *New Orleans* just as she too sent out her ninth salvo. The 1000-pound warhead of the underwater missile set off sympathetic explosions in the forward magazines and gasoline storage tanks. A huge fiery geyser spiraled upward, flinging off flaming fuel and powder, then settled back down to dump a foot of raging water on her decks. Chaplain Howell M. Forgy was dumbfounded as the fires completely dried his sopping wet uniform within seconds. The detonation had severed the bow section forward of Turret 2, which then floated off and sank. Abruptly, her steering and communications failed.

Pensacola, following next in line, swung out to port to pass the battered cruisers and was nearly hit by a salvo from *Minneapolis* that screamed overhead. Hoping to protect the burning ships, the executive officer, Commander Harry Keeler, made the mistake of returning *Pensacola* to base course and at 11:39 she took a torpedo below her mainmast. The captain, Frank L. Lowe—fighting his ship from the sky control platform—was knocked off his feet, and instantly all power, communications, and steering from the bridge failed. The torpedo detonated against a full oil tank and blew oil back into the aft engine room and living compartments, followed immediately by a torrent of water. The upward blast ripped open the main deck and sent a pillar of the mixture soaring. As it came down it coated the ship with a layer of oil, turning into an inferno that burned sailors to death when it ignited. The outer port shaft was torn away and *Pensacola* leaned over by thirteen degrees even as the fires raged.

Honolulu had not as yet fired her guns when she swerved to starboard to avoid *Pensacola* and exposure to her fires. Then, *Honolulu,* with Rear Admiral Mahlon S. Tisdale aboard, commenced a six-minute barrage at another target until it disappeared behind billowing smoke. Just after midnight, Tisdale was ordered by Wright to take command, which he did by ordering destroyers to stand by the maimed ships, and then, laying on speed, took *Honolulu* around Savo in a search for Japanese ships. Instead he found three of the forward destroyers, which joined him.

Last in the cruiser line was *Northampton,* whose guns had helped sink *Takanami.* She had followed *Honolulu* behind the burning cruisers, but did not increase her speed. As she returned to base course, two of *Kawakaze*'s long fish sped in toward her. At 11:48 one impacted 10 feet below the waterline near the aft engine room, and the other 40 feet further back, instantly turning her into a blazing hulk. By 1:15 A.M. of the 29th she was listing by twenty-three degrees despite determined and hectic countermeasures. When she came under fire from Japanese shore guns the captain ordered everyone off except a salvage crew, and soon *Fletcher* and *Drayton* came forward to pick up survivors. By 2:00 Captain Willard A. Kitts, III, and the salvage crew left *Northampton* for the last time. At 3:04 she turned bottom up and sank by the stern.

The awesome torpedo attack had succeeded in sinking *Northampton*, and had blown the bows off *Minneapolis* and *New Orleans*. As Japan's Orita observed, *New Orleans* may have been the only warship ever to ram itself. The bow, separated from the rest of the ship by the explosion, came about out of control and smashed into the chief petty officer's quarters near the stern! Also damaged was the heavy cruiser *Pensacola*. Screened by the other ships, *Honolulu* escaped harm.

Tanaka's resupply mission was repelled, but at the high cost to the Americans of one cruiser sunk and two severely damaged in exchange for the sinking of a single Japanese destroyer. In trying not to repeat the mistakes of previous battles, Wright had made his own. Admittedly, the attack plan had not been his, and he had had little time to get to know his new force. The battle, however, did succeed in its urgent purpose of denying the Japanese forces critically needed resupply and reinforcement, making their position on the island even more perilous.

Wright gracefully accepted full responsibility for the mess he'd gotten his ships into, and escaped censure. Halsey and the Navy, in their arcane need for a scapegoat, reached down the chain of command to lay blame for the fiasco on Cole, commanding *Fletcher.* Cole was censured for launching his torpedoes at "excessive range" and taking his ship around Savo—the same move made by acting Task Force Commander Tisdale without censure. Wright's superiors, in a later stupefying move, awarded him the Navy Cross, second only to the Medal Honor, for his part in the massacre.

The American Navy was not the only force to work in mysterious ways. Despite this astounding victory by probably their best naval combat officer, Tanaka was eventually relieved of his command and transferred to a rear area. This was based on the criticism that he had failed to pursue the attack, despite the fact that he didn't have enough torpedoes to make a second attack. Half of his destroyers had been stripped of their torpedoes to enable them to carry more supply-laden drums. The real reason might have been the long memories of senior officers, who recalled that this was the man who had suggested at the onset that Guadalcanal should be evacuated rather than reinforced.

Air Power

Allied air power, improving in strength, was now far better than during the grim days of October. Eighty-four American, and now New Zealander, planes were on Guadalcanal on November 23. A week later 188 aircraft of all types operated from Henderson Field. In early December the 1st Marine Air Wing was present, along with Marine Air Group 14, the Army's 12th, 68th, and 339th Fighter Squadrons, and B-26 medium attack bombers of the 70th Medium Bombardment Squadron. The buttressed CAF was highly successful in keeping the Tokyo Express resupply effort too little too late. The force was increasingly attacking Japanese land bases and airfields.

With control of the air, the Navy was easily getting troops and supplies safely to the island. B-17s of the heavy bombardment squadrons were drawing patrol duty—the big fortresses had the defensive armament to drive off enemy attacks that was lacking in the PBYs. These bombers could not be used effectively against shore-based establishments farther up the Solomons chain until Henderson Field could be improved enough to handle them. Plans for just that capability had been made, and work was beginning. Rear Admiral McCain had suggested that if Guadalcanal were to be used for further large-scale offensives, aviation gasoline storage tanks with a million-gallon capacity should be constructed, and that plan was being implemented.

The massive Japanese air attacks of October had given way to harassing night air raids. More antiaircraft units with better radar and searchlights were moved to defend Henderson. The annoying "Louie the Louse" and "Washing Machine Charley" continued to disturb the rest of the troops, but caused little damage.

WWII Snapshot—December 1942

South America—The U.S. establishes a Naval Operating Base and an Air Facility at Rio de Janeiro, Brazil, for the purpose of controlling German submarine activity in the South Atlantic.

The United States—Under the stands of a football stadium at the University of Chicago, Italian emigré physicist Enrico Fermi sets up an atomic reactor and produces a self-sustaining nuclear chain reaction. The theory of a making a super nuclear bomb, now fully understood as possible, will be transformed by practical laboratory experiment into reality.

Germany—Another of Hitler's secret weapons, a prototype of the first jet-powered airplane—a remote-controlled rocket—is successfully flown on the 24th.

At a prisoner of war camp at Poniatowa, Poland, 18,000 Soviet POWs are denied all food and deliberately starved to death.

Southern Russia—The Red Army is closing the iron ring around the German 6th Army at Stalingrad. Nazi attempts to support the isolated army by air and break through the ring to relieve the cornered troops fail. The stupefying Russian winter has set in. German officers order that certain deaths be attributed to the freezing cold, and not to starvation.

Southwest Pacific—Major General Edwin F. Harding, commander of the 32nd Division, and Brigadier General Albert W. Waldron have to swim ashore on Papua, New Guinea, after the supply convoy of three trawlers and an ammunition barge is attacked and destroyed by Japanese fighters. Several men and a war correspondent are killed and many wounded. Lost are two 75-mm howitzers, ammunition, medical supplies, and a new portable hospital. This is the first Japanese air activity in a month.

The next day Harding orders the 162nd Battalion of the 32nd Division—mostly National Guard troops from Michigan and Wisconsin—to attack toward Buna. Within a mile of their starting point they are halted by a firestorm of bullets. The "dead" Japanese troops they thought they would find are in fact healthy, well fed, and well armed. That night Harding is astounded to have his 2nd and 3rd Battalions transferred to Major General George A. Vasey's Australian contingent—to be used at Gona!

The Australian 25th Brigade is assigned to Gona, and the 16th have as their objective the village of Sananada. They are stopped well short of their goals on the 19th and 20th of November.

MacArthur sends a message to Harding on the morning of the 20th: TAKE BUNA TODAY AT ALL COSTS. The Area Commander does not seem to understand that Harding's force is pinned down by heavy Japanese fire, with half his troops taken away. Supplies are low and the supporting artillery and tanks needed to reduce the Japanese bunkers have not and maybe will not arrive. Nothing is going right with MacArthur's plans, so Harding begins making command changes.

Major General Robert L. Eichelberger, I Corps commander, is called in on the 30th and given control of the 32nd Division. "Go out there, Bob, and take Buna or don't come back alive," MacArthur tells him. Eichelberger lands at the Dobodura airfield the next morning, and receives the report that the "Ghost Mountain" men of 2nd Battalion, 126th Infantry have moved into Buna Village.

With the Dobodura airfield secured, the supply situation begins to improve. Men are given their first full meal in days on December 3rd. Five Australian Bren gun carriers (lightly armored vehicles) and a 155-mm howitzer with a limited supply of ammo arrive. The first time the Bren carriers go into action they are knocked out in about twenty minutes. The fighting, by both the Australians and Americans, against the entrenched Japanese proceeds slowly. The obdurate enemy, realizing they will not leave New Guinea alive, fight like wildcats from their well protected battlements.

On December 3rd the Australian 30th Brigade—rested up after its ordeal on the Kokoda Trail—is sent in to reinforce the assaults on Gona. The fresh 127th Infantry Regiment, 32nd Division arrives on December 9th. Reinforcements are slowly being provided, despite the heavy casualties being taken in the ferocious fighting. The heat and the rains are compounding the problems caused by malaria and dengue fever. Sick and underfed men, lacking heavy firepower to break through the strong defensive positions, are being ordered to attack through the swampy underbrush.

At last, on December 10th, the Australians take Gona. Their 21st Brigade has suffered 409 battle casualties and the 39th Battalion 121 casualties—forty-one percent of the troops committed to the action. On the 18th, the capture of the small outpost of Haddy's Village claims another 129 Australian casualties.

CHAPTER 17

DECEMBER 1942
THE AMERICAN OFFENSIVE BEGINS

And when he goes to heaven
To Saint Peter he will tell:
Another Marine reporting, sir;
I've served my time in hell.

—Epitaph on grave of Marine PFC Cameron, on Guadalcanal, 1942

The exhausted marines, long overdue for relief, had existed in close proximity to deprivation and destruction for four long months. They had held onto Guadalcanal when few in the world felt they could. For agonizing months there simply hadn't been any replacements available for this battered corps. In early December the Lunga perimeter did not reach much farther than it did in August, although it now extended past the Matanikau to Point Cruz and south to Hill 66. To the east at Koli Point the Seabees were building an airstrip. They were protected by Colonel Tuttle's 147th Infantry and the 9th Defense Battalion (Marines).

Cargo arriving at the Canal was still being moved from the transports in small boats to be unloaded on the beach and then hauled inland. The road system was inadequate for the few trucks that had come in. The chore of getting supplies up to the front lines greatly limited offensive operations.

Malaria was epidemic among the Allies, the Melanesians, and the Japanese, and caused far more casualties than battle wounds. The Japanese were not getting the food and medicine necessary for the troops to maintain offensive operations. At this time most of the men of the Japanese 17th Army suffered from malaria, as well as beri-beri and dysentery, all complicated by malnutrition.

Those first months in the jungles of Guadalcanal experienced by the relative handful of men of the 1st Marine Division and associated forces have few parallels in the history of American warfare—indeed, in world military history. The extended Australian fight for the Kokoda Trail on Papua, New Guinea—the same kind of fight in much the same conditions at about the same time—may be the only similar battle fought in WWII. Both Allied forces were pitifully undermanned, and woefully supplied, equipped, and supported—in contrast to the experienced, tenacious, and courageous Japanese troops facing them.

Contrary to the conclusions of most histories of this landmark campaign, this changeover did not mark the end of the battle for Guadalcanal. The 1st Marine Division had established, held, and expanded the precious perimeter of their original beachhead. Theirs had been primarily a ferocious defensive battle, because they never had the offensive manpower required to drive the Japanese from the island. The fighting for the remaining two months of the campaign moved the Americans to the offensive against stubborn Japanese resistance. In that time the fresh Army and Marine troops would suffer almost as many battle deaths and casualties as those registered in the first four months. Offensive operations necessarily incur more casualties than defensive stands, as the Japanese had learned to their everlasting regret.

"The machine guns and all that," laughed Jim McCarson, now a veteran Raider, "We left them in place—that's what we were told to do. I thought to myself, with all those new weapons they had...well, some of our guns the bullets would come out sideways, they were so worn." Vandegrift had been advised to leave his old and badly worn equipment behind so that when his division reached Australia they could request and obtain new modern gear.

A Tokyo Express resupply group consisting of ten destroyers was spotted coming down the Slot by Coastwatchers and a patrol plane. Eight SBDs and seven TBFs rose up to hit the destroyers—still 160 miles from Tassafaronga—just before the sun disappeared. One was damaged when the CAF swarmed to the attack. Covering Wildcats shot down five Petes trying to protect the fleet. One each SBD, TBF, and Wildcat were lost. Despite continuing daytime air attacks, on the night of the December 3rd the Japanese destroyers unloaded 1,500 supply drums off Tassafaronga. However, only 310 survived CAF strafing attacks.

On the 4th Carlson's Raiders returned to the Lunga perimeter after a month-long sweep around it. Their remarkable escapade had ruined Colonel Shoji's Japanese force, including fresh troops of the 230th Infantry—who had landed a month ago—and the remnants of Kawaguchi's 35th Infantry Brigade. The Melanesian scouts under Vouza had taken part in various Raider ambushes, as well as guiding this "gung ho" Raider battalion—which had previously conducted its famed in-and-out raids on the Japanese-held island of Makin.

In the first of many raids on the 6th, Aircobras from Guadalcanal attacked and strafed the new Japanese airfield, which was being built at Munda with nothing more than picks, shovels, and saws. In spite of cunning camouflage to conceal their progress, the Japanese efforts had been spotted by native scouts and photo reconnaissance. Even with the daily attacks, a crude strip 1,094 by 44 yards—capable of handling thirty Zekes—was completed by December 14th. Antiaircraft batteries and other units also got through to the strip.

A new approach to sending supplies utilizing the drum method—no more than 100 drums to a line and releasing the drums closer to shore—was put into effect December 7th. Again, warned by Coastwatchers of the approach of the reinforcement unit, thirteen VMSB-132 SBDs, led by Major Sailer, found Sato's group at about 6:40 P.M. One destroyer suffered damage from a near miss that killed seventeen men and knocked out an engine, and had to be towed back to the Shortland Islands. In the air attack Sailer's SBD took a hit that slowed him down enough for one of the eight defending Petes to shoot him down, ending his brief but dazzling career.

On the first anniversary of Pearl Harbor eight PT boats of Squadron 3 sortied from their anchorage on Tulagi to meet another Japanese foray down the Slot. At 11:20 P.M. scout PT boats *40* and *48*, commanded by "Stilley" Taylor and Bob Searles, respectively, noticed several warships headed their way, flashed the alarm to the other six boats, and started their attack. Just then the engines of Searles's PT *48* failed, leaving it dead in the water.

Japanese eyes had spotted the plywood pests, and shells began falling near the floundering vessel. Aware that his companion boat was in trouble, Taylor swung back across the bows of the oncoming destroyers to lay a smoke screen, then dashed off to the southwest. The enemy took off in pursuit of Taylor's boat, which managed to evade the wolves nipping at his gunwales. Searles's crew got one engine started and limped off into the lee of Savo Island, finding concealment in the tangled jungle close to shore.

A few minutes after 11:35 the other boats began their attack, and enemy searchlights stabbed out of the darkness, followed by guns opening fire. Jack Searles's PT *59* launched two torpedoes, then swung and raced alongside the length of a destroyer, raking her decks with machine gun fire from a range of about 100 yards. The destroyer holed the "Devil Boat of the Night"—as the Japanese had come to call the plywood monsters—in at least ten spots.

Gunner's Mate 2nd Class Cletus E. Osborne was firing away when an incendiary bullet set off a fire in his ammunition belt. With hot lead buzzing around him, Osborne tore loose the burning belt and tossed it into the sea. He then cleared and reloaded his 50-caliber machine gun and went back to strafing the enemy deck, despite suffering excruciating pain from handling the fiery ammo belt. Almost simultaneously, PT *44* under Lieutenant Frank Freeland and PT *36* under Lieutenant M.G. Pettit zoomed in, each releasing four torpedoes. None of them scored, but the swirling action caused Sato to abandon his resupply mission.

The tide of the battle had swung over to the Americans. They now had the momentum. They were also helped immeasurably by a greatly improved supply situation. The materiel so long denied the ground forces on Guadalcanal was now getting through. This relative freedom of movement on the high seas made possible the long overdue relief of the battered, malaria-ridden, and exhausted Marines after four brutal months of fighting for survival. The Army, accompanied by the fresh 2nd Marine Division (the 2nd Marines stayed behind to join its parent) would take over. Finally the Americans would have sufficient troops and support on the island to move to the irresistible offensive operations. On the 8th the Army's 132nd Regimental Combat Team debarked on Guadalcanal. Army staff officers of Americal Division began taking over combat duties from the 1st Marine Division, now in the process of being relieved.

1st Marine Division Relieved by Army

On December 7th, the first anniversary of the Japanese attack on Pearl Harbor, General Vandegrift sent a message to all the men who had served with him in the Guadalcanal area thanking them for their courage and steadfastness, commending particularly the pilots and "all who labored and sweated within the lines in all manner of prodigious and vital tasks." At the same time he paid tacit tribute to the invaluable contribution of the Coastwatchers. He reminded his troops that their "unbelievable achievements had made 'Guadalcanal' a synonym for death and disaster in the language of our enemy." Indeed, the Japanese now called Guadalcanal "Death Island."

On December 9th Major General Alexander "Sandy" M. Patch took over direction of tactical operations on the Canal from Vandegrift and his battered but unbeaten marines, now headed to Australia for a long needed rest, resupply, and reorganization. Patch operated under the command of Halsey, who gave him a simple mission: "Eliminate all Japanese forces" remaining on Guadalcanal. Vandegrift flew out to Australia at the same time the first elements of the 5th Marines were boarding ships. A medical review a few days before found a third of one unit (probably the 5th) unfit for further combat. The 1st, 11th, and 7th Marines would soon follow, together with all the division's supporting units. The survivors of the island crucible were apathetic and hollow-eyed, exhausted and emaciated young men who had grown frightfully old in four months' time. Their "uniforms" were a mishmash of khaki and green utilities—often torn and frayed—with boondockers held together by what string and remnants of shoelaces they had left. Left behind were 681 buddies buried in the Canal's cemetery. Thirty-one marines would forever be listed as missing on the division's roster.

After being ferried out on the transports that would take them away from this hellhole, many men were so weakened from disease that they could not lift themselves up the nets lowered for them to climb aboard. Some fell into the sea and were rescued by sailors who leaped in after them. Many of the sailors assisting these now almost helpless fighters onto the ship did so with tears flowing down their cheeks. Seeing the plight of these marines, the fresh troops coming ashore had to wonder at what the future held for them.

The Japanese submarine supply run delivered more than 20 tons in three nights without difficulty. American radio eavesdroppers worked out the schedule for delivery. During the night of December 9th, PTs *44* and *59*—setting up an ambush off Kamimbo—were startled to see *I-3* surface between them. The *I-3* had left the Shortlands on the 7th with a load of supplies and medicine. To help get the supplies ashore and a *daihatsu* (landing craft) had been lashed to the deck where the rear gun had been removed. PT *59* sent a torpedo into the sub *I-3* of Commander Ichiro Togami and ripped her open while she tried to unload. All hands were lost. The loss of *I-4* caused the suspension of submarine supply operations.

Tanaka tried again with his destroyers, using five of the eleven as escorts, on the 11th. American intelligence had once again nailed down their position, and fourteen SBDs under Major Robert Shaw found them just at sunset, but failed to cause any damage. One SBD was lost. But the Americans weren't finished. The destroyer transports had dropped off 1,200 drums and were about to withdraw when PTs *37*, *40*, and *48* slipped in and unleashed their torpedoes. One exploded into the flagship *Teruzuki*, ripping out one propeller shaft and the rudder. Leaking oil burst into an incandescent flame, and crept into the ship and blew up an aft magazine. The wounded Tanaka and his staff transferred to *Naganami* at 1:33 A.M. while about 140 crewmen crossed over to *Arashi*.

Roaring in for a piece of the action, Lieutenant Freeland's PT *44* was demolished by gunfire from *Kawakaze* and *Suzukaze*. Only two of the eleven-man crew survived. At 3:15 *Teruzuki* was scuttled, and Tanaka and 154 sailors landed safely at Kamimbo. Only

220 drums of those released were reclaimed by the Japanese on the island. As a result of the PT boat action, there were no further excursions of the Tokyo Express in 1942.

On the 12th the Navy's 18th Seabee Battalion and the 2nd Marine Division's Signal Company arrived on the island. The next day men of the 3rd Battalion, 182nd Infantry and Marine Engineers were added to the buildup of manpower on Guadalcanal. The Army's 35th Regimental Combat Team landed on the Canal, sufficiently increasing the forces available to permit a reconnaissance in force to the northeast side of Mount Austen. Until after the decisive Naval Battle of Guadalcanal in mid-November, the Americans had been unable to move in enough fresh troops and supplies at any one time to initiate and support large-scale offensive operations. The Marines had been forced to fight a prolonged defensive battle—a type of fighting contrary to their stated mission of shock amphibious assaults to establish defensible beachheads that would taken over by Army troops.

Major General Patch estimated there were about 25,000 Japanese of the 17th Army on Guadalcanal but he did not know of the deplorable state of those troops. When the 25th Division arrived, the Allied forces would total about 35,000 men of all units. Patch had the dual mission of protecting the airfields and—when he had sufficient strength—destroying the remaining enemy forces. While he did not think the Japanese were capable of mounting a serious offensive, he did know that they possessed a strong defensive proficiency.

Of the five Army and Marine infantry regiments Patch commanded, on paper, only three had any combat experience. Of those, Colonel Moore's 164th Infantry was at about 60 percent strength and had suffered about 500 combat casualties since their arrival in October. Another 500 had been evacuated as too ill to fight, and malaria infected those who remained. Colonel Arthur's 2nd Marines, on the island since August 7th, were not as bad off, but they were frazzled and riddled with malaria as well. Colonel Jeschke's 8th Marines were ailing, and each day nine or ten men turned themselves in as sick with symptoms of filariasis (elephantiasis), a disease they had been infected with during their stay on Samoa. The morale of the 8th was high despite 213 combat casualties and the illnesses affecting it.

Of the new, untested units, the 182nd Infantry was a battalion short—nearly 1,000 men—of its authorized strength. The 132nd Infantry—the third regiment of the Americal Division—had been on Guadalcanal for only a few days. They were not at all oriented to the conditions on the Canal, and consequently were the least prepared for action. The 147th Infantry (independent), Colonel W.B. Tuttle commanding, was providing the defense for the construction of the large bomber landing strip at Koli Point.

Fighter One had been abandoned because its severe drainage problems had defied correction. Fighter Two had become operational in mid-November. Now, a month later, Brigadier General Woods had 200 aircraft on hand, including 100 fighters. Marine Colonel Perry Smith, headquartered on New Caledonia, ran his force of DC-3 transports—the twin-engined workhorses of the Pacific—on continuous supply and evacuation missions no matter what the weather. They brought in ammunition, bombs, drums of gasoline, barbed wire, and supplies of the greatly desired and appreciated candy bars. They departed with wounded and seriously ill officers and men. By the middle of December they had evacuated nearly three times the number of ailing passengers as had been taken away by ship.

Living conditions had improved slowly, but the ability to acquire better food was even more important. Considerable trading of the ubiquitous souvenirs brought in fresh food from time to time. The basic diet still consisted of vienna sausage, Spam, dehydrated potatoes and rice—which suffered greatly in the preparation—and powdered eggs. This fare almost made the C-rations a gourmet's delight. Still, the quantities were notably better than in the first couple of months following the initial landing.

Mount Austen Offensive

On December 17th units of the Americal Division began a full-scale assault against Japanese troops entrenched around Mount Austen. This menacing nearby landmark had to be secured by the Americans in order to deprive the enemy of a prime observation point. It had long been a great source of intelligence and the most aggravating of the network of enemy strongpoints on Guadalcanal. Two divisions would attack to the west, while a third would defend the Lunga airfields. One division moved south in the Hill 66 area to flank and take Mount Austen, while a second would push along the coast on the Hill 66–Point Cruz line, which had been static for many weeks.

When the marines first landed on Guadalcanal, Mount Austen had been a prime target, but because of faulty intelligence, they felt it was much too far away from the perimeter to be taken. It was not a single peak—as the Americans and the Japanese quickly discovered—but rather a maze of steep interlocking ridges covered with dense jungle. About 1,500 yards northwest of the mountain, across a deep gorge carved by the Matanikau, lay another hill mass, comprised of Hills 43 and 44. A third hill mass, about 900 feet high, lay just north of the first. It would be necessary to move a division in a southwesterly direction to assault Mount Austen. New intelligence indicated that the Japanese were building up their strength in that area. On December 12th the enemy infiltrated the defensive lines to reach Fighter 2 and destroy one P-39 and a gas truck. On the 14th a patrol by elements of the 132nd Infantry (Army) on the northwest slope ran into a force estimated to be of platoon strength, with four machine guns and a few mortars.

The 132nd Infantry, in the west and under the control of Marine Colonel John M. Arthur, had been on the Canal only since December 8th. Under the command of Colonel LeRoy E. Nelson, they had not seen any combat. The 3rd Battalion, led by Lieutenant Colonel William C. Wright, would lead the attack. The 1st Battalion, under Lieutenant Colonel Earl F. Ripstra, would follow in reserve, and Lieutenant Colonel George F. Ferry's 2nd Battalion remained within the perimeter. Offering immediate artillery support were the 105-mm howitzers of the 246th Field Artillery Battalion, and the 75-mm pack howitzers of the 2nd Battalion, 10th Marines, which had just moved over from Tulagi.

In the Spotlight

PFC William T. Paull and the "Lost Battalion"

In the attack on Mount Austen on December 17th, G Battery, 2nd Battalion, 10th Marines, 2nd Marine Division, had been among the forces that landed on August 7th. They were assigned as artillery support for an Army regiment making the assault. Paull, from Helena, Minnesota, was one of these gunners. "Sam Dallas and I were attached to one of the infantry companies of the 164th Army Regiment as forward observers. I developed love and respect for those 'dog-faces.' Marines like to feel superior, but those doggies had as much determination and guts as we did. Sam and I had a built-in advantage since we had been in the islands for over four months and were respected as grizzled veterans. I know that we capitalized on this and told outrageous stories of our heroic deeds.

"I have hazy memories of that long, slow hike up to a ridge overlooking a Japanese strongpoint. The advance up the slope was painful and the column was stopped whenever a Jap sniper fired. When there was a concentration of enemy troops ahead, the lieutenant would ask us to call for artillery fire. This was scary for me...I hadn't been trained for this kind of warfare. Our field exercises back in California taught us how to register our guns on targets that we could see...to direct artillery fire up, down, left, right, and observe the impacts. In Guadalcanal's dense jungle, none of this applied. Our guns were registered on a checkpoint far in advance of our position so we could call fire back toward us in increments of fifty yards. It is spooky when you see and feel artillery shells exploding in the trees only a few yards away and know that you are responsible. Anyway, our shells were ineffective. They were fused to explode at the first resistance, which meant that they blasted all the treetops but didn't do much damage to the snipers and troops below. Among my memories of bad things is the smell of burnt powder and shredded vegetation.

"We finally reached the ridge and dug in. At night we could hear the Japs shouting, 'Maline, you die!' They had snipers placed on their side of the slope, so it was instant suicide to stick your head up to take a peek. We had two army radiomen assigned to us to send our commands back to the gun batteries. Sam and I used their TBX as a screen when we had to make a firing adjustment. I guess we hoped that Japs would hit the radio and put it out of commission. We reasoned that if that happened, we'd be declared unnecessary personnel and sent back down the mountain. This ploy didn't succeed, but after three hairy, scary nights on the ridge Sam and I were relieved by a couple of Army observers and ordered to report back to G Battery.

"We started back down the trail accompanied by two stretcher bearers carrying a wounded soldier. We were almost out of the jungle when snipers opened up on us. Sam was hit and rolled down a steep bank into a little stream. The stretcher bearers ran off the trail with their burden but they weren't able to save the soldier. I jumped behind a fallen log and found myself alongside a decaying Jap corpse.

"This was my peak of terror and horror. It should have been my worst wartime experience. Possibly it was. I was lying alongside a stinking mass of putrefaction and too afraid to move. I thought Sam was dead. I could see that the wounded soldier had been killed and I assumed the other two soldiers were dead too. Then my mind went on automatic pilot. I remained aware of what was happening, but I felt a cool detachment. I seemed to be merely an interested observer.

"Eventually an army patrol came down the trail and cleared out the four snipers that had us pinned down. The two soldiers were unhurt. Sam was hit in the side but he could walk, so we stuck with the patrol until we made it out of the jungle. Sam was bandaged and sent out to a hospital ship and I never saw him again. I hope he recovered and made it back to Arkansas.

"Soon after arriving back at G Battery, I was sent with Andy Anderson, a farmer from North Branch, Minnesota, to set up a forward observation post at the top of a rocky ridge. We dug in just below the crest. The Japs were dug in on the reverse slope. Our job was to send fire commands back to the gun positions and try to blast the Nips out of their positions. This was a pretty tricky exercise! By their very nature, howitzers are more like mortars than cannons. High velocity artillery and naval guns pack a terrible punch but they have a flat trajectory. We could elevate the muzzles of our 75s so that the shells would climb high, then fall back to earth in a steep dive. This enabled us to hit targets sheltered behind a mountain...but there's a trade-off. This high trajectory shooting is much less accurate. The gun muzzles had to be elevated enough so that the shells would clear the top of the ridge, then raised further and further to make the shells fall back toward us, creeping up the reverse slope. This required careful observations on our part and scrupulous accuracy by our gunners at the battery. Even with identical settings, artillery rounds never hit the same place. Many variables cause this: air temperature, humidity, barometric pressure, powder temperature, temperature of the gun barrel, and just a mere fraction of weight difference of the projectiles.

"This didn't cause much of a problem for us during the day. We could observe where the shells were landing and make adjustments. Darkness brought on the excitement...when the gun conducted 'harassing fire'...intermittent firing to keep the enemy awake and uneasy. This ploy may not have worked on the Japs, but it sure kept me in a turmoil. As the air and powder temperatures cooled, the range would gradually shorten up and the shells were whizzing by over our heads closer and closer. We were tormenting more Japs that way, but I didn't appreciate the possibility that our own battery might blast us off the mountain. It never happened, of course, but there were times when I felt I could reach up and caress a projectile as it whispered over our heads.

"By the first of January, the 8th and 6th Regiments of the 2nd Marine Division had arrived from Samoa and New Zealand; the 2nd Division was together for the first time since the war began. Unfortunately for us, the 2nd Division was considered to be fresh and battle ready. Our little detached force was just as dirty, diseased, and battle-weary as the now relieved 1st, but since we made up only a small percentage of the division, we kind of got lost in the shuffle. We were reattached to our division, which was now part of a new organization—*CAMDIV:* Combined Army Marine Division.

"Six men from our instrument section were sent out to establish an observation post near where the Jap lines were supposed to be. The communications section ran a telephone line up to our position and we were left there with a pyramidal tent and a week's provisions. We set up at the edge of a long clearing in the jungle. All we could see was tall grass, trees, and a series of long, low hills about a mile away. There were no identifiable topographical features in the target area for the howitzers to register on, so some lame-brain at Fire Direction Control came up with a great solution—send a patrol out there into no-man's land and plant a flag to serve as a register point. Of course, we got the honor to play heroes and were assigned that scary mission. Four of us reluctantly and cautiously sneaked around the edges of the clearing until we reached the far edge, tied some banners to a few trees, and slipped back to our post as fast as we could. We didn't know if the region contained hundreds of enemy or no Japs. As it turned out, there were only a few snipers left in the area and we didn't encounter any of them. At the time, I thought this was a pretty dumb thing to do. Forty-eight years later, I still think it was a stupid order."

Later Paull took part in the much shorter but equally bloody assault of Tarawa, on November 19, 1943. He also took part in the invasions of Saipan and Guam, and in the battle for Iwo Jima received a field commission to Lieutenant on March 3, 1945.

The operation began on the 17th with a reconnaissance in force around Hill 35 by Love Company and reinforced by about 100 men from King Company. That first day they met no resistance. Early the next day Love Company, still in the lead of the 3rd Battalion, advanced about 1,000 yards southwest from Hill 35. Patrols had pushed ahead 500 yards into the jungle by 9:30 A.M., when fire from well concealed Japanese riflemen and machine gunners sent them to cover to wait for the main body to arrive at 11:30. Wright called for artillery fire into the suspected enemy position but did not attack. The new battalion was exhausted from the difficult climbing in the stifling jungle, and one GI was wounded in the day's action.

The Americans simply underestimated the strength and determination of the Japanese defenses. The enemy had dug fighting emplacements into the hills and camouflaged them so successfully that most of the time they couldn't be spotted until the attackers were right on them. The positions had been excavated and the walls reinforced by as much as two layers of logs, leaving a small firing slit for the guns to cover a critical field of fire. The holes were then covered with logs, and topped with a thick layer of soil and plants for concealment. Only a direct hit with at least a 155-mm shell could destroy the bunker.

Not yet aware of these defensive bastions—the marines in their defensive battles at Alligator Creek, Edson's Ridge, and the big Matanikau fight never had these kind of bunkers, yet had destroyed considerably larger attacking forces—the 132nd Infantry thought an aggressive attack by two battalions would drive the Japanese into the Matanikau River. This conviction recalls the Japanese attitudes in mounting their attacks. Knowing the persistence of the Imperial troops—even when ill and underfed—consideration should have been given to the thought that "just because you can't see them doesn't mean they aren't there."

The attack resumed at about 7:40 A.M. on the 19th after a ten-minute bombing and strafing close air attack by three SBDs, and a five-minute artillery "softening up" blitz on the area a few hundred yards ahead of the main force. Wright, accompanied by a three-man artillery observation party from the 246th Field Artillery Battalion—moved out ahead to take a look, and at about 9:30 the colonel, wearing his insignia of rank, was hit by machine gun fire. The artillery team tried to administer first aid until the medics moved up, but enemy fire kept them back and Wright couldn't be dragged back to safety. He died from loss of blood just before noon.

Command passed to Lieutenant Colonel Louis L. Franco, who was with the rear echelon about 1,000 yards back. The now leaderless attack came to a halt until Franco reached the front in the late afternoon. He sent out a combat patrol that covered the rescue of a wounded man and the retrieval of Wright's body. No ground was gained that day, as Japanese rifle fire from concealed positions stymied movement. Small groups of the enemy infiltrated American lines to harass supply and engineering sections hacking out the supply trail. At 5:00 a previously concealed Japanese machine gun nest opened fire on an area being set up as command post, aid station, and ammo dump, and the area was quickly abandoned.

That night was filled with eruptions of artillery, small arms, and automatic weapons fire as both sides probed for soft spots. The Japanese were particularly adept at seeking out the GI positions, making noise nearby to draw their fire, then eliminating those who responded.

In fierce fighting, the Americans fought their way into the mountain complex, one ridge at a time. By the 20th, engineers had extended a crude jeep trail, now called Wright Road, to key locations along the approach to Hill 35. It was nearly impassable when heavy rain turned the track into a muddy morass. Beyond Hill 35 all ammo, water, food, medical supplies, and replacement equipment—everything—had to be hand carried through the tangled and snarled underbrush. Even with the assistance of native bearers—soon called the "Cannibal Battalion"—the advance movement was difficult. The swampy jungle was no easier for the Americans to traverse than it had been for the Japanese.

Evacuation of the wounded and sick was no easy matter. Stretcher cases were carried the 100 yards back to the battalion aid station. The more serious cases were then toted in relays of 100 yards to a collecting station on Hill 35, from where jeep ambulances took them back to the Lunga perimeter. Carrying the litters up, down, and over the ridges and ravines was so grueling that the four-man litter-bearing teams had to be relieved for a rest after only one or two trips.

When the medics found they were being continually fired upon as they worked, they began to discard their red cross arm bands and carry weapons. Soon two-man escorts armed with rifles and submachine guns had to be provided. Difficult circumstances called for innovation: stretchers were provided with skids to move them down hills, and cablecar-like arrangements were strung over the deeper ravines to move the cumbersome litters.

The Japanese—no longer able to take the offensive, and cut off from relief—dug in at the Gifu Pocket and held up the American advance on Mount Austen. The desperate Japanese enemy troops had no option but to resist and kill as many of their hated foe as they could until they themselves were destroyed.

More determined and resolute patrols on the 23rd, recognizing the problems presented by the carefully concealed Japanese strong points, moved out. Patrols from the 1st Battalion, looking for the Maruyama Trail, penetrated 1,000 yards deeper than before, and then 500 yards further south and west. When the trail was not found, regimental headquarters concluded that the trail did not cross Mount Austen but circled along the southern slopes on its way to the Lunga. A 3rd Battalion patrol moving westward found only deserted enemy outposts around Hill 31. Returning to the Army lines, it encountered small arms fire and killed one of the enemy.

Since the patrol had discovered a relatively safe route to Hill 31, at 10:00 P.M. Colonel Nelson ordered the 3rd Battalion to retrace the route and prepare to attack toward Hill 27 from the north. On the morning of the 24th at 7:30, the 3rd Battalion—with Love Company in the lead—advanced toward Hill 31, arriving there in the afternoon against sporadic resistance. As Franco's men moved up the grassy hillside, they were stopped by heavy machine gun fire from all but hidden positions. The battalion dug in for the night.

Twelve Zekes from the 252nd Air Group flew down to Munda on the 23rd, escorted by nine others. On arrival at the new air base, two Zekes of the group were shot down, and two Wildcats and one Aircobra were lost by the Americans. Nine SBDs, nine P-39s, four P-38 Lightnings, and four Wildcats zoomed in to attack the next morning and found four Zekes in the air. Two of them were shot down, while the Americans bombed and strafed the field, damaging or destroying eleven more planes on the ground. A few days later, on the 27th, the Japanese realized Munda was in fact a liability, and brought their remaining aircraft back to Rabaul. This caused the cancellation of a new type of supply run, which required fighter cover. The air base at Munda, however, remained operational.

Elements of the 132nd Regiment—a former Illinois National Guard unit—were held up a short time before they destroyed a Japanese pillbox on Hill 31, not far from Henderson Field. The night before the action, Staff Sergeant Jack Fitzgerald dreamed that his group of four high school buddies from Chicago would suffer three casualties. In the fighting, a burst of Nambu machine gun fire shattered Fitzgerald's shoulder, and killed Staff Sergeant "Swede" Pearson. Sergeant Richard "Plug" McLaughlin, unwounded, was evacuated because of shell shock and spent most of his adult life in Army and Veterans' mental hospitals. Only Thomas Edwards of the quartet was able to continue fighting.

"Japanese infiltrators and sniper infantrymen were always a problem. They camouflaged themselves and were excellent soldiers...they were cunning, tough and brave. They did a superb job," Fitzgerald later said. He returned to his unit a month after being wounded.

The Gifu

The Americans had located the Gifu, a bristling pocket named after Japan's Gifu prefecture on Honshu island. Their strongest defensive position on the Canal, it was held by about 500 Imperial troops of Colonel Oka's forces. It consisted of a horseshoe-shaped line of about forty-five interconnected, staggered, mutually supporting pillboxes between Hills 31 and 27. Each position had at least one, and sometimes two machine guns, supported by riflemen and light machine guns. While the Japanese machine guns were decidedly inferior to American machine guns, these low-velocity small-caliber weapons were ideal for the kind of fighting that would take place at close range. They gave off very little smoke or flash when they were fired, making them extremely difficult to locate in the tangled jungle. Nests of machine guns and riflemen in front of the fortified bunkers burrowed in around the sprawling trunks of towering banyan and mahogany trees.

Too often the GIs had no idea where such positions were located until bullets ripped into them from the thick undergrowth. They could have used explosive charges to destroy the fortified pillboxes if they could have located them, but they were usually pinned down by heavy fire before they could get close enough to use the dynamite. Mortar fire did not do much damage, and only a direct hit by the heavier artillery shells could destroy the pillboxes. As strong as the positions were, they could not be resupplied or reinforced. American officers thought the west side of the Gifu was relatively weak and could be flanked.

On Christmas Day the 3rd Battalion tried to get behind the positions, but were halted by heavy small arms fire from the all but invisible defensive posts. The day's action convinced Colonel Nelson that the Gifu was a perimeter defense rather than a line. The 3rd Battalion continued its frontal attack the next day, while 1st Battalion—on the 3rd Battalion's left flank—sent out patrols to seek the Japanese flanks. The GIs still held the same positions they had established on the 25th, and Baker Company's search was stopped by machine gun fire. Further attacks continued on the 27th, but were brought to a halt in the face of heavy fire. The 1st Battalion had moved in from too far west, and instead of finding the flank found the main concentration.

When Your Number's Not Up...

"We landed the day after Christmas with the 6th and 10th Marines," related Seabee Fireman 1st Class George T. Wendelken of New York City and now with the 26th Naval Construction Battalion. The husky, freckle-faced redhead had played the part of "Freckles" in the 1925–26 Hal Roach *Our Gang* comedies. "My foxhole was about forty feet from my tent, but I could roll out of my sack and hit it in exactly three steps when that 'Condition Red' sounded."

"One night in January my number came up. I dived for that foxhole, and then blacked out cold. Next morning at ten o'clock the corpsmen found me. Three officers and eighteen men were dead in nearby holes. The bomb must have been a thousand-pounder. Then began the most fearful fifteen days of my life. Bomb fragments had torn hell out of both my legs, and I was paralyzed from the hips down." Freckles continued, "On the twelfth day, however, I was so weak that the corpsmen gave me up. A chaplain came around and prepared me for death.... On the sixteenth day I was moved out of the foxhole to be evacuated in a DC-3 transport.

"There were three transports going out and I was told that I would be placed on the first one, but when the litter bearers carried me up to the plane it was full, and I had to wait for the next plane. That was another break. The first plane was shot down by the Japs. I got the last place on the second plane...."

Yet, his ordeal wasn't over. "While I was in the foxhole I had contracted malignant tertian [malaria] along with my other troubles, so I was sent down to New Zealand. I had dropped off from 168 to 118 pounds, and I was still living on glucose and plasma. Once more the corpsmen gave up on me and I was supposed to die, but unless your number is up all hell can't kill you. I had seven stages of malaria before I could get out of that hospital, but I beat the rap and had the sweet privilege of laying my eyes on these United States again."

Additional patrols by the 132nd on the 28th and 29th had not found any gaps or the flanks of the Gifu, but did find a clear route to Hill 27. The 132nd's 2nd Battalion was given back to Nelson because his superiors demanded that Mount Austen be fully secured. The original assault units had been reduced to 1,541 able-bodied GIs, as the 1st and 3rd Battalions reported fifty-three killed or missing, with 129 wounded and 131 on the sick list. Nelson worked out new plans to hit the northern and eastern slopes of the Japanese stronghold with the 1st and 3rd Battalions, and for Hill 27 to be taken after a looping approach by the 2nd Battalion.

Far away in Tokyo, on December 31, Emperor Hirohito granted approval to the request by the Imperial High Command to give up Guadalcanal and evacuate Japanese troops. This was based on the realization that the time for any meaningful effort to dislodge the Americans had passed. Two incredibly close attempts—which had come within a whisker of victory but instead been crushed—had proven to have been the critical points. These defeats had resulted from faulty low estimates of the American strength—both men and heavy weaponry—and the continued bickering by the commanders involved.

WWII Snapshot—January 1943

The Atlantic and North Africa—Sensing that the course of victory is swinging in favor of the Allies, Roosevelt and Churchill meet on January 14, 1942 in Casablanca—Stalin decides to remain in Russia until the battle of Stalingrad has ended. On the last day of the conference, January 23, Roosevelt proclaims to the world that "Unconditional Surrender" will be the sole condition for ending the war. The Axis Powers will have to admit total defeat in order to prevent a recurrence of the inconclusive, ineffective, and jumbled "peace" that ended WWI. As much as for anything else, the announcement is to assure the paranoid Stalin that America and Britain have no plans for making a separate peace.

These fighting words, which quickly become a catchphrase for the Allied nations, have the ultimate practical effect of ensuring the nearly total destruction of Germany and Japan. Neither of the Axis Powers can accept these terms, which prolongs the duration of the war far beyond humane considerations.

Southern Russia—The totally isolated German 6th Army has been all but destroyed in the frozen wasteland near Stalingrad. More of the trapped Nazi troops are dying from illness, starvation, and the bitter cold than from Soviet bullets and shells. Hitler demands that the more than 100,000 remaining soldiers—who had at one time been so close to victory—die fighting for the Fatherland rather than surrender. This once proud Army of the Third Reich has been written off by the Führer.

The Soviet strength increases daily, while the Nazi troops can not be resupplied nor the badly wounded evacuated.

The once proud and arrogant German armies and their Fascist allies begin a wide withdrawal from the Caucasus region. Unable to penetrate the Stalingrad pocket and relieve the 6th Army, and recognizing that the buildup of massive Soviet forces can not be stopped, Germany faces a greater destruction of its own armies if Stalin's soldiers succeed in cutting off the Nazi thrust to the oil fields.

On January 10, 1943 the Soviet army launches a colossal offensive against the Germans trapped at Stalingrad. The pocket is systematically and gradually compressed despite valiant resistance. The determined offense by the dauntless Russians—who had come so close to defeat—is now irresistible. Only Hitler, back in his bunkers, seems unable to understand that the initiative and momentum have switched to the Soviet Union. Von Paulus decides to surrender the decimated German 6th Army to the Soviet forces on the 31st of December, the same day he is notified of his promotion to Field Marshal. Of the 284,000 men caught in the Red trap, 160,000 have died in the bitter fighting.

Germany—From the 26th on, members of the Hitler Youth, age 15 and up, begin manning the antiaircraft batteries around German cities to free the older men for combat duty.

Southwest Pacific—On Papua the Japanese threat to Port Moresby has been turned back. The Diggers from Down Under have beaten the best troops the Japanese had—and have beaten them in jungle fighting. But their attacks on Japanese fortifications at Gona and Sananada have given them considerable trouble. Manned by picked jungle fighters from Formosa, Gona finally falls on the 22nd. The American attacks on Buna are stalled by fierce Japanese resistance from cleverly concealed bunkers that can't be seen from the air. Allied casualties are mounting, and still the coastal defenses remain in enemy hands.

Buna Village is occupied on December 15, after being abandoned a day earlier by the Japanese. General MacArthur proclaims this a major offensive victory. Still, he is furious that Buna Station hasn't been captured. Major General Eichelberger has not given him the victory he so desperately wants, and he considers relieving Eichelberger. In Tokyo, in mid-November, Lieutenant General Hatazo Adachi is named to take command of the newly formed Japanese 18th Army. Emperor Hirohito has personally charged him with the mission of stopping the American advance on New Guinea at all costs. Attempts to land reinforcements in early December have been turned back by Allied air superiority.

Cape Endaiadere, occupied by the Japanese 229th Infantry's veterans from Sumatra, is overrun on the 18th by the Australians, led and supported by eight tanks. At a nearby objective a column of Australian infantry without tanks is stopped cold after an advance of only 100 yards. When three tanks come up to help, the enemy fortifications are immediately destroyed and the position is taken, but the column loses 171 men in the brief fight—a third of the attacking strength. MacArthur announces another major victory.

On December 28th, Adachi concludes that his forces at Buna can not be reinforced and orders them to withdraw to Sanananda. Eichelberger—frantic that he will be relieved by his commander in chief—plans a new assault. Saturday, January 2, 1943, Allied forces enter the Buna Station fortress. Japanese troops are seen manning small boats or swimming toward Sanananda.

The next day messages of congratulations from the Australian commanders arrive. MacArthur does not acknowledge the victory until the 9th. Sanananda alone remains to be captured, and no one in the front lines thinks it will be easy.

After several weeks of bloody fighting, the Japanese abandon Sanananda and on the 22nd the major fighting is over. Many observers question the need to overpower the positions on the coast when it is evident they could have been bypassed, saving many lives. It is not the tactical skill of the leaders nor the overwhelming superiority of the troops that gains the victory. The Japanese simply lose because of attrition. They run out of men and supplies before the Allies do.

Even MacArthur's loyal staff later admit that he desperately needed a clear-cut victory to atone for his failure in the Philippines, and wanted, most of all, to achieve the first important "land victory" over the Japanese before the Guadalcanal campaign ended. Between mid-November and January 22nd the Allies suffer 6,416 killed, wounded, and missing. An estimated 7,000 Japanese troops are killed at a cost of 3,000 Allied lives. The bloodbath that ends with the capture of Sanananda is a "ghastly nightmare," according to the official Australian history.

It seems that even MacArthur realizes that the shedding of so much blood for a victory isn't the best way to fight this war. He admits his American soldiers were simply not trained nor ready for jungle warfare. The Allied troops never received the supplies and equipment needed to do the job as it should have been done. Never again does he order his troops unprepared into such an appalling meat grinder.

MacArthur becomes the most avid proponent of bypassing Japanese strongholds. His final word on that subject is, "No more Bunas."

Far to the west, in the Philippine Islands, American army officer Captain Ralph B. Prager, back in the mountains of Luzon, radios MacArthur that he has gathered 5,000 Filipinos ready for guerilla actions. Rather than send the supplies as requested, apparently fearing Japanese retaliation on the civilian population, the general directs Prager to continue intelligence operations. The Filipinos, however, want to destroy Japanese troops and installations.

CHAPTER 18

JANUARY 1943
SWEEPING ARMY AND MARINE ASSAULTS

The 27th Regimental Combat Team of the 25th Division arrived on the island on New Year's Day, 1943, the day that Major General Patch relinquished command of the Americal Division to Brigadier General Edmund B. Sebree. On January 2, Patch was named commander of the newly activated XIV Corps on Guadalcanal, in charge of all forces on the island. Although Patch received a steady stream of ground reinforcements and replacements in December, he was not sufficiently prepared to undertake a full-scale offensive until the rest of the 25th Division and the 2nd Marine Division arrived, but he kept all frontline units active in combat and reconnaissance patrols, particularly toward the western flank.

In early January there were 50,000 American troops on the island. This included five Naval Construction Battalions mustering 5,000 officers and men. The Seabees had expanded the roads, and built sanitation systems, bridges, power generation and distribution lines, water systems, and numerous other needed facilities. The first Seabee unit to arrive, the 6th NCB, was depleted by malaria and other diseases that afflicted the marines. It would leave in early January. The 161st Regimental Combat Team, 25th Division, the 6th Marines, and the Headquarters unit of the 2nd Marine Division came ashore on the 4th.

Major General J. Lawton Collins, commander of the 25th Division, said that because of the late diversion of his division to Guadalcanal, the commercial loading of the transports bringing in his men—rather than the preferred combat loading—gave his men a chance to acclimate as they brought their gear ashore in small boats. While the supplies and equipment were unloaded and sorted, the unit had time to conduct some preliminary patrols.

The transports bringing in these reinforcements were supported by seven cruisers and five destroyers of Task Force 67 commanded by Rear Admiral Walden L. Ainsworth and Lee's Task Force 67 with three battleships and four destroyers. After seeing the new troops and supplies safely ashore, Ainsworth left behind four cruisers and three destroyers of his task force and headed for Munda with a bombardment fleet.

Early the next morning at 1:02 Ainsworth's flagship, the cruiser *Nashville*—along with *St. Louis* and *Helena*, escorted by the destroyers *Fletcher* and *O'Bannon*—fired off more than 4,000 shells by 1:50, mostly 6-inch and the rest 5-inch, inflicting heavy damage on Munda airfield. Japanese fighter operations slowed down for a few days, although it took the Japanese only two hours to repair the damage to the field. On hearing of the disruption, Japanese commanders sent a dual search and attack force of fourteen Zekes and four Vals after the American ships.

This Japanese aerial group surprised the American force at 9:36 off Guadalcanal's Cape Hunter, where they had slowed to between 10 and 15 knots to recover their scout planes. A pair of Vals scored near misses on *Honolulu*. Another pair scored one hit on the New Zealander Captain C.A.L. Mansergh's HMNZS *Achilles* with a 250-kilogram bomb that knocked out her Number 3 Turret, and another near miss.

Galloping Horse and Sea Horse

On January 6th, Mike Company, 3rd Battalion, 35th Infantry moved into a staging area near Lunga Point for transportation to a bivouac near Windmill Hill, on the Wright Road northeast of the Gifu. Don Santee had been trained on the 81-mm mortar, which was not suited for this kind of fighting, so he was assigned to a machine gun crew under Sergeant William G. Fournier, Norwich, Connecticut. They were issued C rations to carry with them the next day. Fournier came over and asked Santee, who agreed, if he would move to another squad so that the sergeant could take along his old buddy, Technical Sergeant Lewis "Pop" Hall, Bloom, Ohio.

In the darkness of the next morning the column moved out along the newly cut trail. Santee was carrying two wooden boxes of machine gun ammo besides his usual gear, which made rough going. He recalled, "The trail had been cut on a compass course and led us up and down the steep slopes of the rugged terrain. The heat and humidity took their toll and men began to fall out of the line. The single canteen of water didn't last long and there was no way to replenish, since there were no running streams along our route.... At the end of the first day we had advanced only about two and one-half miles. The jungle was proving to be a formidable foe."

When the advance was resumed on the 9th, the column moved up and down along the hogback hills, and everyone was suffering from lack of water. Mike Company had been attached to King Company, and they were now mixed together. When they stopped for the night, native bearers carried in enough for each man to get one canteen cup and were told it had to last. The next day they were in position to attack.

The quiet was shattered by machine gun fire, followed by rifle fire and exploding grenades. Patrols were sent out ahead of the plodding column. As the day ended without serious action, they descended into a defile with a fair-sized stream at the bottom. One of the ammo boxes was hit by sniper fire. As Santee's group forded the stream, he saw Sergeant Fournier and "Pop" Hall among the detail guarding the crossing. They struggled up a precipitous slope and reached the crest leading to the Sea Horse, their objective. "While using my helmet to scrape out a depression in which to spend the night," said Santee, "I was startled to hear gunfire and explosions from the direction of the place where we had crossed the stream. We could only guess as to what was happening, as nobody was moving in the inky darkness that had fallen." The next day he learned that Fournier and Hall had been killed fighting off the Japanese. "...but for a quirk of fate, I might have been among that small bunch of men who had come under hostile fire there at the stream crossing."

Fournier's machine gun section, charged with covering other battalion units, was attacked by a larger number of Japanese. With his gunner killed, his assistant gunner wounded, and an adjoining gun crew put out of action, he was ordered to withdraw from this hazardous position. He refused to fall back, and instead rushed forward to the idle gun. With the aid of Hall, he propped up the machine gun by the tripod to increase its field of action. Their determined fire inflicted heavy casualties upon the enemy, until both were killed. They were awarded the Medal of Honor, posthumously.

While the 3rd Battalion was circling around to assault Hills 43 and 44, the 2nd Battalion was attacking the Gifu strong point, which remained a hornet's nest of interlocking pillboxes, trenches, and tunnels. In a prolonged battle, Japanese defenders resisted to the last man.

A small U.S. force moved around Cape Esperance on the 9th in two landing crafts and landed at Beaufort Bay on the southwest coast. The object was to explore the Beaufort Trail to determine if any Japanese were in the area.

Later that night PT boats sortied from Tulagi to attack eight Japanese destroyers and damaged *Hatsukaze*. In the sharp action, PT *112* and PT *43* were destroyed.

Japanese positions on Sea Horse fell to the Americans on the 11th, while Japanese defenders on Gifu were surrounded. With Galloping Horse positions now in American hands, new attacks to drive Japanese from coastal areas made slow progress. Nine Japanese destroyers bringing in 600 reinforcements were attacked by PT boats but sustained no damage.

The town of Kokumbona was captured and the Gifu pocket finally cleared of Japanese on the 23rd. With virtually no food or ammunition, the remaining Imperial soldiers had fought to their deaths in another delaying action.

The nearly completed Japanese airstrip at Vila, on Kolombangara Island, was the recipient of a naval bombardment from ships led by Ainsworth.

The battle-weary 2nd Marines had seen their last infantry action on Guadalcanal. A new unit now came into being—a composite Army–Marine division, or CAM division—formed from units of the Americal and 2nd Marine Divisions. They were under the leadership of the 2nd Division, since the Americal had the responsibility to protect the perimeter. Two Army regiments, the 147th and the 182nd Infantry, moved up to attack in line with the 6th Marines still along the coast. The 8th Marines were essentially pinched out of the front lines by a narrowing attack corridor as the inland mountains and hills pressed closer to the coastal trail. The 25th Division, "Tropic Lightning," which was advancing across this rugged terrain, had the mission of outflanking the Japanese in the vicinity of Kokumbona, while the CAM Division drove west. On the 23rd, as the CAM troops approached Kokumbona, the 1st Battalion of the 27th Infantry struck north out of the hills and overran the village site and the Japanese base. There was only slight but steady opposition to the American advance as the enemy withdrew further west toward Cape Esperance.

The island commander's air defense capabilities also grew substantially. The Cactus Air Force, organized into a fighter command and a big bomber command, now operated from the newly redesignated Marine Corps Air Base. The Henderson Field complex included a new airstrip, Fighter Two, replacing Fighter One, which had severe drainage problems. Brigadier General Woods, who had taken over as senior aviator when Geiger returned to Espiritu Santo, was relieved on December 26th by Brigadier General Francis P. Mulcahy, commanding the 2nd Marine Aircraft Wing. New fighter and bomber squadrons from both the 1st and 2nd Wings brought their units forward on a regular basis. The Army had added three fighter squadrons and a medium bomber squadron of B-26s. The Royal New Zealand Air Force brought in a squadron of Lockheed Hudson reconnaissance planes. The Navy added a squadron of consolidated PBY Catalina patrol planes—with their much needed night flying capability—to Guadalcanal's burgeoning air establishment.

When he received intelligence that enemy ships were massing again to the northwest, Patch took steps—as Vandegrift had before him—to guard against overextending his forces in the face of what appeared to be another major enemy attempt to reinforce the Canal. A massive new onslaught against the forces defending Guadalcanal by Japanese troops, planes, and ships was anticipated by the senior commanders. The 25th Division was pulled back to bolster the main perimeter defenses and the CAM Division was ordered to continue its attack. When the marines and soldiers moved to the attack on January 26, they were surprised at the easy going. They gained 1,000 yards the first day and 2,000 yards the next. While pockets of Japanese contested every attack, they did not do so with any substantial strength. On the 25th U.S. forces crossed the Poha River, and two days later they reached the Neuha River.

The Japanese submarine *I-1*, commanded by Lieutenant Commander Eichi Sakamoto, was attacked and destroyed in a surface action with the Royal New Zealand Navy corvette HMNZS *Kiwi* at Kamimbo Bay during the night of the 29th. The *I-1* had left Rabaul on the 24th, and when she arrived off the point there at about 9:00 P.M. she had already been spotted by *Kiwi*. Her rear gun had been removed to make room for a landing craft to take the provisions ashore. When the *I-1*—the sixteen-year-old "grandfather" of the Japanese subs—came under fire she could only use the forward deck gun, and the men manning it were quickly mowed down. Sakamoto was mortally wounded by the shellfire and machine guns.

Kiwi rammed the *I-1* three times trying to sink her, and both sides were by now firing rifles at each other. The Japanese navigator, swinging his sword and seeking hand-to-hand combat, attempted to board the corvette. Another corvette, *Moa*, joined the strange battle and also rammed the beleaguered *I-1*. The Japanese executive officer, now in charge, ran the sub up on the beach. Thirty of his men had been killed, and the remaining fifty splashed ashore to join their comrades on Guadalcanal. Possibly some of the supplies were salvaged shortly after the *I-1* ran aground. The American Navy claimed to have captured important secret documents and codes from the abandoned hulk, but many Japanese reports later disagreed.

The heavy cruiser *Chicago*, a survivor of several battles around Guadalcanal, was torpedoed and later sunk on the 30th by Japanese aircraft. No one thought the fight for Guadalcanal was over and done. Intelligence reported an increased Imperial Naval strength being assembled at Rabaul and Buin. An all-out attack by two aircraft carriers, five battleships, eight cruisers, eleven transports carrying an infantry division, twenty-eight destroyers, 304 land-based aircraft, and more than 150 carrier-based planes was planned. Air attacks had become heavier and more determined against American positions on the island.

To counter the expected massive assault, Major General Patch deployed XIV Corps between the Umasani and the Metapona Rivers, even while continuing pursuit of the 17th Army to Cape Esperance. Halsey's resources had grown considerably, and now included two aircraft carriers, seven battleships, and three escort carriers. Screened by a large force of cruisers and destroyers, there were now a total of six task forces cruising south of the island. By any standard of judgment, a Japanese naval attack against a now considerably better prepared and capable American force promised to be a fierce, bloody, and terrible battle.

The Army's 25th Infantry Division, code named "Lightning," led by Major General Collins, was employed on the 10th and assigned the area east of the 2nd Marine Division along the northwest fork of the Matanikau. Within this area were the Japanese strongholds of Galloping Horse, Sea Horse, and Gifu. Quickly nicknamed "Lightning Joe" by his men, the Louisianan Collins had been in the Army twenty-five years, but had no combat experience. He planned that his 27th Infantry would seize Galloping Horse from the north; the 35th Infantry would block Gifu with one of its battalions, and the other two would move on Sea Horse from the south. The 161st Infantry regiment, a National Guard unit from Washington State, would be in reserve.

"I decided to avoid all frontal attacks and go after the open ridges by flanking maneuvers, keeping out of the low jungle area," Collins stated in *Lightning Joe*, his autobiography. "If we could clear Mount Austen and seize the Sea Horse and Galloping Horse ridges, we could trap the Japanese in the pocketed valleys of the Matanikau, where they could be forced to surrender or be destroyed by artillery and mortar fire, with minimum losses of American lives."

The U.S. Army doctrine was to reduce and eliminate enemy forces with the least possible cost in GI casualties. One marine who participated in the earlier defense of the Lunga perimeter thought that his leaders seemed obsessed with pressing a battle, while disregarding the cost in marine lives. That the marine fighting units did not expect to be involved in prolonged battles—such as that experienced by the 1st Marine Division on Guadalcanal—but rather felt "let's get in and get it over with," partially explains this difference of approach. Both methods were appropriate in the right circumstances, but not in simultaneous actions.

Then the 27th, led by Colonel William A. McCulloch, would push south from Hill 53—the horse's head—and link up with the 35th, under Colonel Robert B. McClure, pushing in from Hill 43. This would cut off contact between the Japanese strongholds, leaving three big pockets which could later be reduced in detail—that is, destroyed and eliminated. Timely logistics was the key to the operation. All the movements spread out from a single precarious jeep "road" that had been hacked through the jungle by the 65th Engineer Battalion. Access to the separate units had to be carved out as they went along. The division supply officer and his resourceful men came up with astounding new ways to move the needed materiel to where it was needed. Throwing away the book, his only criterion regarding how the supplies got through was, "Does it work?" Whether moved on the backs of soldiers, by native carrying parties, by barge or boat up the Matanikau itself, by elevated cable trolleys, or by airdrop, the supplies got through—but at a cost of using men who could have been employed fighting.

In the Spotlight

Army Chaplain Gary Bousman

Chaplain Gary Bousman, attached to the 25th Infantry Division, tells his story in *But You Don't Look Like a Minister*.

"Early in December, 1942, the S.S. *Republic* sailed out of Honolulu. So did several other transports plus one battleship and three destroyers. The 25th Division was at sea.

"The Regimental Special Service Officer (at that time called the Morale Officer) was on another ship in the convoy, and I was asked to take charge of a dozen or more boxes containing books and games. A few days after we sailed, I opened the boxes and discovered that each carton contained several packs of playing cards, checkers, dominoes, books, and bingo games.

"Most of these objects seemed useful as morale-building agents, but at that stage of my life I could not imagine a bunch of grown men playing bingo. In my mind, bingo was kid's stuff. Having spent four years within the sheltering walls of a Protestant seminary, and two years in a somewhat isolated rural community, I did not seem to recognize the gambling potential of the bingo game. For several days, I held back the bingo games, thinking I would insult anyone to whom I offered them.

"Soon after all other games had been distributed, a soldier stopped me and asked if I had any more games. When I told him all that was left were a few bingo games, his face reflected the excitement of a person who had just won a prize in a quiz show. I was surprised to hear him say, 'May I have one, please?'

"As I handed him one of the bingo games, I said to myself, 'Boy, these guys must be bored.' Within a matter of a few hours, word got around that the chaplain had some bingo games, and in no time I became the most popular officer on deck—that is, until all the bingo games had been given away.

"During the rest of the journey, I discovered small clusters of men playing bingo with fascination. In fact, I was told some skipped chow rather than lose their spot in the circle. I do not know whether anyone made much money playing the game, but I was told that the operators were making from thirty to fifty dollars a day—quite a sum for those times. Some of the officers kidded me, saying that I had instigated a vice ring. Others said I should have gone into the 'racket' myself.

"Our destination was 'Cactus'—the military code name for Guadalcanal. It was December 29 when we anchored off the shores of the then famous island.... Two days after landing, on New Year's Eve, we had fireworks—ack, ack. It was our first air raid.

"A few weeks after we landed, I joined the medics at the rear of a long line of marching troops. We were to relieve a unit of the Americal Division facing the Japanese positions. As we marched along the dusty road, the rumble of artillery became more pronounced. Unlike the artillery I had heard in training camps, this was not target practice. It was the real McCoy, and the guns were firing at human targets.

"It is a strange feeling as one marches toward a battlefield. All kinds of thoughts went through my mind. Would I come back on my own, or would I be carried back? What was I doing in this column of soldiers? I was taking part in war, and war is killing, and killing is wrong. Twice in seminary, I had won prizes in the annual oratorical contest, and in both orations I had denounced war as evil and barbarous.

"The next afternoon, I packed my musette bag and walked up the hill designated as military Hill 52. On the aerial photographs, this sector of the island looked like a galloping horse and Hill 52 formed the neck. It was therefore dubbed, 'The Horse's Neck.' Our men had already dug foxhole positions around the crest of the hill, but all was quiet. Quiet is hardly the right word. Officers and men were milling around as if they were at a county fair. When I asked one of the officers what was going on, he explained that this was the forward CP (Command Post). Patrols, he said, were out in front of us.

"'So this is war,' I said to myself.

"A few minutes later, I happened to glance down the slope at one of the machine gun positions near the jungle to our right. Just as I did, I saw the gunner firing into the jungle. For a moment, the meaning of what was going on did not register. Having visited rifle and machine gun ranges in training centers, it was natural to see guns firing. Then it dawned on me that I was seeing, for the first time in my life, a gun firing at a human target, though I could not see the target. Pretty soon several of the guns were firing and above the racket I heard the unmistakable 'ping' sound of bullets passing nearby.

"By this time, I was lying flat on the ground and so was most everyone else. One of the officers nearby made the remark that the enemy shots were wild and high. I stayed on the ground, however. I do not believe I have ever been as homesick as I was at that moment. I wanted to pack up and go home.

"Later I saw a man walk up to the edge of the jungle, poised for action. He peered into the trees as if he were squirrel hunting. 'He's brave,' I thought to myself. 'He's risking his life for the rest of us.' In a few minutes, he was joined by a second GI.

"All of a sudden, both started firing at a tree. It was an awful racket as they emptied the magazines of their M1 rifles. Just as the last shots were fired, a dark object fell to the ground and rolled a few feet in their direction. We all looked at the fallen body, expecting to see a dead enemy sniper. What lay motionless on the ground was a large tropical bird.

"As the two men, with sheepish grins and empty rifles, walked back to the top of the hill, the tension of an earlier moment was broken by laughter, howls, and catcalls.

"'Maybe you'll get the Silver Star,' yelled one soldier.

"Another shouted, 'Hey, do you guys have a hunting license?'

Army and Marine forces began the assault of Japanese defensive strongholds on Galloping Horse and Sea Horse on January 9th. Says Chaplain Gary Bousman, "The next three days were days of action.* My notebook contains many of the details. Here are a few: 'Our medics were kept busy all day...Captain Davis, with the aid of four men from 'G' Company, wiped out a strongly fortified enemy position.... First burial service, for Sergeant George (Red) Thompson of 'E' Company...Lieutenant Weldon Sims killed in heroic attempt to locate an enemy position. The spot on which he was killed to be called 'Sims Ridge.'

"The graves of the men who died on the battlefield were marked with anything we could find—bayonets, helmets, or a couple of sticks tied together as a cross. I collected all personal items found on the dead and tied them up in handkerchiefs. Before long, my musette bag was bulging with such items as pencils, pens, money, pictures, wallets, playing cards, and dice. I doubt whether any clergyman ever transported as much gambling apparatus as I did those days.

"At one burial service, we had to get down on our knees. It was not so much an act of reverence as it was a matter of protection. A sniper would not let up his deadly business while prayers were being said.

"As chaplain, I had to turn in a report on all the men I buried. This report included a description of the place of burial as well as the name, rank, and serial number. Also, there were the letters, KIA—killed in action.

"It was not easy to fill out these reports. Every time I added a name to the list, I thought of the people back home. I was dealing with something more than names, ranks, and serial numbers. They were sons, sweethearts, or husbands. Someone loved each one of them. I knew that within a few days a telegram would be delivered to their homes. I could almost hear the outburst of grief, and see in my mind the tears that would be shed. I wrote the names with a trembling heart.

"By the end of three days of fighting, the Galloping Horse was in our hands, but twenty-seven of our men were buried on its slopes. Though I cannot honestly say I knew all of them personally, a feeling of numbness hung over me for a long time. To accept all this as an act of fate, or the Lord's will, simply did not go down; a feeling of sorrow stuck in my throat."

---

* James Jones, in his novel, *The Thin Red Line,* describes this battle very much the way I [Gary Bousman] remember it. Lieutenant Burns appears in the novel as Lieutenant Brand. Captain Davis and Lieutenant Sims appear in the novel as Captain Gaff and Lieutenant Gray.

The Japanese defensive plan at this time, since it was unlikely that additional reinforcements and supplies could be moved in, seemed to be for the troops to delay the Americans by fighting to the death. This kind of action, which provided a preview of Japanese tactics for the rest of the war, was to make U.S. advances as costly as possible. Infiltration by what few able-bodied Japanese soldiers remained was intended to disrupt the supply line to forward elements, and to engage the Americans in small, intense, but time-consuming skirmishes. These invariably resulted in the destruction of the enemy probe.

The congested terrain of Galloping Horse dictated the way supplies were moved forward, and therefore the deployment of the attack. In getting to the horse's head, the two assaulting battalions moved along different approaches. Lieutenant Colonel Claude Jurney led the 1st Battalion, 27th down the ridge from Hill 66 up the forelegs, and Lieutenant Colonel George E. Bush led his 3rd Battalion, 27th from the high ground east of the Matanikau south along the hind legs, then west toward the head. To complicate matters, scouts reported that a Japanese force was well dug in at the "Water Hole" between the 1st Battalion and Hill 57, its objective.

At 5:50 A.M. on January 10, six battalions of artillery pumped 92.5 tons of shells into the area in twenty-five minutes. Twelve Aircobras dropped their 500-pound bombs on Hill 53, followed by a dozen SBDs dropping three dozen 325-pound depth charges in the area the 1/27 would have to cross. Shortly after 7:30 three companies moved forward against slight opposition from three Japanese machine guns and by 11:40 had occupied Hill 57.

Colonel McCulloch's 27th Infantry led the assault on Galloping Horse at first light on January 10. The six supporting field artillery battalions used an innovation known as "time on target" (TOT), which depended on careful coordination of the firing of all batteries so that projectiles from whatever direction and distance landed at the same time. Usually, rounds fired from the nearest battery struck before those of the main concentration and allowed enemy troops in the open to seek cover. The first bombardment lasted thirty minutes.

The coordinated batteries would fire together to produce a massive barrage for whatever duration was desired. Then they would fire more barrages later at irregular intervals over an extended period of time to mystify the Japanese as to just when a barrage would occur. Equally important to the success of a TOT barrage is that shells come from different guns at different distances firing from different directions. Effective counterbattery fire from Japanese guns would be almost impossible, even if they had had the artillery to use for such purposes. Counterbattery artillery fire means that you seek to destroy the enemy gun batteries that are shelling you, if you can spot them by seeing the flash and smoke from their barrel to establish direction and distance. TOT barrages made it difficult for the enemy to determine the direction and distance.

The 1st and 3rd Battalions led off the 27th Infantry attack, hitting the Galloping Horse at its forelegs and tail. In the early hours the advance was slowed by the steep cliffs, deep ravines, and thick jungle, and as the men moved up the slopes they encountered stiff enemy resistance from hidden bunkers. Heavy fire from rifles, machine guns, and small mortars was expected, but the Americans were surprised to find that the Japanese had also dug in a few 37-mm and 70-mm artillery pieces atop the sharp hills. While the 1st Battalion made better progress than the 3rd, by the second day both units moving inland experienced an equally challenging problem: a shortage of water. The American command had expected the many streams and creeks to provide a sufficient source of water, and they were surprised to find most stream beds dry. Bringing up water for the thirsty soldiers was a laborious task that seriously impeded the attack.

At the end of the second day the 3rd Battalion slumped into a night position more than half a mile short of the head of Galloping Horse, thoroughly exhausted by enemy resistance and an acute shortage of water. Colonel McCulloch pulled the unit back for a rest. Lieutenant Colonel Herbert V. Mitchell's 2nd Battalion, 27th was moved up to continue the advance along the body of the Horse. Easy Company soon stalled against a ridgeline between Hills 52 and 53, where the battle resolved itself into small but intense struggles between fire teams and individuals.

Fire from Japanese snipers in the trees was drawing indiscriminate retaliatory fire that shot up lots of treetops but felled no snipers. Collins, the division commander, had the word sent down that he personally would pay $10 cash to any man who could prove he had shot a Japanese sniper out of a tree. He never had to pay off for a single claim, but managed to save a considerable amount of ammunition that would have been wasted.

On January 12, 1943 Captain Charles W. Davis, Gordo, Alabama, executive officer of 2nd Battalion, 27th Infantry, volunteered to help Fox Company. The unit had been pinned down in a cross fire from Japanese machine guns, which had mortally wounded 1st Lieutenant Robert M. Exton (after whom the ridge was then named). Lieutenant Colonel Mitchell committed the reserve Easy Company to the left of Fox, but it too was unable to move forward because of heavy fire from a concealed strong point. In an amazing demonstration of broken field running over the open ground, Davis led Captain Paul K. Mellichamp and 1st Lieutenant Weldon S. Sims forward to locate the strong point. Sims was shot in the chest and killed. Davis then led Mellichamp back to Fox Company where he called in mortar fire, which failed to knock out the Japanese position.

Early the next morning Mitchell moved part of Easy Company to mount an attack on the ridge from the south. With four other men Davis crawled to a knoll on the south end of the ridge to within ten yards of the enemy strong point. Two Japanese grenades sailed from the emplacement into the small group but failed to explode. The eight grenades Davis and his men tossed back in didn't fail. As Davis jumped up to lead the impromptu assault, his rifle jammed on his first shot, so he drew his pistol and, in clear view on the ridgetop, waved his men forward with the rifle he still held in his left hand. With rifles and pistols blasting the enemy position, Davis and his men wiped out the stubborn enemy. The GIs rushed forward and quickly cleared Sims's Ridge, charged down Galloping Horse, and joined up with Fox Company in a move that broke the enemy resistance. The 27th Infantry had secured its objective. From a nearby hill an astonished General Collins witnessed Davis's dash, for which the young officer received the Medal of Honor.

Later, James Jones of Fox Company, 27th Infantry, would write *The Thin Red Line*, a remarkable fictionalized account of that unit's participation in this campaign. (His previous peacetime service with the 25th Division was the foundation for his earlier novel, *From Here to Eternity*.)

By January 30, the sole front line unit in the American advance was the 147th Infantry; the 6th Marines held positions to its left rear. On January 31 the 2nd Marines and the 1st Battalion, 8th Marines, boarded ship to leave Guadalcanal. Many of these men were so debilitated by malaria and a multitude of other diseases that they could not climb up the loading nets and had to be lifted on board, as had happened with the 1st Marine Division in early December. Observers could not help but comment on the sight of young men grown old "with their skin cracked and furrowed and wrinkled."

The Japanese destroyer transports made their first run to the island on the night of February 1–2, taking out 2,300 men from evacuation positions near Cape Esperance.

During its return from escorting an amphibious landing force around Cape Esperance to land at Verahue on February 1st, the destroyer *De Haven* was sunk by Japanese dive bombers. The Navy laid minefields off Japanese-held beaches. The destroyer *Makigumo* was one of the first victims to be sunk by mines. PT *123* was sunk by a dive bomber, and PT *111* and PT *37* were sunk by gunfire.

General Alphonse DeCarre took over command of the western pursuit from General Sebree on February 1. In the Bonegi River Valley, supported by field artillery and offshore Naval fire, the 1st Battalion, 147th Infantry attacked in an attempt to join up with the 3rd Battalion on the west bank. On reaching the east bank at 3:25 P.M. the Americans encountered resistance by the Japanese delaying force, making the crossing temporarily impossible.

With heavy artillery support, the 1st Battalion of the 147th on February 2 forced a crossing at the Bonegi's mouth. Contact between the 1st and 3rd Battalion was made by 5:10 in the afternoon, south of Tassafaronga. Once the linkup had been made, the 147th estimated that from 700 to 800 Japanese had held the blocking position. They had then withdrawn in an orderly manner but left behind two 70-mm guns, eight 75-mm guns, a radio station, and a mobile machine shop. Two American soldiers had been killed and sixty-seven wounded in the skirmish.

The next day the main body was extending its line south from Tassafaronga Point about 2,300 yards to the west. That gain was increased the following day by about 1,000 more yards to roughly 1,000 yards southeast of the Umasani River. Sporadic fire erupted during the advance, but the soldiers met no heavy resistance.

WWII SNAPSHOT—FEBRUARY 1943

Southern Russia—On February 2nd the victorious Soviet forces at Stalingrad accept the surrender of Field Marshal von Paulus of the German 6th Army. About 90,000 exhausted, starved, and nearly frozen Wehrmacht prisoners begin their long march east across the frozen land headed for POW camps in the wastelands of Siberia. After the war ends, only 10,000 or so survive the forced labor camps to return to their homes in Germany.

The victorious Russian battle for the devastated city of Stalingrad demonstrates that the Nazis' hopes of conquering the Soviet Union are now shattered beyond rejuvenation. Yet Hitler is obsessed with the idea that his battered armies will pull off a miracle and still conquer the Soviets. The two years of futile fighting remaining on the Eastern Front—combined with actions against the American- and British-led Allies in the West—will lead to the utter destruction of Germany.

The Allied policy set at the Casablanca Conference proposed by Churchill and accepted by Roosevelt mandates that only the unconditional surrender of the Axis powers in Europe and Asia can end the war. Any mutually agreeable political cessation of hostilities to end the fighting will not be considered by the Allies. This unusual and unprecedented concept of unconditional surrender—eagerly grasped by the Allies, who at the time are still fighting for their uncertain survival—results in the deliberate and merciless killing of civilian men, women, and children as well as soldiers and sailors, accompanied by the total destruction of the defeated nations' industrial and agricultural capability to sustain life. Never before in the history of mankind had a war of total extinction been waged against an enemy.

The Russian victory at Stalingrad is the turning point—the pivotal WWII battle—in Europe. From January 1943 on, nothing the German armies do can stop the relentless, vengeance-driven advances of the Soviets. While the Nazis claim an infrequent major victory here and there, they are no longer capable of winning the war. Stalin, obsessed with the idea of unconditional surrender, is now determined to destroy Germany. Hitler, still the absolute master of the Third Reich, will never agree to any surrender of Germany, much less an unconditional capitulation.

By now the Soviet forces push the front far beyond Stalingrad. On the 8th of February, Russian armored forces defeat the German armored forces and recapture Kursk, in one of the greatest tank battles ever fought.

North Africa—The American 1st Armored Division meets Rommel's Afrika Corps on the 14th and 15th at the Kasserine Pass in Tunisia, suffering a humiliating defeat, in which many of the U.S. troops break and run. The division commander is sacked, paving the way for the entry of Major General George S. Patton onto the scene.

Despite this stunning victory over the Americans, the Germans will soon have to surrender North Africa. The Nazi government and military are unable to resupply the once nearly invincible German and Italian troops in the Sahara region.

CHAPTER 19

THE JAPANESE ABANDON GUADALCANAL

"Before Guadalcanal the enemy advanced at his pleasure—after Guadalcanal he retreated at ours."

—Admiral "Bull" Halsey

American intelligence had established by the first of February that the Japanese were gathering a fleet of possibly two aircraft carriers, five battleships, eight cruisers, twenty-eight destroyers, eleven transports, 304 land-based aircraft, between 150 and 175 carrier-based combat planes, and a full division at Rabaul and Buin. With the increased intensity of air raids on Henderson Field, Admiral Halsey alerted all his forces that another full-scale counterattack to recapture Guadalcanal could be expected. Solid intelligence could track ship and troop movements, but was not always on firm ground as far as the enemy's actual intentions were concerned. Intelligence gathering was especially difficult when such high-level plans were carried by couriers rather than broadcast.

Halsey began the deployment of six Task Forces to Guadalcanal, totalling two aircraft carriers, three escort carriers, seven battleships, and an array of cruisers and destroyers. The Allied naval forces were increasing in strength and number. The XIV Corps commander Patch would have been negligent had he not heeded the warning of a possible invasion and maneuvered his forces accordingly. Any criticism of the slowness with which his forces moved to engage the enemy in those last days must be tempered with the intelligence estimates provided from higher headquarters.

Few Americans, if any, had any knowledge of the Emperor's approval of the decision to give up Guadalcanal, or the plans being made at Truk, Rabaul, and other affected headquarters. By now the Japanese had come to realize that their campaigns on Papua and Guadalcanal were parts of an integrated whole. It was too late, however, for them to understand that they could have continued their move to capture Port Moresby and—once it had been taken—to recapture Guadalcanal. In retrospect it can be easily seen that the successful capture of either of those objectives would have meant the loss of the other. Unfortunately for the Japanese, they thought they could do both at the same time.

Imperial General Headquarters in Japan became directly involved for the first time. They adopted General Hitoshi Imamura's plan to use the 50,000 troops of his 8th Area Army, including the 17th Army in the Solomons and the 18th Army in eastern New Guinea, and elements of the 4th Air Army. This would be the first time Army aircraft would have been used against the Americans in the South Pacific. Previous offensives to drive the Americans off Guadalcanal had been made at Rabaul and Truk, without consultation with the Imperial General Headquarters.

Imamura's plan was to send two fresh divisions to Guadalcanal, using the airstrip at Munda to provide advanced air support. This massive attack was to have been launched on or about the 1st of February. By this time, however, the insurmountable problems of shipping and supply forced its cancellation. Major General Shuicho Miyazaki, 17th Army chief of staff, stated:

> "The superiority and continuous activity of the American air force [CAF] planes made the seas safe for American movement in any direction and at the same time immobilized the Japanese Army as if it were bound hand and foot."

The large American offensive on January 10 had disrupted or destroyed great segments of the Japanese line and made untenable Hyakutake's plan to hold firm in the Kokumbona area. Reluctantly he ordered his troops to withdraw west to Cape Esperance and conduct a "desperate resistance" to hold on while the plans to withdraw were being implemented. On January 14, 600 men had been put ashore from destroyers at night on Cape Esperance. The Japanese used the buildup of forces and the step-up in air raids to deceive the Allies—one of the few operations that worked in their favor during the long campaign.

When the American 147th Infantry resumed the attack to cross the Bonegi River and capture the high ground to the west, they had been forced to halt in the face of heavy resistance. Despite the support of gunfire from destroyers and two concentrated artillery barrages, they were held back roughly 300 yards east of the mouth of the Bonegi. The 3rd Battalion had crossed the river about 2,500 yards inland from Tassafaronga Point and occupied some of the desired ridges.

Brigadier General DeCarre passed command of the western assaults to Brigadier General Sebree on the 1st of February. On the 2nd the 1st Battalion attempted to join up with the units that had already crossed to the south, and by 3:25 P.M. it had advanced to the east bank before being stopped by the rear guard delaying force recently landed. The next day their attacks succeeded, with 1st Battalion troops crossing the mouth of the Bonegi and shortly after 5:00 P.M. linking up with the 3rd Battalion. An estimate of Japanese strength in the area was more than 700 soldiers. The crossing cost two killed and sixty-seven wounded.

On February 4th, twenty-two Japanese destroyers and one light cruiser conducting their first evacuation run were attacked by CAF dive bombers. Two ships were damaged, and despite night bombing attacks the rest remained in the dangerous waters to pluck troops from the beach. Marine and GI combat patrols searched in this area on the 5th but failed to find or report any organized units.

On the night of February 4–5, the ships returned, taking out most of the Sendai survivors and General Hyakutake and his 17th Army staff. On the 7th, U.S. forces crossed the Umasami River and reached Burina against little opposition. That night, in the final phase of the Japanese evacuation, eighteen destroyers removed the remaining survivors that could be assembled, including the 3,000-man rear guard. In all, the Japanese withdrew about 11,000 men in those three nights and successfully evacuated about 13,000 soldiers from Guadalcanal. Later Hyakutake would remark that if the American forces had moved faster and pressed the battle, his entire Japanese force would have been destroyed on Guadalcanal. The Americans would meet many of these men again in later battles, but not the 600 evacuees who died, too worn and sick to survive their rescue.

By the 8th Patch sensed that the Japanese activity was a cover for the evacuation of the Canal rather than a new invasion. He was deprived of photographic reconnaissance on the 7th and 8th because of a lack of properly equipped P-38 aircraft. His strong suspicion could not be confirmed.

On February 9, American soldiers advancing from east and west linked up at Tenaro Village on Cape Esperance. The only Marine ground unit still in action was the 3rd Battalion, 10th Marines, supporting the advance. Major General Patch could happily report the "complete and total defeat of Japanese forces on Guadalcanal." No organized and combat ready enemy units remained, only isolated stragglers and those dying of wounds, starvation, and illness.

American troops reached Doma Cove. Troops of an amphibious force passed around Cape Esperance and linked up with the main force in Tenaro Village. On February 9, 1943 the bloody Allied Battle for Guadalcanal officially ended; the island was at long last secured. On that day the remainder of the 8th Marines and part of the division's supporting units boarded transports headed for Wellington, New Zealand. The 6th Marines, thankful to have spent only six weeks on the island, were taken off on the 19th. For the first time the 2nd Marines would see New Zealand. On the now legendary Guadalcanal the 2nd Marine Division left behind 263 dead.

Isolated individuals and small pockets of Japanese soldiers who had been left behind had to be mopped up. Many of these were the badly wounded, who either refused evacuation or could not be moved to the pickup points. Some of the stranded troops—once proud and disciplined members of Imperial Japan's glorious and unbeatable armies that were the scourge of Asia and the Pacific—escaped the mopping up operations. These stragglers wandered hopelessly in the jungle for months living off what plants, berries, and animals they could find before finally being captured or killed.

Chapter 20

Call to Arms—Courage and Killing

Green Hell: The Battle for Guadalcanal, is the story of the thousands of Americans, Melanesians, Australians, New Zealanders, and Japanese who were thrown together into a filthy, bloody, and deadly fight for possession of a poor remote island in a faraway corner of the South Pacific. They were average and ordinary men, for the most part, barely trained in the military arts. Only a very few of those who traveled to that faraway land had any idea what fighting in the fetid and swampy jungle would be like.

For the men who participated—both those who survived and those who died—it was a remarkable demonstration of courage and fortitude in overcoming a formidable enemy and unspeakably treacherous terrain. One writer has surmised that the real battle here was of men against the jungle, and that the ideological conflict between Japanese and American troops was a side issue.

"I never had any idea of coming off Guadalcanal alive," remembers Private Jim McCarson. "It never came to my mind that I would get off alive. One time they pushed us back, you know, we advanced to the rear. They cut us off between the river and the ocean and we didn't have any water. I don't think that anybody didn't fear death, but I think everybody was willing to die. Well, I guess the Japs never figured we would turn right around and counterattack. After we started back I actually saw some Japs sitting around. If they had been ready, I think quite possibly we would have lost."

Courage and bravery in the face of death defies precise definition. Some say that one man's bravery means only that he is a little less scared than other men. Others assert that courage is knowingly going into a situation where bullets fly, bombs explode, and death or maiming is a likely possibility. Training a man to face this kind of threat to his existence is virtually impossible. Most soldiers feel that a man who has no fear and is willing to go it alone is certifiably insane. Only groups of men who have been trained to be mutually supportive, who have a basic trust in each other, can do what they have to do in battle.

War correspondent Richard Tregaskis—who wrote *Guadalcanal Diary* soon after the battle—reported on the fear that existed among the men immediately before the landing took place. He mentioned a doctor, whom he had characterized as "scared to death." When he later saw this same man actually under fire, the man acted with great coolness and bravery. This example suggests that the greatest fear stems from unknown threats. Consequently, no man really knows how he will act in combat before the shooting starts. This also means that no man knows how another man will act under fire, with a real enemy trying to kill him.

"You know, when I first came into Guadalcanal, I wondered, could I really kill another human being?" McCarson recalled softly. "I had my doubts, really. One day after things had quieted down, after Bloody Ridge, I had gone back to pick up some stuff by myself. Out of the clear blue sky a young-looking Japanese stepped out. I looked him straight in the eye—I'm sure he was scared as I was—and I don't know whether he went first or I went first, it happened so quick, but I killed him with a shot from a forty-five. I looked down at him, his eyes were closed, he never even twitched. I almost felt sorry for him, but then the memory of that mutilated Marine hanging by his ankles come back to me, wiped it all out."

Much is made of the virtues of patriotism, love of country and flag, and duty to God and the family. These abstract beliefs provide an essential bedrock for the men who take up arms in the armed forces of any nation. But in the heat and savagery of battle six thousand miles from home the motivation to stand fast in a dangerous position—and to keep fighting against seemingly impossible odds—depends almost totally on the loyalty of one man to another, of a man to his unit, and conversely, of a unit to its men.

Loyalty

Too many men, wounded badly enough to be back in a hospital, voluntarily left the hospital, picked up a weapon, and struggled back to their units. Why? Waving the flag, and duty to God and country was not sufficient reason for them to do what they did in these extremes. Instead, as one said, "They really needed me to help out." "My place was with my buddies," said another. Whatever their stated reason, the intense loyalty to the men in their unit was what led these men to leave the safety to which their wounds entitled them.

Military units in which the men had trained together, worked together, and suffered together invariably fared batter in combat. Small unit training was the heart of the Marine Corps doctrine. Considerable effort was expended to place a platoon or a company in difficult training situations to develop reliance on one another. This is one reason the marines insisted on bringing out their dead and wounded despite the difficulties of doing so. Shipmates on a particular vessel relied more on each other than they did on the men on other ships. During the early stages of the war, ships hastily assembled into small fleets went into battle alongside ships they knew nothing about—they had never trained together and had developed no sense of comradeship.

The battles for Guadalcanal, New Guinea, the remainder of the Solomon Islands, and the many ferocious island encounters of the road to Tokyo were primarily small unit battles: squads, platoons, companies, and battalions. When regiments or divisions were committed, the outcome was invariably determined by the small unit actions. That was the nature of warfare in the Pacific—completely unlike the massive land battles of Europe.

The natural attrition of competent, able-bodied men in combat was such that many units needed frequent replacements. One of the great achievements of American industry was the concept of producing interchangeable parts. This concept cannot be reasonably applied to individuals when replenishing the ranks of a particular unit. These replacements may possess the basic military skills, but they have no experience in the unique human interactions of that unit. Consequently, the abilities of replacements were always suspect until they "proved themselves worthy" of belonging to a unit. Such are the demands of war that the veterans in a unit often never even learned the names of replacements who were killed or wounded in their first combat encounter. If a "new guy" survived the rigors for a week or so, he might be considered to have enough savvy to be trusted as part of a unit. The concern was not the bravery or courage of a new man, but rather his dependability. Just being around—"hanging in there" for a week or so—was sufficient demonstration of courage.

On-the-spot leadership of the officers—especially at the small unit level—is critical, and cannot be adequately judged prior to going into combat. Many otherwise qualified officers did not possess what one writer called the "moral courage" to order their men into a perilous situation. They would accept the dangers themselves rather than put their men in jeopardy. This lack of aggressiveness with their men complicated a basic fact in combat: that the casualty rates among young lieutenants and captains were invariably higher than that among their charges. The best of leaders must be able to compel those in his unit to undertake risks for the sake of the unit, even when he is in the front line.

"Chesty Puller was my favorite officer," Private McCarson said later. "There were a lot of good ones, the biggest majority of them. But he was a marine's marine—one tough joker. He wouldn't tell you to do nothing he wouldn't do himself. When he made full colonel and got that driver and vehicle, he walked most of the time right up there with you, not way back there telling you what to do. Men like him could take a bunch of kids and turn them into something pretty doggoned fierce."

A number of higher-ranking officers, who owed their promotions merely to keeping their noses clean and length of service, simply did not have the courage necessary to lead men in combat. They were either hesitant, afraid to make a mistake, or else insensitive to the rigors besetting the men under their command. Too many of these officers went to great lengths to avoid being near the fighting lines. An ineffective officer trying to control a battalion or a regiment from the rear, lacking the courage to go forward to see at first hand the ordeal his men are facing, can cause needless death and suffering in combat.

Most men going into combat do not do so to win medals. The man whose main goal is to win the Medal of Honor, or any of the high awards for heroism, can be a terrible danger to his buddies. He may needlessly expose himself in his quest for glory, placing his unit in grave danger. If he is subsequently wounded, he can easily be responsible for the death or maiming of men trying to come to his aid. When such a man's private personal goal is recognized, the other members of the unit will do anything they can to get rid of him.

Guadalcanal Review

Japanese Army and Navy troops were no longer a threat to the American and Allied forces on Guadalcanal, except as disorganized stragglers. Still, disassociated and starving renegades can kill in their elemental quest for survival. Historian Richard Frank cited a revealing insight by John B. George, a junior army officer who fought the Japanese at Gifu and in Burma:

"...most of us who have fought in the Pacific are ready to admit here and now, away from all the convincing firsthand evidence we have seen—mass starvation, untold suffering, shell shock, cannibalism, mass suicide—that for sheer, bloody, hardened steel guts, the stocky and hard-muscled little Jap doughboy has it all over any of us."

Earlier a soldier of the Army's 164th Infantry Regiment fighting the final battle for Henderson Field noted that if the Japanese had had decent leadership, "they might have beaten us." In the clarity of hindsight the wasteful piecemeal Japanese tactics were forced upon them by the location of the Canal in relation to their main bases. The only realistic approach from Rabaul was down the Slot of the Solomons, if any air support at all was needed, and it obviously was.

Once the United States had established the Cactus Air Force on Guadalcanal, any significant and effective Japanese efforts at reinforcement and resupply were subject to daylight American attacks, which claimed too many men and ships. The great distance from Rabaul to Guadalcanal prevented the Japanese from providing adequate air support for the relatively vulnerable ships and transports. By the time the Japanese began building close-support intermediate bases, the Americans were able to counter these moves.

In many respects, the first landing of Japanese forces, which resulted in the bloody destruction of the Ichiki Force, was a result of arrogance, neglect of basic tactics, and remarkably poor intelligence. The second major effort—against Edson's "Bloody Ridge"—might have achieved the objective of the recapture of Henderson Field. It failed because the Japanese dismissed the ability of the Marines to hold a well prepared defensive position supported by heavy weapons. In both cases, though, the relatively small numbers of Japanese landed to retake the Canal were a consequence of the difficulty of moving men and ships through the Solomon Islands.

Offensive operations against prepared defensive positions were extremely difficult for troops of both armies. In such situations, when the numbers are anywhere near equal, the defenders have the advantage. Ironically, the various elements of the 1st Marine Division, trained for short duration direct assaults, had come to excel in defensive engagements, supporting the foregoing statement. When sufficient numbers of American troops were on hand to begin their offensives in the middle of November, they repeated the same mistakes the Japanese had made earlier. They failed to concentrate their forces, which the tenuous supply problem seemed to dictate, and engaged in bloody piecemeal attacks that failed to gain their objectives.

The American victory evolved finally from the capacity of U.S. forces to move large numbers of fresh troops with their equipment and supplies to the besieged Canal to beat down the increasingly fragmented and starving Japanese resistance. From the American landing on August 7 until the last Japanese troops were evacuated from Guadalcanal, approximately 31,400 sons of Nippon had fought and suffered there. Of those, 20,800 perished, and a small number were captured. The 2,500-man 29th Regiment had only forty-three men able to walk when they were finally withdrawn. Of those who died, only about twenty percent were actual combat casualties.

American troop losses amounted to 1,207 marines, and 562 soldiers. The 1st Marine Division lost more than 650 killed and about thirty-one men permanently missing in action, with 1,278 wounded. This indicates that casualties during the last two months, after the 1st Marine Division was relieved, exceeded the losses of the first four months.

Thirteen American and Australian cruisers that engaged the Japanese Navy around Guadalcanal were sunk or damaged. The losses of sailors were even more telling, for 4,911 died in ship actions. The Japanese Navy lost a minimum of about 3,200 sailors.

Richard Frank's figures are as reliable as any, and were compiled from more complete records. He figures that the American and Allied forces lost a total of about 7,100 men: 1,729 ground, 4,911 sea, and 420 air. He estimates that the Japanese lost no fewer than 30,343 fighting men: 25,600 land, at least 3,543 sea, and roughly 1,200 air. These figures include Australian and New Zealander participants.

Withdrawal of the Japanese forces on Guadalcanal did not make the famous island a place of safety for the Allies. The Japanese were dedicated to retaking Guadalcanal, and continued sending down huge formations of combat aircraft to savage Allied shipping and facilities. Two of the greatest air battles between the Americans and Japanese were fought in the air over the island after the Japanese withdrawal. There was not much realistic hope that the Japanese could regain Guadalcanal, for the island was being converted into a major base to support Allied operations along the Solomon Islands and to Rabaul.

Guadalcanal was the turning point of the Pacific War. The justifiably famed Battle of the Midway in June 1942 blunted the Japanese advance eastward, but did not stop their offensive efforts. They still had available substantial sea, air, and ground forces capable of gaining their objectives against the Allies. The six-month campaign for Guadalcanal and Papua, New Guinea stopped the Imperial forces in their tracks, forcing them to the defensive. From that point on their offensive actions were dreams that could not and did not come true.

GLOSSARY

A-20—Hudson light attack bomber, Army
Aircobra—P-39 or P-400 Army fighter plane
Amphtrak—Amphibious tracked vehicle
Antitank gun—37-mm, small, wheeled, high-velocity cannon
APD—Destroyer transport
Arisaka—Model 38 .256-caliber rifle
Avenger—Grumman TBF torpedo bomber, USN
B-17—Boeing heavy bomber, Army
B-24—Liberator heavy bomber
B-26—Martin Marauder medium bomber
B-29—Superfortress, heavy bomber, Army
BAR—Browning Automatic Rifle: a light machine gun, .30-caliber, thirty-round magazine
Betty—Mitsubishi G4M, Japanese Navy medium high-level or torpedo bomber
Bren—British light machine gun, used by Australian forces
Butai—Japanese unit, or force, as in *Kido Butai*
C-47—Douglas DC-3 Skytrain Transport, USN version R4D
Cactus—Radio code name for Guadalcanal
CAF—Cactus Air Force: aircraft of all services operating from Guadalcanal
CAP—Combat Air Patrol: usually a protective screen over ships, USN
Catalina—*See* PBY, flying boat, USN
Dauntless—*See* SBD dive bomber, USN
Digger—Australian infantryman
Dumbo—PBY equipped for rescue work, USN
F4F —Grumman Wildcat fighter, USN and USMC
F6F—Grumman Hellcat fighter, USN and USMC
Flying Fortress —Boeing B-17 four-engine bomber and reconnaissance plane
Frances—Nakajima P1Y, Japanese Navy all-purpose bomber
Garand M-1—Rifle, .30-caliber, standard issue
Hamp—Mitsubishi Zero, A6M3 Model 32, Japanese Navy, shorter-range version

HMAS—His Majesty's Australian Ship
IJA—Imperial Japanese Army
IJN—Imperial Japanese Navy
Irving—Nakajima J1N, Japanese Navy night fighter
Jake—Japanese Navy float plane
Jill——Nakajima B6N, Japanese Navy, torpedo bomber
Judy—Aichi D4Y, Japanese Navy, dive bomber
Kate —Nakajima B5N, Japanese Navy torpedo bomber
kg—kilogram, approximately 2.2 pounds
Knee mortar—Japanese grenade launcher, with base plate
Long Lance—Type 93 (24-inch warhead) Japanese torpedo
Long Tom—U.S. Artillery, 155-mm howitzer, long-range
"Louie the Louse"—Japanese Scout seaplane; a pest over the Canal
M1—*See* Garand, M1
M3A1—Stuart light tank
Mavis—Nakajima H6K4 Japanese flying boat
Nambu —Model 11 light machine gun, .256-caliber
P-38—Lockheed Lightning fighter, Army
P-400—*See* Aircobra; export version of P-39
Paras—Parachutists, 1st Parachute Battalion
PB4Y—Liberator
PBM-3—Marine or Navy patrol bomber (flying boat)
PBY—Consolidated Catalina flying boat, long-range patrol
PT—Patrol Torpedo Boat, USN
PV-1—Ventura, Navy, medium bomber
R4D—Douglas Skytrain Transport, USN version of DC-3, and C-47
Rufe—Nakajima A6M2-N, Japanese Zero float fighters
SBD —Douglas Dauntless dive bomber, USN and USMC
Seabee—Naval Construction Battalion (CB)
Skytrain—*See* R4D, DC-3, and C-47
SOC—Seagull, Navy, scout observation float plane
Springfield '03—Rifle, .30-caliber, original USMC issue
TBF—Grumman Avenger Torpedo bomber, USN and USMC. Also TBM
TBS—Talk between ships; voice radio
Teleradio—Range of 450 miles for voice transmission and about 600 miles for Morse code. Each unit weighed close to 800 pounds, and was very reliable. The speaker, receiver, and transmitter required heavy batteries and battery recharging engines that ran on benzene.

USS—United States Ship
Val—Aichi D3A1, Japanese Navy dive bomber
VB-5—*Saratoga*'s Bombing Six
VB-6—*Enterprise*'s Bombing Six
VB—Bomber squadron, USN
VC—Composite squadron, USN
VF-5—*Saratoga*'s Fighting Five
VF-6—*Enterprise*'s Fighting Six
VF—Fighter squadron, USN
VMB—Bomber squadron, USMC
VMC—Composite squadron, USMC
VMF—Fighter squadron, USMC
VMF—Fighter squadron, USMC
VMJ—Utility, transport squadron, USMC
VMO—Observation squadron, USMC
VMSB—Dive scout-bomber squadron, USMC
VMT—Torpedo bomber squadron, USMC.
VT—Torpedo bomber squadron, USN
"Washing Machine Charley"—Japanese scout seaplane, IJN, a pest of the Canal
Wildcat—*See* F4F, Grumman Wildcat fighter plane
Zeke—*See* Zero
Zero—Mitsubishi A6M2 Model 21, Japanese Navy fighter

Further Reading

Alexander, Joseph H. 1997. *Storm Landings*. Annapolis, MD: Naval Institute Press.

Ballard, Robert D. 1993. The Lost Ships of Guadalcanal. New York: Madison Press.

Becton, F. Julian, RAdm, with Joseph Morchauser, III. 1980. *The Ship That Would Not Die*. New York: Prentice-Hall.

Belote, James H., and William M. 1975. *Titans of the Seas*. New York: Harper & Row, Publishers.

Bergamini, David. 1971. *Japan's Imperial Conspiracy*. New York: William Morrow and Company, Inc.

Bergerud, Eric. 1996. *Touched With Fire — The Land War in the South Pacific*. New York: Viking.

Brand, Max. 1996. *Fighter Squadron at Guadalcanal*. New York: Pocket Books. (Reprinted by arrangement with Naval Institute Press)

Berry, Henry. 1982. *Semper Fi, Mac*, Living Memories of the U.S. Marines in World War II. New York: Quill, William Morrow.

Breuer, William. 1988. *Devil Boats, The PT War Against Japan*. New York: Jove Books. Presidio Press edition, 1987

Bulkley, Captain Robert J., Jr. 1962. *At Close Quarters*. Washington: Office of Naval History.

Caidin, Martin. 1968. *Flying Forts*. New York: Ballantine Books.

Coggins, Jack. 1972. *The Campaign for Guadalcanal*. Garden City, New York: Doubleday & Company, Inc.

Costello, John. 1981. *The Pacific War*. New York: Rawson, Wade Publishers, Inc.

Craven and Cate. 1950. *Army Air Forces in World War II, Vol. 4, The Pacific: Guadalcanal to Saipan*. Chicago: University of Chicago Press.

Crenshaw, Russell S., Jr. Captain USN (Retired). 1995. *The Battle of Tassafaronga*. Baltimore, MD: The Nautical & Aviation Publishing Company of America.

D'Albas, Captain Andrieu. 1957. *Death of a Navy*. New York: The Devin-Adair Company.

Davis, Burke. 1988. *MARINE! The Life of Chesty Puller*. New York: Bantam Books. First published by Little, Brown and Company, Boston, 1962.

Dull, Paul S. 1978. *A Battle History of the Imperial Japanese Navy (1941–1945)*. Annapolis: Naval Institute Press.

Eichelberger, Robert L. 1950. *Our Jungle Road to Tokyo*. New York: Viking.

Frank, Richard B. 1990. *Guadalcanal*. New York: Random House. Also reprinted by Penguin Books. New York, 1992.

Fuchida, Mitsuo, and Masatake Okumiya. 1982. *Midway*. New York: Ballantine Books. First published by United States Naval Institute, Annapolis, MD, 1955.

Gilbert, Martin. 1989. *The Second World War*. New York: Henry Holt and Company.

Griffith, Samuel B. II, Brigadier General, USMC. 1963. *The Battle for Guadalcanal*. Philadelphia: Lippincott,

Hammel, Eric. 1988. *Guadalcanal - Decision at Sea (The Naval Battle of Guadalcanal, November 13–15, 1942)*. New York: Crown Publishers, Inc.

——1987. *Guadalcanal: Starvation Island*. Crown Publishers.

——1987. *Guadalcanal: The Carrier Battles*, Crown Publishers.

——1995. *Aces Against Japan*, Pocket Books (Simon & Schuster); Novato, CA: Presidio Press, 1992.

Hara, Tameichi, with Fred Saito and Roger Pineau. 1961. *Japanese Destroyer Captain*. New York: Ballantine Books.

Hersey, John. 1943. *Into the Valley*. New York, Alfred A. Knopf.

Holbrook, Heber A. 1981. *The History of the U.S.S. San Francisco in World War II*. Dixon, CA: Pacific Ship and Shore.

Horan, James D. 1945. *Action Tonight*. New York: G.P. Putnam.

Hough, Frank O., Lieutenant Colonel, Major Verle E. Ludwig, and Henry I Shaw. 1958. *U.S. Marine Corps Operations in World War II, Vol. 1: Pearl Harbor to Guadalcanal*. Washington: U.S. Government Printing Office.

Hoyt, Edwin P. 1983. *The Glory of the Solomons*. New York: Stein and Day.

Huie, William Bradford. 1944, *Can Do! The Story of the Seabees*. New York: E. P. Dutton.

Johnson, Frank D. 1980. *United States PT-Boats of World War II In Action*. Poole, Dorset, England: Blanford Press Ltd.

Johnson, Stanley. 1943. *The Grim Reapers*. New York: E. P. Dutton & Co.

Kurzman, Dan. 1995. *Left to Die* (sinking of *Juneau*). Mass Market Paperback.

Laing, William H. 1998. *The Unspoken Bond*. London, Canada: Third Eye Publications.

Leckie, Robert. 1965. *Challenge for the Pacific*. New York, Doubleday & Company, Inc.,

——1957. *Helmet for My Pillow*. New York: Random House,

Lenton, H.T. 1968. *American Battleships, Carriers, and Cruisers*. Garden City, New York: Doubleday & Company.

Lewin, Ronald. 1982. *The American Magic—Codes, Ciphers and the Defeat of Japan*. New York: Farrar Straus Giroux.

Lord, Walter. 1977. *Lonely Vigil: Coastwatchers of the Solomons*. New York: The Viking Press.

Lundstrom, *First South Pacific Campaign*,

MacMillan, George. 1949. *The Old Breed: A History of the First Marine Division in World War II*. Washington, D.C.: Infantry Journal Press.

Mayo, Lida. 1974, *Bloody Buna*. New York: Doubleday & Co,

Miller, Nathan. 1995. *War at Sea*. New York: Scribner.

Miller, Thomas G., Jr. 1969. *The Cactus Air Force*. New York: Harper and Row.

Miller, John, Jr. 1949. *The United States Army in World War II: The War in the Pacific: Guadalcanal: The First Offensive*. Washington, D.C.: Government Printing Office.

Morison, Samuel Eliot. 1963. *The Two-Ocean War*. Boston: An Atlantic Monthly Press Book, Little, Brown and Company.

——1950, 1962. History of United States Naval Operations in World War II, Vol. V: *The Struggle for Guadalcanal*. Boston: The Atlantic Monthly & Little Brown.

Murphy, Edward F. 1990. *Heroes of World War II*. Novato, CA: Presidio Press.

Musicant, Ivan. 1986. *Battleship at War: The Epic Story of the U.S.S. Washington*. New York: Harcourt, Brace Jovanovich.

Orita, Zenji, and Joseph D. Harrington. 1976. *I-Boat Captain*. Canoga Park, CA: Major Books.

Potter, E. B. 1976. *Nimitz*. Annapolis, MD: Naval Institute Press.

Sakai, Saburo, with Martin Caidin and Fred Saito. 1957. *Samurai*. New York: Dutton.

Spector, Ronald H. 1985. *Eagle Against the Sun*. New York: The Free Press, Division of Macmillan.

Stafford, Edward P., Commander, USN. 1964. *The Big E*. New York: Dell Publishing Co., Inc.

Steinberg, Rafael, and the Editors of Time-Life Books. 1978. *Island Fighting*. Alexandria, VA: Time Life Books.

Toland, John. 1970. *The Rising Sun: The Decline and Fall of the Japanese Empire*, Volumes 1 and 2, 1936–1945. New York: Random House.

Tregaskis, Richard. 1943. *Guadalcanal Diary*. New York: Random House.

Vandegrift, A. Archibald, General. 1964. *Once a Marine*. New York: Norton.
van der Vat, Dan. 1991. *The Pacific Campaign: World War II.* New York: Simon & Schuster.

Internet Sources

Green Hell: The Battle for Guadalcanal. Contains additional information, maps, and photographs. http://www.psi-research.com/hellgate/green.htm

Herr, Ernest A. *Horror at Guadalcanal.* http:/www.geocities.com/Pentagon/8548/obannon

Bousman, Jerry, *Chaplain's Story* http://www.geocities.com/Heartland/Plains/6672/canal/chaplain.html

Nichols, John. Guadalcanal: Online http://www.geocities.com/Heartland/Plains/6672/canal_index.html

USMC-50: First Offensive. An excellent overview, with photos. http://sunsite.unc.edu/hyperwar/USMC/USMC-C-Guadalcanal.html

Sullivan Brothers - First Naval Battle of Guadalcanal www.thehistorynet.com/WorldWarII/article...7/1197_side.htm

The U.S. Army Campaigns in World War II. GUADALCANAL. CMH Pub 72-8. [URL: imabbs.army.mil/cmh-pg/guadal.htm]

A Guadalcanal Chronology August 7, 1942–March 6, 1943. Japanese emphasis. [URL: www.friesian.com/history/guadal.htm]

Personal Diaries on Web

J. Rube Garrett http://www.gnt.com/~jrube/index2.html#index

William Paull http://www.sihope.com/~tipi/marine.html

George John Sallet, "The Six Long Years," the naval autobiography starting at age 19, served aboard the destroyer USS *Bagley*, DD386, in the Pacific June 1941–June 1946. http://www.cronab.demon.co.uk/sallet.htm

Michael Phillips mike@cronab.demon.co.uk

INDEX

A

B

H

I

J

K

L

P

Q

R

V

W

Y

Z

WELCOME TO

Hellgate Press

Hellgate Press is named after the historic and rugged Hellgate Canyon on southern Oregon's scenic Rogue River. The raging river that flows below the canyon's towering jagged cliffs has always attracted a special sort of individual — someone who seeks adventure. From the pioneers who bravely pursued the lush valleys beyond, to the anglers and rafters who take on its roaring challenges today — Hellgate Press publishes books that personify this adventurous spirit. Our books are about military history, adventure travel, and outdoor recreation. On the following pages, we would like to introduce you to some of our latest titles and encourage you to join in the celebration of this unique spirit.

Our books are in your favorite bookstore or you can order them direct at ***1-800-228-2275***
or visit our Website at ***http://www.psi-research.com/hellgate.htm***

Army Museums

West of the Mississippi
by Fred L. Bell, SFC Retired

ISBN: 1-55571-395-5
Paperback: $17.95

A guide book for travelers to the army museums of the west, as well as a source of information about the history of the site where the museum is located. Contains detailed information about the contents of the museum and interesting information about famous soldiers stationed at the location or specific events associated with the facility. These twenty-three museums are in forts and military reservations which represent the colorful heritage in the settling of the American West.

Byron's War

I Never Will Be Young Again...
by Byron Lane

ISBN: 1-55571-402-1
Hardcover: $21.95

Based on letters that were mailed home and a personal journal written more than fifty years ago during World War II, *Byron's War* brings the war life through the eyes of a very young air crew officer. It depicts how the life of this young American changed through cadet training, the experiences as a crew member flying across the North Atlantic under wartime hazards to the awesome responsibility assigned to a nineteen year-old when leading hundreds of men and aircraft where success or failure could seriously impact the outcome of the war.

Gulf War Debriefing Book

An After Action Report — **ISBN: 1-55571-396-3**
by Andrew Leyden — **Paperback: $18.95**

Whereas most books on the Persian Gulf War tell an "inside story" based on someone else's opinion, this book lets you draw your own conclusions about the war by providing you with a meticulous review of events and documentation all at your fingertips. Includes lists of all military units deployed, a detailed account of the primary weapons used during the war, and a look at the people, places, and politics behind the military maneuvering.

From Hiroshima with Love

ISBN: 1-55571-404-8
by Raymond A. Higgins — **Paperback: $18.95**

This remarkable story is written from actual detailed notes and diary entries kept by Lieutenant Commander Wallace Higgins. Because of his industrial experience back in the United States and with the reserve commission in the Navy, he was an excellent choice for military governor of Hiroshima. Higgins was responsible for helping rebuild a ravaged nation of war. He developed an unforeseen respect for the Japanese, the culture, and one special woman.

Night Landing

A Short History of West Coast Smuggling — **ISBN: 1-55571-449-8**
by David W. Heron — **Paperback: $13.95**

Night Landing reveals the true stories of smuggling off the shores of California from the early 1800s to the present. It is a provocative account of the many attempts to illegally trade items such as freon, drugs, AK-47s, sea otters, and diamonds. This unusual chronicle also profiles each of these ingenious, but over-optimistic criminals and their eventual apprehension.

Order of Battle

Allied Ground Forces of Operation Desert Storm — **ISBN: 1-55571-493-5**
by Thomas D. Dinackus — **Paperback: $17.95**

Based on extensive research, and containing information not previously available to the public, *Order of Battle: Allied Ground Forces of Operation Desert Storm,* is a detailed study of the Allied ground combat units that served in Operation Desert Storm. In addition to showing unit assignments, it includes the type of insignia and equipment used by the various units in one of the largest military operations since the end of WWII.

Pilots, Man Your Planes!

A History of Naval Aviation — **ISBN: 1-55571- 466-8**
by Wilbur H. Morrison — **Hardbound: $ 33.95**

An account of naval aviation from Kitty Hawk to the Gulf War, *Pilots, Man Your Planes!* tells the story of naval air growth from a time when planes were launched from battleships to the major strategic element of naval warfare it is today. Full of detailed maps and photographs. Great for anyone with an interest in aviation.

K-9 Soldiers

Vietnam and After **ISBN: 1-55571-495-1**

by Paul B. Morgan **Paperback: $13.95**

A retired US Army officer, former Green Beret, Customs K-9 and Security Specialist, Paul B. Morgan has written *K-9 Soldiers.* In his book, Morgan relates twenty-four brave stories from his lifetime of working with man's best friend in combat and on the streets. They are the stories of dogs and their handlers who work behind the scenes when a disaster strikes, a child is lost or some bad guy tries to outrun the cops.

After the Storm

A Vietnam Veteran's Reflection **ISBN: 1-55571-500-1**

by Paul Drew **Paperback: $14.95**

Even after twenty-five years, the scars of the Vietnam War are still felt by those who were involved. *After the Storm: A Vietnam Veteran's Reflection* is more than a war story. Although it contains episodes of combat, it does not dwell on them. It concerns itself more on the mood of the nation during the war years, and covers the author's intellectual and psychological evolution as he questions the political and military decisions that resulted in nearly 60,000 American deaths.

Green Hell

The Battle for Guadalcanal **ISBN: 1-55571-498-6**

by William J. Owens **Paperback: $18.95**

This is the story of thousands of Melanesian, Australian, New Zealand, Japanese, and American men who fought for a poor insignificant island is a faraway corner of the South Pacific Ocean. For the men who participated, the real battle was of man against jungle. This is the account of land, sea and air units covering the entire six-month battle. Stories of ordinary privates and seamen, admirals and generals who survive to claim the victory that was the turning point of the Pacific War.

Oh, What A Lovely War

ISBN: 1-55571-502-8

by Evelyn A. Luscher **Paperback: $14.95**

This book tells you what history books do not. It is war with a human face. It is the unforgettable memoir of British soldier Gunner Stanley Swift through five years of war. Intensely personal and moving, it documents the innermost thoughts and feelings of a young man as he moves from civilian to battle-hardened warrior under the duress of fire.

Through My Eyes

91st Infantry Division, Italian Campaign 1942-1945 **ISBN: 1-55571-497-8**

by Leon Weckstein **Paperback: $14.95**

Through My Eyes is the true account of an Average Joe's infantry days before, during and shortly after the furiously fought battle for Italy. The author's front row seat allows him to report the shocking account of casualties and the rest-time shenanigans during the six weeks of the occupation of the city of Trieste. He also recounts in detail his personal roll in saving the historic Leaning Tower of Pisa.